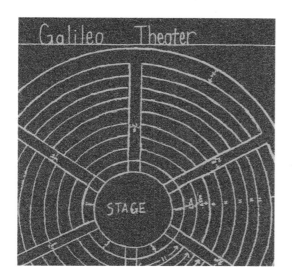

Galileo Theater

STAGE

PERFORMANCE

Volume 3 ▪ High School

STANDARDS

NEW
STANDARDS™

English Language Arts

Mathematics

Science

Applied Learning

Support for the development of the New Standards performance standards was provided by:

The Pew Charitable Trusts,
John D. and Catherine T. MacArthur Foundation,
William T. Grant Foundation,
and the
New Standards partners.

ISBN 1-889630-53-5

INTRODUCTION

ABOUT NEW STANDARDS

New Standards is a collaboration of the Learning Research and Development Center of the University of Pittsburgh and the National Center on Education and the Economy, in partnership with states and urban school districts. The partners are building an assessment system to measure student progress toward meeting national standards at levels that are internationally benchmarked.

The Governing Board includes chief state school officers, governors and their representatives, and others representing the diversity of the partnership, whose jurisdictions enroll nearly half of the Nation's students.

New Standards was founded by Lauren Resnick, Director of the Learning Research and Development Center (LRDC), and Marc Tucker, President of the National Center on Education and the Economy (NCEE). The Executive Director is Eugene Paslov. New Standards staff is based at the LRDC and NCEE as well as the American Association for the Advancement of Science, the Fort Worth Independent School District, the National Council of Teachers of English, and the University of California Office of the President. Technical studies are based at LRDC and Northwestern University, with an advisory committee of leading psychometricians from across the nation.

The New Standards assessment system has three interrelated components: performance standards, an on-demand examination, and a portfolio system.

The **performance standards** are derived from the national content standards developed by professional organizations, e.g., the National Council of Teachers of Mathematics, and consist of two parts:

 Performance descriptions—descriptions of what students should know and the ways they should demonstrate the knowledge and skills they have acquired in the four areas assessed by New Standards—English Language Arts, Mathematics, Science, and Applied Learning—at elementary, middle, and high school levels.

 Work samples and commentaries—samples of student work that illustrate standard-setting performances, each accompanied by commentary that shows how the performance descriptions are reflected in the work sample.

The performance standards were endorsed unanimously by the New Standards Governing Board in June 1996 as the basis for the New Standards assessment system.

The on-demand examination, called the **reference examination** because it provides a point of reference to national standards, is currently available in English Language Arts and Mathematics at grades 4, 8, and 10. It assesses those aspects of the performance standards that can be assessed in a limited time frame under standardized conditions. In English Language Arts, this means reading short passages and answering questions, writing first drafts, and editing. In Mathematics, this means short exercises or problems that take five to fifteen minutes and longer problems of up to forty-five minutes. The reference examination stops short of being able to accommodate longer pieces of work—reading several books, writing with revision, conducting investigations in Mathematics and Science, and completing projects in Applied Learning—that are required by New Standards performance standards and by the national content standards from which they are derived.

The **portfolio system** complements the reference examination. It provides evidence of achievement of the performance standards that depend on extended pieces of work (especially those that show revision) and accumulation of evidence over time. In 1995-96, 3,000 teachers and almost 60,000 students participated in a field trial of the portfolio system. The portfolio system includes instructions for students, teachers, and administrators and example portfolios that contain concrete examples of expectations for students and teachers to refer to as they prepare portfolios.

The 1995-96 portfolio field trial was the second year of field testing the system in English Language Arts and Mathematics, and the first year of developmental testing for Science and Applied Learning. The materials used in the 1995-96 trial were revised to take account of the experience of the first year, with the goal of making the portfolio system easier to understand and implement.

ABOUT THE PERFORMANCE STANDARDS

We have adopted the distinction between content standards and performance standards that is articulated in *Promises to Keep: Creating High Standards for American Students* (1993), a report commissioned by the National Education Goals Panel. Content standards specify "what students should know and be able to do"; performance standards go the next step to specify "how good is good enough."

These standards are designed to make content standards operational by answering the question: how good is good enough?

Where do the performance standards come from?

These performance standards are built directly upon the consensus content standards developed by the national professional organizations for the disciplines. The Mathematics performance standards are based directly on the content standards produced by the National Council of Teachers of Mathematics (1989). (See "Introduction to the Mathematics performance standards," page 48.) Similarly, the performance standards for English Language Arts were developed in concert with the content standards produced by the National Council of Teachers of English and the International Reading Association (1996). (See "Introduction to the English Language Arts performance standards," page 20.)

The Science performance standards are built upon the National Research Council's *National Science Education Standards* (1996) and the American Association for the Advancement of Science's Project 2061 *Benchmarks for Science Literacy* (1993). (See "Introduction to the Science performance standards," page 80.)

The case of the Applied Learning performance standards is a little different. Applied Learning focuses on connecting the work students do in school with the demands of the twenty-first century workplace. As a newer focus of study, Applied Learning does not have a distinct professional constituency producing content standards on which performance standards can be built. However, the Secretary's Commission on Achieving Necessary Skills (SCANS) laid a foundation for the field in its report, *Learning a Living: A Blueprint for High Performance* (1992) which defined "Workplace Know-how." We worked from this foundation and from comparable international work to produce our own "Framework for Applied Learning" (New Standards, 1994). The Applied Learning performance standards have been built upon this framework. (See "Introduction to the Applied Learning performance standards," page 106.)

STANDARDS FOR STANDARDS

In recent years several reports on standards development have established "standards for standards," that is, guidelines for developing standards and criteria for judging their quality. These include the review criteria identified in *Promises to Keep*, the American Federation of Teachers' "Criteria for High Quality Standards," published in *Making Standards Matter* (1995), and the "Principles for Education Standards" developed by the Business Task Force on Student Standards and published in *The Challenge of Change* (1995). We drew from the criteria and principles advocated in these documents in establishing the "standards" we have tried to achieve in the New Standards performance standards.

Standards should establish high standards for all students.

The New Standards partnership has resolved to abolish the practice of expecting less from poor and minority children and children whose first language is not English. These performance standards are intended to help bring all students to high levels of performance.

Much of the onus for making this goal a reality rests on the ways the standards are implemented. The New Standards partners have adopted a Social Compact, which says in part, "Specifically, we pledge to do everything in our power to ensure all students a fair shot at reaching the new performance standards...This means they will be taught a curriculum that will prepare them for the assessments, that their teachers will have the preparation to enable them to teach it well, and there will be...the resources the students and their teachers need to succeed."

There are ways in which the design of the standards themselves can also contribute to the goal of bringing all students to high levels of performance, especially by being clear about what is expected. We have worked to make the expectations included in these performance standards as clear as possible. For some standards it has been possible to do this in the performance descriptions. For example, the Reading standard includes expectations for students to read widely and to read quality materials. Instead of simply exhorting them to do this, we have given more explicit direction by specifying that students should be expected to read at least twenty-five books each year and that those books should be of the quality and complexity illustrated in the sample reading list provided for each grade level. In Mathematics, we have gone beyond simply listing problem solving among our expectations for students. We set out just what we mean by problem solving and what things we expect students to be able to do in problem solving and mathematical reasoning. In addition, by providing numerous examples we have indicated the level of difficulty of the problems students are expected to solve.

The inclusion of work samples and commentaries to illustrate the meaning of the standards is intended to help make the standards clearer. Most of the standards are hard to pin down precisely in words alone. In the Writing standard, for example, the work samples show the expected qualities of writing for the various kinds of writing required and the commentaries explain how these qualities are demonstrated in the work samples. The work samples and commentaries are an integral part of the performance standards.

The work samples will help teachers, students, and parents to picture work that meets standards and to establish goals to reach for. Students need to know what work that meets standards looks like if they are to strive to produce work of the same quality. They also need to see themselves reflected in the work samples if they are to believe that they too are capable of producing such work. We have included work samples drawn from a diverse range of students and from students studying in a wide variety of settings.

Standards should be rigorous and world class.

Is what we expect of our students as rigorous and demanding as what is expected of young people in other countries—especially those countries whose young people consistently perform as well as or better than ours?

That is the question we are trying to answer when we talk about developing world class standards.

Through successive drafts of these performance standards, we compared our work with the national and local curricula of other countries, with textbooks, assessments, and examinations from other countries and, where possible, with work produced by students in other countries. Ultimately, it is the work students produce that will show us whether claims for world class standards can be supported.

We shared the *Consultation Draft* with researchers in other countries and asked them to review it in terms of their own country's standards and in light of what is considered world class in their field. Included among these countries were Australia, Belgium, Canada, the Czech Republic, Denmark, England and Wales, Finland, France, Germany, Japan, the Netherlands, New Zealand, Norway, Poland, Scotland, Singapore, Sweden, and Switzerland. We asked these reviewers to tell us whether each standard is at least as demanding as its counterparts abroad and whether the set of standards represents an appropriately thorough coverage of the subject areas. We also shared the *Consultation Draft* with recognized experts in the field of international comparisons of education, each of whom is familiar with the education systems of several countries.

Our reviewers provided a wealth of constructive responses to the *Consultation Draft*. Most confined their responses to the English Language Arts, Mathematics, and Science standards, though several commended the inclusion of standards for Applied Learning. The reviewers supported the approach we adopted to "concretize" the performance standards through the inclusion of work samples (similar

approaches are being used in some other countries, notably England and Wales and Australia). Some of the reviewers were tentative in their response to the question of whether these performance standards are at least as demanding as their counterparts, noting the difficulty of drawing comparisons in the absence of assessment information, but offered comparative comments in terms of the areas covered by the standards. Some provided a detailed analysis of the performance descriptions together with the work samples and commentaries in terms of the expectations of students at comparable grade levels in other countries.

The reviews confirmed the conclusion we had drawn from our earlier analyses of the curricula, textbooks, and examinations of other countries: while the structure of curricula differs from country to country, the expectations contained in these performance standards represent a thorough coverage of the subject areas. No reviewer identified a case of significant omission. In some cases, reviewers noted that the range of expectations may be greater in the New Standards performance standards than in other countries; for example, few countries expect young people to integrate their learning to the extent required by the standards for investigation in New Standards Mathematics. At the same time, a recent study prepared for the Organisation for Economic Co-operation and Development reports that many countries are moving towards expecting students to engage in practical work of the kind required by the New Standards Science standards (Black and Atkin, 1996). The reviews also suggest that these performance standards contain expectations that are at least as rigorous as, and are in some cases more rigorous than, the demands made of students in other countries. None of the reviewers identified standards for which the expectations expressed in the standards were less demanding than those for students in other countries.

We will continue to monitor the rigor and coverage of the New Standards performance standards and assessments in relation to the expectations of students in other countries. In addition to the continued collection and review of materials from other countries, our efforts will include a review of the New Standards performance standards by the Third International Mathematics and Science Study, collaboration with the Council for Basic Education's plan to collect samples of student work from around the world, continued review of the American Federation of Teachers' series, *Defining World Class Standards*, and collaborative efforts with visiting scholars at the Learning Research and Development Center.

Standards should be useful, developing what is needed for citizenship, employment, and life-long learning.

We believe that the core disciplines provide the strongest foundation for learning what is needed for citizenship, employment, and life-long learning. Thus, we have established explicit standards in the core areas of English Language Arts, Mathematics,

and Science. But there is more. In particular, it is critical for young people to achieve high standards in Applied Learning—the fourth area we are working on.

Applied Learning focuses on the capabilities people need to be productive members of society, as individuals who apply the knowledge gained in school and elsewhere to analyze problems and propose solutions, to communicate effectively and coordinate action with others, and to use the tools of the information age workplace.

Applied Learning is not about "job skills" for students who are judged incapable of, or indifferent to, the challenges and opportunities of academic learning. They are the abilities all young people will need, both in the workplace and in their role as citizens. They are the thinking and reasoning abilities demanded both by colleges and by the growing number of high performance workplaces, those that expect people at every level of the organization to take responsibility for the quality of products and services. Some of these abilities are familiar; they have long been recognized goals of schooling, though they have not necessarily been translated clearly into expectations for student performance. Others break new ground; they are the kinds of abilities we now understand will be needed by everyone in the near future. All are skills attuned to the real world of responsible citizenship and dignified work that values and cultivates mind and spirit.

Many reviewers of drafts of these performance standards noted the absence of standards for the core area of social studies, including history, geography, and civics. At the time we began our work, national content standards for those areas were only in early stages of development; we resolved to focus our resources on the four areas we have worked on. As consensus builds around content standards in this additional area, we will examine the possibilities for expanding the New Standards system to include it.

Standards should be important and focused, parsimonious while including those elements that represent the most important knowledge and skills within the discipline.

As anyone who has been involved in a standards development effort knows, it is easier to add to standards than it is to limit what they cover. It is especially easier to resolve disagreements about the most important things to cover by including everything than it is to resolve the disagreements themselves. We have tried not to take the easier route. We adopted the principle of parsimony as a goal and have tried to practice it. At the same time, we have been concerned not to confuse parsimony with brevity. The performance descriptions are intended to make explicit what it is that students should know and the ways they should demonstrate the knowledge and skills they have acquired. For example, the standards relating to conceptual understanding in Mathematics spell out the expectations of students in some detail.

The approach we have adopted distinguishes between standards as a means of organizing the

STANDARDS FOR STANDARDS

knowledge and skills of a subject area and as a reference point for assessment, on the one hand, and the curriculum designed to enable students to achieve the standards, on the other. The standards are intended to focus attention on what is important but not to imply that the standards themselves should provide the organizing structure for the curriculum. In English Language Arts, for example, we have established a separate standard for conventions, grammar, and usage. This does not imply that conventions, grammar, and usage should be taught in isolation from other elements of English Language Arts. In fact, all of the work samples included in this book to illustrate the Conventions standard also illustrate parts of the Writing standard. What we are saying is that the work students do should be designed to help them achieve the Conventions standard. This means that conventions, grammar, and usage should not only be among the things assessed but should also be a focus for explicit reporting of student achievement.

Standards should be manageable given the constraints of time.

This criterion follows very closely on the last one, but focuses particularly on making sure that standards are "doable." One of the important features of our standards development effort is the high level of interaction among the people working on the different subject areas. We view the standards for the four areas as a set at each grade level; our publication of the standards by grade level reflects this orientation. This orientation has allowed us to limit the incidence of duplication across subject areas and to recognize and use opportunities for forging stronger connections among subject areas through the work that students do. A key to ensuring the standards are manageable is making the most of opportunities for student work to do "double" and even "triple duty." Most of the work samples included in this book demonstrate the way a single activity can generate work that allows students to demonstrate their achievement in relation to several standards within a subject area. Several of the work samples show how a single activity can allow students to demonstrate their achievement in relation to standards in more than one subject area. (See, for example, "Interview With Aspirin," page 96.)

Standards should be adaptable, permitting flexibility in implementation needed for local control, state and regional variation, and differing individual interests and cultural traditions.

These standards are intended for use in widely differing settings. One approach to tackling the need for flexibility to accommodate local control, state and regional variation, and differing individual interests and cultural traditions, is to make the standards general and to leave the job of translating the standards into more specific statements to the people who use them. We have not adopted that approach. These standards need to be specific enough to guide the New Standards assessment system; we have tried to

make them specific enough to do so. We have also tried to achieve the degree of specificity necessary to do this without unduly limiting the kinds of flexibility outlined above. Most of the standards are expressed in a way that leaves plenty of room for local decisions about the actual tasks and activities through which the standards may be achieved.

However, the specificity needed for standards intended to guide an assessment system does place some limits on flexibility. To tackle these apparently contradictory demands on the standards, we have adopted the notion of "substitution." This means that when users of these standards identify elements in the standards that are inconsistent with decisions made at the local level, they can substitute their own. An example of this is the Reading standard in English Language Arts. The Reading standard includes the requirement that students should read the equivalent of twenty-five books each year and specifies that they should read material of the quality and complexity illustrated in the sample reading list. We have included the reading list so as to be clear about the quality of reading material we are talking about at each grade level. But we do not claim that the titles on this list are the only ones that would be appropriate. Thus, users who have established their own reading lists and are satisfied with them can replace the lists provided with their own. There is, however, one important proviso: substitution only works when what is substituted is comparable with the material it replaces both in terms of the quality and the quantity of expectation.

Standards should be clear and usable.

Making standards sufficiently clear so that parents, teachers, and students can understand what they mean and what the standards require of them is essential to the purpose for establishing standards in the first place. It is also a challenge because while all of these groups need to understand what the standards are, the kinds of information they need are different. The most obvious difference is between the way in which the standards need to be presented to elementary school students so that they know what they should be striving to achieve and the way in which those same standards need to be presented to teachers so that they can help their students get there. If the standards were written only in a form that elementary school students could access, we would have to leave out information teachers need to do their job.

These standards are being presented in several formats. This version of the standards is written primarily for teachers. It includes technical language about the subject matter of the standards and terms that educators use to describe differences in the quality of work students produce. It could be described as a technical document. That does not mean that parents and students should not have access to it. We have tried to make the standards clear and to avoid jargon, but they do include language that may be difficult for students to comprehend and more detail

than some parents may want to deal with.

The standards are also included in the portfolio materials provided for student use. In these materials, the standards are set out in the form of guides to help students select work to include in their portfolios.

A less technical version of the standards is in preparation. It is being written with parents and the community in general in mind. The standards will be the same but they will be explained in more generally accessible language.

Standards should be reflective of broad consensus, resulting from an iterative process of comment, feedback, and revision including educators and the general public.

This publication is the result of progressive revisions to drafts over a period of eighteen months. Early drafts were revised in response to comment and feedback from reviewers nominated by the New Standards partners and the New Standards advisory committees for each of the subject areas, as well as other educators.

The *Consultation Draft*, published in November 1995, was circulated widely for comment. Some 1,500 individuals and organizations were invited to review the *Draft*. The reviewers included nominees of professional associations representing a wide range of interests in education, subject experts in the relevant fields, experienced teachers, business and industry groups, and community organizations. In addition, we held a series of face-to-face consultations to obtain responses and suggestions. These included detailed discussions with members of key groups and organizations and a series of meetings at which we invited people with relevant experience and expertise to provide detailed critique of the *Consultation Draft*. We also received numerous responses from people who purchased the *Consultation Draft* and who took the trouble to complete and return the response form that was included with each copy.

The process of revision of the performance standards was further informed by a series of independently-conducted focus group meetings with parents and other members of the community in several regions of the country and with teachers who were using the *Consultation Draft*.

The reviewers provided very supportive and constructive commentary on the *Consultation Draft*, both at the broad level of presentation and formatting of the performance standards and at the detailed level of suggestions for refinements to the performance descriptions for some of the standards. These comments have significantly informed the revisions made to the standards in the preparation of this publication.

HOW TO READ THESE PERFORMANCE STANDARDS

The standards for high school are set out in an overview on page 19. The overview provides the names of the standards for each of the four areas: English Language Arts, Mathematics, Science, and Applied Learning. To help you navigate your way through the book, a different color is used for each area.

High school level means the end of tenth grade.

The standards for high school are set at the level of achievement expected of students at approximately the end of tenth grade or the end of the common core. (For a definition of common core, see "Introduction to the performance standards for Mathematics," page 48.) Some students will achieve this level of performance earlier than the end of tenth grade. Some students will reach it later than the end of tenth grade. What is important is that students have the opportunity to meet the standards. (See "Deciding what constitutes a standard-setting performance," page 12.)

Each standard is identified by a symbol.

Turn to the performance descriptions for English Language Arts on pages 22-27. There are seven standards for English Language Arts, each identified by a symbol. The symbol for the Reading standard is **E1**. This symbol appears throughout the book wherever there is a reference to this standard.

1 **Most standards are made up of several parts.**

Most of the standards are made up of several parts, for example, the Reading standard has three parts. Each part is identified by a lower case letter; for example, the part of the Reading standard that refers to reading informational materials is **E1c**. These symbols are used throughout the book wherever there is a reference to the relevant part of a standard.

Performance descriptions tell what students are expected to know and be able to do.

Each part of a standard has a performance description. The performance description is a narrative description of what students are expected to know and be able to do. It is shown in color.

2 **Examples are the kinds of work students might do to demonstrate their achievement of the standards.**

Immediately following the performance descriptions for the standard are examples of the kinds of work students might do to demonstrate their achievement. The examples also indicate the nature and complexity of activities that are appropriate to expect of students at the grade level. However, we use the word "example" deliberately. The examples are intended only to show the kinds of work that students might do and to stimulate ideas for further kinds of work. None of the activities shown in the examples is necessarily required to meet the standard.

3 **Cross-references highlight the links between the examples and the performance descriptions.**

The symbols that follow each example show the part or parts of the standard to which the example relates.

4 **Cross-references also highlight links among the standards.**

Often the examples that go with the English Language Arts performance descriptions include cross-references to other parts of the English Language Arts standards.

5 **Cross-references also highlight opportunities for connecting activities across subject areas.**

Some cross-references shown following the examples identify parts of standards in other subject areas. These cross-references highlight examples for which the same activity may enable students to demonstrate their achievement in more than one subject matter.

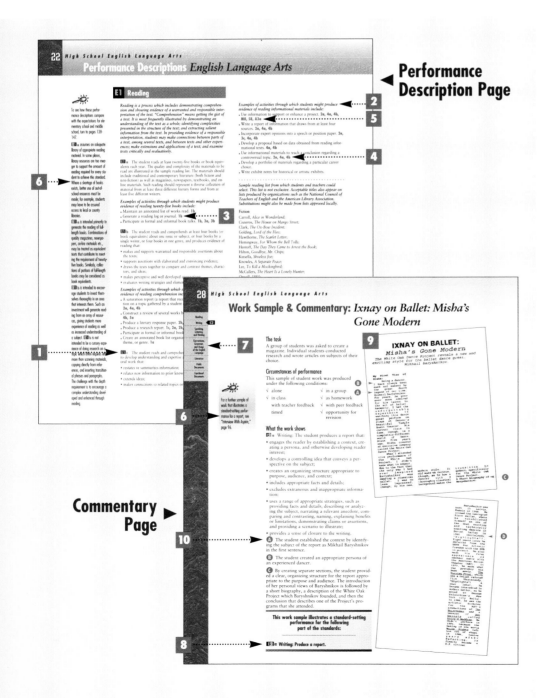

Performance Description Page

Commentary Page

HOW TO READ THESE PERFORMANCE STANDARDS

Some cross-references are to Applied Learning.

Some of the cross-references are to Applied Learning. Applied Learning is not a subject area in its own right. Applied Learning activities are expected to draw on subject matter from English language arts, mathematics, science, or other subjects. Generally, they will take place as part of studies within one or more subjects. The cross-references show activities that may provide a vehicle for students to demonstrate achievement of standards within one or more subject areas as well as standards for Applied Learning.

Some cross-references also show the possibilities for using work from Mathematics or Science to demonstrate their achievement of English Language Arts standards, and vice versa.

We have not tried to highlight every possible cross-reference, only to give an indication of the possibilities. The potential of these examples for realizing the possibilities of enabling students to demonstrate their achievement in more than one subject area depends to a large extent on the specific tasks that are presented to students.

6 Margin notes draw attention to particular aspects of the standards.

The notes in the margin draw attention to particular aspects of the standards, such as the resources to which students need access in order to meet the requirements of the standards.

Comparing the grade levels.

Each page showing performance descriptions has a note in the margin that directs attention to the Appendices which show the performance descriptions at each of the three grade levels: elementary, middle, and high school.

Work samples and commentaries.

Work samples and commentaries appear on the pages immediately following the performance descriptions.

7 Standards are highlighted in the bar at the side of the page.

The bar along the side of the pages showing student work highlights the standards that are illustrated by each work sample.

8 The box at the bottom of the page shows what is illustrated in the work sample.

The shaded box at the bottom of the page lists the parts of the standards that are illustrated in the work sample.

9 Work samples illustrate standard-setting performances.

Each work sample is a genuine piece of student work. We have selected it because it illustrates a standard-setting performance for one or more parts of the standards. (See "Not all performance standards are the same," page 10.)

10 The commentary explains why the work illustrates a standard-setting performance.

The commentary that goes with each work sample identifies the features of the work sample that illustrate the relevant parts of the standards. The commentary explains the task on which the student worked and the circumstances under which the work was completed. It draws attention to the qualities of the work with direct reference to the performance descriptions for the relevant standards.

The commentary also notes our reservations about the work.

The commentary also draws attention to any reservations we have about the student work. (See "Genuine student work," page 12.)

Performance Standards = performance descriptions + work samples + commentaries on the work samples.

Performance standards are, therefore, made up of a combination of performance descriptions, work samples, and commentaries on the work samples:

• The performance descriptions tell what students should know and the ways they should demonstrate the knowledge and skills they have acquired.

• The work samples show work that illustrates standard-setting performances in relation to parts of the standards.

• The commentaries explain why the work is standard-setting with reference to the relevant performance description or descriptions.

Each of these is an essential component of a performance standard.

Most work samples illustrate a standard-setting performance for parts of more than one standard.

Most work samples illustrate the quality of work expected for parts of more than one standard. For example, some of the work samples selected to illustrate parts of **E2**, Writing, also illustrate a standard-setting performance for one or both parts of **E4**, Conventions, Grammar, and Usage of the English Language, or for part of **E5**, Literature, or, possibly, all of these.

"Dreams: Can Money Make Them Come True?" (see page 40) is an example of a work sample that illustrates parts of more than one standard in English Language Arts.

A work sample may illustrate standards from more than one subject area.

Similarly, a work sample may illustrate parts of standards in more than one subject area. For example, a project completed for **M8**, Putting Mathematics to Work, might also illustrate the report writing part of **E2**, Writing. It might also qualify as a project within the requirements of **A1**, Problem Solving.

"Interview With Aspirin" (see page 96) is an example of a work sample that illustrates parts of standards from more than one subject area.

Reading **E1**
Writing **E2**
Speaking, Listening, and Viewing **E3**
Conventions, Grammar, and Usage of the English Language **E4**
Literature **E5**
Public Documents **E6**
Functional Documents **E7**

Number and Operation Concepts **M1**
Geometry & Measurement Concepts **M2**
Function & Algebra Concepts **M3**
Statistics & Probability Concepts **M4**
Problem Solving & Mathematical Reasoning **M5**
Mathematical Skills & Tools **M6**
Mathematical Communication **M7**
Putting Mathematics to Work **M8**

Physical Sciences Concepts **S1**
Life Sciences Concepts **S2**
Earth and Space Sciences Concepts **S3**
Scientific Connections and Applications **S4**
Scientific Thinking **S5**
Scientific Tools and Technologies **S6**
Scientific Communication **S7**
Scientific Investigation **S8**

Problem Solving **A1**
Communication Tools and Techniques **A2**
Information Tools and Techniques **A3**
Learning and Self-management Tools and Techniques **A4**
Tools and Techniques for Working With Others **A5**

NOT ALL PERFORMANCE STANDARDS ARE THE SAME

As you read these performance standards, you will notice that the standards are not all the same. The most obvious difference is in the way in which the performance descriptions for the standards are written. We did not impose a single style on the way in which the standards were written although we probably intended to do so when we began work. The reason we abandoned the idea of a single style is that during the course of the development process, it became increasingly apparent that the various standards are different in nature and have different purposes that lend themselves to different kinds of presentation. But the style we have adopted for each standard is not entirely idiosyncratic. There are some patterns that help make sense of the different styles and of the nature and purposes of the standards for which those styles have been used.

The first distinction that most people notice is the difference between the way the performance descriptions for the Mathematics and Science standards are written, on the one hand, and the way the performance descriptions for the English Language Arts and Applied Learning standards are written, on the other. But closer inspection reveals that the differences among the standards do not fall out as neatly as that division would suggest. Each subject area includes different styles of standards and the styles apply across subject areas.

We have identified four categories or kinds of standards, distinguished by their relationship to products of student learning and by the range of evidence required to demonstrate achievement of the standards. The distinctions are broad rather than neat, and we have sought only to define them generally rather than precisely. These differences among the standards have consequences for what it means to "meet a standard" and, therefore, for the ways in which we can use samples of student work to illustrate standard-setting performances.

Standards that describe a piece of work or a performance

One kind of standard is characterized by **E2**, Writing. Each part of this standard literally describes a piece of work that students are expected to produce and the knowledge and skills that should be evident in that work. For this kind of standard there is a one to one relationship between each part of the standard and a piece of work.

Standards that fit this category generally are the parts of **E1**, **E2**, **E3**, **E5**b, **M8**, **S8**, **A1**, **A2**, and **A5**.

Standards of this kind have several features:

• A single piece of work can meet the standard. In fact all of the requirements of the standard usually must be evident in a single piece of work for it to be judged as meeting the standard.

• The qualities that must be evident in a piece of work for it to meet the standard can be stated explicitly and are listed in bullet points as part of the performance description. These qualities can be thought of as assessment criteria or as a rubric for work that meets the standard.

Work samples and commentaries to illustrate standard-setting performances for standards of this kind include: "Ixnay on Ballet: Misha's Gone Modern," page 28, "Compost," page 104, and "Caring for Your Campus Lawn," page 118.

Standards that describe conceptual understanding

A second kind of standard is characterized by **M1**, Number and Operation Concepts. This standard describes conceptual understanding.

Standards that fit this category are **E5**a, **M1**, **M2**, **M3**, **M4**, **S1**, **S2**, **S3**, and **S4**.

These standards have several features:

• The standard is made up of a number of distinct parts. It is most unlikely that any single piece of work will demonstrate all parts of the standard. In fact, it is common for a single piece of work to relate only to some aspects of one part of the standard. Thus, the standard can usually only be met by multiple pieces of work.

• Conceptual understanding is developmental. Any one piece of work may contain elements of conceptual understanding that are below what is expected for the grade level and elements that either meet or exceed what is expected for the grade level. Judging whether the work is "good enough" often means making an on-balance judgment. The developmental nature of conceptual understanding makes it difficult to specify in more than general terms the qualities that need to be present in a piece of work for it to be judged as "good enough." These expectations need to be defined concept by concept.

In **M1**, **M2**, **M3**, and **M4**, the expectations have been defined more closely through progressive drafts of these performance standards.

S1, **S2**, **S3**, and **S4** are derived from the *National Science Education Standards* and the *Benchmarks for Science Literacy*, each of which contains detailed explication of the concepts and the expectations of students for conceptual understanding at different grade levels.

Work samples and commentaries to illustrate standard-setting performances for standards of this kind include: "Dreams: Can Money Make Them Come True?" page 40, "Cubes," page 64, and "Density of Sand," page 86.

Standards that describe skills and tools

The third kind of standard is made up of the standards that describe skills and tools, such as analytical skills. It is characterized by **S6**, Scientific Tools and Technologies.

Standards that fit this category generally are **E4**, **M5**, **M6**, **M7**, **S5**, **S6**, **S7**, **A3**, and **A4**.

These standards have several features:

• As with the standards that describe conceptual understanding, it is most unlikely that any single piece of work will demonstrate all parts of the standard. In fact, it is common for a single piece of work to relate only to some aspects of one part of the standard. Thus, the standard can only be met by multiple pieces of evidence.

• Also, like conceptual understanding, use of skills and tools is developmental. Any one piece of work may contain evidence of use of skills and tools that is below what is expected for the grade level and evidence of use that either meets or exceeds what is expected for the grade level. Deciding whether the work is "good enough" often means making an on-balance judgment.

• What distinguishes these standards from the other kinds is the body of evidence needed to demonstrate that the standard has been met. Here, sufficiency refers not only to the idea of coverage but also to a notion of consistency of application. We want to be confident that the work in question is representative of a body of work.

Ideally, work that provides evidence for these standards also provides evidence for other standards. This is the case for all of the work samples in this book that illustrate parts of these standards.

Work samples and commentaries to illustrate standard-setting performances for standards of this kind include: "School Bond Levy," page 36, "Galileo's Theater," page 76, and "Are Oysters Safe to Eat?" on page 94.

Standards that describe an accomplishment based on effort

The fourth category is closely related to the first, standards that describe a piece of work or a performance; it could be regarded as a sub-category of those standards. It is characterized by **E1**a, Read at least twenty-five books or book equivalents each year.

This part of the Reading standard is designed to encourage and reward effort. It is designed on principles similar to those that apply to the merit badges that have long formed a part of the system of encouragement and rewards for young people in community youth organizations like the Boy Scouts of America and the Girl Scouts of the U.S.A. The twenty-five book requirement is designed to encourage students to develop a habit of reading by requiring that they read a lot. The requirement is challenging, especially since the reading is expected to be of the quality of the materials included in the sample

reading list, but it is also confined. This part of the standard is not made more complex by requirements for evidence of depth of reading and comprehension. The message is, if you invest the effort, you will meet the requirement.

An example of a work sample and commentary to illustrate a standard-setting performance for this part of the Reading standard is "Books, Tomes, Novels, Treasures," page 46.

The differences among standards described here have implications for their assessment. (See "How the assessments are connected to the performance standards," page 14.)

THE WORK SAMPLES

The work samples and commentaries form an essential element of the performance standards because they give concrete meaning to the words in the performance descriptions and show the level of performance expected by the standards.

Genuine student work

In all cases, the work samples are genuine student work. While they illustrate standard-setting performances for parts of the standards, many samples are not "perfect" in every respect. Some, for example, include spelling errors, clumsy grammatical constructions, or errors of calculation. We think it is important that the standards be illustrated by means of authentic work samples and accordingly have made no attempt to "doctor" the work in order to correct these imperfections: the work has been included "warts and all." Where errors occur, we have included a note drawing attention to the nature of the mistakes and commenting on their significance in the context of the work. In some cases, for example, the work was produced as a first draft only (in which case it would be expected that the errors would be corrected in work presented as finished work), or there is evidence in the rest of the work to suggest that an error was a slip rather than an error in conceptual understanding.

In other words, we have tried to adopt reasonable expectations for correctness, but not to overlook errors where they arise. We have also resolved to apply those expectations consistently to all the work samples. We have paid attention to spelling, for example, not only in the work samples included to illustrate the English Language Arts standards, but also in those samples included to illustrate standards in the other subject areas. Similarly, we reviewed all work samples for accuracy in relation to mathematical and scientific content.

Work produced by a diverse range of students

The work samples in this book were produced by a diverse range of students in a wide variety of settings. The work comes from places as different from one another as rural communities in Vermont and Iowa, urban communities in Fort Worth, Pittsburgh, San Diego, and New York City, and suburban communities in Washington, California, and Colorado. It comes from students with a wide range of cultural backgrounds, some of whom have a first language other than English. And it comes from students studying in regular programs and from students studying in special education programs. Some of the work was produced under examination conditions in timed settings; most of it was produced in the context of on-going class work and extended projects. Most of the work was produced in school, but some samples were produced through out-of-school programs, such as 4-H and a community youth program.

What unites the work samples is that they all help to illustrate the performance standards by demonstrating standard-setting performances for parts of one or more of the standards.

Deciding what constitutes a standard-setting performance

The work samples published in this book were selected from a much wider range of samples. The samples came from students working on producing New Standards portfolios, from students' work on New Standards reference examinations, from other work produced by students in the classrooms of schools of the states and urban school districts that form the New Standards partnership, and from work produced by students in schools that are involved in related programs.

The collections of student work were reviewed through a variety of strategies to tap the judgment of teachers and subject experts about the "level of performance" at which each of the standards for high school should be set. We define the high school level as being the expectations for student performance at approximately the end of tenth grade or the end of the common core. (For a definition of common core, see "Introduction to the performance standards for Mathematics," page 48.) We used grade level as our reference point because it is in common use and most people understand it. However, "at approximately the end of tenth grade" begs some questions. Do we mean the level at which our tenth graders currently perform? Or, do we mean the level at which our tenth graders might perform if expectations for their performance were higher and the programs through which they learn were designed to help them meet those higher expectations? And, do we mean the level at which the highest-achieving tenth graders perform or the level at which most tenth graders perform?

We established our expectations in terms of what we should expect of students who work hard in a good program; that is, our expectations assume that students will have tried hard to achieve the standards and they will have studied in a program designed to help them to do so. These performance standards are founded on a firm belief that the great majority of students can achieve them, providing they work hard, they study a curriculum designed to help them achieve the standards that is taught by teachers who are prepared to teach it well, and they have adequate resources to succeed.

Some of the work samples included in this book were also included in the *Consultation Draft*; some appeared in earlier drafts as well. The appropriateness of these work samples as illustrating standard-setting performances has been the subject of extensive review, through discussions among our subject advisory committees and through round table discussions among experienced teachers and subject experts. Some of the work samples included in earlier drafts did not pass the scrutiny of these reviews and are not included in this book. Many of the new work samples were identified in the course of meetings set up to score portfolios produced through the New Standards portfolio field trial in 1995-96; others were identified in the process of scoring tasks on New Standards reference examinations. These scor-

ing meetings involve multiple scoring and discussion of samples among experienced teachers and subject experts. Cross-referencing the selection of work samples to illustrate the performance standards with the scoring of work produced through the two elements of the New Standards assessment system is critical to ensuring the development of coherence among all the parts of the system.

We used this process of progressive iterations of review of work samples, both in relation to the performance descriptions and in relation to our definition of high school level, to arrive at agreement about the meaning of high school level.

Inevitably, agreement about what work constitutes a standard-setting performance was easiest to achieve for those parts of the standards that relate to familiar kinds of expectations for student work. The parts of the Writing standard that refer to familiar and often-practiced kinds of writing such as narrative account are good examples of this. Not only did we have access to a wide range of samples from which to choose, but teachers and experts in the field have a long tradition of discussion and assessment of the features of good writing for a narrative account. Work samples to illustrate some other parts of the standards are much harder to find; for example, work samples to illustrate the investigations and projects standards in Mathematics and Science and work samples to illustrate each of the Applied Learning standards. Overall, we had access to relatively few work samples for Science and Applied Learning, since work on these areas within the New Standards system is at an early stage by comparison with the work in English Language Arts and Mathematics.

The comprehensiveness of the work samples

This book contains more than thirty samples of student work and additional samples are contained in the videotape that accompanies the book. We have sought to include work samples that illustrate standard-setting performances for each of the standards and for as many of the parts of the standards as possible. The range of work samples has been expanded considerably over progressive drafts of the standards. But the collection is still not comprehensive. We have included work samples to illustrate only some parts of the conceptual understanding standards in Mathematics and Science, for example, and work samples to illustrate only some of the kinds of projects and investigations included in those standards.

Limiting the number of samples was a deliberate decision. We decided that we would make best use of a print format by seeking to illustrate as many parts of the standards as possible but restricting the overall number of work samples to a manageable number. We also decided to restrict the work samples to samples that illustrate standard-setting performances in relation to parts of the standards, rather than include work samples that illustrate performances that are not of sufficient quality or that exceed expectations for the standards. (With regard to the latter point,

collections of work samples that illustrate performances at a range of performance levels do exist within the New Standards system, as part of the Released Tasks and scoring guides for the reference examinations and in the example portfolios; see page 16.)

It is arguable whether any given collection of work samples, regardless of how large, would be adequate for illustrating every part of the standards. Similarly, it is arguable whether any such collection could also demonstrate the range of ways that students might produce work that illustrates standard-setting performances and illustrate the standards more fully by including work that demonstrates a range of levels of performance. To be really useful, such a collection would also need to be capable of being updated to include more effective illustrations of the standards as work that serves the purpose becomes available— a need that we have already noted exists in relation to some of the standards. A publication format that could perform all of those functions presents a tall order, indeed. However, electronic formats hold the promise of making it possible to build a collection of this sort and to make it easily accessible. We hope to make use of the potential of electronic formats in the future.

HOW WILL THE PERFORMANCE STANDARDS BE USED?

The primary audience for these performance standards is teachers. We hope that teachers will use the standards to:

- Help students and parents understand what work that meets standards looks like;

- Inform discussions with their colleagues as they plan programs to help students learn to high standards;

- Challenge assumptions about what we can expect from students;

- Communicate the meaning of high standards to district administrators, school board members, and the public so they can work together to build learning environments that challenge all students.

New Standards will use the performance standards to provide:

- The basis of design specifications for the New Standards assessment system;

- The basis for reporting student scores on assessments within the New Standards system; and

- The basis for linking the New Standards assessment system with the standards and assessment systems of the members of the New Standards partnership.

Assessment based on standards

Performance standards define a student's academic responsibilities and, by implication, the teaching responsibilities of the school. How do we determine whether students have lived up to their academic responsibilities? We assess their work—is it "good enough" by comparison with the standards.

Assessment that serves the purpose of telling us how well students are performing by comparison with standards (standards-referenced assessment) differs from assessment designed to compare students to average performances (norm-referenced assessment). New Standards assessments are standards-referenced assessments. They start with performance standards and they take seriously the type, quality, and balance of performances spelled out by the standards. Assessment systems of this kind look a lot like a sampling of questions and assignments from a standards-based curriculum.

Common examples of standards-referenced examinations are the Advanced Placement (AP) exams of the College Board. The Scholastic Achievement Test (SAT), also from the College Board, is a contrasting example of a norm-referenced test. The AP exams look like the work (type, quality, and balance) students do in the AP courses whereas the SAT looks very different from the work students do in their college preparatory courses. Other well established standards-based examinations include licensure exams for many occupations such as pilots, architects, and electricians.

Unlike the AP or licensure exams, with explicit courses of study that have been debated and agreed upon in an open, public forum (e.g., the College Board, the state bar association or the board of realtors), many individual teacher's grades are based solely on their experience as students and teachers. Unless they participate in an external program like the AP or the International Baccalaureate, teachers rarely have the opportunity to see or discuss an end-of-course examination with others who teach the same course, no less to apply common criteria for marking. Even in the case of high school courses with departmental final examinations, the majority of the feedback to students throughout the school year is based on their individual teacher's judgment. And in the vast majority of the instances, especially in the elementary and middle school years, the individual teacher's standards apply almost exclusively.

It can be argued that the teacher, the person closest to the student's work, is in the best position to assess the student's accomplishment. However, the problem with an assessment system based on individual teacher judgment is that students in different classes, with different teachers, in different schools, work to widely varying standards. There is no common reference for teachers, students, or the public to compare performance across individuals or classrooms. This leads to wide variation in expectation and opportunity. Students get good grades one year for trying hard, then fail the following year for being too far below the average on a test.

New Standards has designed an assessment system that provides a common reference point for students, parents, teachers, and the public who want to judge student performance on the quality and quantity of student work that is expected at a particular level. The New Standards assessment system is based on these performance standards. It has three parts: reference examinations, portfolios, and teacher assessment. While each part of the system can be used independently, the most complete picture of performance referenced to the performance standards comes from using all three.

How the assessments are connected to the performance standards

The performance standards define a domain of expected student performances. Take the Reading standard as an example (see page 22). This standard begins with a definition of reading that describes what we expect students to *be able to do* at approximately the end of tenth grade or the end of the common core. The performance descriptions go on to spell out expectations for what students *will accomplish* in terms of the quantity, quality, range, and concentration of their reading. Furthermore, students are expected to *put their reading to work* and the standards say so; students have to produce work based on their reading of specific types of text.

We assess the different elements of the domain defined by a standard by using assessment methods appropriate to the expected performances.

In the English Language Arts reference examination

students read a selection of grade-level appropriate passages. The passages include both literary and informational selections and may include selections from public documents and functional documents. Students answer two types of questions about the passages. One type of question assesses "understanding of the text as a whole" as described in the definition in the Reading standard. These are straightforward questions about the gist of the text. Some of these questions ask students to write a few sentences; some are multiple choice. The second type of question about the same passages asks students to analyze the text, draw reasonable conclusions, and make interpretations—behaviors that characterize what competent readers do.

To demonstrate their achievement of the Reading standard students must also show what they have accomplished—just as people do when they apply for a job. Assessing actual accomplishments means evaluating a selection of student work according to criteria derived directly from the performance descriptions for the standards. New Standards portfolios are organized around "exhibits," each focused on an area of performance. The reading exhibit in the English Language Arts portfolio requires that students include at least four pieces of work that demonstrate their accomplishments in responding to literary and informational texts of appropriate complexity and in interpreting public documents and functional documents. The portfolio includes criteria for judging the entries in this exhibit. These criteria are drawn directly from the relevant performance descriptions. The criteria can be used by the student for self-assessment, by the teacher for feedback and grading, and by independent external scorers to report on achievement of standards to the public.

A further requirement of the reading exhibit in the portfolio, again based directly on the performance standards, is certification of what the student has read. The first part of the Reading standard (**E1**a) requires that students read at least twenty-five books or book equivalents each year. The reading must include a range of literary forms and works from several writers. Students are also required to read in depth (**E1**b). The appropriate assessor for these requirements is the teacher or another adult close to the student who can verify the student's claims for meeting this requirement. This component of the system for assessing achievement of the Reading standard is designed to work like a merit badge in the style of the awards developed by the Girl Scouts of the U.S.A. and the Boy Scouts of America.

In summary, students' achievement of the Reading standard is assessed through a combination of methods:

• The reference examination provides evidence of comprehension, analysis, and interpretation of literary and informational texts, related to the Reading standard as a whole and particularly to **E1**c. (These parts of the reference examination also provide evidence of the first part of the Literature standard, **E5**a. Depending on the selection of texts, they may also

provide evidence for the first part of the Public Documents standard, **E6**a, and the first part of the Functional Documents standard, **E7**a.)

• The reading exhibit for the portfolio provides evidence of working with literary and informational texts, related to **E5**a and **E1**c. (Entries included in this exhibit also demonstrate accomplishment in relation to **E5**a, **E6**a, and **E7**a and may be used to fulfill part of the requirements of the writing exhibit.)

• Teacher assessment, in the form of certification included in the reading exhibit, provides verification of students' claims regarding the twenty-five book requirement, related to **E1**a and **E1**b.

This example of how reading is assessed in the New Standards system illustrates several important points. First, the assessment methods and instruments suit the part of the standard to be assessed. Second, the criteria for judging achievement of the standard are drawn as directly as possible from the performance descriptions of the relevant standard. Third, comprehensive assessment of student achievement of the performance standards requires an appropriate combination of external on-demand assessments like the reference examination, externally-set auditable criteria like the portfolio, and teacher assessment.

The assessments are built on the basic principle that students who work hard in a good program should be able to achieve the performance standards. Students who do what is asked of them, read what they are assigned, do their homework, study for examinations, participate in class, and so on, have a right to expect all this work to pay off in learning. If it does not, there is something wrong with the program.

These standards expect students to work hard. For example, the Science standards include an expectation that every student will complete one science investigation in each of the years leading up to graduation chosen from the following: experiment, fieldwork, design, or secondary research. This requirement is demanding for all students, but doable. Most current college bound students are not asked do this much, let alone students who are not intending to go to college. This is not because these students are not capable of doing the work, but because their programs are not organized to give them the opportunity. However, virtually any student who works hard in a good program can produce investigations such as those identified above that meet standards for quality. By setting expectations like this, standards are raised for all students.

Raising standards for all students has important implications for the quality of curriculum and instruction. Indeed, one of the most important reasons for setting high standards is to challenge the system to perform for the students. Appropriate assessments based on these high standards can give the system feedback on how well it is doing and what it has to do next.

HOW WILL THE PERFORMANCE STANDARDS BE USED?

The reference examinations

Mathematics

The Mathematics reference examinations are targeted for grades 4, 8, and 10. Each examination consists of extended response and short answer items. Student responses are scored both holistically and dimensionally.

Students receive three scores for the Mathematics reference examination: one for understanding of mathematical concepts, one for mathematical skills, and one for problem solving and reasoning and mathematical communication.

Standards defining mathematics scores

SCORE	STANDARDS INCLUDED IN SCORE
Conceptual Understanding	**M1**, **M2**, **M3**, **M4**
Mathematical Skills	**M6**
Problem Solving and Reasoning/ Mathematical Communication	**M5**, **M7**

English Language Arts

The English Language Arts reference examinations are targeted for grades 4, 8, and 10. Each examination includes open-ended responses, short answer responses, essay questions, and multiple choice items. The student responses are scored holistically on two of these forms; the multiple choice responses are scanned.

Students receive four scores for the English Language Arts reference examination: one for writing, one for reading for basic understanding, one for interpretation and analysis of reading, and one for conventions, grammar, and usage of the English language.

Standards defining English Language Arts scores

SCORE	STANDARDS INCLUDED IN SCORE
Reading: Basic Understanding	**E1**
Reading: Inference and Analysis	**E1**
Writing	**E2**
Writing Conventions	**E4**

The criteria for scoring each task, for example, the writing sample or responses to the reading questions, are defined by rubrics for each score level (usually 0 to 5) and by anchor examples of student performance at each level. Trained scorers use these rubrics and anchor examples to score responses with high reliability.

Released Tasks from the reference examinations, complete with anchor examples and rubrics, are available to assist teachers and students to prepare for the examinations. The Released Tasks also include examples of student responses scored at each of the performance levels.

Each student's level of performance on the reference examination is determined by decision rules for profiles of scores on sets of items or tasks. These rules were established by panels of judges based on the stated expectations of the performance standards, with allowance made for the usual effects of the test-taking situation.

Levels of performance

For each standards-based score, there are five levels of student performance:

H—Achieved the Standard with Honors means that in addition to meeting the standards, a number of the student's responses exceeded the basic criteria for meeting the standard or displayed features characteristic of advanced knowledge and skill.

S—Achieved the Standard means that the student's performances met the standards as set out in the New Standards performance standards.

N—Nearly Achieved the Standard means that the student's performances almost but did not quite meet the performance standards.

B—Below the Standard means that the student's performances clearly did not meet the performance standards.

L—Little Evidence of Achievement means that the student's performances demonstrated little or none of the knowledge and skill expected by the performance standards.

The portfolio system

The portfolio system complements the reference examination by requiring selections of student work that provide evidence of achievement of the performance standards. The portfolios are organized into exhibits; each focuses on an area of performance and includes clear criteria for assessment. The structure and content of the exhibits parallels the structure of the performance standards. Each exhibit is composed of one or more entries; the entry slips tell students exactly what is required and how it will be assessed. The criteria come directly from the performance descriptions for the standards. For example, the middle school Mathematics portfolio has five exhibits drawn directly from the performance standards as is shown in the chart on the next page.

Mathematics portfolio

EXHIBIT	ENTRIES	STANDARD	EXHIBIT REQUIREMENTS
Conceptual Understanding	• Number and Operations • Geometry and Measurement • Functions and Algebra • Probability and Statistics	**M1** **M2** **M3** **M4**	To demonstrate conceptual understanding, students are required to provide evidence that they can use the concept to solve problems, represent it in multiple ways (through numbers, graphs, symbols, diagrams, or words, as appropriate), and explain it to someone else. The student must include at least two problems, and may include a third if necessary, to provide evidence of all three ways of demonstrating conceptual understanding (using, representing, and explaining).
Problem Solving	• Four problems	**M5**	The student must include four problems which, taken together, show the full range of problem solving required by the performance standard, including formulation, implementation, and conclusion. Problem solving is defined as using mathematical concepts and skills to solve non-routine, usually realistic, problems that challenge the student to organize the steps to follow for a solution.
Skills and Communication	• Skills • Communication Entries submitted for the other three exhibits are cited as evidence. A few additional pieces of work may be included here to fill important gaps.	**M6** **M7**	Entry Slips list skills from **M6** (e.g., compute accurately with rational numbers, use equations, formulas, and simple algebraic notation, use geometric shapes and terms correctly) and **M7** (e.g., present mathematical procedures and results clearly, systematically, and correctly; use mathematical language and representations with accuracy: numerical tables and equations, formulas, functions, algebraic equations, charts, graphs, and diagrams).
Project	• At least one large scale project each year	**M8**	This exhibit requires students to put their mathematics to work. Entry slips state criteria, from **M8**, for assessing the following kinds of projects: data study, mathematical model of a physical system, design of a physical structure, management and planning analysis, pure mathematics investigation, and history of a mathematical idea.
Work in Progress	• No entries submitted		Students keep sample work during the year as candidates for selecting as entries.

Portfolios put the standards directly in the hands of students. They help students manage their responsibility for producing work that achieves the performance standards. They also provide a focus for conversations among teachers and students about how the students' work shows evidence of meeting the performance standards and about the further work students need to do to meet the standards.

The portfolio system includes exhibit instructions and entry slips for students, and materials for teachers, including scoring materials. The scoring materials include procedures, criteria, and example exhibits of student work.

Linking the New Standards system with partners' standards and assessment systems

"Linking" is the process of establishing the extent and degree of match between the New Standards system and those of the New Standards partners. It is an essential step in the process of enabling our partners to make decisions about their use of the New Standards system, either in part or as a whole.

Linking is crucial for assuring that student work is assessed according to the same standards that guided its production.

The performance standards provide the initial point of reference for the linking process. While comprehensive linking of assessment systems requires the further step of linking scores on performances, linking standards is a necessary first step and provides a good indication of the potential for linking New Standards with partners' systems.

The ones I favor the most
be the ones written by [...]
and Mary Higgins Clark. I
I felt that I was able
and comprehend the choi[...]
my teacher had me rea[...]
exception of Jane Eyre, I
of them. In the beginning
write how easily distra[...]
when I'm reading litera[...]
specific class. This is e[...]
the warm weather and [...]
CD I received for my
of the reasons I'm so
meditation, besides gettin[...]

Galileo Theater

STAGE

[...]nd Microscope:

[...]looked like spiders with front claws. These we[...]
[...]gy book they do not have the upright tail with[...]
[...] front and the two segment body similar to a [...]
[...]tch and hold food

[...]se we recognized right away. They were by fa[...]
[...]stification book says they are omnivores (like [...]
[...]ful wound. We did not want to find out and vot[...]
[...]d to like the apple peal the best. We could alwa[...]
[...]nd leave fruit out of one bottle to find out if th[...]

Application Project
Proposal Paper

Have you ever wanted to go for a ride into the [...]
drive an almost non-polluting vehicle? For my applicati[...]
to build a full size, fully drivable, fully operational solar/[...]
currently, and will continue to build, and improve an ele[...]
with the aid of 4 other students, and the watchful eye[...]
motor, a speed control, and two batteries from R.U.[...]
In return, we must build an electric or, solar-electric ve[...]
jumped at the rare opportunity to build the Electro-[...]
it took us until after December to get a team togethe[...]
This is the main reason that I have started my applica[...]
middle of building this vehicle.

There are many skills that have helped me along [...]
many new skills I have acquired while building this vehic[...]
important skills I have are those pertaining to my fami[...]
tools (saws, drills, grinders, sanders, etc.) used to fab[...]
have been around these different tools all of my life si[...]
a custom woodworking company. I have also taken m[...]

OVERVIEW OF THE PERFORMANCE STANDARDS

The high school standards are set at a level of performance approximately equivalent to the end of tenth grade or the end of the common core. (For a definition of common core, see "Introduction to the performance standards for Mathematics," page 48.) It is expected that some students might achieve this level earlier and others later than this grade. (See "Deciding what constitutes a standard-setting performance," page 12.)

E English Language Arts

E1 Reading
E2 Writing
E3 Speaking, Listening, and Viewing
E4 Conventions, Grammar, and Usage of the English Language
E5 Literature
E6 Public Documents
E7 Functional Documents

M Mathematics

M1 Number and Operation Concepts
M2 Geometry and Measurement Concepts
M3 Function and Algebra Concepts
M4 Statistics and Probability Concepts
M5 Problem Solving and Mathematical Reasoning
M6 Mathematical Skills and Tools
M7 Mathematical Communication
M8 Putting Mathematics to Work

S Science

S1 Physical Sciences Concepts
S2 Life Sciences Concepts
S3 Earth and Space Sciences Concepts
S4 Scientific Connections and Applications
S5 Scientific Thinking
S6 Scientific Tools and Technologies
S7 Scientific Communication
S8 Scientific Investigation

A Applied Learning

A1 Problem Solving
A2 Communication Tools and Techniques
A3 Information Tools and Techniques
A4 Learning and Self-management Tools and Techniques
A5 Tools and Techniques for Working With Others

Introduction to the performance standards for

English Language Arts

The performance standards for English Language Arts define high standards of literacy for American students. The standards focus on what is central to the domain; they are built around reading, writing, speaking, listening, and viewing; and they acknowledge the importance of conventions, literature, public discourse, and functional documents. The standards were developed with the help of classroom teachers and content experts in concert with both the National Council of Teachers of English and the International Reading Association.

The performance standards represent a balanced view of what students should know and the ways they should demonstrate the knowledge and skills they have acquired in this domain. Students are expected to read both literature and informational texts. They are required to produce writing that is traditionally associated with the classroom, including narratives and reports, and they are also expected to exhibit increasing expertise in producing and critiquing public and functional documents. In addition, students are expected to become proficient speakers, to hone their listening skills, and to develop a critical awareness of viewing patterns and the influence of media on their lives. The work students produce in both written and spoken formats is expected to be of high quality in terms of rhetorical structures as well as the conventions of the English language.

The five standards for English Language Arts are as follows:

E1 Reading;

E2 Writing;

E3 Speaking, Listening, and Viewing;

E4 Conventions, Grammar, and Usage of the English Language;

E5 Literature.

At the high school level, two additional standards are added:

E6 Public Documents;

E7 Functional Documents.

The expansion of literacy at the high school level reflects the growing need for students to understand the range of materials they must deal with throughout their lives. Both public documents and functional documents are introduced in the Reading standard at the middle school level where students are required

to demonstrate a familiarity with these kinds of texts. It is important that the middle school standard anticipates the advanced degree of understanding expected at the high school level where students are expected both to critique and produce materials of these kinds.

The first part of the Reading standard, **E1** a, requires students to read a wide range of materials by a range of authors on different subjects. The requirement here is fairly simple: read twenty-five books of the quality illustrated in the sample reading list. Too often students are not given the opportunity to read full length books because of curricular restraints, a lack of resources, or a lack of access to books. The missed opportunity results in a tremendous loss of potential literacy skills that can only be developed when students become habitual readers. The requirement to read twenty-five books a year provides all students the opportunity to become habitual readers and represents a realistic and worthwhile goal that can be reached if students simply invest the effort. The sample reading list is included to provide an indication of the quality and complexity of the materials students are expected to read. Any or all of the specific works on the list may be substituted with other works providing the works that are substituted are of comparable quality and complexity to those that are replaced.

The second part of the Reading standard, **E1** b, requires students to "go deep" in at least one area of interest. We know that students who read regularly tend to read what interests them; note the trends in the work sample, "Books, Tomes, Novels, Treasures," page 46. This part of the Reading standard is intended to encourage all students to do what good readers do and pursue themes, authors, and genres that are of interest to them.

The third part of the Reading, **E1** c, standard requires students to work with informational materials in order to develop understanding and expertise about the topics they investigate. This area of informational materials is of great importance, and for too long it has been neglected in the school curriculum. Its inclusion as a separate part of the Reading standard indicates our desire that more attention be given to reading a broad range of materials written for a variety of audiences and purposes.

The Writing standard, **E2**, requires students to demonstrate accomplishment in six types of writing. Each of these writing types is defined by a distinct set of criteria, though there is clearly some overlap. The use of criteria specific to the writing types is meant to ensure that students become familiar with the strategies that characterize specific writing forms and to encourage students to use these criteria when they review and revise their work. All of the commentaries on the work samples related to the Writing standard use the language of these criteria and make

explicit how the student work sample illustrates an accomplished example. The types of writing included in this standard are all forms of writing commonly produced both in and out of school.

The Speaking, Listening, and Viewing standard, **E3**, is the only standard that has changed dramatically from previous drafts of these performance standards. The primary change is that the speaking and listening parts of the standard now revolve around a variety of social situations: one-to-one interaction, group discussion, and oral presentation, and that the viewing part of the standard now asks for evidence of an awareness of media influences. The attention to viewing represents a growing awareness that the media play an integral part in most students' lives and that students require increasingly sophisticated tools for dealing with media influences.

The Conventions, Grammar, and Usage of the English Language standard, **E4**, is listed as a separate standard even though the parts of the standard are always assessed in either a written or spoken context. The first part of the standard indicates the expectation that students should be able to represent themselves appropriately using standard English. The second part of the standard reflects the understanding that high quality work most often comes about as a result of a sustained effort represented by numerous drafts of a particular piece of work. In classrooms where high quality work is consistently produced, the revision process is most often an integral part of the curriculum.

The Literature standard, **E5**, like the Conventions standard, is listed separately even though it could easily be broken into two pieces and placed respectively within the Reading and Writing standards. However, for many people who go through school, the study of literature is the only situation in which they have the chance to explore the big ideas and the themes that emerge from social and political conflict, both in their own writing and in the writing of others. An understanding of these ideas and themes is integral for students who will one day be responsible for the negotiation of meaning important to a democracy. The first part of the Literature standard asks students to explore and critique the writing of others with these kinds of critical skills in mind. The second part of the standard asks students to produce literature with the hope that doing this will help students better understand the world that shapes both their literature and the literature of professional writers.

The Public Documents standard, **E6**, addresses the increasing need to prepare students to deal with the complexities involved in being a citizen in a democracy by focusing on those texts that address issues in the pubic sphere. Integral to active citizenship is an understanding of both the issues being addressed and the methods by which these issues are presented.

Students need to be able to examine critically the evidence presented to them, determine the types of evidence that are acceptable in formulating various arguments, and to make informed judgments about issues that impact them. To do so, students must learn to read with a critical eye the arguments made by other people. The first part of the Public Documents standard asks students to offer a critique of a document that addresses a current issue; the second part asks students to write responsibly about an issue currently being debated in the public sphere.

The Functional Documents standard, **E7**, recognizes the increasing need people have to communicate with one another. In the emerging literacy of a technological world, documents such as the instructions for programming a VCR, computer manuals, and corporate memoranda each serve the purpose of helping someone get something done. Students who will be asked to function efficiently in such a world need to be adept with the literacy such a world brings, which means they need to become skilled at "reading" materials such as charts and graphs, reference materials for large, complex procedures, and memoranda and other correspondence that contain the information they need to do their jobs successfully. Students must also understand how to participate in such a world as contributors, whether that means producing a set of instructions or communicating a body of data graphically. The first part of the Functional Documents standard asks students to critique a functional document in terms of its effectiveness in accomplishing its purpose; the second part asks students to successfully prepare a document that has as its primary purpose the goal of getting something done.

Performance Descriptions *English Language Arts*

E1 Reading

To see how these performance descriptions compare with the expectations for elementary school and middle school, turn to pages 138-147.

E1 a assumes an adequate library of appropriate reading material. In some places, library resources are too meager to support the amount of reading required for every student to achieve this standard. Where a shortage of books exists, better use of out-of-school resources must be made; for example, students may have to be assured access to local or county libraries.

E1 a is intended primarily to generate the reading of full-length books. Combinations of quality magazines, newspapers, on-line materials etc., may be treated as equivalent texts that contribute to meeting the requirement of twenty-five books. Similarly, collections of portions of full-length books may be considered as book equivalents.

E1 b is intended to encourage students to invest themselves thoroughly in an area that interests them. Such an investment will generate reading from an array of resources, giving students more experience of reading as well as increased understanding of a subject. **E1 b** is not intended to be a cursory experience of doing research on a topic which often requires little more than scanning materials, copying directly from references, and inserting transitional phrases and paragraphs. The challenge with the depth requirement is to encourage a complex understanding developed and enhanced through reading.

Reading is a process which includes demonstrating comprehension and showing evidence of a warranted and responsible interpretation of the text. "Comprehension" means getting the gist of a text. It is most frequently illustrated by demonstrating an understanding of the text as a whole; identifying complexities presented in the structure of the text; and extracting salient information from the text. In providing evidence of a responsible interpretation, students may make connections between parts of a text, among several texts, and between texts and other experiences; make extensions and applications of a text; and examine texts critically and evaluatively.

E1 a The student reads at least twenty-five books or book equivalents each year. The quality and complexity of the materials to be read are illustrated in the sample reading list. The materials should include traditional and contemporary literature (both fiction and non-fiction) as well as magazines, newspapers, textbooks, and on-line materials. Such reading should represent a diverse collection of material from at least three different literary forms and from at least five different writers.

Examples of activities through which students might produce evidence of reading twenty-five books include:
▲ Maintain an annotated list of works read. **1b**
▲ Generate a reading log or journal. **1b**
▲ Participate in formal and informal book talks. **1b, 3a, 3b**

E1 b The student reads and comprehends at least four books (or book equivalents) about one issue or subject, or four books by a single writer, or four books in one genre, and produces evidence of reading that:
• makes and supports warranted and responsible assertions about the texts;
• supports assertions with elaborated and convincing evidence;
• draws the texts together to compare and contrast themes, characters, and ideas;
• makes perceptive and well developed connections;
• evaluates writing strategies and elements of the author's craft.

Examples of activities through which students might produce evidence of reading comprehension include:
▲ A saturation report (a report that recounts substantial information on a topic gathered by a student over a period of time). **1c, 2a, 4a, 4b**
▲ Construct a review of several works by a single author. **2b, 4a, 4b, 5a**
▲ Produce a literary response paper. **2b, 4a, 4b, 5a**
▲ Produce a research report. **1c, 2a, 2b, 4a, 4b, 5a, M8f**
▲ Participate in formal or informal book talks. **1a, 1c, 3a, 3b, 5a**
▲ Create an annotated book list organized according to author, theme, or genre. **1a**

E1 c The student reads and comprehends informational materials to develop understanding and expertise and produces written or oral work that:
• restates or summarizes information;
• relates new information to prior knowledge and experience;
• extends ideas;
• makes connections to related topics or information.

Examples of activities through which students might produce evidence of reading informational materials include:
▲ Use information to support or enhance a project. **2a, 4a, 4b, M8, S8, A3a**
▲ Write a report of information that draws from at least four sources. **2a, 4a, 4b**
▲ Incorporate expert opinions into a speech or position paper. **2e, 3c, 4a, 4b**
▲ Develop a proposal based on data obtained from reading informational texts. **4a, 4b**
▲ Use informational materials to reach a conclusion regarding a controversial topic. **2e, 4a, 4b**
▲ Develop a portfolio of materials regarding a particular career choice.
▲ Write exhibit notes for historical or artistic exhibits.

....

This is a sample reading list from which the students and teachers could select. This list is not exclusive. Acceptable titles also appear on lists produced by organizations such as the National Council of Teachers of English and the American Library Association. Substitutions might also be made from lists approved locally.

Fiction

Carroll, *Alice in Wonderland;*
Cisneros, *The House on Mango Street;*
Clark, *The Ox-Bow Incident;*
Golding, *Lord of the Flies;*
Hawthorne, *The Scarlet Letter;*
Hemingway, *For Whom the Bell Tolls;*
Hentoff, *The Day They Came to Arrest the Book;*
Hilton, *Goodbye, Mr. Chips;*
Kinsella, *Shoeless Joe;*
Knowles, *A Separate Peace;*
Lee, *To Kill a Mockingbird;*
McCullers, *The Heart Is a Lonely Hunter;*
Orwell, *1984;*
Paulsen, *Canyons;*
Portis, *True Grit;*
Potok, *Davita's Harp;*
Stoker, *Dracula;*
Wartski, *A Boat to Nowhere;*
Welty, *The Golden Apples.*

Non-Fiction

Angell, *Late Innings;*
Angelou, *I Know Why the Caged Bird Sings;*
Ashe, *Days of Grace;*
Beal, *"I Will Fight No More Forever": Chief Joseph and the Nez Perce War;*
Bishop, *The Day Lincoln Was Shot;*
Bloom, *The Closing of the American Mind;*
Campbell, *The Power of Myth;*
Covey, *Seven Habits of Highly Effective People;*
Galarza, *Barrio Boy;*
Hawking, *A Brief History of Time;*
Houston, *Farewell to Manzanar;*
Kennedy, *Profiles in Courage;*
Kingsley and Levitz, *Count Us In: Growing Up With Down Syndrome;*
Kingston, *Woman Warrior;*
Mazer, ed., *Going Where I'm Coming From;*

English Language Arts

Momaday, *The Way to Rainy Mountain*;
Rodriquez, *Hunger of Memory*;
Sternberg, *User's Guide to the Internet*;
Wright, *Black Boy*.

Poetry

Angelou, *I Shall Not be Moved*;
Bly, ed., *News of the Universe*;
Cummings, *Collected Poems*;
Dickinson, *Complete Poems*;
Randall, ed., *The Black Poets*;
Carruth, ed., *The Voice That Is Great Within Us*;
Hughes, *Selected Poems*;
Knudson and Swenson, eds., *American Sports Poems*;
Longfellow, *Evangeline*;
Wilbur, *Things of This World*.

Drama

Christie, *And Then There Were None*;
Hansberry, *A Raisin in the Sun*;
McCullers, *The Member of the Wedding*;
Pomerance, *The Elephant Man*;
Rose, *Twelve Angry Men*;
Rostand, *Cyrano de Bergerac*;
Shakespeare, *Romeo and Juliet; Julius Caesar*;
Van Druten, *I Remember Mama*;
Wilder, *The Skin of Our Teeth*;
Wilson, *The Piano Lesson*.

Folklore/Mythology

Evslin, *Adventures of Ulysses*;
Pinsent, *Greek Mythology*;
Stewart, *The Crystal Cave*;
Burland, *North American Indian Mythology*;
White, *The Once and Future King*.

Modern Fantasy and Science Fiction

Adams, *Watership Down*;
Asimov, *Foundation*;
Bradbury, *The Martian Chronicles*;
Clarke, *2001: A Space Odyssey*;
Clarke, *Childhood's End*;
Frank, *Alas, Babylon*;
Herbert, *Dune*;
Lewis, *Out of the Silent Planet*;
McCaffrey, *Dragonflight*;
Twain, *A Connecticut Yankee in King Arthur's Court*;
Verne, *20,000 Leagues Under the Sea*.

Magazines and Newspapers

Omni;
Sports Illustrated;
Literary Cavalcade (Scholastic);
National Geographic;
Smithsonian;
Newsweek;
Time.

Other

Computer manuals; instructions; contracts; technical materials.

E2 Writing

Writing is a process through which a writer shapes language to communicate effectively. Writing often develops through a series of initial plans and multiple drafts and through access to informed feedback and response. Purpose, audience, and context contribute to the form and substance of writing as well as to its style, tone, and stance.

E2 a The student produces a report that:

• engages the reader by establishing a context, creating a persona, and otherwise developing reader interest;

• develops a controlling idea that conveys a perspective on the subject;

• creates an organizing structure appropriate to purpose, audience, and context;

• includes appropriate facts and details;

• excludes extraneous and inappropriate information;

• uses a range of appropriate strategies, such as providing facts and details, describing or analyzing the subject, narrating a relevant anecdote, comparing and contrasting, naming, explaining benefits or limitations, demonstrating claims or assertions, and providing a scenario to illustrate;

• provides a sense of closure to the writing.

Examples of reports include:

• An I-search essay (an essay that details a student's search for information as well as the information itself; I-search papers are developed through a variety of means, e.g., interviews, observation, as well as traditional library research). **1c, 4a, 4b**

▲ A saturation report (a report that recounts substantial information on a topic gathered by a student over a period of time). **1c, 4a, 4b**

▲ A report produced as part of studies in subjects such as science, social studies, and mathematics. **1c, 4a, 4b, M7b, M7e, M7g, S7a, S7b, S7c**

▲ A formal or informal research paper. **1c, 4a, 4b, 5a**

▲ An investigative report for a newspaper. **1c, 4a, 4b**

E2 b The student produces a response to literature that:

• engages the reader through establishing a context, creating a persona, and otherwise developing reader interest;

• advances a judgment that is interpretive, analytic, evaluative, or reflective;

• supports a judgment through references to the text, references to other works, authors, or non-print media, or references to personal knowledge;

• demonstrates understanding of the literary work through suggesting an interpretation;

• anticipates and answers a reader's questions;

• recognizes possible ambiguities, nuances, and complexities;

• provides a sense of closure to the writing.

Examples of responses to literature include:

▲ An evaluation of a piece of literature or several pieces of literature. **1b, 4a, 4b, 5a**

▲ A comparison of a piece of literature with its media presentation. **1b, 3d, 4a, 4b, 5a**

▲ A response that focuses on personalizing the theme of a literary work. **1b, 4a, 4b, 5a**

▲ An analysis of the significance of a section of a novel in terms of its significance to the novel as a whole. **1b, 4a, 4b, 5a**

▲ An evaluation of the role played by setting in a novel. **1b, 4a, 4b, 5a**

(Continued overleaf)

Samples of student work that illustrate standard-setting performances for these standards can be found on page 28-47.

The examples that follow the performance descriptions for each standard are examples of the work students might do to demonstrate their achievement. The examples also indicate the nature and complexity of activities that are appropriate to expect of students at the high school level.

The cross-references that follow the examples highlight examples for which the same activity, and possibly even the same piece of work, may enable students to demonstrate their achievement in relation to more than one standard. In some cases, the cross-references highlight examples of activities through which students might demonstrate their achievement in relation to standards for more than one subject matter.

E2 b is meant to expand the repertoire of responses students traditionally write when they respond to literature. This type of response requires an understanding of writing strategies.

Performance Descriptions *English Language Arts*

E2 Writing continued

To see how these performance descriptions compare with the expectations for elementary school and middle school, turn to pages 138-147.

The examples that follow the performance descriptions for each standard are examples of the work students might do to demonstrate their achievement. The examples also indicate the nature and complexity of activities that are appropriate to expect of students at the high school level.

The cross-references that follow the examples highlight examples for which the same activity, and possibly even the same piece of work, may enable students to demonstrate their achievement in relation to more than one standard. In some cases, the cross-references highlight examples of activities through which students might demonstrate their achievement in relation to standards for more than one subject matter.

▲ An analysis of the effect of a minor character on the plot of a novel. **1b, 4a, 4b, 5a**

▲ An interpretation of a recurring motif in a novel or a play. **1b, 4a, 4b, 5a**

▲ A comparison of two critical interpretations of a poem or a work of fiction. **1b, 4a, 4b, 5a**

E2 c The student produces a narrative account (fictional or auto-biographical) that:

• engages the reader by establishing a context, creating a point of view, and otherwise developing reader interest;

• establishes a situation, plot, point of view, setting, and conflict (and for autobiography, the significance of events and of conclusions that can be drawn from those events);

• creates an organizing structure;

• includes sensory details and concrete language to develop plot and character;

• excludes extraneous details and inconsistencies;

• develops complex characters;

• uses a range of appropriate strategies, such as dialogue, tension or suspense, naming, pacing, and specific narrative action, e.g., movement, gestures, expressions;

• provides a sense of closure to the writing.

Examples of narrative accounts include:

▲ A biographical account. **4a, 4b, 5b**

▲ A fiction or non-fiction story. **4a, 4b, 5b**

▲ A personal narrative. **4a, 4b, 5b**

▲ A narrative poem or song based on a modern hero. **4a, 4b, 5b**

▲ A historical account. **1c, 4a, 4b**

▲ A parody of a particular narrative style, e.g., fable, soap opera. **4a, 4b, 5b**

E2 d The student produces a narrative procedure that:

• engages the reader by establishing a context, creating a persona, and otherwise developing reader interest;

• provides a guide to action for a complicated procedure in order to anticipate a reader's needs; creates expectations through predictable structures, e.g., headings; and provides smooth transitions between steps;

• makes use of appropriate writing strategies, such as creating a visual hierarchy and using white space and graphics as appropriate;

• includes relevant information;

• excludes extraneous information;

• anticipates problems, mistakes, and misunderstandings that might arise for the reader;

• provides a sense of closure to the writing.

Examples of narrative procedures include:

▲ A set of rules for organizing a class meeting. **4a, 4b, 7b**

▲ A set of instructions for playing computer games. **4a, 4b, 7b**

▲ A set of instructions for using media technology. **4a, 4b, 7b**

▲ A lab report. **4a, 4b, 58**

▲ A report of a mathematical investigation. **4a, 4b, M8**

▲ A set of instructions for conducting searches on the Web. **4a, 4b, 7b**

E2 e The student produces a persuasive essay that:

• engages the reader by establishing a context, creating a persona, and otherwise developing reader interest;

• develops a controlling idea that makes a clear and knowledgeable judgment;

• creates an organizing structure that is appropriate to the needs, values, and interests of a specified audience, and arranges details, reasons, examples, and anecdotes effectively and persuasively;

• includes appropriate information and arguments;

• excludes information and arguments that are irrelevant;

• anticipates and addresses reader concerns and counter-arguments;

• supports arguments with detailed evidence, citing sources of information as appropriate;

• uses a range of strategies to elaborate and persuade, such as definitions, descriptions, illustrations, examples from evidence, and anecdotes;

• provides a sense of closure to the writing.

Examples of persuasive essays include:

▲ A position paper. **4a, 4b**

▲ A problem-solution paper. **4a, 4b**

▲ An opening statement for a debate. **4a, 4b, 3c**

▲ An evaluation of a product or policy. **4a, 4b, A1a**

▲ A critique of a public policy. **4a, 4b, 6b**

▲ An editorial on a current issue that uses reasoned arguments to support an opinion. **4a, 4b, 6b**

E2 f The student produces a reflective essay that:

• engages the reader by establishing a context, creating a persona, and otherwise developing reader interest;

• analyzes a condition or situation of significance;

• develops a commonplace, concrete occasion as the basis for the reflection, e.g., personal observation or experience;

• creates an organizing structure appropriate to purpose and audience;

• uses a variety of writing strategies, such as concrete details, comparing and contrasting, naming, describing, creating a scenario;

• provides a sense of closure to the writing.

Examples of reflective essays include:

▲ An analysis of the significance of a proverb or quotation. **4a, 4b**

▲ A report about a concrete occasion and its implications over time. **2a, 4a, 4b**

▲ An essay comparing a school issue to broader societal concerns. **4a, 4b, 6b**

▲ A paper explaining how some experiences, conditions, or concerns have universal significance. **4a, 4b**

▲ A self-reflective essay evaluating a portfolio to be submitted. **4a, 4b**

▲ A comparison of a scene from a work of fiction with a lesson learned from a personal experience. **2b, 4a, 4b**

▲ A paper about a common childhood experience from a more adult perspective. **4a, 4b, 5b**

English Language Arts

E3 Speaking, Listening, and Viewing

Speaking, listening, and viewing are fundamental processes which people use to express, explore, and learn about ideas. The functions of speaking, listening, and viewing include gathering and sharing information; persuading others; expressing and understanding ideas; coordinating activities with others; and selecting and critically analyzing messages. The contexts of these communication functions include one-to-one conferences, small group interactions, large audiences and meetings, and interactions with broadcast media.

E3 a The student participates in one-to-one conferences with a teacher, paraprofessional, or adult volunteer, in which the student:

- initiates new topics in addition to responding to adult-initiated topics;
- asks relevant questions;
- responds to questions with appropriate elaboration;
- uses language cues to indicate different levels of certainty or hypothesizing, e.g., "what if...," "very likely...," "I'm unsure whether...";
- confirms understanding by paraphrasing the adult's directions or suggestions.

Examples of one-to-one interactions include:

▲ Analytical discussion of movies or television programs in a one-to-one situation. **3d, 4a, 4b**

▲ Student-teacher conferences regarding a draft of an essay, the student's progress on a mathematics assignment, or the state of a science project. **4b**

▲ Assessment interview by a teacher about an author or book. **1b, 5a**

E3 b The student participates in group meetings, in which the student:

- displays appropriate turn-taking behaviors;
- actively solicits another person's comment or opinion;
- offers own opinion forcefully without dominating;
- responds appropriately to comments and questions;
- volunteers contributions and responds when directly solicited by teacher or discussion leader;
- gives reasons in support of opinions expressed;
- clarifies, illustrates, or expands on a response when asked to do so; asks classmates for similar expansions;
- employs a group decision-making technique such as brainstorming or a problem-solving sequence (e.g., recognize problem, define problem, identify possible solutions, select optimal solution, implement solution, evaluate solution);
- divides labor so as to achieve the overall group goal efficiently.

Examples of activities involving group meetings include:

▲ Develop and negotiate a classroom rubric.
▲ Engage in classroom town meetings.
▲ Participate in book talks with other students. **1a, 1b, 1c, 5a**
▲ Work as part of a group to solve a complex mathematical task.
▲ Role-play to better understand a certain historical event. **1c**
▲ Participate in peer writing response groups. **4b**

E3 c The student prepares and delivers an individual presentation, in which the student:

- shapes information to achieve a particular purpose and to appeal to the interests and background knowledge of audience members;
- shapes content and organization according to criteria for importance and impact rather than according to availability of information in resource materials;

- uses notes or other memory aids to structure the presentation;
- develops several main points relating to a single thesis;
- engages the audience with appropriate verbal cues and eye contact;
- projects a sense of individuality and personality in selecting and organizing content, and in delivery.

Examples of presentations include:

▲ An individual talk which develops several main points relating to a single thesis (e.g., describing a problem and evaluating alternative solutions to that problem, or explaining several causes leading to a historical event, or constructing different types of argument all supporting a particular policy). **4a, 4b**

▲ A public panel discussion during which each member of the panel speaks about a particular area of expertise relating to the overall topic. **4a**

▲ A forum discussion during which audience members question and respond to panelists during the presentation. **4a, A2a**

▲ A simulated congress (e.g., Model United Nations) in which each participant "represents" the interests of a particular constituency. **4a**

E3 d The student makes informed judgments about television, radio, and film productions; that is, the student:

- demonstrates an awareness of the presence of the media in the daily lives of most people;
- evaluates the role of the media in focusing attention and in forming opinion;
- judges the extent to which the media are a source of entertainment as well as a source of information;
- defines the role of advertising as part of media presentation.

Examples of activities through which students might produce evidence of making informed judgments about television, radio, and film production include:

▲ Maintain a week's log to document personal viewing habits, and analyze the information collected in the log.
▲ Summarize patterns of media exposure in writing or in an oral report. **2a, 3c, 4a, 4b**
▲ Analyze the appeal of popular television shows and films for particular audiences. **2a, 4a, 4b**
▲ Explain the use of "propaganda techniques" (e.g., bandwagon, glittering generalities, celebrity) in television commercials. **2a, 4a, 4b**
▲ Analyze the characteristics of different television genres (e.g., the talk show, the situation comedy, the public affairs show). **2a, 4a, 4b**

E3 e The student listens to and analyzes a public speaking performance; that is, the student:

- takes notes on salient information;
- identifies types of arguments (e.g., causation, authority, analogy) and identifies types of logical fallacies (e.g., ad hominem, inferring causation from correlation, over-generalization);
- accurately summarizes the essence of each speaker's remarks;
- formulates a judgment about the issues under discussion.

Examples of activities through which students might provide evidence of analysis of public speaking include:

▲ Take notes of a meeting of a local government council or of an institution's governing body.
▲ Make a report detailing testimony from a local trial. **2a, 4a, 4b**
▲ Analyze an address by a political leader. **4a, 4b, 6a**

Samples of student work that illustrate standard-setting performances for these standards can be found on pages 28-47.

For samples of student work that illustrate standard-setting performances for **E3 a** and **E3 b** refer to the videotape accompanying this book.

The work students produce to meet the English Language Arts standards does not all have to come from an English class. Students should be encouraged to use work from subjects in addition to English to demonstrate their accomplishments. The work samples include some examples of work produced in other classes that meet requirements of these standards. See page 45.

Performance Descriptions *English Language Arts*

To see how these performance descriptions compare with the expectations for elementary school and middle school, turn to pages 138-147.

The examples that follow the performance descriptions for each standard are examples of the work students might do to demonstrate their achievement. The examples also indicate the nature and complexity of activities that are appropriate to expect of students at the high school level.

The cross-references that follow the examples highlight examples for which the same activity, and possibly even the same piece of work, may enable students to demonstrate their achievement in relation to more than one standard. In some cases, the cross-references highlight examples of activities through which students might demonstrate their achievement in relation to standards for more than one subject matter.

These standards allow for oral performances of student work wherever appropriate.

E4 Conventions, Grammar, and Usage of the English Language

Having control of the conventions and grammar of the English language means having the ability to represent oneself appropriately with regard to current standards of correctness (e.g., spelling, punctuation, paragraphing, capitalization, subject-verb agreement). Usage involves the appropriate application of conventions and grammar in both written and spoken formats.

E4 a The student independently and habitually demonstrates an understanding of the rules of the English language in written and oral work, and selects the structures and features of language appropriate to the purpose, audience, and context of the work. The student demonstrates control of:

• grammar;
• paragraph structure;
• punctuation;
• sentence construction;
• spelling;
• usage.

Examples of activities through which students might demonstrate an understanding of the rules of the English language include:

▲ Demonstrate in a piece of writing the ability to manage the conventions, grammar, and usage of English so that they aid rather than interfere with reading. **2a, 2b, 2c, 2d, 2e, 2f, 3d, 5a, 5b, 6b, 7b**

▲ Independently and accurately proofread the student's own writing or the writing of others, using dictionaries, thesauruses, and other resources as appropriate. **2a, 2b, 2c, 2d, 2e, 2f, 3d, 5a, 5b, 6b, 7b**

▲ Observe the conventions of language during formal oral presentations. **3c**

▲ Demonstrate use of a variety of sentence patterns for stylistic effect. **2a, 2b, 2c, 2d, 2e, 2f, 3c, 3d, 5a, 5b, 6b, 7b**

E4 b The student analyzes and subsequently revises work to clarify it or make it more effective in communicating the intended message or thought. The student's revisions should be made in light of the purposes, audiences, and contexts that apply to the work. Strategies for revising include:

• adding or deleting details;
• adding or deleting explanations;
• clarifying difficult passages;
• rearranging words, sentences, and paragraphs to improve or clarify meaning;
• sharpening the focus;
• reconsidering the organizational structure;
• rethinking and/or rewriting the piece in light of different audiences and purposes.

Examples of activities through which students might provide evidence of analyzing and revising written work include:

▲ Incorporate into revised drafts, as appropriate, suggestions taken from critiques made by peers and teachers. **2a, 2b, 2c, 2d, 2e, 2f, 3c, 3d, 5a, 5b, 6b, 7b**

▲ Produce a series of distinctly different drafts that result in a polished piece of writing or presentation. **2a, 2b, 2c, 2d, 2e, 2f, 3c, 3d, 5a, 5b, 6b, 7b**

▲ Critique the writing or presentation of a peer.

▲ Describe the reasons for stylistic choices made as a writer or presenter. **2a, 2b, 2c, 2d, 2e, 2f, 3c, 3d, 5a, 5b, 6b, 7b**

▲ Produce a series of papers on the same topic, each serving a different purpose. **2a, 2b, 2c, 2d, 2e, 2f, 3d, 5a, 5b, 6b, 7b**

E5 Literature

Literature consists of poetry, fiction, non-fiction, and essays as distinguished from instructional, expository, or journalistic writing.

E5 a The student responds to non-fiction, fiction, poetry, and drama using interpretive, critical, and evaluative processes; that is, the student:

• makes thematic connections among literary texts, public discourse, and media;
• evaluates the impact of authors' decisions regarding word choice, style, content, and literary elements;
• analyzes the characteristics of literary forms and genres;
• evaluates literary merit;
• explains the effect of point of view;
• makes inferences and draws conclusions about fictional and non-fictional contexts, events, characters, settings, themes, and styles;
• interprets the effect of literary devices, such as figurative language, allusion, diction, dialogue, description, symbolism;
• evaluates the stance of a writer in shaping the presentation of a subject;
• interprets ambiguities, subtleties, contradictions, ironies, and nuances;
• understands the role of tone in presenting literature (both fictional and non-fictional);
• demonstrates how literary works (both fictional and non-fictional) reflect the culture that shaped them.

Examples of responding to literature include:

▲ Analyze stereotypical characters in popular fiction. **1b, 2b, 4a, 4b**

▲ Evaluate the effect of literary devices in a number of poems by one author or poems on a common topic. **1b, 2b, 4a, 4b**

▲ Compare the literary merits of two or more short stories, biographies of one individual, novels, or plays. **1b, 2b, 4a, 4b**

▲ Compare two different video presentations of a literary work. **1b, 2b, 3d, 4a, 4b**

▲ Compare two works written in different time periods on the same topic or theme. **1b, 2b, 4a, 4b**

▲ Evaluate the persona of the writer. **1b, 2b, 4a, 4b**

▲ Compare two literary texts that share a similar theme. **1b, 2b, 4a, 4b**

▲ Analyze the author's point of view toward an issue raised in one of an author's works. **1b, 2b, 4a, 4b**

▲ Analyze the literary, cultural, and social context of a literary work. **1b, 2b, 4a, 4b**

E5 b The student produces work in at least one literary genre that follows the conventions of the genre.

Examples of literary genres include:
▲ A reflective essay. **2f, 4a, 4b**
▲ A memoir. **4a, 4b**
▲ A short story. **2c, 4a, 4b**
▲ A short play. **4a, 4b**
▲ A poem. **4a, 4b**
▲ A vignette. **4a, 4b**

E6 Public Documents

A public document is a document that focuses on civic issues or matters of public policy at the community level or beyond. These documents, ranging from speeches to editorials to radio and television spots to pamphlets, do at least one of the following: take issue with a controversial public policy; suggest an alternative course of action; analyze and defend a contemporary public policy; define a public problem and suggest policy.

E6 a The student critiques public documents with an eye to strategies common in public discourse, including:

• effective use of argument;
• use of the power of anecdote;
• anticipation of counter-claims;
• appeal to audiences both friendly and hostile to the position presented;
• use of emotionally laden words and imagery;
• citing of appropriate references or authorities.

Examples of activities through which students might provide evidence of critiquing public documents include:

▲ Analyze a political speech. **1c, 3e**
▲ Evaluate an editorial. **1c**
▲ Examine campaign literature to determine underlying assumptions. **1c, 2a**
▲ Examine a range of articles published in a magazine or newspaper and drawing inferences about the political stance of that magazine or newspaper. **1c, 2a**

E6 b The student produces public documents, in which the student:

• exhibits an awareness of the importance of precise word choice and the power of imagery and/or anecdote;
• utilizes and recognizes the power of logical arguments, arguments based on appealing to a reader's emotions, and arguments dependent upon the writer's persona;
• uses arguments that are appropriate in terms of the knowledge, values, and degree of understanding of the intended audience;
• uses a range of strategies to appeal to readers.

Examples of public documents include:

▲ A proposal for changing an existing social or school policy. **2e, 4a, 4b**
▲ An analysis of a state policy. **4a, 4b**
▲ A policy statement that closely examines a significant public policy and proposes a change. **4a, 4b**
▲ A letter to an elected official taking a position on an issue or concern. **4a, 4b**
▲ A press release announcing a policy. **4a, 4b**

E7 Functional Documents

A functional document is a document that exists in order to get things done, usually within a relatively limited setting such as a social club, a business, an office, a church, or an agency. These often take the form of memoranda, letters, instructions, and statements of organizational policies. Functional documents require that particular attention be paid to issues of layout, presentation, and particularly to audience and the way different audiences will interact with the documents.

E7 a The student critiques functional documents with an eye to strategies common to effective functional documents, including:

• visual appeal, e.g., format, graphics, white space, headers;
• logic of the sequence in which the directions are given;
• awareness of possible reader misunderstandings.

Examples of activities through which students might provide evidence of critiquing functional documents include:

▲ Analyze a manual.
▲ Analyze a contract.
▲ Evaluate a loan application.
▲ Critique tax documents.

E7 b The student produces functional documents appropriate to audience and purpose, in which the student:

• reports, organizes, and conveys information and ideas accurately;
• includes relevant narrative details, such as scenarios, definitions, and examples;
• anticipates readers' problems, mistakes, and misunderstandings;
• uses a variety of formatting techniques, such as headings, subordinate terms, foregrounding of main ideas, hierarchical structures, graphics, and color;
• establishes a persona that is consistent with the document's purpose;
• employs word choices that are consistent with the persona and appropriate for the intended audience.

Examples of functional documents include:

▲ A summary of a meeting. **4a, 4b**
▲ A manual. **2d, 4a, 4b, A1**
▲ A proposal. **4a, 4b, A1**
▲ A set of instructions. **2d, 4a, 4b, A1**
▲ A recommendation. **4a, 4b, A1**

Samples of student work that illustrate standard-setting performances for these standards can be found on pages 28-47.

Much writing can be classified as belonging to the public arena. At the high school level, students should address issues which are of national importance in work directed toward accomplishment of **E6**.

Functional writing, as described in **E7**, is ordinarily considered technical writing. As such, functional documents are often not part of the typical English curriculum. New Standards requires students to demonstrate proficiency with functional documents because such writing is of increasing importance to the complex literacy of our culture.

Reading
Writing E2
Speaking, Listening, and Viewing
Conventions, Grammar, and Usage of the English Language
Literature
Public Documents
Functional Documents

Work Sample & Commentary: *Ixnay on Ballet: Misha's Gone Modern*

For a further sample of work that illustrates a standard-setting performance for a report, see "Interview With Aspirin," page 96.

The task

A group of students was asked to create a magazine. Individual students conducted research and wrote articles on subjects of their choice.

Circumstances of performance

This sample of student work was produced under the following conditions:

√ alone √ in a group
√ in class √ as homework
   with teacher feedback √ with peer feedback
   timed √ opportunity for revision

What the work shows

E2 a Writing: The student produces a report that:

• engages the reader by establishing a context, creating a persona, and otherwise developing reader interest;

• develops a controlling idea that conveys a perspective on the subject;

• creates an organizing structure appropriate to purpose, audience, and context;

• includes appropriate facts and details;

• excludes extraneous and inappropriate information;

• uses a range of appropriate strategies, such as providing facts and details, describing or analyzing the subject, narrating a relevant anecdote, comparing and contrasting, naming, explaining benefits or limitations, demonstrating claims or assertions, and providing a scenario to illustrate;

• provides a sense of closure to the writing.

A The student established the context by identifying the subject of the report as Mikhail Baryshnikov in the first sentence.

B The student created an appropriate persona of an experienced dancer.

C By creating separate sections, the student provided a clear, organizing structure for the report appropriate to the purpose and audience. The introduction of her personal views of Baryshnikov is followed by a short biography, a description of the White Oak Project which Baryshnikov founded, and then the conclusion that describes one of the Project's programs that she attended.

This work sample illustrates a standard-setting performance for the following part of the standards:

E2 a Writing: Produce a report.

IXNAY ON BALLET:
Misha's Gone Modern

The White Oak Dance Project reveals a new and exciting style for the ballet dance great, Mikhail Baryshnikov.

My First View of Misha:

B **A** Being a dancer, I have always been awed and amazed by the great dance legend of our time, Mikhail Baryshnikov. For years, he grew ever more admired for his talent in the art of ballet. Recently, I had the unforgettable experience of watching this dance great perform on stage at Denver's beautiful Temple Buell Theater. His current claim to fame, though, is a completely different world of dance. About five years ago, Misha created an exclusive company called the White Oak Dance Project.

When I attended this performance of the White Oak Project, I didn't know what to expect, due to the fact that the only way I had ever imagined Baryshnikov was dancing a classical ballet. I was no less impressed, though, by his new, modern style. It did make me curious, though, as to how a dancer with a thoroughly classical background makes the transition to modern, specifically for the White Oak Dance Project.

A Short Biography of Baryshnikov: **C**

Baryshnikov was born in Latvia, Russia in 1948. He joined the Leningrad Kirov Ballet, where he established himself as one of the most exciting and technically exacting dancers in Soviet ballet in 1966 (Hertelendy, "Highlights"). Eight years later he defected from the USSR for artistic freedom with the KGB in pursuit. He also made his first appearance as *danseur noble* with the American Ballet Theater (ABT). In 1977, he made what was probably his best movie, The Turning Point, which was a ballet-related film (Hertelendy, "Highlights"). A year later, he became interested in modern ballet, so he moved to George Balanchine's New York City Ballet. In 1980, he was the artistic director for the ABT's productions of The Nutcracker and a version of Don Quixote called Kitry's Wedding. He didn't perform in 1984, because the making of the movie White Nights left him out of shape. In 1986, twelve years after defecting, he finally became a U.S. citizen **D**

Ixnay on Ballet: Misha's Gone Modern

Reading

E2 ▶ Writing

Speaking, Listening, and Viewing

Conventions, Grammar, and Usage of the English Language

Literature

Public Documents

Functional Documents

[Ticket stub:]
EB0501E MEZZ B   D 201   N-PKC
42.50   42.50   MEZZANINE
MEZZ B
CO BALLET PRESENTS
BARYSHNIKOV PRODUCTIONS
WHITE OAK DANCE PROJECT
TEMPLE BUELL THEATRE
14TH & CURTIS
MON MAY 1, 1995 8:00PM
CA 14X
D 201
CBA0828
015MAR5

(Hertelendy, "Highlights"). In February of the next year, he was forced to move on toward his career as a modern dancer by multiple injuries and operations to his right knee. In 1990, he created the White Oak Dance Project (Hertelendy, "Highlights").

The White Oak Project:
The company is made up of anything but young dancers. The average age is 36 years, which, for as dancer, if near the age of retirement (Hertelendy, "Experience"). This hasn't deterred audiences from flocking to see the dance legend and his eleven fellow dancers (program, "White Oak"). When it was first born, though, the company had fourteen members, and has at times been as small as seven dancers

(Hertelendy, "Experience"). It has been nearly a sellout in more than ninety cities, including New York City (Duffy, 1).
New York City has been given the reputation of dance

capital of the world, and rightfully so, considering both the quantity and quality of companies that originate and perform there. No problem for White Oak. They simply waited a few years for the group to mature and tackled the picky, snobbish audiences and critics successfully. They spent almost $500,000 for a week at the Lincoln Center (Duffy, 1). The money was returned to them, though, by the run

being sold out before opening night.

The Program:
The program I was fortunate enough to attend was one of a tour involving twelve pieces, four of which were presented at the May first performance (program, "White Oak"). One of these twelve pieces is called "Signals," choreographed in the early 1970's by Merce Cunningham, who is now 76 years old (Duffy, 1). This piece was wall received by critics for its new score and costumes and its mesmerizing moves. Cunningham is an entirely unique choreographer. He does not think of music and steps, but of time. "Given ten seconds," he once said, "the dancer has to define the phrase and accent something within the time" (Duffy, 1). Karen Panasewicz calls the piece, "unmistakable" (interview, Panasewicz). His inspiration for this piece was found in his observations of groups of chairs in paris park. "Sometimes full, sometimes not," he said, "people come and go and converse- only this time,

they dance" (Duffy, 2).
Another piece on tour, titled "Pergolesi," was created by Twyla Tharp, who is now 52 years old (Green, 1). It was originally choreographed in 1992 as a duet for Tharp and

Baryshnikov and was titled "Bare Bones." It was reworked, though, as a solo for Misha on the tour. Occasionally, though, Baryshnikov dances with an invisible partner. This is Tharp's way of proving that it is still her piece (Duffy, 3). The

dance is twenty minutes, and is the longest solo he has ever done (Green, 1). He says it is the "biggest amount of dancing I ever did non-stop. It requires the same amount of concentration as anything in ballet" (Green, 1). Tharp first worked with Misha in 1976 when she created "Push Comes to Shove" for the ABT (Green, 1).
My personal favorite piece, titled "A Suite of Dances," was a solo by Baryshnikov set to Bach cello music (program, "White Oak"). This piece was created by Jerome Robbins, who is now 76 years old (Duffy, 3). Robbins found it to be an inspiration and joy to work with Misha. He said of the dancer, "If I think it is too dark, he lightens it, and vice versa. A great, great artist" (Duffy, 3). The friendship between these two artists began in 1979, when Baryshnikov was invited by President Carter to perform at the White House, where the available space to work with is extremely limited (Duffy, 5). Robbins, taking pity on Baryshnikov, became a sort of

stage manager to help him put on a successful production.
"Mosaic and United," a piece created for five dancers, was choreographed by Mark Morris (program, "White Oak"). Baryshnikov and Morris have worked together since 1988, when Morris created the ensemble work, "Drink Me Only With Thine Eyes" for the ABT (Green, 1). After Baryshnikov left the ABT in 1989, the two men founded White Oak together (Green, 1). Thus, the first season was devoted in its entirety to Morris's choreography. This piece was not as well appreciated and received by critics and critical observers, though (Duffy, 3). Says Karen Panasewicz, "That ("Mosaic and United") was a disappointing surprise. No very exciting" (interview, Panasewicz).

A New View of Misha: ◀
The identifying point for this ensemble from other groups organized by celebrities is the seriousness and intelligence of its programs and the fact that the ensemble comes first (Duffy, 5). Though Baryshnikov is so well known and admired, and he may have solos, he also performs in smaller roles in dances such as "Signals" and "Behind White Lilies" (Duffy, 5). The Program booklet also, is listed alphabetically, with Baryshnikov *second* in the list.
I greatly admire him for not losing this amount of modesty through his difficult, and yet very flattering career. It can't be easy to convert not only one's style of dancing, but also his attitude from that of a soloist to that of a member of a group. This gives me even more respect for him as a person and a dancer.

D **E** The student used a range of strategies, including the incorporation of appropriate facts and details not only about Baryshnikov's early years but also about his defection from the USSR to the American Ballet Theater. Facts and details are also provided about the White Oak Project.

F The report identifies specific pieces from the White Oak Project's performances in a manner similar to that used by reviewers and writers in professional publications. It provides the title of the piece, the name of the choreographer, and some specific details of the performance, such as a quotation from Baryshnikov about the piece "Bare Bones."

G The student made the assertion that "A Suite of Dances" was her favorite of the performance she attended. Her persona of a knowledgeable dancer makes the judgment reliable.

H The student waited until the end to address a fairly technical question regarding the difficulty Baryshnikov must have faced personally and professionally in making the switch from dancing as "a soloist to that of a member of a group." Dealing with this question last allowed her to address a specialized question from an informed position, and provided a sense of closure to the work.

Work Sample & Commentary: *Two Poems About Sports*

Reading

Writing · **E2**

Speaking, Listening, and Viewing

Conventions, Grammar, and Usage of the English Language · **E4**

Literature · **E5**

Public Documents

Functional Documents

The task
In an on-demand situation, students were asked to discuss the meaning they found in two poems and to justify or explain how they arrived at such a meaning.

Circumstances of performance
This sample of student work was produced under the following conditions:

√ alone in a group

√ in class as homework

with teacher feedback with peer feedback

√ timed opportunity for revision

The writing was completed in forty-five minutes with no opportunities for review and revision.

What the work shows

E2 b Writing: The student produces a response to literature that:

- engages the reader through establishing a context, creating a persona, and otherwise developing reader interest;
- advances a judgment that is interpretive, analytic, evaluative, or reflective;
- supports a judgment through references to the text, references to other works, authors, or non-print media, or references to personal knowledge;
- demonstrates understanding of the literary work through suggesting an interpretation;
- anticipates and answers a reader's questions;
- recognizes possible ambiguities, nuances, and complexities;
- provides a sense of closure to the writing.

A The opening engages the reader by citing the titles of the two poems under consideration and establishing a context through discussion of their shared content.

This work sample illustrates a standard-setting performance for the following parts of the standards:

E2 b Writing: Produce a response to literature.

E4 a Conventions: Demonstrate an understanding of the rules of the English language.

E5 a Literature: Respond to non-fiction, fiction, poetry, and drama.

B The student analyzed the authors' craft and advanced an interpretation in which he considered aspects of both poems.

C The interpretive judgments are supported through reference to the texts.

The writer analyzed the author's craft and interpreted both poems in terms of:
D mood; and
E attitude.

The writer recognized nuances that are reflected in:
F symbols; and
G common themes.

E4 a Conventions, Grammar, and Usage of the English Language: The student independently and habitually demonstrates an understanding of the rules of the English language in written or oral work, and selects the structures and features of language appropriate to the purpose, audience, and context of the work. The student demonstrates control of:

- grammar;
- paragraph structure;
- punctuation;
- sentence construction;
- spelling;
- usage.

Two Poems About Sports

Reading

E2 Writing

Speaking, Listening, and Viewing

E4 Conventions, Grammar, and Usage of the English Language

E5 Literature

Public Documents

Functional Documents

[Handwritten student essay, first column:]

lingers an aura of failure and sadness, which in its way connects with the seriousness of the first poem. One very important aspect that is prominent in both poems is a focus on what was, face turned towards memories of the past. For instance, the author of "To an Athlete" focuses in the sixth stanza on the past glory of the dead boy, the "still-defended challenge cup." And in the last stanza there is the second mention of the prized laurel wreath of victory, how it crowns his head still. This is a symbol of "don't forget what he accomplished". This message is achieved in a slightly different manner when Mr. Updike writes in "Ex-Ball Player" "he dribbles an inner tube," But most of us remember anyway. Since Flick is still alive, he himself is able to reminisce about glory gone by (equal to the narrator's reverie in the first poem). He (Flick) does not think highly of his present job—it is evident that no one does. So indeed he often dreams of how things once were—again, turning towards the past. He doesn't concentrate much on his present occupation, but rather imagines the gas pumps as basketball players and the rows of candy boxes as a cheering audience. It is

[Second column top:]

different from the first poem's way of expressing memory, yet it is much the same because of the similar situations. If Flick died, probably someone would reminisce about his high school glory at his grave in much the same way as the author does in that poem.

Both poems end on a nicer tone than they felt midway through. In "Ex-Ball Player" Mr. Updike mentions bluntly that "he never earned a trade, he just sells gas, checks oil, and changes flats." But the voice we hear at the finale of the poem is one with a smile in it, talking about applauding Necco Wafers™. Even the first poem ends on a lighter nuance of color than the rest, using words like "unwithered" to indicate that the boy's memory will stay among the townspeople.

* also equating past with present, laying a distinct tie between the two; in the first stanza the narrator speaks of the day the boy won the race and was carried shoulder-high among a throng of admirers. In the second stanza about the funeral, the boy was again brought home shoulder-high (in a casket) and through a crowd of admirers ("the road all runners come").

[Bottom boxed handwritten section, G:]

In "Ex-Ball" too, there is again equating present to past, achieved when Flick imagines the basketball game using objects from the present.

So the two poems do have many similarities and parallels, the most important of which I have pointed out to you today.

[Printed commentary, left column:]

In almost error free writing, the student managed spelling, punctuation, usage, grammar, and sentence structure. The few errors he made can be attributed to the nature of the task, which was given in a timed writing situation. The writing was completed in forty-five minutes with no opportunities for review and revision.

E5 a   Literature: The student responds to non-fiction, fiction, poetry, and drama using interpretive, critical, and evaluative processes; that is, the student:

- makes thematic connections among literary texts, public discourse, and media;
- evaluates the impact of authors' decisions regarding word choice, style, content, and literary elements;
- analyzes the characteristics of literary forms and genres;
- evaluates literary merit;
- explains the effect of point of view;
- makes inferences and draws conclusions about fictional and non-fictional contexts, events, characters, settings, themes, and styles;
- interprets the effect of literary devices, such as figurative language, allusion, diction, dialogue, description, symbolism;
- evaluates the stance of a writer in shaping the presentation of a subject;

[Printed commentary, right column:]

- interprets ambiguities, subtleties, contradictions, ironies, and nuances;
- understands the role of tone in presenting literature (both fictional and non-fictional);
- demonstrates how literary works (both fictional and non-fictional) reflect the culture that shaped them.

H   The student made the inference that each poem focuses on the past and yet has a distinct tie to the present.

I   The student interpreted the effect of literary devices, such as rhyme.

Work Sample & Commentary: *Ronnie*

Reading

Writing   **E2**

Speaking, Listening, and Viewing

Conventions, Grammar, and Usage of the English Language   **E4**

Literature

Public Documents

Functional Documents

The task

Students were asked to submit a narrative account about someone who had been an influence in their lives.

Circumstances of performance

This sample of student work was produced under the following conditions:

√ alone   in a group

√ in class   √ as homework

   with teacher feedback   √ with peer feedback

   timed   √ opportunity for revision

What the work shows

E2 ‹ Writing: A narrative account (fictional or autobiographical) that:

- engages the reader by establishing a context, creating a point of view, and otherwise developing reader interest;
- establishes a situation, plot, point of view, setting, and conflict (and for autobiography, the significance of events and of conclusions that can be drawn from those events);
- creates an organizing structure;
- includes sensory details and concrete language to develop plot and character;
- excludes extraneous details and inconsistencies;
- develops complex characters;
- uses a range of appropriate strategies, such as dialogue, tension or suspense, naming, pacing, and specific narrative action, e.g., movement, gestures, expressions;
- provides a sense of closure to the writing.

A The account engages the reader by establishing the initial context of seeing the "Camaro with a broken headlight," as well as "Ronnie the alcoholic," as familiar to the narrator. The narrator's familiarity with an awkward situation creates the tone for the narrative

---

This work sample illustrates a standard-setting performance for the following parts of the standards:

E2 ‹ Writing: Produce a narrative account.

E4 α Conventions: Demonstrate an understanding of the rules of the English language.

10/6/95

Ronnie

A Erica and Kesha (my two cousins) and I were walking back from the park in Bradsfordsville, Kentucky, when we saw it. The white 1989 Camero with a broken headlight on the right side. I'd seen that car before, earlier that day sitting in the same spot. My mom was talking to whoever was inside. Probably a childhood friend, I thought. We walked over to the car, not knowing who he was. My mom saw us and gave us a look like please go away, but we **B** didn't. For the first time we saw who was in the car when we walked up to the car. It was Ronnie, a childhood friend of my mom, Ronnie the alcoholic.

Ronnie was having his seventeenth beer for the day when we saw him. My mom was talking to him about his life, and why he was **E** where he was, where he messed up, and where he went wrong. Ronnie kept saying,"My life isn't worth living anymore, Patti. I should just end it. Here I am, forty years old and an alcoholic for almost twenty years." I remember looking at him and thinking "Is he serious? What will he do?" As we sat there hearing Ronnie talk about his life, I just kept feeling sorry for him. He had been an alcoholic since the Vietnam war. He told us in a drunken **D** state,"How can you fight a war and kill people? How can you just kill innocent people? Wives? Little children with cute smiles and innocent faces? I ask you, how can anyone do that?" He continued, sobbing,"How could I look at little children knowing I just **F** killed one of their parents?" Then he came out of the stare he had been in and said,"Will you help me? Please?"

B The scene with the broken-down car where Ronnie is first identified creates a situation for the plot by displaying the narrator's prior knowledge of the main character of the story.

C The inclusion of sensory details, such as a careful description of the character's clothing and physical characteristics, helps to develop the character of Ronnie. These descriptions further the plot by providing motivations for Ronnie's actions.

The student employed an effective writing strategy by using dialogue:

D to develop the complexity of the main character; and

E **F** to build suspense at appropriate moments in the plot.

G The account closes appropriately by telling the reader where the events of the story have led the main character, as well as how this encounter with Ronnie affected the narrator's life.

Ronnie

Reading

E2 ▶ Writing

Speaking,
Listening,
and Viewing

Conventions,
Grammar,
E4 ▶ and Usage
of the English
Language

Literature

Public
Documents

Functional
Documents

E4 a Conventions, Grammar, and Usage of the English Language: The student independently and habitually demonstrates an understanding of the rules of the English language in written and oral work, and selects the structures and features of language appropriate to the purpose, audience, and context of the work. The student demonstrates control of:

- grammar;
- paragraph structure;
- punctuation;
- sentence construction;
- spelling;
- usage.

The student created sentence structures appropriate to the informal nature of this narrative account, including effective fragments.

My mom spoke after clearing her throat,"Yes Ronnie I'll help you." She ran up to my grandparent's house while Kesha, Erica, and I sat there listening to Ronnie. While we were there, he kept mumbling,"I can do this" over and over. Finally, my mom came back from my grandparent's house. "We need to go to Lexington to the Rehab. Center there." Lexington was an hour away from Bradsfordsville. My mom didn't want us to go, but she needed someone to keep her awake because it was an all night thing.

C ▶ When Ronnie got out of the car, I finally got a good look at him. He was wearing a plain white shirt with several different stains on it. His shorts were cut off from sweat pants and were blue. His blue blood shot eyes had told me he hadn't slept in a while. His face had a five o'clock shadow, and his tan skin was slightly dirty. His sandy blond hair was messed up, and his facial expression was of total confusion. He smelled like Coors Light and Camel cigarettes.

I slept on the way up to Lexington. When arrived at the hospital, I looked at the clock and it read 12:45. We walked into the Emergency Room and asked for a nurse to do a physical on Ronnie. Two hours after Ronnie's physical, which took an hour itself, a nurse told us that they wouldn't take Ronnie because he had no insurance. They told us of a detoxification center about ten minutes from the hospital on the bad side of town. When we arrived at the place, I got really scared. It was three o'clock in the morning, and we were in a place that looked like the ghetto on a gangster movie. It was really scary.

It wasn't until 7:00 that morning, that we were back in

Bradsfordsville. We left Ronnie at the place in Lexington. I really didn't want to leave him, but we had to. I wrote about Ronnie because he really influenced my life. He showed me what **G** ▶ "rock bottom" is and showed me the courage to bring his life up out of the gutter. I respect him for stopping his alcoholism and changing his life to make it better. Ronnie is doing well now. He goes to AA meetings and is in a job training program. He has overcome his troubles and making a life for himself, and anyone who does that earns my respect.

Work Sample & Commentary: *Blue-gray Eyes*

Reading

Writing **E2**

Speaking, Listening, and Viewing

Conventions, Grammar, and Usage of the English Language **E4**

Literature

Public Documents

Functional Documents

The task
Students were asked to write a descriptive essay.

Circumstances of performance
This sample of student work was produced under the following conditions:

√ alone   in a group

   in class   √ as homework

   with teacher feedback   with peer feedback

   timed   √ opportunity for revision

What the work shows

E2 d Writing: The student produces a narrative procedure that:

- engages the reader by establishing a context, creating a persona, and otherwise developing reader interest;

- provides a guide to action for a complicated procedure in order to anticipate a reader's needs; creates expectations through predictable structures, e.g., headings; and provides smooth transitions between steps;

- makes use of appropriate writing strategies, such as creating a visual hierarchy and using white space and graphics as appropriate;

- includes relevant information;

- excludes extraneous information;

- anticipates problems, mistakes, and misunderstandings that might arise for the reader;

- provides a sense of closure to the writing.

A The student created a thoroughly engaging persona by employing two different types of language—popular music lyrics and a narrative about painting a room—in such a way that a non-literary procedure becomes literary.

B The reader's interest is engaged by the use of lyrics from popular songs to organize the essay and to reflect an attitude toward the procedure.

C A clear guide for a complicated procedure is provided through the use of smooth transitions between steps.

This work sample illustrates a standard-setting performance for the following parts of the standards:

E2 d Writing: Produce a narrative procedure.

E4 a Conventions: Demonstrate an understanding of the rules of the English language.

11-16-95
Descriptive Essay

A "...Blue-gray eyes...they change with the color..., Change with the sun...they run with the sight, They change with the wind...but they're always bright, Bright eyes...Blue Denim, Bright eyes...Blue Denim..."

The chorus to "Blue Denim," a song off Stevie Nicks' CD *Street Angel*, blares for probably the twenty-fifth time from my CD player. I'm singing right along, having the whole CD memorized by now, along with 10,000 Maniacs' *Our Time In Eden*, Enya's *Watermark*, and Diana Ross & The Supremes, all of which I've been listening to almost constantly since they arrived in the mail from BMG. At the moment I'm putting on the finishing touches to the paint on the loft walls of my room, and I look like I just walked out **J** of a paint ball war in which the other team had a smashing victory using slightly peachish-white paint (though this is nothing compared to what I looked like during the texturing stage).

C The very first step in finishing the walls in my room was to pack up all my stuff and **E** move it out. Hah! Easier said than done. I am a pack rat. I love to sort and organize and derive great pleasure from getting rid of things, but it doesn't happen very often. Once everything was neatly packed into boxes and set in safe, semi-out-of-the-way places, my dad came in to put up the sheet rock. When it was up, the whole thing was my baby.

I spent about a day caulking the walls. The sheet rock had been hard to put up because the board behind it couldn't always be found on the first bang of the hammer, so there were lots of extra dents to be filled with putty. Dabbing a bit of putty, smoothing it

D The student provided a clear sense of closure by reflecting on the experience and by ending with lyrics that are appropriate to the reflection.

Blue-gray Eyes

Reading

E2 Writing

Speaking, Listening, and Viewing

Conventions, Grammar, and Usage of the English Language

E4

Literature

Public Documents

Functional Documents

over, dabbing a bit of putty, smoothing it over. Then there were the corners (my favorite), and the seams that had to be covered with tape and smoothed over with putty...

(B) "You win a prize for that, for telling lies like that so well that I believed it. I never felt cheated. You were the chosen one, the pure eyes of Noah's dove. Choir boys and angles stole your lips and your halo..." ("Noah's Dove" - 10,000 Maniacs)

Once all the walls were caulked, they had to be textured. I sat on the flour, which was covered in plastic drop cloths, and experimented with different textures and techniques on an extra piece of sheet rock. I decided to go with an original design of my own that consisted of interweaving rainbow-shaped strokes made with a small hand broom. I mixed **(F)** up a bunch of plaster with just the right consistency (it was different every time) and got to work. I spent hours sitting on the flour making strokes with the broom, standing **(K)** making stokes with the broom, balancing on the ladder making strokes with the broom, and stooping in my loft making strokes with the broom. Every once in a while there would be some bugs, cobwebs, or dried bits of plaster that would get stuck in a stroke, and I'd have to pick them out and redo it. Whenever I got plaster somewhere it wasn't supposed to be, I just wiped it off on myself. I could be washed. Between mixing plaster and wiping things **(G)** off, I was soon covered. It was all over my shirt, shorts, legs, arms, hands, feet, tools, and there was even a little bit in my hair. Nobody could deny that I had been deeply involved in my task. After two or three days of texturing, I was finally done...

"For love, forget me, I didn't mean for him to get me. Get up in the morning, and I'm filled with desire. No, no I can't stop the fire, love is a real live fire. Love is a burning sensation, far beyond imagination. Love is like an itching in my heart, tearing it all apart, an itching in my heart, and baby·I can't scratch it..." ("Love Is Like An Itching In My Heart" - Diana Ross & The Supremes)

Then I started the painting. First, there was the coat of white primer, which thankfully didn't take very long. Then there were the two coats of slightly peach tinted white paint (you know, one of those twenty-five new shades of white), which I managed to slop all over the drop cloths and myself. We have this great roller with a long handle that I **(I)** got to use, and attempt to maneuver when that nice long handle was hitting some large space occupying object, such as a bookshelf or desk. "I will not become frustrated. I will **(L)** not become frustrated..." I had to wait in between coats for the paint to dry and spent a few wonderful nights sleeping on the couch so I wouldn't become intoxicated by the fumes. I unfortunately am not a morning person. The rest of my family are.

I'm wearing my plastering/painting clothes now for the last time in what I hope is a long time, and I'm pretty much done. I've managed not to drive myself crazy with all this **(D)** time alone to think, with the aid of what is now very well-known music to me. I have gained quite a bit of experience in caulking, artistically texturing, and painting, and above all, I can now be very proud of myself for a great accomplishment all my own... "Let me sail, let me sail, let the Orinoco flow; let me reach, let me beach on the shores of Tripoli; let me sail, let me sail, let me crash upon your shore; let me reach, let me beach far beyond the Yellow Sea..." ("Orinoco Flow" - Enya)

E4 a Conventions, Grammar, and Usage of the English Language: The student independently and habitually demonstrates an understanding of the rules of the English language in written or oral work, and selects the structures and features of language appropriate to the purpose, audience, and context of the work. The student demonstrates control of:

- grammar;
- paragraph structure;
- punctuation;
- sentence construction;
- spelling;
- usage.

The work displays a controlled, sophisticated use of sentence structures, including:

(E) the effective use of fragments;

(F) parenthetical comments; and

(G) effective repetitive elements.

(H) The student made one spelling mistake which may have been merely a typographical error ("flour" instead of "floor").

(I) This error in usage does not detract from the excellent control exhibited overall.

The student made use of a variety of language features such as:

(J) effective word choice to create sensory appeals;

(K) parallelism; and

(L) interior monologue.

Work Sample & Commentary: *School Bond Levy*

Reading

Writing ◀ **E2**

Speaking, Listening, and Viewing

Conventions, Grammar, and Usage of the English Language ◀ **E4**

Literature

Public Documents

Functional Documents

The task

Students were asked to write a persuasive essay based on research.

Circumstances of performance

This sample of student work was produced under the following conditions:

√ alone   in a group

   in class   as homework

   with teacher feedback   with peer feedback

   timed   √ opportunity for revision

What the work shows

E2 e **Writing:** The student produces a persuasive essay that:

- engages the reader by establishing a context, creating a persona, and otherwise developing reader interest;

- develops a controlling idea that makes a clear and knowledgeable judgment;

- creates an organizing structure that is appropriate to the needs, values, and interests of a specified audience, and arranges details, reasons, examples, and anecdotes effectively and persuasively;

- includes appropriate information and arguments;

- excludes information and arguments that are irrelevant;

- anticipates and addresses reader concerns and counter-arguments;

- supports arguments with detailed evidence, citing sources of information as appropriate;

- uses a range of strategies to elaborate and persuade, such as definitions, descriptions, illustrations, examples from evidence, and anecdotes;

- provides a sense of closure to the writing.

Ⓐ The essay engages the reader by establishing the context of identifying the facilities that the bond levy will add or improve, and by taking a clear stand on the issue. The persona is that of a serious, reasonable individual willing to address opposing viewpoints.

This work sample illustrates a standard-setting performance for the following parts of the standards:

E2 e **Writing:** Produce a persuasive essay.

E4 a **Conventions:** Demonstrate an understanding of the rules of the English language.

School Bond Levy

The ＿＿＿ School Board has recently proposed a bond levy to add new facilities as well as conduct some major repairs to the school. The bond includes building a new gymnasium, a new science room and lab, a new Media Center/Library, new Chapter 1 and Special Education classrooms, and other facilities such as more parking space, an increase in storage area, and new locker rooms. Along with new construction, the board is proposing to remodel facilities such as the drama/music areas, the entire roof, the heating system, the school kitchen, and present gym as well. This bond allowing ＿＿＿ School to add more facilities should be passed in order for young students to be provided with a better education.

Several arguments have been brought up concerning the levy since it failed in the March election. Some say that the school doesn't need to have brand new facilities and better classrooms, but it does. Just this year the school had to shut down for days at a time as a result of a malfunction of the heating system. The roof of the library also had a leaking problem all winter long. The leaking has actually caused the ceiling tiles to rot to the point where they are having to be removed. It isn't safe to sit underneath them because, in fact, they have fallen to tables where students had been working only minutes before.

Another issue that people may be concerned with is the money that taxpayers have to put up for the building. The cost of the project in its entirety will be 2.9 million dollars, meaning that for the next 25 years, taxpayers would pay 40 cents more per thousand dollars in property tax than they do this year. The project does cost a significant amount of money, but the school needs it. If something isn't done now, then the facilities such as the library, the science room and others will continue to grow

Ⓐ

Ⓒ

Ⓑ

Ⓑ The essay's organization takes into consideration its audience of adults concerned with accelerating tax levies. For example, paragraph three deals with costs by detailing the actual dollar amount needed, and by arguing that current low interest rates and expenses make additions and repairs more cost effective today than they would be in the future.

All of the information and arguments included are relevant to the purpose of the essay.

Ⓒ The student anticipated reader concerns about the need for repairs by recounting in detail the results of a heating system failure and the unsafe conditions in the library.

School Bond Levy

Reading

E2 Writing

Speaking,
Listening,
and Viewing

Conventions,
Grammar,
and Usage
of the English
Language

E4

Literature

Public
Documents

Functional
Documents

steadily worse. The construction and remodeling needs to be done eventually, so why not now, when interest rates are low and expenses are also low. Superintendent_____ _____ commented that it would cost the taxpayers much less money now than ten years from now. Another reason that this is a good time to pass this bond is that the results of Ballot Measure 5 are going into effect at the same time as the levy. As it stands now, property tax rates will go down another $2.50 by next year; however, if taxpayers don't mind paying what they do now and can handle a 40 cent increase, then the school can be that much better.

Many other good reasons we exist for funding this construction now. For one, better facilities will be made available to everyone: staff members, students, and community members. The new gym will allow student athletes to have earlier practices and more time for homework. With only one gym in a K-12 school system, the junior high has to practice in the morning before school, starting at 6:30 A.M., meaning that both the girls and boys teams had to practice at the same time, with half of the court for the girls half for the boys. After school, the high school girls would practice from 3:30 to 5:30 P.M. The varsity boys would then start at 5:30 or 6:00 and go until 7:30. After that, the junior varsity boys would come in for an hour and a half. It's absurd to think that student athletes can make good use of their time with a schedule like that. If the bond were to pass, both the new gym and the present gym would be used for practices and athletes wouldn't have to wait so long to practice every day.

Another reason that the gym should be built is that it is no longer adequate. The bleachers are too close to the court and so there is no room to walk by without getting in the way during a game. The gym also poses a problem for the cheerleaders. As it is now, there is no room for them to cheer. They have to stand on one of the ends which, of course, is right in the way of people walking by. If a new gym were built, enough room would be provided surrounding the court that there wouldn't be any of the problems there are now.

Another advantage to the bond proposal is that it would provide more space in the school. The school has always been small, which is in some ways nice, but it needs to expand. The lack of space is a problem because everyone is crammed into one little hallway trying to make it around from class to class. As it is, there isn't enough room for the library to just be a library or the kitchen to just be a kitchen. Students can't even go to the library when they need to because Health, Media, and other classes are held there. The Satellite Learning classroom, which shares a space with the kitchen, usually has a difficult learning atmosphere each day people prepare food for the hot lunch program. Another problem area is the current science room and lab. Lab facilities are outdated and cannot be replaced for a variety of reasons related to the plumbing and electrical systems. Both science teachers have said publicly that the chemical storage room is inadequate and unsafe. The science curriculum is a core part of students' education and they deserve good facilities.

It is clear then, that _____ School needs significant improvements in which case the bond must be passed. As a community, education is an essential part of the future. In the past, _____ has relied in the timber industry for employment, but times are changing and the younger generations need to be better prepared to meet the challenges that arise. For example, they need to able to take part in a variety of activities and be able to achieve in many different areas. If the school is inadequate, how can the younger generations be provided with the education and training they need to be successful in the future?

D The arguments are supported with clear, detailed evidence in which the student provided an account of the total costs and the results of Ballot Measure 5.

E The student cited scheduling difficulties resulting from having only one gym. The arguments are supported with effective illustrations showing why more space is needed.

Detailed information is included in an effort to persuade the audience, particularly those who voted against the initial bond initiative.

F The student used an effective strategy in closing the argument with an emotional plea: "If the school is inadequate, how can the younger generations be provided with the education and training they need to be successful in the future?"

E4 a Conventions, Grammar, and Usage of the English Language: The student independently and habitually demonstrates an understanding of the rules of the English language in written or oral work, and selects the structures and features of language appropriate to the purpose, audience, and context of the work. The student demonstrates control of:

- grammar;
- paragraph structure;
- punctuation;
- sentence construction;
- spelling;
- usage.

In almost error free writing, the student managed grammar, usage, spelling, punctuation, sentence construction, and paragraph structure.

Work Sample & Commentary: *As a Reader*

Reading

Writing **E2**

Speaking, Listening, and Viewing

Conventions, Grammar, and Usage of the English Language

Literature

Public Documents

Functional Documents

The task

Students were asked to write an essay reflecting upon their English Language Arts portfolio and their progress throughout the year in reading, writing, speaking, and listening.

Circumstances of performance

This sample of student work was produced under the following conditions:

√ alone   in a group

√ in class   √ as homework

   with teacher feedback   with peer feedback

   timed   √ opportunity for revision

What the work shows

E2 f Writing: The student produces a reflective essay that:

• engages the reader by establishing a context, creating a persona, and otherwise developing reader interest;

• analyzes a condition or situation of significance;

• develops a commonplace, concrete occasion as the basis for the reflection, e.g., personal observation or experience;

• creates an organizing structure appropriate to purpose and audience;

• uses a variety of writing strategies, such as concrete details, comparing and contrasting, naming, describing, creating a scenario;

• provides a sense of closure to the writing.

The work engages the reader with a highly self-conscious voice that offers a reflection of the past year. The focus on literacy skills narrows the scope of the work and helps to keep it interesting.

A The student included an analysis of her abilities and her performances as a reader, writer, listener, and speaker, including details, such as the strategies she used to improve her concentration.

B The reflections are grounded in commonplace occasions, such as reading at the dinner table, providing an additional context for the student's comments.

This work sample illustrates a standard-setting performance for the following part of the standards:

E2 f Writing: Produce a reflective essay.

Reflective Essay

F As a reader, I love all types of literature. The ones I favor the most would always be the ones written by Micheal Crichton and Mary Higgins Clark. In English Class, I felt that I was able to read, enjoy and comprehend the choices of literature my teacher had me read. With the exception of Jane Eyre, I enjoyed everyone of them. In the beginning of the year I wrote how easily distracted I can be when I'm reading literature for a specific class. This is even more true with the warm weather and a new Beatles CD I received for my by birthday. One **A** of the reasons I'm so interested in meditation, besides getting rid of unwanted pressure, is so I can learn to concentrate on one particular thing. I always seem to be having hundreds of thought all jumbled up in my head. Besides reading books, I also love reading magazines. I will never get tired of receiving a brand new National Geographic Society magazine. Even reading the paper at the

B dinner table has become a habit for me. At first my parents told me to put it away, but they don't say anything more about the issue. I guess because I can do the balancing act of eating, reading and having a nice conversation with my parents. As you can see I love to read just about anything and anywhere.

G As a writer, I find myself to be a **C** real creative writer. As a child I was always told I had a wonderful imagination I hope I'll never lose it. Writing creative stories seem to come real easy to me. The only obstacle I always have to try to overcome is the grammar **D** involved. I am so bad when it comes to correcting the grammar of one of my papers. Despite all the fuss over grammar, I still want to become a photo journalist for **E** the National Geographic Society This flaming dream of mine has been smoldered by a few people who don't believe in dreaming. Fortunately, both my parents support my dreams one hundred per cent. My father always brings up the fact that

High School English Language Arts 39

Reading

Writing

Speaking, Listening, and Viewing

Conventions, Grammar, and Usage of the English Language

Literature

Public Documents

Functional Documents

As a Reader

we're in America now and I should follow my dreams no matter what others may say. Another dream of mine is to write a book that millions will enjoy. Unlike most people, I'm not interested in making millions of dollars. However, to make money by doing something I love does sound real nice. Since I love to make people laugh as well as being creative, I think the book I will write will have people die of laughing.

As a speaker, I've been told that I have a nice, clear, projective voice. That is when I'm not petrified with fear of talking in front of a large crowd of people. I think I speak much better when I'm faced with just a small group. People, especially one particular teacher, have told me I do a great job of talking. That is I don't mumble, stutter, talk too fast or too slow. Despite all these great compliments that make me blush, I still feel I am too quiet. Sometimes, I even think about taking elocution classes. No matter how many people reassure me, I am still self-

C D E The student engaged the reader by identifying both her strengths: "I find myself to be a real creative writer," and her weaknesses: "The only obstacle I always have to try to overcome is the grammar involved." She considered both her strengths and her weaknesses in discussing her plan to become a photo journalist for the National Geographic Society.

The student created an organizing structure by narrating and reflecting as:

F a reader;

G a writer;

H a speaker; and

I a listener.

J The student employed concrete details as a writing strategy to communicate the nature of the work represented in her portfolio.

K The work incorporates a scenario about being a good listener and does so in a way that effectively illustrates the point.

This work contains a small number of errors, such as "conscience" instead of "conscious," that do not detract from the overall quality of the work.

conscience about my Khmer accent. I think I still have one. I hope it isn't wrong to want to get rid of this, but I do. One thing I try to do to practice my speaking in public is to read book out loud. Of course, I do this in the privacy of my bedroom. I occasionally practice on easy books, because their simple phrases can turn out to be killer tongue twisters.

As a listener, I think I'm great. I don't yawn, roll my eyes or look completely exhausted when someone is giving a public speech. That is, not excessively. I don't want to do something to someone else, and then have them do it right back to me. I was raised to live by the Golden Rule, and I will never forget it. When I listen to people during a close conversation, I try to look in their eyes as often as possible. Sometimes I have to look away, because I get an eerie feeling. I also don't like standing too close to another person during a conversation. I try to stay quiet, but not too quiet. If I don't say anything the other person may get the

impression I'm not listening. However, I don't want the other's story to turn into one of my own, by interrupting too many times at the wrong moments. I think great listening is a craft that must be learned and practised.

Work Sample & Commentary: *Dreams: Can Money Make Them Come True?*

Reading

Writing E2

Speaking, Listening, and Viewing

Conventions, Grammar, and Usage of the English Language E4

Literature E5

Public Documents

Functional Documents

The task

Students were asked to read *A Raisin in the Sun* and to write an analysis of one or more elements of the play.

Circumstances of performance

This sample of student work was produced under the following conditions:

√ alone

√ in class

with teacher feedback

timed

in a group

√ as homework

with peer feedback

√ opportunity for revision

What the work shows

E2 b Writing: The student produces a response to literature that:

- engages the reader through establishing a context, creating a persona, and otherwise developing reader interest;

- advances a judgment that is interpretive, analytic, evaluative, or reflective;

- supports a judgment through references to the text, references to other works, authors, or non-print media, or references to personal knowledge;

- demonstrates understanding of the literary work through suggesting an interpretation;

- anticipates and answers a reader's questions;

- recognizes possible ambiguities, nuances, and complexities;

- provides a sense of closure to the writing.

A The title and first paragraph provide a clear context to engage the reader: the conflicts and connections between money and dreams. This context is maintained throughout the essay.

B The essay advances an interpretive judgment regarding the theme of *A Raisin in the Sun*.

C The judgment about the play is supported through references to the text.

February 27, 1996

Dreams: Can Money Make Them Come True?

A If you were to listen in on a typical conversation between two people today, one topic is bound to come up sooner or later: money. People talk about their jobs and money. People talk about their plans and money. People talk about their families and money. People talk about their dreams and, you guessed it, money.

Money is definitely important. It puts a roof over our heads, food on our tables, and clothing on our backs. But money also provides people with a means to achieve their goals. People often rely on money to make life better and help their dreams come true, but is it really the stuff dreams are made of?

B This reliance on money to make goals realities is a theme in the play by Lorraine Hansberry entitled *A Raisin in the Sun*. In this drama, the Younger family struggles to survive life in their crummy Southside apartment in Chicago around the 1950s. When the family receives the ten thousand dollar insurance check from the death of Walter Lee Younger Sr., they are forced to decide which dreams they should use the money to make come true and which ones should just stay dreams.

C Beneatha Younger, Walter Sr. and Lena's daughter, has a passion for medicine and longs to be a doctor. When she was young, Bennie witnessed a sledding accident involving another of the neighborhood children that mangled the child's face and she was amazed when he came back from the hospital with only a small scar. She tells her friend, Joseph Asagai, how she felt by saying "... that was what one person could do for another, fix him up—sew up

---

D The student demonstrated an understanding of the play by suggesting an interpretation and then defending it with an appropriate argument.

E The student recognized the complexities inherent in this literary work by closing with a discussion of the importance of "people and their actions" as opposed to money alone.

This work sample illustrates a standard-setting performance for the following parts of the standards:

E2 b Writing: Produce a response to literature.

E4 a Conventions: Demonstrate an understanding of the rules of the English language.

E5 a Literature: Respond to non-fiction, fiction, poetry, and drama.

Dreams: Can Money Make Them Come True?

Reading

E2 Writing

Speaking, Listening, and Viewing

E4 Conventions, Grammar, and Usage of the English Language

E5 Literature

Public Documents

Functional Documents

the problem, make him all right again. That was the most marvelous thing in the world. . . . I wanted to do that" (83) . Now, Bennie wants to be a healer and to help other people because she believes that is the best thing she can do for her fellow human beings. However, medical school costs a lot of money—money the Youngers don't have—until the insurance check arrives. Now, that money can be used to make Bennie's doctor dreams come true, and she is counting on it happening.

Walter Lee Younger Junior, Lena's older child, has plans of his own. He dreams of going into business for himself instead of being a rich man's chauffeur. He tells his mother "'. . . I open and close car doors all day long. I drive a man around in his limousine and I say, 'Yes, sir; no, sir; very good, sir; shall I take the Drive, sir?' Mama, that ain't no kind of job . . . that ain't nothing at all" (42) . Walter wants to be a business man, not someone else's servant, so he plans to use the insurance money to invest in a liquor store with some of his friends. But without the money, his grand schemes aren't possible.

Walter is also motivated to go into business because he wants to give his family a better life. One morning, his son Travis needs fifty cents for school. Ruth Younger, Walter's wife, told Travis that they didn't have fifty cents for him to take, and when Walter finds out he says, "What you tell the boy things like that for?" (12) and proceeds to give his son the money. He continued, "In fact, here's another fifty cents. . . . Buy yourself some fruit today—or take a taxicab to school or something!" (12) Walter wants to be able to give his son all the money he will ever need, like most parents do. Later on, he states that, "This morning, I was lookin' in the mirror and thinking about it . . . I'm thirty-five years old, I been married eleven years and I got a boy who sleeps in the living room . . . —and all I got to give him is stories about how rich white people live . . ." (14). Walter doesn't want his child to have to sleep on the couch in the living room, and he sees the insurance money as his means to achieve the life he believes his family should have and dreams of them living.

In another scene, Walter and Travis are talking and the boy tells his father that he wants to be a bus driver when he grows up. Walter is surprised and tells Travis that that isn't big enough (63). Walter says:

> You wouldn't understand yet, son, but your daddy's gonna make a transaction . . . a business transaction that's going to change our lives. . . . And—and I'll say, all right son—it's your seventeenth birthday, what is it you've decided? . . . Just tell me where you want to go to school and you'll *go*. Just tell me, what it is you want to be—and you'll be it. . . . You just name it son . . . and I hand you the world! (64)

D ⤑ Walter longs to be able to give his son the best and make Travis' dreams come true, and money is what he believes will make that possible. He is relying on the insurance money to give Travis the things Walter envisions for him.

Walter also wants to give Ruth the things he feels she deserves. He said:

> . . . I want to hang some real pearls round my wife's neck. Ain't she supposed to wear no pearls? Somebody tell me—tell me, who decides which women is supposed to wear pearls in this world. I tell you I am a *man*—and I think my wife should wear some pearls in this world! (91)

Walter doesn't think it's fair that other men can afford to buy pearls for their wives and he can't. He longs to be able to buy Ruth everything he feels she should have, but he needs money to do that. Again, he is putting his trust in the insurance money and its ability to make the situation improve.

Ruth herself feels like Walter in that she wants a better life for her family. When Ruth Younger discovers she is pregnant, she hopes some of the money could be used to support the new baby. But, she knows they can't afford to add another person to the family, even with the inheritance, so she decides to get an abortion. Lena tells Walter that, "When the world gets ugly enough—a woman will do anything for her family. *The part that's already living*" (43).

E4 a Conventions, Grammar, and Usage of the English Language: The student independently and habitually demonstrates an understanding of the rules of the English language in written or oral work, and selects the structures and features of language appropriate to the purpose, audience, and context of the work. The student demonstrates control of:

- grammar;
- paragraph structure;
- punctuation;
- sentence construction;
- spelling;
- usage.

Through virtually error free writing, the student demonstrated the ability to manage the conventions of grammar and usage.

Dreams: Can Money Make Them Come True?

Reading

Writing ◄ **E2**

Speaking, Listening, and Viewing

Conventions, Grammar, and Usage of the English Language ◄ **E4**

Literature ◄ **E5**

Public Documents

Functional Documents

E5 a Literature: The student responds to non-fiction, fiction, poetry, and drama using interpretive, critical, and evaluative processes; that is, the student:

• makes thematic connections among literary texts, public discourse, and media;

• evaluates the impact of authors' decisions regarding word choice, style, content, and literary elements;

• analyzes the characteristics of literary forms and genres;

• evaluates literary merit;

• explains the effect of point of view;

• makes inferences and draws conclusions about fictional and non-fictional contexts, events, characters, settings, themes, and styles;

• interprets the effect of literary devices, such as figurative language, allusion, diction, dialogue, description, symbolism;

• evaluates the stance of a writer in shaping the presentation of a subject;

• interprets ambiguities, subtleties, contradictions, ironies, and nuances;

• understands the role of tone in presenting literature (both fictional and non-fictional);

• demonstrates how literary works (both fictional and non-fictional) reflect the culture that shaped them.

F The student made and supported a series of inferences about the characters in *A Raisin in the Sun.*

G The student found a connection between dreams and money in the play.

H The student concluded with a declaration about society that stems directly from her reading of the play.

Ruth desperately wants to keep her baby, but she knows the rest of her family will suffer if she does. They just don't have the financial means to take care of another Younger and Ruth is aware of the added problems a new baby would cause everyone, but she still wishes the insurance money will provide her with a way to keep the child. She feels that her future, dreams, and even the life of her child depend on money.

People do expect money to make things in life better and even rely on it to do so. But, can money live up to people's expectations? Or can something else—like people, and especially loved ones—be the real key to dreams coming true?

G ┈┈► This idea shows up toward the end of the play. The stress of living in conditions like the Youngers do eventually gets to people, and deciding what to do with the money only made things worse. Lena doesn't like what is happening to her family, so she goes out and buys a newer, bigger house. She states that:

> I—I just seen my family falling apart today . . . just falling to pieces in front of my eyes . . . We couldn't have gone on like we was today. We was going backwards 'stead of forwards—talking 'bout killing babies and wishing each other was dead . . . When it gets like that in life—you just got to do something different, push on out and do something bigger. (58)

Lena wants the best for her children, too, just like Walter and Ruth, and she realizes that they can't go on in that apartment any longer, so she uses her money to try and make the dreams she has for her family come true, once again demonstrating how people rely on money to achieve goals.

The only drawback to Lena's solution is that the new house is located in an all-white neighborhood, and a man named Mr. Lindner comes to try and persuade the Youngers not to move. He offers to buy the house back from them for more than it is worth. At the end of the play, after Walter losses the insurance money, he decides to accept Mr. Lindner's offer to give

---

the Youngers the money for the house. When he announces his decision to the rest of the family, Lena talks to him about pride. She tells him, "I come from five generations of people who was slaves and sharecroppers—but ain't nobody in my family never let nobody pay 'em no money that was a way of telling us we wasn't fit to walk on this earth" (91). Even though the money they would get from the deal could be used to make the family's future more like the one they want, money isn't as important to the family as pride. The money—which can help ◄┈┈ **F** make dreams come true—can't take the place of the people in the family and their attitudes.

When Lindner arrives, Walter changes his mind and tells the man that ". . . we have decided to move into our house because my father—my father—he earned it" (95). Walter realizes that his mother is right, and when he changes his mind, the rest of the family is happy and proud. As they leave the small, cramped apartment for the last time, Lena states that, "He finally come into his manhood today, didn't he? Kind of like a rainbow after the rain. . . ." (97)

E ┈┈► The money did help the family get out of their unhappy situation, but Walter's behavior made the family's real dreams come true.

People in society today rely on money to make things better and to help them achieve their goals. In some cases, money can do just that, and many dreams wouldn't come true if not for money. But in the end, it's people who make life worth living and cause fantasies to

H ┈┈► become reality. People and their actions are more special than anything money can buy.

Work Sample & Commentary: *Tall Tale*

Reading

Writing

Speaking,
Listening,
and Viewing

Conventions,
Grammar,
and Usage
of the English
Language

E5 ▶ Literature

Public
Documents

Functional
Documents

The task

Students were asked to read and listen to a series of tall tales and then to write a tall tale using their knowledge of content and the style associated with that genre.

Circumstances of performance

This sample of student work was produced under the following conditions:

√ alone   in a group

√ in class   √ as homework

   with teacher feedback   √ with peer feedback

   timed   opportunity for revision

What the work shows

E5 b Literature: The student produces work in at least one literary genre that follows the conventions of the genre.

The work demonstrates the student's understanding of the style associated with tall tales.

The work incorporates a dialect appropriate to the time and place depicted in the narrative.

(A) The student's use of colloquialisms and repeated phrases emphasized the oral nature of the genre.

The tall tale includes features the student identified as being common to the genre; for example, it includes a heroine who has unusual adventures and is accompanied by an animal companion.

(B) The work describes how a real geographical feature was created by the actions of a tall tale character rather than natural forces.

(C) The story accounts for all the natural elements for which the character is purported to be responsible, providing a clear sense of closure.

Nov. 30, 1995

Tall Tale

(A) This here paper's the story of Miss Angela Carmody. What's that you say? Who's Angela Carmody? Why, only the prettiest, most kind-hearted woman that ever lived, and the best darn singer you ever did hear. Well, pull up a chair and listen a spell while I tell her tale.

No one quite knows where little Angela grew up, only that it was in a cabin somewheres in the great Sierra Nevadas. She had hair as blonde as the California beaches and eyes green like the greenest leaves on the greenest trees. She had the most beautiful voice; she sang so sweet. Her parents took to callin' her Angela 'cause even when she were a youngun' her cry was pretty to hear, like a baby angel from Heaven.

When she was just a small thing, she wandered out in the forest. She felt happy, like a young gal should, and she let out with a most wonderful melody. She perched herself on a rock and soon, all the creatures on that big mountain were gathered around just a'listenin' to her song. The cougars and the bears sat right alongside the deer most peaceful-like. The birds in the trees chirped along, too.

When the song was over, one voice kept on a'singing. Who's throat it was coming out of and where the one ownin' the throat was was a mystery. All of the sudden, a huge shadow covered Angela and the animals. When they looked up, they saw a gigantic bird float gracefully by. Angela added her sweet voice making it a doozy of a duet. The bird landed next to the child and the tune stopped while them two studied each other. The creature was indeed huge, with feathers exactly the same shade o' green as Angela's eyes. They were a perfect pair.

Angela named her new pal Emmy 'cause her feathers reminded the girl of emeralds. Angela climbed on Emmy's back and off they flew. Them two visited far off places all over the world, and people in each city stopped to hear 'em sing. The girl and her bird got to be quite famous over them years.

When Angela got to be older, she got to wonderin' about her old home and family. So, Emmy, she a'headed back to the Sierra Nevadas and Angela's cabin. But on the way, a man huntin' bears let a shot go wild up into the air and the bullet hit the great green bird. She fell out of the sky and landed in a hanging valley high in the mountains. Poor Emmy and Angela had sung their last duet.

The girl buried her friend on the spot where they landed, then sat herself down **(B)** and cried. She cried and cried and cried. Her tears ran together and tumbled over the edge of the cliff becomin' a waterfall—Yosemite Falls, to be exact. And to this very day, **(C)** that waterfall still comes down from the Sierra Nevadas, and the grass on top of that big hill grows green as emeralds. They say if a body listens hard enough, they can still hear Angela's sad solo sung for her fallen friend...

This work sample illustrates a standard-setting performance for the following part of the standards:

E5 b Literature: Produce work in at least one literary genre that follows the conventions of the genre.

Work Sample & Commentary: *Living Rooms as Classrooms*

Reading

Writing

Speaking, Listening, and Viewing

Conventions, Grammar, and Usage of the English Language

Literature

Public Documents **E6**

Functional Documents

The task

Students were asked to read and respond to a newspaper article. They were asked to pay particular attention to the way the articles were written and the implications underlying the arguments.

Circumstances of performance

This sample of student work was produced under the following conditions:

√ alone   in a group

√ in class   √ as homework

   with teacher feedback   with peer feedback

   timed   √ opportunity for revision

What the work shows

E6 a Public Documents: The student critiques public documents with an eye to strategies common in public discourse, including:

- effective use of argument;
- use of the power of anecdote;
- anticipation of counter-claims;
- appeal to audiences both friendly and hostile to the position presented;
- use of emotionally laden words and imagery;
- citing of appropriate references or authorities.

A The student identified certain aspects of the argument being considered and responded responsibly, stating agreement with two of the aspects, but not the third.

B The student made use of emotionally charged words and imagery to present a counter-argument.

C The work appeals to both friendly and hostile audiences by clearly identifying the point of disagreement and then discussing it in a reasonable manner.

"Living rooms As Classrooms" discussed a type of education that was unknown to me. In some instances, I feel that home schooling is a good alternative to public education. Yet many questions arise as I read this article.

First of all, my questions begin with one word: Why? As I read on, this question was answered with answers such as to keep children away from school violence, health reasons, or religious reasons. The only answer I disagreed with was school violence. I disagree because wherever a person may go, they may encounter violence. Sheltering the child now is not going to benefit them in the long run.

The article, written by Bill Schackner, was based on a home-schooled student, Jesse Richman. A statement that Richman made was that he did not feel he missed anything by not attending school, and also he did not feel isolated. I don't understand how he can feel this way. By not going to school, Richman probably never got to see the diverse number of people a public school has to offer. He never got to meet the school snob, the class clown, the jock, the nerd, etc. He never had the chance to attend a <u>real</u> discussion group, where teens stated their mind without censoring their opinions because their parents were around. Many of his socializing skills may not have been developed simply because he didn't go to school. For all Richman knows, he may have missed meeting that special someone just because he didn't go to school.

In conclusion, I feel that home schooling can be a good method for educating children. Many children in society today do need one-on-one teaching. Yet many things happen-

particularly in high school- that a teen must, or should experience. Besides, going to a dance at a church function just doesn't hold a candle to the Senior Prom.

This work sample illustrates a standard-setting performance for the following part of the standards:

E6 a **Public Documents: Critique public documents.**

Work Sample & Commentary: *Please Post: Caring For Your Campus Lawn*

Reading

Writing

Speaking, Listening, and Viewing

Conventions, Grammar, and Usage of the English Language

Literature

Public Documents

E7 Functional Documents

The task

In a chemistry class, students were asked to determine the most effective, economical, and environmentally safe grass fertilizer for their school district. The students were to produce an analytical report with detailed procedures and conclusions and to make a recommendation to the school district's Grounds and Maintenance Department. The document included here is the instructional piece that was produced in response to the research. The knowledge necessary to produce the document came out of a substantial research effort.

Circumstances of performance

This sample of student work was produced under the following conditions:

alone	√ in a group
√ in class	√ as homework
√ with teacher feedback	√ with peer feedback
timed	√ opportunity for revision

What the work shows

E7 b Functional Documents: The student produces functional documents appropriate to audience and purpose, in which the student:

- reports, organizes, and conveys information and ideas accurately;

- includes relevant narrative details, such as scenarios, definitions, and examples;

- anticipates readers' problems, mistakes, and misunderstandings;

- uses a variety of formatting techniques, such as headings, subordinate terms, foregrounding of main ideas, hierarchical structures, graphics, and color;

- establishes a persona that is consistent with the document's purpose;

- employs word choices that are consistent with the persona and appropriate for the intended audience.

The organization of the work into three brief sections serves to communicate a great deal of information in a limited space.

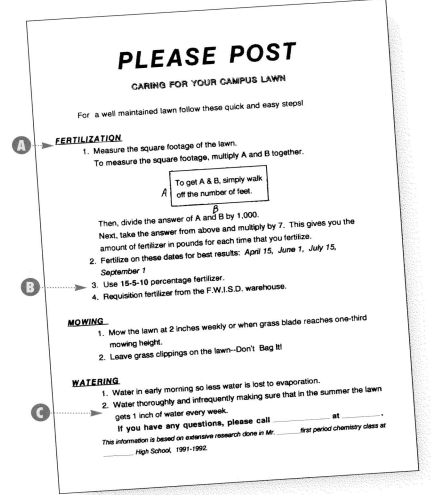

A The "Fertilization" section includes clear instructions for determining the amount of fertilizer for a lawn.

The students used several layers of headings, indicated by changes in the font size, type, and placement.

The persona of the piece is clear and direct, thus diminishing the opportunity for misunderstanding.

B The trade language used, such as "15-5-10 percentage fertilizer," is appropriate for the audience of the Grounds and Maintenance Department.

C The information that the Grounds and Maintenance Department would already have is not included, e.g., the rationale for fertilization dates is left out, which is appropriate for the expert audience but would not be appropriate for a novice audience.

This piece of work was completed as part of an Applied Learning project. See page 118 for commentary on the project as a whole.

This work sample illustrates a standard-setting performance for the following part of the standards:

E7 b Functional Documents: Produce a functional document.

Work Sample & Commentary: *Books, Tomes, Novels, Treasures*

Reading ◀ **E1**

Writing

Speaking, Listening, and Viewing

Conventions, Grammar, and Usage of the English Language

Literature

Public Documents

Functional Documents

The task

Students were asked to submit a log of reading done both in and out of school.

Circumstances of performance

This sample of student work was produced under the following conditions:

√ alone in a group

√ in class √ as homework

 with teacher feedback with peer feedback

 timed opportunity for revision

What the work shows

E1 a **Reading:** The student reads at least twenty-five books or book equivalents each year. The quality and complexity of the materials to be read are illustrated in the sample reading list. The materials should include traditional and contemporary literature (both fiction and non-fiction) as well as magazines, newspapers, textbooks, and on-line materials. Such reading should represent a diverse collection of material from at least three different literary forms and from at least five different writers.

The reading log provides evidence that the student met the goal of reading twenty-five books of the appropriate quality of literature for the high school standard. In fact, some of the literature on his list is included in many college level courses. The reading log also shows the variety of texts the student engaged in from fiction, classic literature, and informational materials.

Books Tomes Novels TREASURES

The following list includes a selection of my favorite books that I've read during American Studies (An advanced placement class composed of History and English.) as well as on my own during the past year.

<u>The Oedipus Plays of Sophocles</u>, Sophocles
"Oedipus the King",
"Oedipus at Colonus",
"Antigone". –We as a nation a very concerned with family values today, and often want to return to the "old days." Wouldn't Oedipus and his family give us an extremely unpleasant suprise!
<u>The Giver</u>, Lois Lowry–For Jonas and his family, life is perfect...but where is it taking them?!?!
<u>The Scarlet Letter</u>, Nathaniel Hawthorne–"A" is for adultery, as well as agony, angellic and anaclitic.
<u>Rappaccini's Daughter</u>, Nathaniel Hawthorne–Rappaccini was torn between the love he felt for his daughter and his beloved plants.
<u>Come Spring</u>, Ben Ames Williams–Life was not easy in the backwoods of Maine in the late 1700's. They were rich in family, faith, and in the hope of the coming spring.
<u>Brave New World</u>, Aldous Huxley–Life is wonderful...as long as it feels that way!
<u>Heart of Darkness</u>, Joseph Conrad–We never know what will change with the weather, in the jungles of inner Africa.
<u>The Secret Sharer</u>, Joseph Conrad–Relationships form, like two ships colliding in the night.
<u>Night</u>, Elie Wiesel–Life must go on with visions of burning babies and rooms of death. Always remember...never forget!
<u>Demian</u>, Hermann Hesse–The sky is the limit for those who find spirituality in themselves.
<u>Siddhartha</u>, Hermann Hesse–If the Buddah is truly divine, then frienship must be his master.
<u>Steppenwolf</u>, Hermann Hesse–Terror is nothing to be afraid of...until it looks you in the face.
<u>The Tempest</u>, William Sakespeare–The fantasy based on the colonization of America. Shall Prospero choose love over vengeance?
<u>The Taming of the Shrew</u>, William Shakespeare–If you think Katharine is a shrew....meet Bianca!
<u>Twelfth Night</u>, William Shakespeare, Poor Maivolio, learn a lesson from Viola and Sebastian.
<u>Macbeth</u>, William Shakespeare, By the twitching of my thumbs, something wicked this way comes. Something WICKED this way comes!
<u>Immortal Wife</u>, Irving Stone, John C. Fremont conquered the west, his wife placed him on a pedestal.
<u>Those Who Love</u>, Irving Stone, John and Abigail Adams were married in law and patriotism.
<u>The President's Lady</u>, Irving Stone, Oh, in 1814 we took a little trip, along with Andrew Jackson down the mighty Mississipp...
<u>Cold Sassy Tree</u>, Olive Ann Burns, Everyone felt sorry for Grandpa after Grandma died...until he brought

E1 b **Reading:** The student reads and comprehends at least four books (or book equivalents) about one issue or subject, or four books by a single writer, or four books in one genre, and produces evidence of reading that:

• makes and supports warranted and responsible assertions about the texts;

• supports assertions with elaborated and convincing evidence;

• draws the texts together to compare and contrast themes, characters, and ideas;

• makes perceptive and well developed connections;

• evaluates writing strategies and elements of the author's craft.

The reading log shows evidence that the student read four or more books in one genre. He fulfilled the requirement by reading a number of plays, including several groups of plays within more specific categories, such as Greek tragedy.

This work sample illustrates a standard-setting performance for the following parts of the standards:

E1 a **Reading: Read at least twenty-five books or book equivalents each year.**

E1 b **Reading: Read and comprehend at least four books about one issue or subject, or four books by a single writer, or four books in one genre.**

Books, Tomes, Novels, Treasures

E1 ▶ Reading

Writing

Speaking,
Listening,
and Viewing

Conventions,
Grammar,
and Usage
of the English
Language

Literature

Public
Documents

Functional
Documents

home his new wife! News travels fast in Alabama!

Hopkins of the Mayflower, Margaret Hodges, The story of a man who wanted more, and achieved it.

Constance, Patricia Clapp, Life was hard in early Plymouth, but life is always hard when you're fourteen.

Arundel, Kenneth Roberts, Life was dull for Steven...until Benedict Arnold came along!

Frankenstein, Mary Shelley, Victor had created a monster...inside himself!

Walden, Henry David Thoreau-Lay back in a rowboat and let yourself drift...

Volatile Truths, Martin Bickman-A study of Thoreau's Walden, and what inspired him.

Spoon River Anthology, Edgar Lee Masters-All, all are sleeping, sleeping, sleeping on the hill.

Silas Marner, Silas Marner-Silas is a miser even without his gold, until a child appeared.

The Client, John Grisham-The mob is always listening!

Midnight in the Garden of Good and Evil, John Berendt, Savannah is a beautiful town...until skeletons start falling out of closets...literally!

Seed of Sarah, Judith Isaacson-The courageous story of a young Jewish girl trying to survive in Nazi prison and death camps.

Suivez la Piste, Emile de Harven-Fait attention le virus dangereux!

Un Bouquet, Hermin Dubus-Monologues et d'a propos pour toutes les fetes de l'annee.

Le Fantome de l'Opera, Gaston Leroux-L'histoire triste d'un homme, a demi monstre et a demi enfant.

24 Favorite One-Act Plays,

"27 Wagons Full of Cotton"-Tennessee Williams

"Spreading the News"-Lady Gregory

"A Marriage Proposal"-Anton Chekhov

"In the Shadow on the Glen"-J.M. Synge

"Cathleen ni Houlihan"-W.B. Yeats

"The Jest of Hahalaba"-Lord Dunsany

"Trifles"-Susan Glaspell

"The Happy Journey"-Thornton Wilder

"The Ugly Duckling"-A.A. Milne

"The Flattering Word"-George Kelly

"The Tridget of Greva"-Ring Lardner

"The Moon of the Caribbees"-Eugene O'Neil

"The Still Alarm"-George S. Kaufman

"The Devil and Daniel Webster"-Stephen Vincent Benet

"The Apollo of Bellac"-Jean Giraudoux

"A Memory of Two Mondays"-Arthur Miller

"Glory in the Flower"-William Inge

"Hands Across the Sea"-Noel Coward

"Here We Are"-Dorothy Parker

"Sorry, Wrong Number"-Lucille Fletcher

"The Browning Version"-Terence Rattigan

"A Florentine Tradgedy"-Oscar Wilde

"The Maker of Dreams"-Oliphant Down

"The Traveler"-Marc Connelly

This Same Sky, Compiled by Naomi Shihab Nye-A collection of poems from around the world.

Introduction to the performance standards for
Mathematics

Building directly on the National Council of Teachers of Mathematics (NCTM) Curriculum Standards, the Mathematics performance standards present a balance of conceptual understanding, skills, and problem solving.

The first four standards are the important conceptual areas of mathematics:

M1 **Number and Operation Concepts;**

M2 **Geometry and Measurement Concepts;**

M3 **Function and Algebra Concepts;**

M4 **Statistics and Probability Concepts.**

These conceptual understanding standards delineate the important mathematical content for students to learn. To demonstrate understanding in these areas, students need to provide evidence that they have used the concepts in a variety of ways that go beyond recall. Specifically, students show progressively deeper understanding as they use a concept in a range of concrete situations and simple problems, then in conjunction with other concepts in complex problems; as they represent the concept in multiple ways (through numbers, graphs, symbols, diagrams, or words, as appropriate) and explain the concept to another person.

This is not a hard and fast progression, but the concepts included in the first four standards have been carefully selected as those for which the student should demonstrate a robust understanding. These standards make explicit that students should be able to demonstrate understanding of a mathematical concept by using it to solve problems, representing it in multiple ways (through numbers, graphs, symbols, diagrams, or words, as appropriate), and explaining it to someone else. All three ways of demonstrating understanding—use, represent, and explain—are required to meet the conceptual understanding standards.

Establishing separate standards for these areas is a mechanism for highlighting the importance of these areas, but does not imply that they are independent of conceptual understanding. As the work samples that follow illustrate, good work usually provides evidence of both.

Like conceptual understanding, the definition of problem solving is demanding and explicit. Students use mathematical concepts and skills to solve nonroutine problems that do not lay out specific and detailed steps to follow; and solve problems that

---

Complementing the conceptual understanding standards, M5 - M8 focus on areas of the mathematics curriculum that need particular attention and a new or renewed emphasis:

M5 **Problem Solving and Mathematical Reasoning;**

M6 **Mathematical Skills and Tools;**

M7 **Mathematical Communication;**

M8 **Putting Mathematics to Work.**

---

make demands on all three aspects of the solution process—formulation, implementation, and conclusion. These are defined in **M5**, Problem Solving and Mathematical Reasoning.

The importance of skills has not diminished with the availability of calculators and computers. Rather, the need for mental computation, estimation, and interpretation has increased. The skills in **M6**, Mathematical Skills and Tools, need to be considered in light of the means of assessment. Some skills are so basic and important that students should be able to demonstrate fluency, accurately and automatically; it is reasonable to assess them in an on-demand setting, such as the New Standards reference examination. There are other skills for which students need only demonstrate familiarity rather than fluency. In using and applying such skills they might refer to notes, books, or other students, or they might need to take time out to reconstruct a method they have seen before. It is reasonable to find evidence of these skills in situations where students have ample time, such as in a New Standards portfolio. As the margin note by the examples that follow the performance descriptions indicates, many of the examples are performances that would be expected when students have ample time and access to tools, feedback from peers and the teacher, and an opportunity for revision. This is true for all of the standards, but especially important to recognize with respect to **M6**.

M7 includes two aspects of mathematical communication—using the language of mathematics and communicating about mathematics. Both are important. Communicating about mathematics is about ideas and logical explanation. The travelogue approach adopted by many students in the course of describing their problem solving is not what is intended.

M8 is the requirement that students put many concepts and skills to work in a large-scale project or investigation, at least once each year, beginning in the fourth grade. The types of projects are specified; for each, the student identifies, with the teacher, a clear purpose for the project, what will be accom-

plished, and how the project involves putting mathematics to work; develops a question and a plan; writes a detailed description of how the project was carried out, including mathematical analysis of the results; and produces a report that includes acknowledgment of assistance received from parents, peers, and teachers.

The examples

The purpose of the examples listed under the performance descriptions is to show what students might do or might have done in achieving the standards, but these examples are not intended as the only ways to demonstrate achievement of the standard. They are meant to illustrate good tasks and they begin to answer the question, "How good is good enough?" "Good enough" means being able to solve problems like these.

Each standard contains several parts. The examples below are cross-referenced to show a rough correspondence between the parts of the standard and the examples. These are not precise matches, and students may successfully accomplish the task using concepts and skills different from those the task designer intended, but the cross-references highlight examples for which a single activity or project may allow students to demonstrate accomplishment of several parts of one or more standards.

The purpose of the samples of student work is to help to explain what the standards mean and to elaborate the meaning of a "standard-setting performance." Few pieces of work are so all-encompassing as to qualify for the statement, "meets the standard." Rather, each piece of work shows evidence of meeting the requirements of a selected part or parts of a standard. Further, most of these pieces of work provide evidence related to parts of more than one standard. It is essential to look at the commentary to understand just how the work sample helps to illuminate features of the standards.

Resources

We recognize that some of the standards presuppose resources that are not currently available to all students. The New Standards partners have adopted a Social Compact, which says, in part, "Specifically, we pledge to do everything in our power to ensure all students a fair shot at reaching the new performance standards…This means that they will be taught a curriculum that will prepare them for the assessments, that their teachers will have the preparation to enable them to teach it well, and there will be an equitable distribution of the resources the students and their teachers need to succeed."

The NCTM standards make explicit the need for calculators of increasing sophistication from elementary to high school and ready access to computers. Although a recent National Center for Education Statistics survey confirmed that most schools do not have the facilities to make full use of computers and video, the New Standards partners have made a commitment to create the learning environments where students can develop the knowledge and skills that are delineated here. Thus, **M6**, Mathematical Skills and Tools, assumes that students have access to computational tools at the level spelled out by NCTM. This is not because we think that all schools *are* currently equipped to provide the experiences that would enable students to meet these performance standards, but rather that we think that all schools *should be* equipped to provide these experiences. Indeed, we hope that making these requirements explicit will help those who allocate resources to understand the consequences of their actions in terms of student performance.

The high school standards reflect what students are expected to know and be able to do after a three-year core program in high school mathematics as defined by the NCTM standards, independent of the specific curriculum they study or its sequencing: traditional Algebra I, Geometry, Algebra II; or (Integrated) Mathematics I, II, III.

Performance Descriptions *Mathematics*

M1 Number and Operation Concepts

The student demonstrates understanding of a mathematical concept by using it to solve problems, by representing it in multiple ways (through numbers, graphs, symbols, diagrams, or words, as appropriate), and by explaining it to someone else. All three ways of demonstrating understanding—use, represent, and explain—are required to meet this standard.

The student produces evidence that demonstrates understanding of number and operation concepts; that is, the student:

M1 a Uses addition, subtraction, multiplication, division, exponentiation, and root-extraction in forming and working with numerical and algebraic expressions.

M1 b Understands and uses operations such as opposite, reciprocal, raising to a power, taking a root, and taking a logarithm.

M1 c Has facility with the mechanics of operations as well as understanding of their typical meaning and uses in applications.

M1 d Understands and uses number systems: natural, integer, rational, and real.

M1 e Represents numbers in decimal or fraction form and in scientific notation, and graphs numbers on the number line and number pairs in the coordinate plane.

M1 f Compares numbers using order relations, differences, ratios, proportions, percents, and proportional change.

M1 g Carries out proportional reasoning in cases involving part-whole relationships and in cases involving expansions and contractions.

M1 h Understands dimensionless numbers, such as proportions, percents, and multiplicative factors, as well as numbers with specific units of measure, such as numbers with length, time, and rate units.

M1 i Carries out counting procedures such as those involving sets (unions and intersections) and arrangements (permutations and combinations).

M1 j Uses concepts such as prime, relatively prime, factor, divisor, multiple, and divisibility in solving problems involving integers.

M1 k Uses a scientific calculator effectively and efficiently in carrying out complex calculations.

M1 l Recognizes and represents basic number patterns, such as patterns involving multiples, squares, or cubes.

Examples of activities through which students might demonstrate understanding of number and operation concepts include:

▲ Show how to enlarge a picture by a factor of 2 using repeated enlargements at a fixed setting on a photocopy machine that can only enlarge up to 155%. Do the same for enlargements by a factor of 3, 4, and 5. **1a, 1c, 1g, 1h**

▲ Discuss the relationship between the "Order of Operations" conventions of arithmetic and the order in which numbers and operation symbols are entered in a calculator. Do all calculators use the same order? **1a, 1c, 1k**

▲ Give a reasoned estimate of the volume of gasoline your car uses in a year. How does this compare to the volume of liquid you drink in a year? (Balanced Assessment) **1a, 1c, 2k**

▲ Show that there must have been at least one misprint in a newspaper report on an election that says: Yes votes - 13,657 (42%); No votes - 186,491 (58%). Suggest two different specific places a misprint might have occurred. (Balanced Assessment) **1a, 1f, 1g, 1h**

▲ Make and prove a conjecture about the sum of any sequence of consecutive odd numbers beginning with the number 1. **1a, 1l**

▲ It is sometimes convenient to represent physical phenomena using logarithmic scales. Discuss why this is so, and illustrate with a description of pH scales (acidity), decibel scales (sound intensity), and Richter scales (earthquake intensity). **1b, 1c, 1d, 1e**

▲ What proportion of two digit numbers contain the digit 7? What about three digit numbers? **1d, 1e, 1i**

▲ Figure out how many pages it would take to write out all the numbers from 1 to 1,000,000. (Balanced Assessment) **1d, 1e, 1l**

▲ If 10% of U.S. citizens have a certain trait, and four out of five people with the trait are men, what proportion of men have the trait and what proportion of women have the trait? Explain whether the answer depends on the proportion of U.S. citizens who are women and, if so, how. (Balanced Assessment) **1f, 1g, 1h**

▲ Simpson's Paradox is this: X may have a better record than Y in each of two possible categories but Y's overall record for the combined categories may be better than X's. Explain how this can happen. **1g**

▲ Find a simple relationship between the least common multiple of two numbers, the greatest common divisor of the two numbers, and the product of the two numbers. Prove that the relationship is true for all pairs of positive integers. **1j**

To see how these performance descriptions compare with the expectations for elementary school and middle school, turn to pages 148-159.

The examples that follow the performance descriptions for each standard are examples of the work students might do to demonstrate their achievement. The examples also indicate the nature and complexity of activities that are appropriate to expect of students at the high school level. Depending on the nature of the task, the work might be done in class, for homework, or over an extended period.

The cross-references that follow the examples highlight examples for which the same activity, and possibly even the same piece of work, may enable students to demonstrate their achievement in relation to more than one standard. In some cases, the cross-references highlight examples of activities through which students might demonstrate their achievement in relation to standards for more than one subject matter.

M2 Geometry and Measurement Concepts

The student demonstrates understanding of a mathematical concept by using it to solve problems, by representing it in multiple ways (through numbers, graphs, symbols, diagrams, or words, as appropriate), and by explaining it to someone else. All three ways of demonstrating understanding—use, represent, and explain—are required to meet this standard.

The student produces evidence that demonstrates understanding of geometry and measurement concepts; that is, the student:

M2 a Models situations geometrically to formulate and solve problems.

M2 b Works with two- and three- dimensional figures and their properties, including polygons and circles, cubes and pyramids, and cylinders, cones, and spheres.

M2 c Uses congruence and similarity in describing relationships between figures.

M2 d Visualizes objects, paths, and regions in space, including intersections and cross sections of three dimensional figures, and describes these using geometric language.

M2 e Knows, uses, and derives formulas for perimeter, circumference, area, surface area, and volume of many types of figures.

M2 f Uses the Pythagorean Theorem in many types of situations, and works through more than one proof of this theorem.

M2 g Works with similar triangles, and extends the ideas to include simple uses of the three basic trigonometric functions.

M2 h Analyzes figures in terms of their symmetries using, for example, concepts of reflection, rotation, and translation.

M2 i Compares slope (rise over run) and angle of elevation as measures of steepness.

M2 j Investigates geometric patterns, including sequences of growing shapes.

M2 k Works with geometric measures of length, area, volume, and angle; and non-geometric measures such as weight and time.

M2 l Uses quotient measures, such as speed and density, that give "per unit" amounts; and uses product measures, such as person-hours.

M2 m Understands the structure of standard measurement systems, both SI and customary, including unit conversions and dimensional analysis.

M2 n Solves problems involving scale, such as in maps and diagrams.

M2 o Represents geometric curves and graphs of functions in standard coordinate systems.

M2 p Analyzes geometric figures and proves simple things about them using deductive methods.

M2 q Explores geometry using computer programs such as CAD software, Sketchpad programs, or LOGO.

Examples of activities through which students might demonstrate understanding of geometry and measurement concepts include:

▲ A model tower is made of small cubes of the same size. There are four types of cubes used in the tower: vertex, edge, face, and interior, having respectively 3, 2, 1, and 0 faces exposed. If a new tower, of the same shape but three times as tall, is to be built using the same sort of cubes, show how the numbers of each of the four types of cubes need to be increased. Generalize to a tower n times as tall as the original. **2a, 2b, 2c, 2d, 2j, 2n**

▲ Figure out which of two ways of rolling an 8.5" by 11" piece of paper into a cylinder gives the greater volume. Is there a way to get even greater volume using a sheet of paper with the same area but different shape? (Balanced Assessment) **2a, 2b, 2d, 2e**

▲ Explain which is a better fit, a round peg in a square hole or a square peg in a round hole. Go on to the case of a cube in a sphere vs. a sphere in a cube. (Balanced Assessment) **2a, 2b, 2e, 2f**

▲ Suppose that you are on a cliff looking out to sea on a clear day. Show that the distance to the horizon in miles is about equal to 1.2 $\sqrt{h}$, where h is the height in feet of the cliff above sea level. Derive a similar expression in terms of meters and kilometers. (Balanced Assessment) **2a, 2d, 2f**

▲ Can a cube be dissected into four or fewer congruent square-base pyramids? What about triangle-base pyramids? In each case, show how it can be done or why it cannot be done. **2a, 2b, 2d, 2p**

▲ Given three cities on a map, find a place that is the same distance from all of them. Determine if there is always such a place. Are there ever many such places? (Balanced Assessment) **2a, 2b, 2d, 2p**

▲ A circular glass table top has broken, and all you have is one piece. The piece contains a section of the circular edge, but not the center. Describe and apply two different methods for finding the radius of the original top (so that you can order a new top). (Balanced Assessment) **2a, 2b, 2p**

▲ An isosceles trapezoid has height h and bases of lengths b and c. What must be the relationship among the lengths h, b, and c if we are to be able to inscribe a circle in the trapezoid? **2a, 2b, 2p**

▲ Explore the relation between the length of a person's shadow (made by a streetlight) and the person's height and distance from the light. Extend the analysis to include the rate of change of shadow length when the person is moving. (Balanced Assessment) **2a, 2g, 2l**

Samples of student work that illustrate standard-setting performances for these standards can be found on pages 58-79.

Performance Descriptions *Mathematics*

M3 Function and Algebra Concepts

The student demonstrates understanding of a mathematical concept by using it to solve problems, by representing it in multiple ways (through numbers, graphs, symbols, diagrams, or words, as appropriate), and by explaining it to someone else. All three ways of demonstrating understanding—use, represent, and explain—are required to meet this standard.

The student produces evidence that demonstrates understanding of function and algebra concepts; that is, the student:

M3 a Models given situations with formulas and functions, and interprets given formulas and functions in terms of situations.

M3 b Describes, generalizes, and uses basic types of functions: linear, exponential, power, rational, square and square root, and cube and cube root.

M3 c Utilizes the concepts of slope, evaluation, and inverse in working with functions.

M3 d Works with rates of many kinds, expressed numerically, symbolically, and graphically.

M3 e Represents constant rates as the slope of a straight line graph, and interprets slope as the amount of one quantity (y) per unit amount of another (x).

M3 f Understands and uses linear functions as a mathematical representation of proportional relationships.

M3 g Uses arithmetic sequences and geometric sequences and their sums, and sees these as the discrete forms of linear and exponential functions, respectively.

M3 h Defines, uses, and manipulates expressions involving variables, parameters, constants, and unknowns in work with formulas, functions, equations, and inequalities.

M3 i Represents functional relationships in formulas, tables, and graphs, and translates between pairs of these.

M3 j Solves equations symbolically, graphically, and numerically, especially linear, quadratic, and exponential equations; and knows how to use the quadratic formula for solving quadratic equations.

M3 k Makes predictions by interpolating or extrapolating from given data or a given graph.

M3 l Understands the basic algebraic structure of number systems.

M3 m Uses equations to represent curves such as lines, circles, and parabolas.

M3 n Uses technology such as graphics calculators to represent and analyze functions and their graphs.

M3 o Uses functions to analyze patterns and represent their structure.

Examples of activities through which students might demonstrate understanding of function and algebra concepts include:

▲ A used car is bought for $9,500. If the car depreciates at 5% per year, how much will the car be worth after one year? Five years? Twelve years? n years? (College Preparatory Mathematics) **3a, 3b, 3c**

▲ Express the diameter of a circle as a function of its area and sketch a graph of this function. **3a, 3b, 3c, 3h**

▲ If a half gallon carton of milk is left out on the counter, its temperature T in degrees Fahrenheit can be approximated by the formula $T = 70 - (^{500}/_t)$, where t is the time in minutes it has been out of the refrigerator. (This formula works as long as t is greater than about 20 minutes.) Find a formula that will let you figure out how long the milk has been there from its temperature T. Graph this formula. (College Preparatory Mathematics) **3a, 3b, 3c, 3h**

▲ Use measurements from shopping carts that are nested together to find a formula for the number of carts that will fit in a space of any given length, and a formula for the amount of space needed for any given number of carts. (Balanced Assessment) **3a, 3b, 3c, 3f, 3h**

▲ Express the concentration of bleach as a function of the amount of water added to three liters of a 12% solution of bleach. **3a, 3b, 3c, 1h**

▲ The quantity $1 + x$ is sometimes used as an approximation for the quantity $^1/_{(1+x)}$ if x is positive and small (much less than 1). Use graphs to show why this makes sense. Over what range of values of x does this approximation yield less than a 5% error? Find the sum of the infinite geometric series $1 + x + x^2 + x^3 + ...$ (assuming $0 < x < 1$) and show how it sheds light on why the approximation works. **3b, 3c, 3g, 3h, 3i**

▲ Design a staircase that rises a total of 11 feet, given that the slope must be between .55 and .85, and that the rise plus the run on each step must be between 17 and 18 inches. (Balanced Assessment) **3c, 3h, A1a**

▲ You have a green candle 12.4 cm tall that cost $0.45; after burning for four minutes it is 11.2 cm tall. You also have a red candle 8.9 cm tall that cost $0.40; after burning for ten minutes it is 7.5 cm tall. Analyze the burning rates with functions and graphs. If they are both lit at the same time, predict when (if ever) they will be the same height, and when each will burn down completely. Which costs less per minute to use? (College Preparatory Mathematics) **3d, 3e, 3f**

To see how these performance descriptions compare with the expectations for elementary school and middle school, turn to pages 148-159.

The examples that follow the performance descriptions for each standard are examples of the work students might do to demonstrate their achievement. The examples also indicate the nature and complexity of activities that are appropriate to expect of students at the high school level. Depending on the nature of the task, the work might be done in class, for homework, or over an extended period.

The cross-references that follow the examples highlight examples for which the same activity, and possibly even the same piece of work, may enable students to demonstrate their achievement in relation to more than one standard. In some cases, the cross-references highlight examples of activities through which students might demonstrate their achievement in relation to standards for more than one subject matter.

M4 Statistics and Probability Concepts

The student demonstrates understanding of a mathematical concept by using it to solve problems, by representing it in multiple ways (through numbers, graphs, symbols, diagrams, or words, as appropriate), and by explaining it to someone else. All three ways of demonstrating understanding—use, represent, and explain—are required to meet this standard.

The student demonstrates understanding of statistics and probability concepts; that is, the student:

M4 a Organizes, analyzes, and displays single-variable data, choosing appropriate frequency distribution, circle graphs, line plots, histograms, and summary statistics.

M4 b Organizes, analyzes, and displays two-variable data using scatter plots, estimated regression lines, and computer generated regression lines and correlation coefficients.

M4 c Uses sampling techniques to draw inferences about large populations.

M4 d Understands that making an inference about a population from a sample always involves uncertainty and that the role of statistics is to estimate the size of that uncertainty.

M4 e Formulates hypotheses to answer a question and uses data to test hypotheses.

M4 f Interprets representations of data, compares distributions of data, and critiques conclusions and the use of statistics, both in school materials and in public documents.

M4 g Explores questions of experimental design, use of control groups, and reliability.

M4 h Creates and uses models of probabilistic situations and understands the role of assumptions in this process.

M4 i Uses concepts such as equally likely, sample space, outcome, and event in analyzing situations involving chance.

M4 j Constructs appropriate sample spaces, and applies the addition and multiplication principles for probabilities.

M4 k Uses the concept of a probability distribution to discuss whether an event is rare or reasonably likely.

M4 l Chooses an appropriate probability model and uses it to arrive at a theoretical probability for a chance event.

M4 m Uses relative frequencies based on empirical data to arrive at an experimental probability for a chance event.

M4 n Designs simulations including Monte Carlo simulations to estimate probabilities.

M4 o Works with the normal distribution in some of its basic applications.

Examples of activities through which students might demonstrate understanding of statistics and probability concepts include:

▲ Compare a frequency distribution of salaries of women in a company with a frequency distribution of salaries of men. Describe and quantify similarities and differences in the distributions, and interpret these. **4a, 4f**

▲ Analyze and interpret prominent features of a scatter plot of several hundred data points, each giving the age of death of a person and the average number of cigarettes smoked per day by that person. **4b, 4f**

▲ Make an estimate of the number of beads in a large container using the following method. Select a sample of beads, mark these beads, return them to the container, and mix them in thoroughly. Then re-sample and count the proportion of marked beads. Compare your result with another method of estimating the number, for example, one based on weighing the beads. **4c**

▲ Two integers, each between 1 and 9 are selected at random, and then added. Determine the possible sums and the probability of each. Generalize to two integers between 1 and n. Generalize to three integers between 1 and 9. (Balanced Assessment) **4h, 4i, 4j**

▲ Suppose it is known that 1% of $100 bills in circulation are counterfeit. Suppose also that there is a quick test for counterfeit bills, but that the test is imperfect: 5% of the time the test gives a false negative (pronouncing a counterfeit bill as genuine) and 15% of the time the test gives a false positive (pronouncing a genuine bill as counterfeit). Find the probability that a bill that tests negative is actually counterfeit. Find the probability that a bill that tests positive is actually genuine. **4h, 4j, 4l**

▲ Player A has a one out of six chance of hitting the target on any throw, while player B has a two out of ten chance. They alternate turns, with A going first. The first one to hit the target wins. Who is favored? **4i, 4j**

▲ In a game, you toss a quarter (diameter 24 mm) onto a large grid of squares formed by vertical and horizontal lines 24 mm apart. You win if the quarter covers an intersection of two lines. What are the odds of winning? Express your answer in terms of π. **4l, 4m**

Samples of student work that illustrate standard-setting performances for these standards can be found on pages 58-79.

Performance Descriptions *Mathematics*

M5 Problem Solving and Mathematical Reasoning

The student demonstrates problem solving by using mathematical concepts and skills to solve non-routine problems that do not lay out specific and detailed steps to follow, and solves problems that make demands on all three aspects of the solution process— formulation, implementation, and conclusion.

Formulation

M5 a The student participates in the formulation of problems; that is, given the statement of a problem situation, the student:

- fills out the formulation of a definite problem that is to be solved;
- extracts pertinent information from the situation as a basis for working on the problem;
- asks and answers a series of appropriate questions in pursuit of a solution and does so with minimal "scaffolding" in the form of detailed guiding questions.

Implementation

M5 b The student makes the basic choices involved in planning and carrying out a solution; that is, the student:

- chooses and employs effective problem solving strategies in dealing with non-routine and multi-step problems;
- selects appropriate mathematical concepts and techniques from different areas of mathematics and applies them to the solution of the problem;
- applies mathematical concepts to new situations within mathematics and uses mathematics to model real world situations involving basic applications of mathematics in the physical and biological sciences, the social sciences, and business.

Conclusion

M5 c The student provides closure to the solution process through summary statements and general conclusions; that is, the student:

- concludes a solution process with a useful summary of results;
- evaluates the degree to which the results obtained represent a good response to the initial problem;
- formulates generalizations of the results obtained;
- carries out extensions of the given problem to related problems.

Mathematical reasoning

M5 d The student demonstrates mathematical reasoning by using logic to prove specific conjectures, by explaining the logic inherent in a solution process, by making generalizations and showing that they are valid, and by revealing mathematical patterns inherent in a situation. The student not only makes observations and states results but also justifies or proves why the results hold in general; that is, the student:

- employs forms of mathematical reasoning and proof appropriate to the solution of the problem at hand, including deductive and inductive reasoning, making and testing conjectures, and using counterexamples and indirect proof;
- differentiates clearly between giving examples that support a conjecture and giving a proof of the conjecture.

To see how these performance descriptions compare with the expectations for elementary school and middle school, turn to pages 148-159.

The examples that follow the performance descriptions for each standard are examples of the work students might do to demonstrate their achievement. The examples also indicate the nature and complexity of activities that are appropriate to expect of students at the high school level. Depending on the nature of the task, the work might be done in class, for homework, or over an extended period.

The cross-references that follow the examples highlight examples for which the same activity, and possibly even the same piece of work, may enable students to demonstrate their achievement in relation to more than one standard. In some cases, the cross-references highlight examples of activities through which students might demonstrate their achievement in relation to standards for more than one subject matter.

Examples of activities through which students might demonstrate facility with problem solving and mathematical reasoning include:

- A regular hexagon "rolls" around a stationary regular octagon of the same side length until it returns to its starting position. Figure out how many times the hexagon (i) rotates about the octagon and (ii) revolves on its axis. Generalize to an m-gon rolling around an n-gon. (Balanced Assessment) **5a, 5b, 5c, 5d, 1j**
- Create a mathematical model that will give an estimate for the volume of a bottle, given a front view and top view of the bottle drawn to scale. Repeat for bottles of different shapes. (New Standards Released Task) **5a, 5b, 2a, 2b, 2d, 2e**
- Classify quadrilaterals according to two criteria: the number of right angles, and the number of pairs of parallel sides. For every possible combination of number of right angles and number of pairs of parallel sides, either give an example of such a quadrilateral, or show why such an example is impossible. (New Standards Released Task) **5b, 5d, 2b, 2p**
- An earthquake generates two types of "waves" that travel through the Earth: "P-waves," which travel at 5.6 km/sec, and "S-waves," which travel at 3.4 km/sec. After an earthquake, the P-waves arrive at one recording station 15 seconds before the S-waves. Use functions, graphs, and equations to explain how far the recording station was from the epicenter of the earthquake. Show the flaw in this attempted solution: "The epicenter is 33 km away because the difference in velocities is 2.2 km/sec, and in 15 seconds that's 33 km." **5a, 5b, 5c, 3a**
- Analyze the relationship between the number of pairs of eyelet holes in a shoe and the length of the shoelace. (New Standards Released Task) **5a, 5b, 5c, 3a, 3f**
- In a game for many players in which each player rolls three dice and adds the three numbers, show how to assign scores to each possible sum so that sums with the same probability get the same score, sums with twice the probability get half the score, and so on. **5a, 5b, 5c, 5d, 4h, 4l**
- Investigate different ways of running a wire from the floor at one corner of a room to the ceiling at the opposite corner. Find the shortest wire under each of the following restrictions: (i) you can only run the wire along the edges of walls; (ii) you can also run the wire across the face of a wall; (iii) you can even run the wire through the air. (Balanced Assessment) **5b, 5c, 2d, 2f, 3b, 3h**
- Explore rectangular spaces enclosed by line segments laid out on a square lattice of dots. Check that the numbers of line segments, dots, and spaces enclosed seem to be related by the formula $L + 1 = D + S$. Justify this formula by reasoning as follows: the formula holds for the simplest arrangement of line segments and dots, and it is not changed through any of the possible ways of adding to an arrangement. (Balanced Assessment) **5d**

M6 Mathematical Skills and Tools

The student demonstrates fluency with basic and important skills by using these skills accurately and automatically, and demonstrates practical competence and persistence with other skills by using them effectively to accomplish a task, perhaps referring to notes, or books, perhaps working to reconstruct a method; that is, the student:

M6 a Carries out numerical calculations and symbol manipulations effectively, using mental computations, pencil and paper, or other technological aids, as appropriate.

M6 b Uses a variety of methods to estimate the values, in appropriate units, of quantities met in applications, and rounds numbers used in applications to an appropriate degree of accuracy.

M6 c Evaluates and analyzes formulas and functions of many kinds, using both pencil and paper and more advanced technology.

M6 d Uses basic geometric terminology accurately, and deduces information about basic geometric figures in solving problems.

M6 e Makes and uses rough sketches, schematic diagrams, or precise scale diagrams to enhance a solution.

M6 f Uses the number line and Cartesian coordinates in the plane and in space.

M6 g Creates and interprets graphs of many kinds, such as function graphs, circle graphs, scatter plots, regression lines, and histograms.

M6 h Sets up and solves equations symbolically (when possible) and graphically.

M6 i Knows how to use algorithms in mathematics, such as the Euclidean Algorithm.

M6 j Uses technology to create graphs or spreadsheets that contribute to the understanding of a problem.

M6 k Writes a simple computer program to carry out a computation or simulation to be repeated many times.

M6 l Uses tools such as rulers, tapes, compasses, and protractors in solving problems.

M6 m Knows standard methods to solve basic problems and uses these methods in approaching more complex problems.

Examples of activities through which students might demonstrate facility with mathematical skills and tools include:

▲ Given that Celsius temperature C can be computed from the Fahrenheit temperature F by the formula $C = (\frac{5}{9})(F-32)$, find a formula for computing F from C. **6a**

▲ If the temperature of an aluminum bar is increased from 0 to T degrees Celsius, its length is increased by a factor of aT, where $a = 23.8 \times 10^{-6}$ is the coefficient of thermal expansion for aluminum. By how many millimeters would a 1 meter bar increase if raised from 0 to 40 degrees Celsius? **6a**

▲ Use the local phone book to find the approximate relative frequency of last names beginning with each of the 26 letters of the alphabet. Make a histogram and a circle graph of this information. Decide how you would divide the names into four roughly equal groups. **6a, 6b, 6g**

▲ The braking distance in feet for a car is given by the formula $0.026 \, s^2 + st$, where s is the speed of the car in feet per second, and t is the reaction time in seconds of the driver. What is the braking distance at a speed of 60 miles per hour if the reaction time is ¾ second? **6a, 6c**

▲ Write the general equation for a straight line that uses as parameters the x-intercept A and the y-intercept B. **6a, 6g**

▲ Make a one-tenth size scale diagram of an archery target with these specifications: There are five target regions, bounded by concentric circles with radii equal to 10 cm, 15 cm..., 35 cm. Compute the area of each region. **6d, 6e**

▲ Given the riser height and tread width of the steps on stairs of many kinds, make a scatter plot of the data. Find a line that seems to fit the data in two ways, by eye and using a calculator that can compute a regression line. Compare the result with the rule of thumb that riser height plus tread width should range from about 40 to 45 cm. **6g**

▲ The function $V = x (40 - 2x) (30 - 2x)$ gives the volume in cubic centimeters of a tray of depth x formed from a rectangle of dimensions 30 cm by 40 cm. Graph this function. What is the volume if the depth is 10 cm? What is the largest volume such a tray can have? What depth gives this largest volume? **6g, 6h, 6j**

▲ Describe an algorithm for converting any distance given in miles and feet to decimal miles, and another algorithm for converting the other way. Do the same for converting decimal hours to hours, minutes, and seconds. **6i**

Samples of student work that illustrate standard-setting performances for these standards can be found on pages 58-79.

To see how these performance descriptions compare with the expectations for elementary school and middle school, turn to pages 148-159.

The examples that follow the performance descriptions for each standard are examples of the work students might do to demonstrate their achievement. The examples also indicate the nature and complexity of activities that are appropriate to expect of students at the high school level. Depending on the nature of the task, the work might be done in class, for homework, or over an extended period.

The cross-references that follow the examples highlight examples for which the same activity, and possibly even the same piece of work, may enable students to demonstrate their achievement in relation to more than one standard. In some cases, the cross-references highlight examples of activities through which students might demonstrate their achievement in relation to standards for more than one subject matter.

M7 Mathematical Communication

The student uses the language of mathematics, its symbols, notation, graphs, and expressions, to communicate through reading, writing, speaking, and listening, and communicates about mathematics by describing mathematical ideas and concepts and explaining reasoning and results; that is, the student:

M7 a Is familiar with basic mathematical terminology, standard notation and use of symbols, common conventions for graphing, and general features of effective mathematical communication styles.

M7 b Uses mathematical representations with appropriate accuracy, including numerical tables, formulas, functions, equations, charts, graphs, and diagrams.

M7 c Organizes work and presents mathematical procedures and results clearly, systematically, succinctly, and correctly.

M7 d Communicates logical arguments clearly, showing why a result makes sense and why the reasoning is valid.

M7 e Presents mathematical ideas effectively both orally and in writing.

M7 f Explains mathematical concepts clearly enough to be of assistance to those who may be having difficulty with them.

M7 g Writes narrative accounts of the history and process of work on a mathematical problem or extended project.

M7 h Writes succinct accounts of the mathematical results obtained in a mathematical problem or extended project, with diagrams, graphs, tables, and formulas integrated into the text.

M7 i Keeps narrative accounts of process separate from succinct accounts of results, and realizes that doing so can enhance the effectiveness of each.

M7 j Reads mathematics texts and other writing about mathematics with understanding.

Examples of activities through which students might demonstrate facility with mathematical communication include:

- Discuss the mathematics underlying a sign along a highway that says "7% Grade Next 3 Miles." Use representations such as tables, formulas, graphs, and diagrams. Explain carefully concepts such as slope, steepness, grade, and gradient. (Balanced Assessment) **7b, 7e**
- Suppose in a certain country every adult gets married, and every married couple keeps having children until they have a daughter, then stops. Describe the effect on the population and the ratio of males to females over time. Assume a probability of one-half that a birth is a girl. **7c, 7d, 7e**
- Design a unit of instruction for middle school about proportional relationships. Show the relevance and interconnection of concepts such as percent, ratio, similarity, and linear functions. **7f**
- Prepare review materials that summarize the basic skills and tools used in an instructional unit from a mathematics text (assuming the unit does not already have such a summary). **7f**
- Read a book written for the general public that discusses different advanced fields of mathematics and report on one of these fields. **7j**

M8 Putting Mathematics to Work

The student conducts at least one large scale investigation or project each year drawn from the following kinds and, over the course of high school, conducts investigations or projects drawn from at least three of the kinds.

A single investigation or project may draw on more than one kind.

M8 a Data study, in which the student:

- carries out a study of data relevant to current civic, economic, scientific, health, or social issues;
- uses methods of statistical inference to generalize from the data;
- prepares a report that explains the purpose of the project, the organizational plan, and conclusions, and uses an appropriate balance of different ways of presenting information.

Examples of data study projects include:

- Carry out a study of the circulation of books in a library based on type of book and number of users, and showing the progression over a period of years. **3k, 4a, 4f, 4g, 5**
- Carry out a study of the students in a district in terms of their proficiency in using writing in mathematics, and how that proficiency changed over a period of years. **3k, 4a, 4g, 5**
- Carry out a study of several kinds of data about auto races and trends in these data over a number of years. **3k, 4a, 4g, 5**
- Carry out a study of the circulation of books in a library over a period of time. Represent the relative number of borrowers for each type of book and analyze any change over time. Represent the number of borrowers for the most popular book titles and look for a correlation with the number of copies of each title the library has. **4a, 4b, 4g, 5**
- Analyze selected newspapers and magazines for accuracy and clarity of graphical presentations of data, discussing the most common and effective types of presentation used, and identifying misleading graphical practices. **4f, 5, 7a, 7b**

M8 b Mathematical model of a physical system or phenomenon, in which the student:

- carries out a study of a physical system or phenomenon by constructing a mathematical model based on functions to make generalizations about the structure of the system;
- uses structural analysis (a direct analysis of the structure of the system) rather than numerical or statistical analysis (an analysis of data about the system);
- prepares a report that explains the purpose of the project, the organizational plan, and conclusions, and uses an appropriate balance of different ways of presenting information.

Examples of mathematical modeling projects include:

- Analyze the change in shape undergone under thermal expansion of a long bridge. **2a, 2b, 3a, 3b, 3e, 3f, 3i, S1b, S1e**
- Analyze the characteristics of an irrigation system for large fields that has a central water feed and rotating spray arms that sweep out a circle. **2a, 2b, 2e, 2l, 3a, 3d, 5**
- Construct pendulums with various lengths of rods and masses of bobs. Measure their periods when released from various heights. Determine which of these parameters the period depends on. Create a formula for the period in terms of these parameters, and compare these results with the analysis of a pendulum in a physics book. **3a, 3b, 3h, 3i, 3n, 5, S1d, S1e**

M8 c Design of a physical structure, in which the student:

- creates a design for a physical structure;
- uses general mathematical ideas and techniques to discuss specifications for building the structure;
- prepares a report that explains the purpose of the project, the organizational plan, and conclusions, and uses an appropriate balance of different ways of presenting information.

Examples of projects to design a physical structure include:

- ▲ Make a plan for the layout of a housing development to be created on a large tract of land, according to given specifications such as lot size, house setbacks, and street widths. Take into consideration given information on the relation between development cost and possible sale prices. **2a, 2b, 2e, 2k, 2n, 3a, 3i, 5**
- ▲ Design and make a model for a wheelchair access ramp to an 11' high platform, given that the ramp must fit in a 30' by 30' space and must conform to the provisions of the Americans with Disabilities Act. **2a, 2g, 2i, 3a, 3b, 3c, 5, A1a**
- ▲ Design seating plans for a large theater given specifications on the size and shape of the space, the allowable width of aisles, the required spacing between rows, and the allowable sizes and spacing of seats. Find the plan that allows for the maximum number of seats. Suggest how that plan might have to be modified to take other features into consideration, such as staggering seats in successive rows for better viewing. **2a, 2b, 3a, 3e, 5**

M8 d Management and planning analysis, in which the student:

- carries out a study of a business or public policy situation involving issues such as optimization, cost-benefit projections, and risks;
- uses decision rules and strategies both to analyze options and balance trade-offs; and brings in mathematical ideas that serve to generalize the analysis across different conditions;
- prepares a report that explains the purpose of the project, the organizational plan, and conclusions, and uses an appropriate balance of different ways of presenting information.

Examples of management and planning projects include:

- ▲ Create a schedule for practices and events at the school gymnasium and swimming pool, taking into account home and away games, junior varsity and varsity, and boys' and girls' teams. **1i, 3a, 3i, 5, A1c**
- ▲ Make a business plan for publication of a magazine, taking into account different requirements in the production of the magazine, such as quality of paper, use of color, cover stock, and the relationship between selling price and circulation. **3a, 3i, 5, A1a**

M8 e Pure mathematics investigation, in which the student:

- carries out a mathematical investigation of a phenomenon or concept in pure mathematics;
- uses methods of mathematical reasoning and justification to make generalizations about the phenomenon;
- prepares a report that explains the purpose of the project, the organizational plan, and conclusions, and uses an appropriate balance of different ways of presenting information.

Examples of pure mathematics projects include:

- ▲ Carry out an investigation of the many properties of Pascal's triangle. **1b, 1i, 1l, 3a, 3b, 3i, 3o, 5**
- ▲ Create a schedule for a ping-pong tournament among ten players in which each player plays each other player exactly once. Arrange the schedule so that no players have to sit out while others are playing. Try to do the same for a tournament with sixteen players. Then (this is much harder) say what you can about the general case of a tournament with 2n players. Create effective and revealing representations for the schedules. (Balanced Assessment) **1i, 5, A1c**
- ▲ Make a study of different mathematical types of spirals, the properties they share, and the ways in which they are different. **2o, 3m, 5**
- ▲ Make an inquiry into what distributions of objects of two colors result in a probability of roughly ½ that the objects are the same color when two of the objects are selected at random. (For example, three of one color and six of another color is such a distribution.) **4h, 4i, 4j, 4k, 4l, 5**

M8 f History of a mathematical idea, in which the student:

- carries out a historical study tracing the development of a mathematical concept and the people who contributed to it;
- includes a discussion of the actual mathematical content and its place in the curriculum of the present day;
- prepares a report that explains the purpose of the project, the organizational plan, and conclusions, and uses an appropriate balance of different ways of presenting information.

Examples of historical projects include:

- ▲ Read and report on the history of the Pythagorean Theorem, including a discussion of some of the basic ways of proving the theorem and of its uses within and outside mathematics. **2f, 2p, 5, 7e, 7j**
- ▲ Carry out a historical study of the concept of "function" in mathematics, including a report on the most important function concepts and types currently in use. Base part of the work on interviews with people from other fields who use mathematics in their work. **3, 5, 7e, 7j**

Samples of student work that illustrate standard-setting performances for these standards can be found on pages 58-79.

Work Sample & Commentary: *How Much Gold Can You Carry Out?*

Number and Operation Concepts M1

Geometry & Measurement Concepts

Function & Algebra Concepts

Statistics & Probability Concepts

Problem Solving & Mathematical Reasoning

Mathematical Skills & Tools M6

Mathematical Communication M7

Putting Mathematics to Work

The task

How Much Gold Can You Carry Out?

A vault contains a large amount of gold and you are told that you may keep as much as you can carry out, under the following conditions:

On the first trip you may only take one pound.

On each successive trip you may take out half the amount you carried out on the previous trip.

You take one minute to complete each trip.

Explain how much gold you can carry out, and how long it will take to do it.

Also, determine your hourly rate of earnings if you work only fifteen minutes. Use the current value of gold, $350 per ounce. What would be your hourly rate if you work for twenty minutes? What if you worked for an entire hour?

The quotations from the Mathematics performance descriptions in this commentary are excerpted. The complete performance descriptions are shown on pages 50-57.

This task, in different variants, is commonly seen in classrooms. It is designed to show how very rapidly a quantity shrinks if it is halved over and over. Similar tasks show how very rapidly a quantity grows if it is doubled over and over. These tasks illustrate exponential decay and growth. The fanciful context makes the task memorable. Still, the context is easily stripped away to get at the underlying mathematics required to answer the questions.

How Much Gold Can You Carry Out?

On my first trip I will take out 16 oz. of gold. On the second trip I will take out only 8 oz. On the third only 4, then 2, then 1, then 1/5 and so on. I made a table of the amount of gold that I took out on each trip which is on the attached sheet. You can see how many ounces of gold I took out on each trip.

I added up the amount of gold made in each of the first 15 trips, which represents the first 15 minutes I worked because each trip is one minute, and got a total of 31.999023 ounces. Gold is worth $350 an ounce, so I made $11,199.66. Since I only worked for 1/4 of an hour my hourly wage is $44,798.63. I also added the amount of gold in each of the first 20 trips, which represents 20 minutes of work, and got a total of 31.999969 ounce. That means I took out $11,199.98 worth of gold. But since I worked for 1/3 of an hour this time my hourly wage is now $33,599.97.

I continued the table a little further to see the total amount that I was going to take out. On the 26th trip I found that all of the amounts of gold gathered added up to 32 ounce which yielded $11,200. After this point the amount of gold that I am taking out is immeasurable and has no effect on the total any more, adding .000002 of an ounce makes no sense because it is so small. After an hour of working I would still have only $11,200 worth of gold, so I would make $11,200 an hour if I work for a full hour.

I also found that after working for more than 20 minutes I take out less than a cent worth of gold on each trip. So I would probably stop at this point because I would be taking out fractions of pennies which are worthless.

I found that if I worked for 15 minutes I would be making $44,798.63 an hour and for 20 minutes $33,599.97 an hour. If I work for a full hour I would be getting $11,200 worth. I also found that after 20 minutes of working I will be taking out gold worth only fractions of pennies and it's not worth it.

This work sample illustrates a standard-setting performance for the following parts of the standards:

M1 a **Number and Operation Concepts:** Use addition, multiplication, and division in forming and working with numerical and algebraic expressions.

M1 c **Number and Operation Concepts:** Have facility with the mechanics of operations as well as understanding of their typical meaning and uses in applications.

M1 e **Number and Operation Concepts:** Represent numbers in decimal form.

M1 h **Number and Operation Concepts:** Understand numbers with specific units of measure, such as numbers with rate units.

M6 a **Mathematical Skills and Tools:** Carry out numerical calculations effectively.

M7 b **Mathematical Communication:** Use mathematical representations with appropriate accuracy.

M7 e **Mathematical Communication:** Present mathematical ideas effectively.

Circumstances of performance

This sample of student work was produced under the following conditions:

√ alone   in a group

   in class   √ as homework

   with teacher feedback   with peer feedback

   timed   opportunity for revision

Mathematics required by the task

The key requirement in the problem statement is "Explain how much gold you can carry out, and how long it will take to do it." Since the amount of gold starts at 1 pound on the first trip, and is cut in half for each successive trip, finding the quantity of gold that can be carried out amounts to finding this sum:

$$1 + \tfrac{1}{2} + \tfrac{1}{4} + \tfrac{1}{8} + \tfrac{1}{16} + \ldots.$$

If this is approached as a practical problem, all that is required is to compute these terms until they get too small to be practical, then add them up. "Too small to be practical" might be interpreted as "too small to be represented on a calculator." On a calcu-

How Much Gold Can You Carry Out?

lator with an 8-digit display, this happens after about 25 terms of this series. That is, $\frac{1}{2^{24}}$ comes out as 0.0000001 on the calculator, while $\frac{1}{2^{25}}$ comes out as 0.0000000. When all the terms up to $\frac{1}{2^{24}}$ are added up, the sum comes to 1.9999999, but when all the terms up to $\frac{1}{2^{25}}$ are added, the sum comes to 2.0000000. All these quantities are in pounds. (To treat these issues fully, we would need to address questions such as how many digits are stored but not shown on a calculator.)

As a practical problem, then, the answer is that a little less than 2 pounds can be carried out, and that after about 25 minutes the 2 pound figure has almost been reached, and the amounts to be carried out per trip are probably too small to measure. In fact, after just 8 minutes more than 1.99 pounds can be taken out, as can be determined by summing the terms up to $\frac{1}{128}$. In summary, the mathematics required to work the task as this sort of practical problem is an organized application of arithmetic: taking powers, reciprocals, and summing.

A mathematically more powerful solution would be the summation of the full infinite series. This is a geometric series with factor $\frac{1}{2}$, and the sum of such an infinite series with first term 1 is $\frac{1}{1-1/2} = 2$ by a formula often developed in high school texts. Such an approach would give evidence of **M3**g (Function and Algebra Concepts: Uses...geometric sequences and their sums...). The student work shown here did not take this approach.

What the work shows

M1a Number and Operation Concepts: The student uses addition...multiplication, and division...in forming and working with numerical and algebraic expressions.

M1c Number and Operation Concepts: The student has facility with the mechanics of operations as well as understanding of their typical meaning and uses in applications.

M1e Number and Operation Concepts: The student represents numbers in decimal...form....

M1h Number and Operation Concepts: The student understands...numbers with specific units of measure, such as numbers with...rate units.

M6a Mathematical Skills and Tools: The student carries out numerical calculations...effectively, using...pencil and paper, or other technological aids, as appropriate.

A The table is organized by its first column, the trip number. The second column is the weight of gold taken out on the trip with that number, the third column is a running sum of the weights in the second column, and the last column gives the value in $ of the gold taken out up to that point. It is formed by multiplying the weight in ounces given in the third column by the cost of gold per ounce ($350).

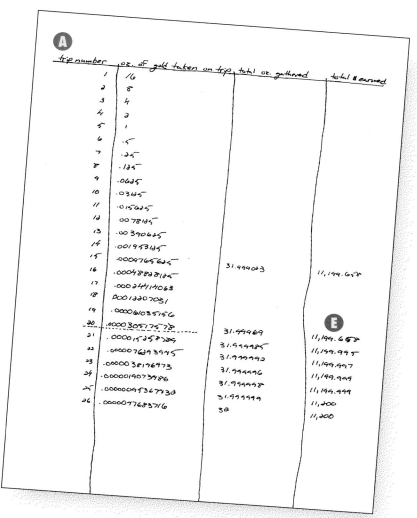

trip number	oz. of gold taken on trip	total oz. gathered	total $ earned
1	16		
2	8		
3	4		
4	2		
5	1		
6	.5		
7	.25		
8	.125		
9	.0625		
10	.03125		
11	.015625		
12	.0078125		
13	.00390625		
14	.001953125		
15	.0009765625		
16	.00048828125	31.999023	11,199.658
17	.000244140063		
18	.000122070031		
19	.000061035156		
20	.0000305175578	31.99969	11,199.658
21	.00001525878289	31.999985	11,199.995
22	.0000076293945	31.999992	11,199.995
23	.00000381469073	31.999993	11,199.997
24	.0000019073986	31.999996	11,199.999
25	.000000953367730	31.999998	11,199.999
26	.0000007768371(6)	31.999999	11,200
		32	11,200

B A further step appears in the text of the response, though not in the table; the hourly rate earned at various stages is figured by dividing the value in $ of the gold taken out by the time in hours up to that point.

C The student has expressed the 1 pound weight as 16 ounces. This is sensible, since it means that the numbers obtained in the repeated halving are larger and hence easier to work with: 16, 8, 4, 2, 1, $\frac{1}{2}$,..., as opposed to 1, $\frac{1}{2}$, $\frac{1}{4}$, $\frac{1}{8}$,.... Note the misprint here: $\frac{1}{8}$ should be .5, as it is in the table.

How Much Gold Can You Carry Out?

M1 h Number and Operation Concepts: The student understands…numbers with specific units of measure, such as numbers with…rate units.

B Here the weight has been converted to its monetary value using the given price of $350 per ounce. The hourly *rate* of earnings has been figured by dividing the monetary value by the time in hours (first converting 15 minutes to 0.25 hours, etc.).

D Notice that the largest total the student found was 32 ounces, but that there is no justification given that the total could not go higher. A justification would require showing that 32 is the sum of the geometric series with first term 16 and common factor ½. The student interpreted the problem in practical terms, and the references to amounts that are eventually "immeasurable" or "so small" refer to practicalities, not to the mathematics of the situation. The student did not deal with the issue of whether the amounts 32 oz. and $11,200 actually would be *reached* on the 26th trip, or whether these are figures that have been rounded up. See the discussion above in "Mathematics required by the task."

E There is a misprint here. Line 20 should be $11,199.989.

M7 b Mathematical Communication: The student uses mathematical representations with appropriate accuracy, including numerical tables….

M7 e Mathematical Communication: The student presents mathematical ideas effectively…in writing.

The student wrote a coherent explanation of the steps taken to solve the problem and produced a clearly labeled table.

Work Sample & Commentary: *Miles of Words*

The task

Miles of Words

In this task you are asked to read a passage from a magazine article and then use mathematics to assess the reasonableness of its claim that forty thousand words were uttered in a 200 mile train journey.

The following appeared in *The New Yorker*, October 17, 1994:

I met Dodge on an Amtrak train in Union Station, Washington, in January of 1993…He came into an empty car and sat down beside me, explaining that the car would before long fill up. It did. He didn't know me from Chichikov, nor I him…Two hundred miles of track lie between Union Station and Trenton, where I got off, and over that distance he uttered about forty thousand words. After I left him, I went home and called a friend who teaches Russian literature at Princeton University, and asked her who could help me assess what I had heard,….

Discuss in detail the statement:

"over that distance he uttered about forty thousand words."

Is this statement reasonable? Why or why not? Show all of your calculations and explain your reasoning.

Reprinted with permission from The Balanced Assessment Project, University of California, Berkeley, CA 94720.

This work sample illustrates a standard-setting performance for the following parts of the standards:

M2 l Geometry and Measurement Concepts: Use quotient measures that give "per unit" amounts.

M2 m Geometry and Measurement Concepts: Understand unit conversions.

M3 a Function and Algebra Concepts: Model given situations with formulas and functions, and interpret given formulas and functions in terms of situations.

M3 d Function and Algebra Concepts: Work with rates of many kinds.

M5 a Problem Solving and Mathematical Reasoning: Formulation.

M6 b Mathematical Skills and Tools: Use a variety of methods to estimate the values of quantities met in applications.

M7 e Mathematical Communication: Present mathematical ideas effectively.

This task helps answer these things about students' understanding:

1. Given a specific question based on a selection from a written text, can students figure out what information from the text is relevant and what mathematics is needed to answer the question? (Here the mathematics is about rate relationships.)

2. Can students work with the mechanics of these rate relationships and arrive at correct results that answer the given question?

In short, the task requires students to (1) formulate and set up a problem from a given context, and then (2) solve the problem.

Circumstances of performance

This sample of student work was produced under the following conditions:

√ alone   in a group

in class   √ as homework

with teacher feedback   with peer feedback

timed   opportunity for revision

Mathematics required by the task

To get to the mathematical heart of the task, students need to make reasonable estimates of the rate of speed s of a train (in miles per hour) and the rate r of normal speech (in words per minute). Using these estimates, students need to:

(i) Find the time T required to travel a given distance D at the estimated rate of speed s, using the relationship $T = D/s$.

(ii) Find the number of words N that can be spoken in that time T at the estimated rate r, using the relationship N = rT.

Combining (i) and (ii) gives the formula $N = r/s (D)$, expressing the number of words N in terms of the estimated rate of speed s, the estimated rate of speech r, and the given distance D. Since s, r, and D are known, the formula can be used to see if the 40,000 words mentioned in the article is reasonable.

(Interestingly, the quotient r/s of the rates r and s is itself a rate, "words per mile." Other students working on this task made use of this rate in their analysis.)

Students also need to make appropriate unit conversions: the time T they find will be in hours, and they

The quotations from the Mathematics performance descriptions in this commentary are excerpted. The complete performance descriptions are shown on pages 50-57.

Miles of Words

will have to convert this to minutes before they use it to find the rate in "words per minute."

As individual exercises, (i) and (ii) above would be too simple for high school. But the "Miles of Words" task requires students to do more than work these as routine exercises. Students must formulate the problem from the context, make estimates, set up their own version of (i) and (ii), and then combine them. What is being assessed in the task is this whole process.

What the work shows

M2 l Geometry and Measurement Concepts: The student uses quotient measures, such as speed,…that give "per unit" amounts….

M2 m Geometry and Measurement Concepts: The student understands…unit conversions….

A The student immediately followed the computation $^{200m}/_{35mph} = 5.71$…hours" with a multiplication by the conversion factor "60 minutes per hour," and immediately followed this with "= 342.857… minutes." The calculations are correct, but this use of a conversion factor in a train of equalities is not ideal. It is clearer to keep the unit conversions separate from the other calculations. In fact, the student did keep the unit conversion separate below when using the conversion factor "60 sec/min."

M3 a Function and Algebra Concepts: The student models given situations with formulas and functions, and interprets given formulas and functions in terms of situations.

M3 d Function and Algebra Concepts: The student works with rates of many kinds, expressed numerically [and] symbolically….

A The student found the time of travel from the formula (time) = $^{distance}/_{speed}$.

B The student found the speaking rate required to support the claim from the formula $^{number\ of\ words}/_{time}$.

Number and Operation Concepts

Geometry & Measurement Concepts **M2**

Function & Algebra Concepts **M3**

Statistics & Probability Concepts

Problem Solving & Mathematical Reasoning **M5**

Mathematical Skills & Tools **M6**

Mathematical Communication **M7**

Putting Mathematics to Work

C The first thing I thought about when I recieved this problem was how long would it take the train to travel these 200 miles? I know from personal experience that this particular train has a cruising speed of around 55 miles per hour (I have traveled on the Amtrak train from Philadelphia to Washington several times). However, the train must also start and stop many times, so its actual speed will be considerably less. I have no way to accurately estimate what its average speed, including stops, would be, but I do know from having taken both the train and a car between these two points that the train is not twice as slow as the car. So, I will say that the trains average speed is 35 mph, which I believe to be less than its actual speed.

Using this number, I made the following calculations

A $\dfrac{200\ m}{35\ mph} = 5.71...hours \times 60\,min\ per\ hour = 342,857...\ mins.$

$342.857... mins \times 60\ sec/min = 20,571\ seconds$

So, it would be fairly generous to say that the man the author met had 20,571 seconds to speak.

B $\dfrac{40,000\ words}{20,571\ seconds} = 1.94\ \dfrac{words}{second}$

Next, I attempted to speak at this rate for one minute. I discovered that it is possible to talk

D at this speed, but it is not comfortable or normal speech, and is very hard to comprehend. From the authors comments, he was impressed by something the man said, which implies that he understood what was being said. Therefore, I conclude that the person he met could not have spoken 40000 words over the 200 miles, unless he was intentionally speaking very fast, or the train broke down or stopped for an unusual amount of time at one of its stops.

M5a Problem Solving and Mathematical Reasoning: Formulation. Given the basic statement of a problem situation, the student:

- fills out the formulation of a definite problem that is to be solved;

- extracts pertinent information from the situation as a basis for working on the problem;

- asks and answers a series of appropriate questions in pursuit of a solution and does so with minimal "scaffolding" in the form of detailed guiding questions.

The response shows that the student read the written passage from the article, focused on what is relevant to the given question, and formulated and solved a particular problem involving rates in order to answer this question. The work involved is very different from solving a fully formulated mathematics problem.

M6b Mathematical Skills and Tools: The student uses a variety of methods to estimate the values, in appropriate units, of quantities met in applications....

C The student suggested and supported an estimate for the rate of speed of the train.

D The student concluded that a speaking rate of 2 words per second is too fast to be reasonable. This is puzzling, since rates of 3 words per second are commonly judged to be representative of actual speech. Yet, the student gathered data on which to base this opinion.

M7e Mathematical Communication: The student represents mathematical ideas effectively...in writing.

The response gives a clear indication of what the student did to solve the problem, and of the result.

A **B** **C** The response does not have a consistent approach to the number of significant digits used. The estimate given of a train's average speed (about 35 mph) is very rough (perhaps ± as much as 20 mph), but the time is reported later as 342.857 minutes. After carrying out exact calculations with this number, the result is appropriately rounded up to 2 words/second. It would have been more reasonable to use only one significant digit in all calculations.

There are two misspellings ("recieved" in the first line, "acctual" at the end of the first paragraph) and a punctuation error ("trains" should have an apostrophe), but these do not detract from communicating the meaning.

Number and Operation Concepts

Geometry & Measurement Concepts

Function & Algebra Concepts

Statistics & Probability Concepts

Problem Solving & Mathematical Reasoning

Mathematical Skills & Tools

Mathematical Communication

Putting Mathematics to Work

Work Sample & Commentary: *Cubes*

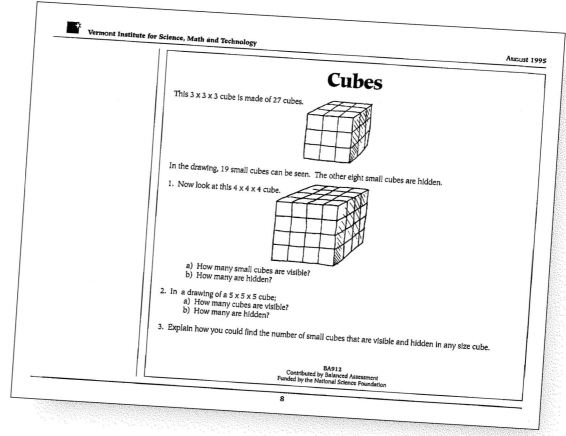

Number and Operation Concepts

Geometry & Measurement Concepts **M2**

Function & Algebra Concepts **M3**

Statistics & Probability Concepts

Problem Solving & Mathematical Reasoning

Mathematical Skills & Tools **M6**

Mathematical Communication **M7**

Putting Mathematics to Work

The quotations from the Mathematics performance descriptions in this commentary are excerpted. The complete performance descriptions are shown on pages 50-57.

This 3 x 3 x 3 cube is made of 27 cubes.

In the drawing, 19 small cubes can be seen. The other eight small cubes are hidden.

1. Now look at this 4 x 4 x 4 cube.

   a) How many small cubes are visible?
   b) How many are hidden?

2. In a drawing of a 5 x 5 x 5 cube;
   a) How many cubes are visible?
   b) How many are hidden?

3. Explain how you could find the number of small cubes that are visible and hidden in any size cube.

BA912
Contributed by Balanced Assessment
Funded by the National Science Foundation

8

This work sample illustrates a standard-setting performance for the following parts of the standards:

M2 b Geometry and Measurement Concepts: Work with three dimensional figures and their properties.

M2 d Geometry and Measurement Concepts: Visualize objects in space.

M2 i Geometry and Measurement Concepts: Investigate geometric patterns.

M3 a Function and Algebra Concepts: Model given situations with formulas.

M3 b Function and Algebra Concepts: Use basic types of functions.

M3 h Function and Algebra Concepts: Use and manipulate expressions involving variables.

M3 i Function and Algebra Concepts: Represent functional relationships.

M3 o Function and Algebra Concepts: Use functions to analyze patterns and represent their structure.

M6 e Mathematical Skills and Tools: Make and use rough sketches or schematic diagrams to enhance a solution.

M7 c Mathematical Communication: Organize work and present mathematical procedures and results clearly, systematically, succinctly, and correctly.

The task

Students were given the task displayed here.

This task requires an interesting combination of geometry (spatial visualization) and algebra (expressing the general relationship symbolically).

Circumstances of performance

This sample of student work was produced under the following conditions:

√ alone   in a group

   in class   √ as homework

   with teacher feedback   with peer feedback

   timed   opportunity for revision

Mathematics required by the task

The idea at the heart of the task is the following fact about three-dimensional geometry: A large cube which is made up as an "n by n by n" assembly of small, identical cubes contains exactly n^3 small cubes. The task statement illustrates an isometric diagram of such large cubes for the case n = 3 and n = 4.

Cubes

It is necessary to visualize this situation spatially to appreciate another important fact. The small cubes that are hidden from view in an isomeric diagram of a large n by n by n cube actually form a large (n-1) by (n-1) by (n-1) cube. This means that there is a total of $(n-1)^3$ small cubes that are hidden from view.

Finally, an algebraic representation seems essential to express the generalization asked for in Question 3. For example, the number of visible cubes in a large n by n by n cube can be expressed as the total number of cubes minus the number of invisible cubes:

total # of cubes - # of hidden cubes = # of visible cubes

$$n^3 - (n-1)^3 = 3n^2 - 3n + 1$$

(These expressions make sense if and only if n is a whole number.)

The student work illustrates another way in which the visible cubes are counted directly.

What the work shows

M2b Geometry and Measurement Concepts: The student works with...three dimensional figures and their properties, including...cubes....

M2d Geometry and Measurement Concepts: The student visualizes objects...in space....

M2j Geometry and Measurement Concepts: The student investigates geometric patterns, including sequences of growing shapes.

Throughout the response, the student worked with the structure of large cubes built up from smaller cubes, visualizing them in terms of the small cubes that are visible and those that are hidden, and representing the visible and hidden cubes in large cubes of various sizes.

M3a Function and Algebra Concepts: The student models given situations with formulas..., and interprets given formulas...in terms of situations.

M3b Function and Algebra Concepts: The student...uses basic types of functions...[including] cube....

M3h Function and Algebra Concepts: The student...uses and manipulates expressions involving variables...in work with formulas....

M3i Function and Algebra Concepts: The student represents functional relationships in formulas [and] tables....

M3o Function and Algebra Concepts: The student uses functions to analyze patterns and represent their structure.

A Here the student began to formulate the generalization asked for in Question 3 of the task. The variable "x" was chosen to represent the number of small cubes making up each dimension of the large

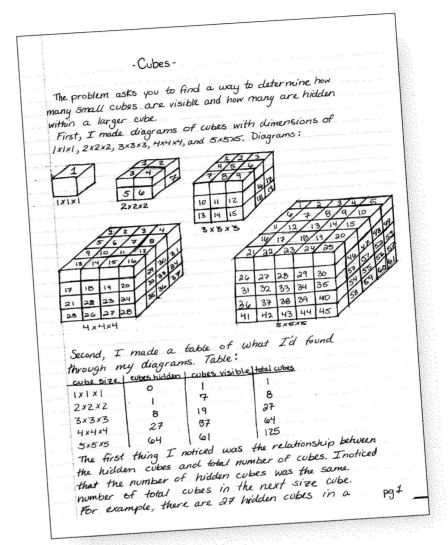

Number and Operation Concepts

M2 Geometry & Measurement Concepts

M3 Function & Algebra Concepts

Statistics & Probability Concepts

Problem Solving & Mathematical Reasoning

M6 Mathematical Skills & Tools

M7 Mathematical Communication

Putting Mathematics to Work

cube. (The variable "n" would be more in keeping with standard practice.) The total number of small cubes in a large "x by x by x" cube is given as x^3, while the number of hidden cubes is given as $(x-1)^3$. The latter fact was based on the empirical observation "I noticed that the number of hidden cubes was the same number of cubes in the next size cube."

B Expressing the number of visible cubes is harder than expressing the number of hidden cubes. The student expressed the number of visible cubes directly by summing the number of cubes on the three visible faces (and making sure not to count the same cube more than once):

- top face: x^2

- front face: $x(x-1) = x^2 - x$

- side face: $(x-1)(x-1) = x^2 - 2x + 1$

Summing these gives the total number of visible cubes: $3x^2 - 3x + 1$.

Cubes

The same result could have been obtained a little more easily by subtracting the number of hidden cubes (which is $(x-1)^3$) from the total number of cubes (which is x^3).

Ⓐ It is not clear how the student arrived at the cubic function given in the response. Is it an observation that the numerical entries in the "total cubes" column of the table are all perfect cubes: $1 = 1^3$, $8 = 2^3$, $27 = 3^3$, etc.? Or is it the geometrical insight that an n by n by n large cube has n^3 small cubes in it? The difference between these two possible ways of seeing the cubic pattern is the difference between:

(i) data analysis (get numerical data from the geometrical situation case by case, then forget the situation and analyze the data numerically); and

(ii) "structural analysis" (directly analyze the geometric structure of the situation).

M6 e Mathematical Skills and Tools: The student makes and uses rough sketches, schematic diagrams…to enhance a solution.

The student made effective use of diagrams as a way of illustrating and hence visualizing the structure of the large cubes. The small cubes in the diagrams are numbered systematically, indicating an organized process of using the diagrams to reveal the pattern.

M7 c Mathematical Communication: The student organizes work and presents mathematical procedures and results clearly, systematically, succinctly, and correctly.

The diagrams are connected and interpreted with explanatory text.

Ⓐ 4×4×4 cube and 27 total cubes in a 3×3×3 cube. So I found that the formula; $(x-1)^3$ will tell you how many hidden cubes there are in a certain size cube. "x" equals the dimension of one side of a cube.

You can also find a formula for the number of visible cubes. Take a look at the diagram of a 3×3×3 cube. Diagram:

Again, "x" equals the dimension of one side of a cube. The top of this cube is equal to x^2, side A is equal to x^2-x, and side B is equal to x^2-2x+1.

equation: $x^2 + x^2 - x + x^2 - 2x + 1 \Rightarrow 3x^2 - 3x + 1$
The equation or formula for finding the number of visible cubes is $3x^2 - 3x + 1$. If I say x=3, and put that in the formula; $3(3^2) - 3(3) + 1 \Rightarrow 27 - 9 + 1 \Rightarrow 19$. So there are 19 visible cubes. To find the number of hidden cubes I put x=3 into $(x-1)^3 \Rightarrow (3-1)^3 \Rightarrow 2^3 \Rightarrow 8$. I find there **Ⓑ** are 8 hidden cubes. If I add those 8 to the 19 visible cubes, I get a total of 27 cubes in a 3×3×3 cube. We can see this is correct because the total number of cubes can be found by $x^3 \Rightarrow 3^3 \Rightarrow 27$.

The formulas I found in this problem could also be expressed as functions. I could have written the formula for hidden cubes as $\Rightarrow h(x) = (x-1)^3$ and the formula for visible cubes as $\Rightarrow v(x) = 3x^2 - 3x + 1$.

pg 2

Work Sample & Commentary: *Shopping Carts*

The task

Shopping Carts

In this task you are asked to think mathematically about shopping carts. You are asked to create a rule that can be used to predict the length of storage space needed given the number of carts.

The diagram below shows a drawing of a single shopping cart.

It also shows a drawing of 12 shopping carts that have been "nested" together.

The drawings are accurately scaled to ¼₄ the **real size.**

Reprinted with permission from The Balanced Assessment Project, University of California, Berkeley, CA 94720.

This work sample illustrates a standard-setting performance for the following parts of the standards:

M2 k Geometry and Measurement Concepts: Work with geometric measures of length.

M2 n Geometry and Measurement Concepts: Solve problems involving scale.

M3 a Function and Algebra Concepts: Model given situations with formulas and functions.

M3 f Function and Algebra Concepts: Use linear functions as a mathematical representation of proportional relationships.

M3 h Function and Algebra Concepts: Manipulate expressions involving variables.

M5 b Problem Solving and Mathematical Reasoning: Implementation.

M6 l Mathematical Skills and Tools: Use tools in solving problems.

M7 c Mathematical Communication: Organize work and present mathematical procedures and results clearly, systematically, succinctly, and correctly.

---

1. Create a rule that will tell you the length S of storage space needed for carts when you know the number N of shopping carts to be stored. You will need to show *how* you built your rule; that is, we will need to know what information you drew upon and how you used it.

2. Now create a rule that will tell you the number N of shopping carts that will fit in a space S meters long.

The diagram, as reproduced here, is 45% as large as the original task prompt the students worked from.

About the task

This task is designed to see if students can recognize the proportional relationship inherent in this situation (the increase in the length of a nested row of carts is proportional to the number of carts added) and express it in terms of a linear formula or function.

Once students have completed the task as given, it is natural to ask them to look for other examples (in the real world), of structures which, similar to a row of nested shopping carts, can be represented by linear functions of the form y = A + b n.

In their examples, y, A, and b should have a clear geometric meaning that they identify, and n should represent the number of identical components in the structure. Their examples can be represented in a diagram similar to the shopping carts diagram.

Circumstances of performance

This sample of student work was produced under the following conditions:

√ alone　　　　　　　in a group

　in class　　　　　√ as homework

√ with teacher feedback　　with peer feedback

　timed　　　　　　√ opportunity for revision

Mathematics required by the task

There are two relevant lengths in this task, the full length (call it L) of a single cart, and the amount (call it d) that each new cart in a row sticks out beyond the others. Since the drawing is accurately scaled to ¼₄th full size, L and d can be found by measuring the drawing and multiplying by 24.

Each new cart added to a row adds the fixed amount d to the length of the row. This means that the length S of a row of carts is a linear function of the number n of carts in the row, and that the slope of this function is d. Since the full length of a single cart is L, this function can be written as:

S = L + d (n-1).

The quotations from the Mathematics performance descriptions in this commentary are excerpted. The complete performance descriptions are shown on pages 50-57.

Number and Operation Concepts

M2 Geometry & Measurement Concepts

M3 Function & Algebra Concepts

Statistics & Probability Concepts

M5 Problem Solving & Mathematical Reasoning

M6 Mathematical Skills & Tools

M7 Mathematical Communication

Putting Mathematics to Work

Shopping Carts

Using the full-size measurements in centimeters of L and d for the shopping cart pictured, the function is:

$$S = 96 + 28.8 (n-1).$$

The reason n-1 appears in this formula instead of n is that the contribution of the first cart is contained in the number L. A way of writing the function using n instead of n-1 is:

$$S = (L-d) + d \, n = 67.2 + 28.8 \, n.$$

It is important to note that the function here is *discrete*: it is meaningful in this context only for the natural numbers n = 1, 2, 3,.... In particular, n = 0 gives a result, S = L-d, which has no direct meaning in this context; (it would mean the length of a row of 0 carts).

What the work shows

M2k Geometry and Measurement Concepts: The student works with geometric measures of length....

M2n Geometry and Measurement Concepts: The student solves problems involving scale...in... diagrams.

A The student recognized the two lengths needed to work the problem, measured them from the diagram, and used the given 1 to 24 scale of the diagram to convert these to full size measurements.

B The student said the two answers arrived at were "fairly close." To be more precise, the answers given in the response agree to two significant digits. Actually, it would have made sense to limit all numbers in the work to two significant digits. After all, the measurements used were made from a small diagram and could not be very accurate.

M3a Function and Algebra Concepts: The student models given situations with formulas and functions....

C The student was clear about interpreting the mathematics in terms of the situation, for example, by saying "The 96 is the length of the first cart and the 28.8 (n-1) is the length added by all the additional carts after the first."

M3f Function and Algebra Concepts: The student...uses linear functions as a mathematical representation of proportional relationships.

D The student created a simple formula that describes the given situation, and that shows that the length of a row after the first cart is proportional to the number (n-1) of carts after the first.

Shopping carts

Each shopping cart in the picture, when measured with a ruler is about 4 cm long. Since the drawings are accurately scaled to $\frac{1}{24}$th the real size, each cart is 96 cm long.

A I also measured how much of a cart sticks out when two shopping carts are nested together. This length is about 1.2 cm long. To attain the accurate size, I multiplied 1.2 by 24 and got 28.8 cm. So the length of two carts nested together is 124.8 centimeters. Each additional cart would add an extra 28.8 cm.

D Thus: (in centimeters)

$$S = 96 + 28.8 (n-1);$$

when S = length of storage space and n = number of shopping carts to be stored.

C The 96 is the length of the first cart and the 28.8(n-1) is the length added by all the additional carts after the first.

When you get this answer, you would convert it to meters by dividing it by 100.

However, to make this problem even simpler, you can put the rule into meters.

Thus: (in meters)

$$S = 0.96 + 0.288 (n-1)$$

So, we will test these rules by using the diagram. When measuring all the way across the 12 shopping carts, I get about

Shopping Carts

M3 h Function and Algebra Concepts: The student...manipulates expressions involving variables...in work with formulas, functions, [and] equations....

E Having expressed the length S in terms of the number n of carts, using the formula
S = 0.96 + 0.288 (n-1), the student re-expressed this formula to express the number n in terms of the length S. In the language of the student: "...let's convert the equation."

F This formula should indicate in some way that n must be an integer, perhaps simply saying that any non-integer result must be rounded down to the nearest integer.

M5 b Problem Solving and Mathematical Reasoning: Implementation. The student chooses and employs effective problem solving strategies in dealing with... non-routine problems.

In a situation that was unfamiliar the student chose and applied appropriate mathematics that closely modeled the situation.

M6 l Mathematical Skills and Tools: The student uses tools such as rulers...in solving problems.

A The student recognized the two lengths needed to work the problem, measured them from the diagram, and used the given 1 to 24 scale of the diagram to convert these to full size measurements.

M7 c Mathematical Communication: The student organizes work and presents mathematical procedures and results clearly, systematically, succinctly, and correctly.

The student presented an orderly approach to the problem, explained the steps of the solution process clearly and concisely, and arrived at a result that is correct.

Number and Operation Concepts

M2 Geometry & Measurement Concepts

M3 Function & Algebra Concepts

Statistics & Probability Concepts

M5 Problem Solving & Mathematical Reasoning

M6 Mathematical Skills & Tools

M7 Mathematical Communication

Putting Mathematics to Work

16.9 cm. So the real size is approximately 405.6 cm. To get meters divide by 100: 4.056 meters.

By using the meter rule:
$$S = 0.96 + 0.288(n-1)$$
$$S = 0.96 + 0.288(12-1)$$
$$S = 0.96 + 0.288(11)$$
$$S = 0.96 + 3.168$$
$$S = 4.128 \text{ meters}$$

B The 2 answers I have gotten are fairly close, so I know that my rule is probably accurate.

To find n by knowing S, let's convert the equation.

E
$$S = 0.96 + 0.288(n-1)$$
$$S - 0.96 = 0.288n - 0.288$$
$$S - 0.96 + 0.288 = 0.288n$$
$$S - 0.672 = 0.288n$$
So →
$$n = \frac{S - 0.672}{0.288}$$
F

Work Sample & Commentary: *Grazing Area*

The task

A cow is secured by a 50 foot long rope that is tied to a stake. The stake is placed 10 feet from the corner of a 20 foot by 40 foot barn. A line from the stake to the corner makes a 135 degree angle with the sides of the barn.

Under these conditions, how much area does the cow have to graze in?

The quotations from the Mathematics performance descriptions in this commentary are excerpted. The complete performance descriptions are shown on pages 50-57.

Although the context of the task is somewhat fanciful, it is a situation that can be visualized concretely in a definite way, and the requirements for a solution are quite clear: the area of a particular plot of grass needs to be found. Moreover, finding this area requires a thorough understanding of important ideas from geometry. In short, in spite of the fanciful context, the task provides the opportunity for demonstrating good use of sound mathematics.

This work sample illustrates a standard-setting performance for the following parts of the standards:

M2 a Geometry and Measurement Concepts: Model situations geometrically to formulate and solve problems.

M2 b Geometry and Measurement Concepts: Work with two dimensional figures and their properties.

M2 e Geometry and Measurement Concepts: Know and use formulas for area.

M2 f Geometry and Measurement Concepts: Use the Pythagorean Theorem in many types of situations.

M2 g Geometry and Measurement Concepts: Work with similar triangles, and extend the ideas to include simple uses of the three basic trigonometric functions.

M3 a Function and Algebra Concepts: Model given situations with formulas and functions.

M5 a Problem Solving and Mathematical Reasoning: Formulation.

M5 b Problem Solving and Mathematical Reasoning: Implementation.

M6 c Mathematical Skills and Tools: Evaluate and analyze formulas and functions of many kinds.

M6 e Mathematical Skills and Tools: Make and use rough sketches or schematic diagrams to enhance a solution.

M7 h Mathematical Communication: Write succinct accounts of the mathematical results obtained in a mathematical problem or extended project.

I have a cow. Her name is Daisy, and she enjoys eating the wildflowers that grow in abundance around my 20' × 40' barn. In order to maximize this pleasurable experience for her, I decided to tie her to a 50' rope and attach the other end to a corner of my barn. Unfortunately, the most delectable flowers are located 60' from the corner of the barn, and seeing as I did not have a longer piece of rope, I securely planted a post 10' from the corner of the barn and at an angle of 135° from each side of the barn. I attached Daisy to this post. To properly provide for Daisy's needs, I must calculate how many square feet she has to graze on, and thereby decide how much supplementary nutrition she will require.

For starters, I drew a diagram of the situation. From this diagram, I saw that at a certain angle, Daisy's rope would hit the 20' side of the barn and she could wrap around the corner of the barn and graze there (area D). The same was true for the 40' side of the barn (area E). When the rope was taunt against the corner of the 20' side of the barn, a triangle (△A) resulted. Likewise, when the rope was taunt against the 40' side of the barn, another triangle (△B) resulted. (The remaining area is area C.)

What makes the task specifically a problem solving task is that the details of just how this area is to be found are not at all clear at the start. It is not just a matter of plugging numbers into area formulas. Students must figure out on their own exactly what to do to arrive at a result. In this task, this is a process with many steps.

The task is quite useful for seeing whether students who have learned how to do some things in geometry (such as finding lengths, angles, and areas) can apply what they have learned in a new and non-routine situation.

Circumstances of performance

This sample of student work was produced under the following conditions:

alone	√ in a group
in class	√ as homework
√ with teacher feedback	with peer feedback
timed	√ opportunity for revision

Grazing Area

The student work is an excerpt from a long-term project that was completed over a four-week period. During this time, one class per week was allocated to completion of the project. The students worked in groups of three or four, and each student did a separate write-up. No teacher or adult help was provided until near the end, when there was an opportunity to revise the work. The project was included by the student in a portfolio of work in mathematics.

Mathematics required by the task

The task requires strong understanding of specific key ideas from geometry, listed below. Still, the conceptual understanding of geometry required is far greater than a list like this might suggest. Finding any of these lengths, angles, or areas in a one-step problem is far easier than creating and carrying out the complex hierarchy of steps needed to arrive at a solution here.

Finding lengths:

- knowing the lengths of two sides of a right triangle, use the Pythagorean Theorem to find the length of the third side;

- knowing the hypotenuse of an isosceles right triangle, find the side lengths;

Finding angles:

- knowing two angles of a triangle, find the third;

- knowing an angle, find the supplementary angle;

- knowing the angle of a sector of a circle, find the angle of the complementary sector;

- knowing the length of two sides of a right triangle, use the inverse of the tangent function to find the acute angles;

Finding areas:

- knowing the base and height of a triangle, find its area;

- knowing the angle and radius of a sector of a circle, find its area.

What the work shows

M2a Geometry and Measurement Concepts: The student models situations geometrically to formulate and solve problems.

A The response is built on a complex and effective geometric model of the problem situation. The model consists of a division of the region into five separate regions each of which consists of a triangle or a circle sector, and the introduction of techniques to find the area of each.

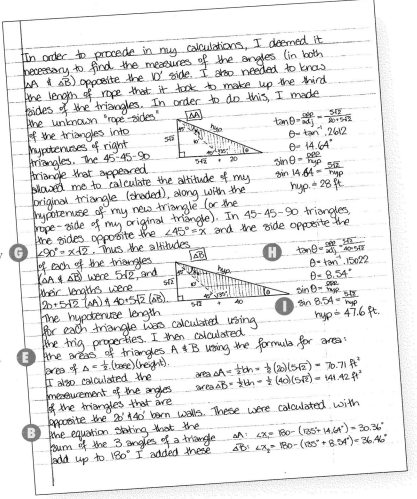

M2b Geometry and Measurement Concepts: The student works with two...dimensional figures and their properties, including polygons and circles....

Throughout the work, the student used knowledge of two dimensional figures and their properties. For example:

B knowing two angles of a triangle, the student found the third; and

C knowing the angle of a sector of a circle, the student found the angle of the complementary sector.

D The angle θ in triangle A is actually supplementary to the *sum* of 90° and the angle of arc D. (Similarly for triangle B and the angle of arc E.)

Number and Operation Concepts

M2 Geometry & Measurement Concepts

M3 Function & Algebra Concepts

Statistics & Probability Concepts

M5 Problem Solving & Mathematical Reasoning

M6 Mathematical Skills & Tools

M7 Mathematical Communication

Putting Mathematics to Work

Grazing Area

M2e Geometry and Measurement Concepts: The student knows [and] uses...formulas for...area...of many types of figures.

Throughout the work, the student used knowledge of area formulas. For example:

E knowing the base and height of a triangle, the student found its area; and

F knowing the angle and radius of a sector of a circle, the student found its area. This is a key part of the response, and the student managed it nicely. The result being used is that the area of a sector of a circle with angle θ (in degrees) and radius r is $\theta/360 \, \pi r^2$.

M2f Geometry and Measurement Concepts: The student uses the Pythagorean Theorem in many types of situations....

G Knowing the lengths of two sides of a right triangle (or knowing the length of the hypotenuse of an isosceles right triangle), the student used the Pythagorean Theorem to find the length of the third side. The response cites and uses a specific rule about 45°, 45°, 90° triangles: the hypotenuse of an isosceles right triangle is $\sqrt{2}$ times the leg. This rule can be derived using the Pythagorean Theorem.

M2g Geometry and Measurement Concepts: The student works with similar triangles, and extends the ideas to include simple uses of the three basic trigonometric functions.

H Knowing the length of two sides of a right triangle, the student used the inverse of the tangent function to find the acute angle. This is the one place in the solution where use of trigonometry is necessary. The student found an acute angle of a right triangle by using a calculator and the inverse tangent function to solve for θ in the defining formula for the tangent: $\tan \theta = {}^{opp}/_{adj.}$. This is possible since the opposite (opp.) and adjacent (adj.) sides are both known. (The calculation is shown in the response for both triangles A and B, though the step is not mentioned in the prose explanation.)

I Here the student used trigonometry again, this time to find the hypotenuse knowing the angle and the opposite side. This is fine. But the hypotenuse could have also been found without trigonometry by the Pythagorean Theorem, since both the opposite and the adjacent sides are known. (The hypotenuse lengths of triangles A and B are not used until later when triangles D and E are treated.)

The response uses the symbol ≐ (an equals sign with a dot over it) to mean "is approximately equal to" in cases where decimals are rounded off. Actually, this symbol should have been used in more of the cases here, since all the decimals have been rounded off.

C two angles together and subtracted their sum from 360° to get the measurement of the angle made by circle C. This angle was divided by 360° to find the fraction of a circle that C made up. I then multiplied this fraction by the area of the circle with radius 50' (area = πr²). Area C ended right before the rope wrapped around the barn on either side and created smaller arcs with shorter radii (areas D & E). For sections D & E, the rope left over (creating a new radius) was the 50' rope minus the hypotenuses of the two triangles A & B. I also found the angles θ that I had found earlier helpful in calculating the measures of the angles which were parts of the arcs of areas D & E. The angle θ (in both D & E) was supplementary to the 90° angle the barn made and the angle of arc D or E. Thus I calculated the percentages of a circle that each area (D or E) uses and multiplied this fraction by the area of a complete circle of that radius. To find the total grazing area, I simply added up all of my individual segments, triangles A & B, and circle-pieces C, D & E

$C's \angle = 360 - (x_1 + x_2)$
$= 360 - (30.36 + 36.46)$
$= 293.18°$

$\frac{293.18}{360} = \%$ of circle grazed
$= .8144$ or 81.44%

area of $C = \pi r^2 \times .8144 = \pi \cdot 50^2 \cdot .8144$
$= 6396.2 \, ft^2$

$\angle y_1 = 180 - (90° + 14.64°) = 75.36°$
$\%$ of circle $= \frac{75.36}{360} = 20.93\%$
$r = 50 - hyp = 50 - 28 = 22'$
area of $D = \pi r^2 \cdot .2093 = \pi \cdot 22^2 \cdot .2093$
$= 318.3 \, ft^2$

$\angle y_2 = 180 - (90° + 8.54°) = 81.46°$
$\%$ of circle $= \frac{81.46}{360} = 22.63\%$
$r = 50 - hyp = 50 - 47.6 = 2.4 \, ft$
area of $E = \pi r^2 \cdot .2263 = \pi \cdot 2.4^2 \cdot .2263$
$= 4.09 \, ft^2$

$A = 70.71$
$B = 141.42$
$C = 6396.20$
$D = 318.30$
$+ E = 4.09$

TOTAL AREA ≐ $6930.72 \, ft^2$

Grazing Area

M3 a Function and Algebra Concepts: The student models given situations with formulas and functions….

M5 a Problem Solving and Mathematical Reasoning: Formulation. The student…asks and answers a series of appropriate questions in pursuit of a solution and does so with minimal "scaffolding" in the form of detailed guiding questions.

M5 b Problem Solving and Mathematical Reasoning: Implementation. The student…

• chooses and employs effective problem solving strategies in dealing with non-routine and multi-step problems;

• selects appropriate mathematical concepts and techniques from different areas of mathematics and applies them to the solution of the problems;

• …uses mathematics to model real-world situations….

A The student organized the task by clearly identifying five regions (labeled A to E) whose area needed to be found. From this point on, the response represents a continual process of setting up a relationship and using it to find an unknown, then setting up a new relationship using what was just found to find another unknown, and so on for many steps.

J The student indicated that the experience of working on this extended task was a rich and rewarding one and echoed the language of the standard.

M6 c Mathematical Skills and Tools: The student evaluates and analyzes formulas and functions of many kinds….

M6 e Mathematical Skills and Tools: The student makes and uses rough sketches, schematic diagrams…to enhance a solution.

In working toward a final answer, the response makes continual use of formulas in conjunction with accompanying explanatory diagrams.

M7 h Mathematical Communication: The student writes succinct accounts of the mathematical results obtained in a mathematical problem or extended project, with diagrams,…tables, and formulas integrated into the text.

The response integrates a prose description of the solution process and of the mathematical results used with the presentation of formulas, equations, and diagrams. The result is a clear and easy-to-follow exposition of a complex problem.

The word "taunt" should be "taut"; but this does not detract from successful communication.

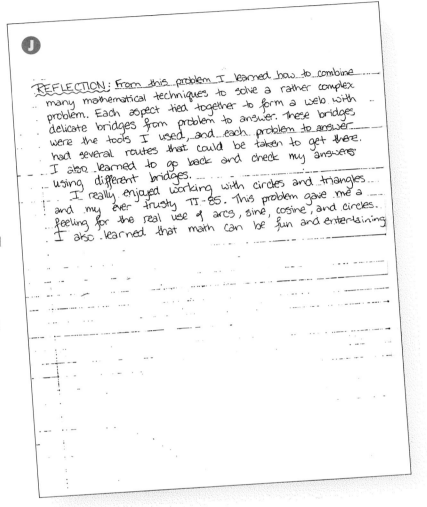

J REFLECTION: From this problem I learned how to combine many mathematical techniques to solve a rather complex problem. Each aspect tied together to form a web with delicate bridges from problem to answer. These bridges were the tools I used, and each problem to answer had several routes that could be taken to get there. I also learned to go back and check my answers using different bridges.
I really enjoyed working with circles and triangles and my ever trusty TI-85. This problem gave me a feeling for the real use of arcs, sine, cosine, and circles. I also learned that math can be fun and entertaining.

Number and Operation Concepts

M2 Geometry & Measurement Concepts

M3 Function & Algebra Concepts

Statistics & Probability Concepts

M5 Problem Solving & Mathematical Reasoning

M6 Mathematical Skills & Tools

M7 Mathematical Communication

Putting Mathematics to Work

Work Sample & Commentary: *Dicing Cheese*

Number
and Operation
Concepts

Geometry &
Measurement ◄ **M2**
Concepts

Function &
Algebra ◄ **M3**
Concepts

Statistics &
Probability
Concepts

Problem
Solving &
Mathematical ◄ **M5**
Reasoning

Mathematical ◄ **M6**
Skills & Tools

Mathematical ◄ **M7**
Communication

Putting
Mathematics
to Work

The quotations from the Mathematics performance descriptions in this commentary are excerpted. The complete performance descriptions are shown on pages 50-57.

The task

Dicing Cheese

You have a large rectangular block of cheese. You know its volume, V in cubic centimeters. Using a special cheese dicing machine, you cut the whole block up into small cubes, all exactly the same size.

When you spread these small cubes out one layer thick, with no spaces in between, they completely fill a flat, rectangular tray. You know the area, A of the tray in square centimeters.

1. In terms of V and A, find the length of the side of one of these small cubes.

2. In terms of V and A, find how many cubes were made.

This task about area and volume may appear to be rather simple. It involves only basic, rectangular shapes, and the only formulas needed are the most elementary ones (formulas for the volume of a cube

This work sample illustrates a standard-setting performance for the following parts of the standards:

M2 a Geometry and Measurement Concepts: Model situations geometrically to formulate and solve problems.

M2 b Geometry and Measurement Concepts: Work with three dimensional figures and their properties.

M2 e Geometry and Measurement Concepts: Know and use formulas for area, surface area, and volume.

M2 k Geometry and Measurement Concepts: Work with geometric measures of length, area, and volume.

M3 a Function and Algebra Concepts: Model given situations with formulas.

M3 h Function and Algebra Concepts: Define, use, and manipulate expressions involving variables.

M5 a Problem Solving and Mathematical Reasoning: Formulation.

M5 b Problem Solving and Mathematical Reasoning: Implementation.

M5 c Problem Solving and Mathematical Reasoning: Conclusion.

M6 a Mathematical Skills and Tools: Carry out symbol manipulations effectively.

M7 c Mathematical Communication: Organize work and present mathematical procedures and results clearly, systematically, succinctly, and correctly.

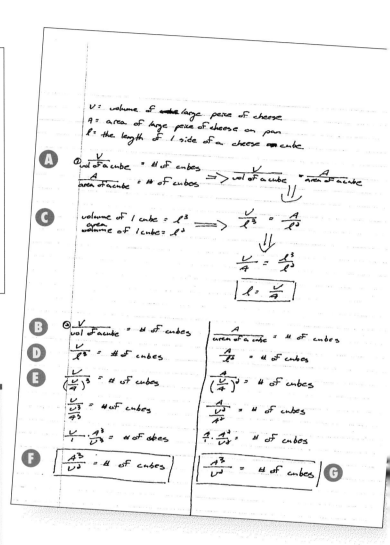

and the area of a face of a cube). Yet the task deeply probes students' conceptual understanding of area and volume. Anyone who has merely memorized formulas will make little headway here.

Circumstances of performance

This sample of student work was produced under the following conditions:

√ alone   in a group

√ in class   as homework

  with teacher feedback   with peer feedback

√ timed   opportunity for
                            revision

Mathematics required by the task

The task asks the student to express the number n of cubes and their side length l in terms of the total volume V and the total area A they cover. One way to proceed is to write down these observations about the volume V and the area A:

1. Since the volume of one small cube is l^3, the total volume is $V = nl^3$.

Dicing Cheese

2. Since the area of a face of one cube is l^2, the total area they cover is $A = nl^2$.

Eliminating n from these two equations allows us to express l in terms of V and A, while eliminating l allows us to express n in terms of V and A.

It is interesting that there are many approaches quite different from this one that students use to solve this problem. For example, looking at the cubes spread out on the tray as a rectangular solid, its volume can be written as $V = l$ A. This gives the length l immediately in terms of V and A as $l = \frac{V}{A}$. Another method uses "dimensional analysis" to argue that $l = \frac{V}{A}$ (perhaps with a dimensionless constant) is the only possible formula for l in terms of V and A that has the right units (the right "dimensions"). "Dimensional analysis" is a technique that keeps track of the "dimensions" of quantities. For example, volume has the dimensions L^3 (where L stands for length), area has the dimensions L^2, and speed has the dimensions $\frac{L}{T}$ (where T stands for time). These dimensions can be operated on algebraically. Hence, a volume divided by an area has the dimensions $\frac{L^3}{L^2} = L = $ length.

One feature of the task that needs comment is the fact that specific numbers are not given for V and A. The task is designed to assess students' abilities to deal with the abstractness of this "numberless" formulation. Assigning specific numbers would make the task somewhat easier. For example, in another version of the task that was used with other students, the specific values A = 9,000 square centimeters and V = 5,400 cubic centimeters were given. This made it easier for the students to create a concrete picture of the situation, and hence easier to get started.

What the work shows

M2a Geometry and Measurement Concepts: The student models situations geometrically to formulate and solve problems.

A **B** To start off both questions, the student used these facts about the whole mass of cheese:

- The number of small cubes is equal to the total volume V divided by the volume of one cube.

- The number of small cubes is equal to the total area A covered divided by the face area of one cube.

M2b Geometry and Measurement Concepts: The student works with...three dimensional figures and their properties, including...cubes....

M2k Geometry and Measurement Concepts: The student works with geometric measures of length, area, volume....

This is evident throughout the student work.

M2e Geometry and Measurement Concepts: The student knows [and] uses...formulas for...area, surface area, and volume of many types of figures.

C **D** To continue, the student used the area and volume formulas for a cube of side length l:
volume = l^3 area of a face = l^2

M3a Function and Algebra Concepts: The student models given situations with formulas....

M3h Function and Algebra Concepts: The student defines [and] uses...variables...in work with formulas....

Throughout, the response uses relevant formulas for area and volume and their interrelation in the derivation of formulas for the side length l and the number of cubes n.

M3h Function and Algebra Concepts: The student defines, uses, and manipulates expressions involving variables...in work with formulas...[and] equations....

E The student substituted the result obtained for Question 1, namely $l = \frac{V}{A}$ into the equations of Question 2.

F **G** The second result is obtained by manipulation and substitution:
# of cubes = $\frac{A^3}{V^2}$

M5a Problem Solving and Mathematical Reasoning: Formulation. The student...asks and answers a series of appropriate questions in pursuit of a solution and does so with minimal "scaffolding" in the form of detailed guiding questions.

M5b Problem Solving and Mathematical Reasoning: Implementation. The student...selects appropriate mathematical concepts and techniques from different areas of mathematics and applies them to the solution of the problem....

M5c Problem Solving and Mathematical Reasoning: Conclusion. The student...concludes a solution process with a useful summary of results....

The response shows the formulation and implementation of an approach to a difficult and non-routine problem, and clearly indicates the results of this approach.

F **G** There are two independent derivations of the second result, one starting with the area A and the other starting with the volume V.

M6a Mathematical Skills and Tools: The student carries out...symbol manipulations effectively....
E

M7c Mathematical Communication: The student organizes work and presents mathematical procedures and results clearly, systematically, succinctly, and correctly.

Although the response is brief, it is easy to follow and to the point.

Number and Operation Concepts

M2 Geometry & Measurement Concepts

M3 Function & Algebra Concepts

Statistics & Probability Concepts

M5 Problem Solving & Mathematical Reasoning

M6 Mathematical Skills & Tools

M7 Mathematical Communication

Putting Mathematics to Work

Work Sample & Commentary: *Galileo's Theater*

The quotations from the Mathematics performance descriptions in this commentary are excerpted. The complete performance descriptions are shown on pages 50-57.

The task

This is a design task. Students are asked to create a design for a theater that conforms to several specified constraints. Interpreting and implementing these specifications requires significant knowledge of concepts and terminology from geometry and algebra.

The task asks for a theater design "with the greatest seating capacity" given the specified constraints. This will be interpreted as requiring a demonstration, in the work, that the choices being made in making the design do in fact contribute to increased seating capacity. It is felt to be too difficult, in this complex situation, to require an actual proof that the design produced has the greatest possible capacity.

This work sample illustrates a standard-setting performance for the following parts of the standards:

M2 a **Geometry and Measurement Concepts: Model situations geometrically to formulate and solve problems.**

M2 b **Geometry and Measurement Concepts: Work with two dimensional figures and their properties.**

M2 e **Geometry and Measurement Concepts: Know, use, and derive formulas for circumference.**

M3 a **Function and Algebra Concepts: Model given situations with formulas.**

M3 i **Function and Algebra Concepts: Represent functional relationships in formulas and tables.**

M5 b **Problem Solving and Mathematical Reasoning: Implementation.**

M5 c **Problem Solving and Mathematical Reasoning: Conclusion.**

M6 b **Mathematical Skills and Tools: Round numbers used in applications to an appropriate degree of accuracy.**

M6 e **Mathematical Skills and Tools: Make and use rough sketches or precise scale diagrams to enhance a solution.**

M7 a **Mathematical Communication: Be familiar with basic mathematical terminology.**

M7 h **Mathematical Communication: Write succinct accounts of the mathematical results obtained in a mathematical problem or extended project.**

Designing a Theater for Galileo

You and your architectural engineering team are competing for the contract to design a new circular theater with a revolving center stage. The theater is to be built beneath the great dome R-3 at the lunar space port Galileo. The Arts Director of Galileo has asked each potential engineering team to submit its design and its calculations for the new theater. Although overall design is important, the job will go to the team that produces the design with the greatest seating capacity. The director has given you the following restrictions and guidelines.

1. The theater must contain only one level and seat at least 1000 people.
2. The stage should be at least 10 meters in diameter.
3. The outer diameter of the theater interior should be at most 42 meters.
4. The seating should be divided into sections by equally spaced aisles radiating from center stage. There should be no fewer than four radial aisles and no more than eight radial aisles. Each radial aisle should be at least 1 meter in width.
5. There should be two concentric aisles. The innermost concentric aisle around the stage should be at least 1 meter wide and at most 2 meters wide. The outer concentric aisle should be at least 2 meters wide and at most 4 meters wide and should ring the perimeter of the theater.

6. Safety codes at the lunar colony require that each seat be at least 60 centimeters wide and that each seating position be at least 90 centimeters in depth.
7. Safety codes require that there be no more than 30 seats in any row.

Your job is to draw a scaled plan of the theater, including seating, aisles, and the stage. Your plan should maximize seating capacity. You will need to calculate the following with calculations that verify your seating capacity.

1. The number of rows and the number of seats in each row
2. The width at the stage end of each radial aisle and the width at the back end of each radial aisle; the width of the concentric aisles
3. Total seating capacity for your plan

There is a hint leading to a possible solution for this problem in the Hints section.

The assignment text in the work sample titled "Designing a Theater for Galileo," from *Discovering Geometry*. Used by permission of Key Curriculum Press, P.O. Box 2304 Berkeley, CA 94702, 1-800-995-MATH.

Circumstances of performance

This sample of student work was produced under the following conditions:

alone	√ in a group
√ in class	√ as homework
√ with teacher feedback	with peer feedback
timed	√ opportunity for revision

The students had a week to complete the task, and then a week to revise based on teacher feedback. They worked in groups, but then each student submitted a separate response.

Number and Operation Concepts

Geometry & Measurement Concepts **M2**

Function & Algebra Concepts **M3**

Statistics & Probability Concepts

Problem Solving & Mathematical Reasoning **M5**

Mathematical Skills & Tools **M6**

Mathematical Communication **M7**

Putting Mathematics to Work

Galileo's Theater

Mathematics required by the task

The task requires students to do careful work, all based on the complex specifications given for the theater, that involves the geometry of circles and the division of line segments into parts:

- Lay out concentric circular rings that will serve as rows of seats and find the maximum number of rows possible, subject to a given minimum depth of a row of 90 centimeters.

- Divide the concentric rings into sections separated by radial aisles and calculate the resulting length of the seating section in each row, subject to a given minimum aisle width of 1 meter.

- Calculate the number of seating positions possible in each section, subject to a given minimum seat width of 60 centimeters and a given maximum number of seats per section of 30.

- Among possible ways of laying out such a theater, make choices that increase seating capacity.

The core mathematical concepts needed to do this work are few and simple. They are principally:

- Find the circumference C of a circle from its radius r or its diameter d:

   ($C= 2\pi r = \pi d$).

- Find the number N of seats of width 60 centimeters in a section of length L meters: (N = the greatest whole number less than or equal to $L/0.6$).

Taken in isolation these concepts are straightforward. However, in this task students need to use them repeatedly and appropriately in a complex setting. This need provides much more of a challenge than the mathematical concepts themselves. As a result, the task requires quite a bit of "problem solving" ability such as understanding the situation, constructing and testing mathematical models of the situation, and finding the optimal model (since "the job will go to the team that demonstrates the design with the greatest seating capacity").

What the work shows

M2a Geometry and Measurement Concepts: The student models situations geometrically to formulate and solve problems.

M2b Geometry and Measurement Concepts: The student works with two...dimensional figures and their properties, including...circles....

M2e Geometry and Measurement Concepts: The student knows, uses, and derives formulas for... circumference....

The whole project is a complex geometric model based on circles that was created in response to a request for a design meeting detailed, specified constraints.

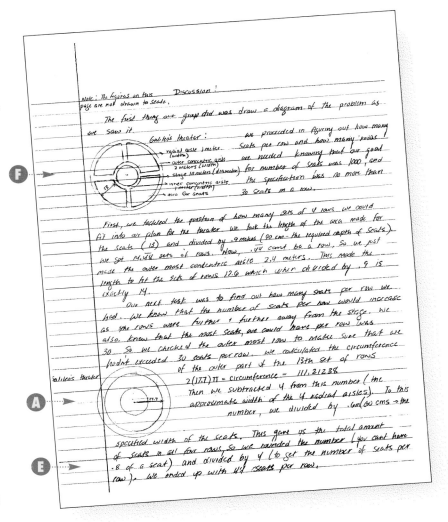

A Note that the radius of 17.7m used here results from work shown earlier on the page: 5 (stage) + 1 (aisle) + 12.6 (set of 14 rows) - 0.9 (last row) = 17.7 meters.

The use made here of the 17.7m dimension in calculating the circumference is a step repeated several times throughout the work.

M3a Function and Algebra Concepts: The student models given situations with formulas....

M3i Function and Algebra Concepts: The student represents functional relationships in formulas [and] tables...and translates between these.

B The formula produced by the student is the heart of the response. This formula provides an effective mechanism for counting the number of seats in each row in terms of the radius of the row. The student used the formula to construct the table on the next page showing the seating capacity for a section in each of the 14 rows of the theater. The formula produced by the student had to be applied many times for the aisles of different radii. The student apparently carried out these computations by hand. This is fine, but it would also have been an ideal place to let technology do some of the work by using a spreadsheet. The advantage would be that the effect of changes in the input (here the radii) could have been quickly determined.

Galileo's Theater

M5b Problem Solving and Mathematical Reasoning: Implementation. The student...

- chooses and employs effective problem solving strategies in dealing with non-routine and multi-step problems;

- selects appropriate mathematical concepts and techniques from different areas of mathematics and applies them to the solution of the problem;

- ...uses mathematics to model real world situations....

Throughout the work, the student responded to a non-routine task in a way that shows careful planning, use of many kinds of given information from a real situation, selection of appropriate mathematics from **M2** and **M3**, and employment of results from one step as input to the next step.

The student also made many choices dictated by the goal that the theater should have "the greatest seating capacity" consistent with the given space. For example, the response uses the smallest allowed dimension (90 cm) for the depth of a row, thus yielding the maximum number of rows.

C Still, the response does not take the next step in attempting to create the greatest seating capacity, namely pursuing alternate ways of meeting the constraints of the design and comparing them for the resulting seating capacity. This portion of the work shows the steps taken to meet the constraint on the maximum number of seats (30) allowed per row. The student found that a 4-aisle design would give 44 seats in the last row of each section, that a 5-aisle design would give 35, and that a 6-aisle design would give 29. The choice of a 6-aisle design thus seems natural. Still, it seems necessary to note that other possibilities were not explored in the response. For example, if 5 radial aisles are used, and are made wider toward the rear of the theater to limit the number of seats per row in a section to 30, then a total capacity of 1,585 can be reached. And with a 6-aisle design, if the seats are pushed rearward as far as possible (by making the outside concentric aisle width its minimum of 2 m) there are 1,614 seats possible, which is 60 more than the response's 1,554 seats in a design using a rear aisle width of 2.4 m. In this sense the student did not do full justice to the goal of obtaining the greatest seating capacity. Nevertheless, the maximum seating requirement here is a very difficult one to meet and justify, and the fact that this student did not fully accomplish this does not detract from the fact that the response illustrates the indicated portions of **M5**.

Number and Operation Concepts

Geometry & Measurement Concepts **M2**

Function & Algebra Concepts **M3**

Statistics & Probability Concepts

Problem Solving & Mathematical Reasoning **M5**

Mathematical Skills & Tools **M6**

Mathematical Communication **M7**

Putting Mathematics to Work

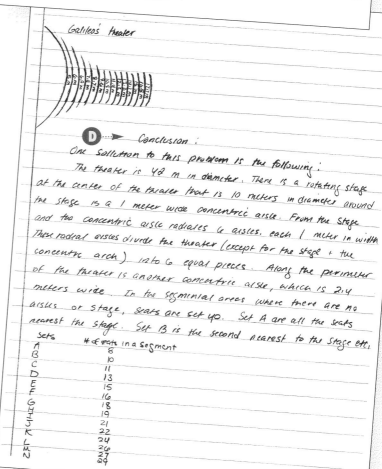

C 44 was too many seats (the total could not exceed 30). We decided to change the number of radial aisles. So we went through the same procedure as we had done with 4 radial aisle only with 5 instead. Still, there were too many (35). With 6 radial aisles, though, there were only 29 seats.

Galileo's theater

The next thing we accomplished was writing down, and arriving at the exact number of seats per row. We did this by taking the radius of the particular circle we were looking at, finding the circumference, subtracting 6 (number of radial aisles), dividing by .6 (m), then dividing by 6.

B $$\frac{\left(\frac{2\pi r - 6}{.6}\right)}{6} = P \; (\# \; \text{seats in 1 row})$$

By multiplying each P by 6 (there are 6 of these segments with P number of seats) and taking the sum of everything, we found the total seating capacity of our theater (1554 seats).

Galileo's theater

D Conclusion:

One solution to this problem is the following:

The theater is 42 m in diameter. There is a rotating stage at the center of the theater that is 10 meters in diameter. Around the stage is a 1 meter wide concentric aisle. From the stage and the concentric aisle radiates 6 aisles, each 1 meter in width. These radial aisles divide the theater (except for the stage + the concentric arch) into 6 equal pieces. Along the perimeter of the theater is another concentric aisle, which is 2.4 meters wide. In the segmental areas where there are no aisles or stage, seats are set up. Set A are all the seats nearest the stage. Set B is the second nearest to the stage etc.

sets	# of seats in a segment
A	8
B	10
C	11
D	13
E	15
F	16
G	18
H	19
I	21
J	22
K	24
L	26
M	27
N	29

Galileo's Theater

M5c Problem Solving and Mathematical Reasoning: Conclusion. The student...concludes a solution process with a useful summary of results....

D The conclusion summarizes the results obtained.

M6b Mathematical Skills and Tools: The student rounds numbers used in applications to an appropriate degree of accuracy.

E This remark "you can't have .8 of a seat" should actually say "you can't have .7 of a seat" since it refers to the fractional part of the number ≈ 178.7 seats obtained in the calculation mentioned previously. Still, the rounding down to an integer value is correct.

M6e Mathematical Skills and Tools: The student makes and uses rough sketches...or precise scale diagrams to enhance a solution.

F G H

M7a Mathematical Communication: The student is familiar with basic mathematical terminology....

A Here and throughout the work, the student used terminology such as "radial aisles" in an appropriate and consistent way.

M7h Mathematical Communication: The student writes succinct accounts of the mathematical results obtained in a mathematical problem or extended project, with diagrams,...tables, and formulas integrated into the text.

The student produced a clear explanation of the thinking that went into the design, together with diagrams showing features of the design and a formula for the crucial calculation of the number of seats in a row. Particularly good examples of communication include:

D E The student explained in words where the result of "44 seats per row" came from. The explanation amounts first to the calculation $\frac{2\pi(17.7)\,-4}{(0.6)} \approx 178.7$, rounded down to 178 seats in the last row, then the calculation $\frac{178}{4} = 44.5$, rounded down to 44 seats per section. A little thought shows that this is equivalent to the one step calculation $\frac{2\pi(17.7)-4}{(0.6)\,(4)} \approx 44.7$, rounded down to 44 seats. This calculation is crucial to the whole problem. The response gives an explicit formula for this calculation for the 6-aisle case.

D The conclusion summarizes the results obtained. The word "sollution" in the final paragraph should be "solution."

H

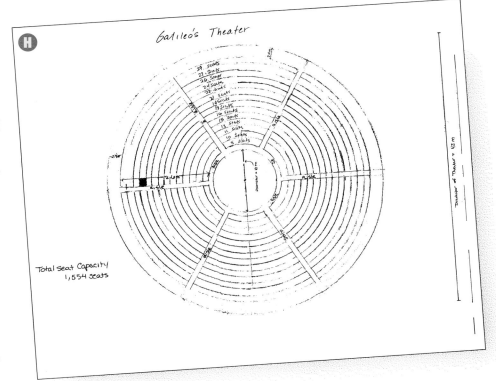

Galileo's Theater

Total seat Capacity
1,554 seats

Number and Operation Concepts

M2 Geometry & Measurement Concepts

M3 Function & Algebra Concepts

Statistics & Probability Concepts

M5 Problem Solving & Mathematical Reasoning

M6 Mathematical Skills & Tools

M7 Mathematical Communication

Putting Mathematics to Work

Introduction to the performance standards for

Science

There are two widely used and respected national documents in science which we have taken into account: the National Research Council (NRC) *National Science Education Standards* (1996) and the American Association for the Advancement of Science (AAAS) Project 2061 *Benchmarks for Science Literacy* (1993). We found the AAAS analysis of the Benchmarks and the NRC Draft to be helpful in seeing the substantial degree of agreement between the two documents. We also consulted New Standards partner statements about standards and international documents, including the work of the Third International Mathematics and Science Study and the Organisation for Economic Co-operation and Development. Many of these sources, like the *Benchmarks*, give greater emphasis to technology and the applications of science than does the NRC.

The framework for the Science performance standards reflects New Standards partner representatives' distillation of these several sources of guidance:

S1 **Physical Sciences Concepts;**

S2 **Life Sciences Concepts;**

S3 **Earth and Space Sciences Concepts;**

S4 **Scientific Connections and Applications;**

S5 **Scientific Thinking;**

S6 **Scientific Tools and Technologies;**

S7 **Scientific Communication;**

S8 **Scientific Investigation.**

As the amount of scientific knowledge explodes, the need for students to have deep understanding of fundamental concepts and ideas upon which to build increases; as technology makes information readily available, the need to memorize vocabulary and formulas decreases. There is general agreement among the science education community, in principle, that studying fewer things more deeply is the direction we would like to go. The choices about what to leave out and what to keep are hotly debated. There are 855 benchmarks and the content standards section of the NRC standards runs nearly 200 pages, so there are still choices to be made in crafting a reasonable set of performance standards.

When the goal is deep understanding, it is necessary to revisit concepts over time. Students show progressively deeper understanding as they use the concept in a range of familiar situations to explain observations and make predictions, then in unfamiliar situations; as they represent the concept in multiple ways (through words, diagrams, graphs, or charts), and explain the concept to another person. The conceptual understanding standards make explicit that students should be able to demonstrate understanding of a scientific concept "by using a concept accurately to explain observations and make predictions and by representing the concept in multiple ways (through words, diagrams, graphs, or charts, as appropriate)." Both aspects of understanding—explaining and representing—are required to meet these standards.

For most people and most concepts, there is a progression from phenomenological to empirical to theoretical, or from a qualitative to a quantitative understanding. We have chosen one important concept, density, to illustrate the progression. To do this we use "Flinkers" at the elementary school level (see Volume 1, page 136), "Discovering Density" at the middle school level (see Volume 2, page 101), and "The Density of Sand" at the high school level (see page 86). The expectation for any particular concept at any particular level can only be described with a satisfactory degree of precision and accuracy in the degree of detail adopted by AAAS and NRC; we strongly urge users of these performance standards to consult either or both of those documents for guidance on other concepts.

Complementing the conceptual understanding standards, S5-S8 focus on areas of the science curriculum that need particular attention and a new or renewed emphasis:

S5 **Scientific Thinking;**

S6 **Scientific Tools and Technologies;**

S7 **Scientific Communication;**

S8 **Scientific Investigation.**

Establishing separate standards for these areas is a mechanism for highlighting the importance of these areas, but does not imply that they are independent of conceptual understanding. The NRC standards, by declaring that inquiry is not only a teaching method but also an object of study, should put the time-worn "content versus process" debate to rest, and focus effort on combining traditionally defined content with process. As the work samples that follow illustrate, good work usually provides evidence of both.

Resources

Reviewers of drafts of these performance standards have pointed out that our expectations are more demanding, both in terms of student time and access to resources, than they consider reasonable for all students. We acknowledge the distance between our goals and the status quo, and the fact that there is a tremendous disparity in opportunities between the most and least advantaged students. We think that there are at least two strategies that must be pursued to achieve our goals—making better use of existing, out-of-school resources and making explicit the connection between particular resources and particular standards.

Best practice in science has always included extensive inquiry and investigation, but it is frequently given less emphasis in the face of competing demands for student time and teacher resources. An elementary teacher faced with the unfamiliar territory of project work in science or a secondary teacher faced with the prospect of guiding 180 projects and investigations can legitimately throw up his or her hands and cry, "Help!" Youth and community-based organizations, such as the Boy Scouts of America, Girl Scouts of the U.S.A., and 4-H, have science education on their agenda. Thus, we have incorporated examples of projects and investigations that are done outside of school to make clear that help is available.

We acknowledge that some of the performance descriptions and examples presuppose resources that are not currently available to all students, even those who take advantage of the out-of-school opportunities available to them. Yet, New Standards partners have adopted a Social Compact, which says, in part, "Specifically, we pledge to do everything in our power to ensure all students a fair shot at reaching the new performance standards...This means that they will be taught a curriculum that will prepare them for the assessments, that their teachers will have the preparation to enable them to teach it well, and there will be an equitable distribution of the resources the students and their teachers need to succeed."

All of the district, state, and national documents in science make explicit the need for students to have hands-on experience and to use information tools. Thus, for example, **S6**, Scientific Tools and Technologies, makes explicit reference to using telecommunications to acquire and share information. A recent National Center for Education Statistics survey recently reported that only 50% of schools and fewer than 9% of instructional rooms currently have access to the Internet. We know that this is an equity issue—that far more than 9% of the homes in the United States have access to the Internet and that schools must make sure that students' access to information and ideas does not depend on what they get at home—so we have crafted performance standards that would use the Internet so that people will make sure that all students have access to it. Since the New Standards partners have made a commitment to create the learning environments where students can develop the knowledge and skills that are delineated here, we hope that making these requirements explicit will help those who allocate resources to understand the consequences of their actions in terms of student performance.

Performance Descriptions *Science*

To see how these performance descriptions compare with the expectations for elementary school and middle school, turn to pages 160-167.

The Science standards are founded upon both the National Research Council's *National Science Education Standards* and the American Association for the Advancement of Science's Project 2061 *Benchmarks for Science Literacy*. These documents, each of which runs to several hundred pages, contain detail that amplifies the meaning of the terms used in the performance descriptions.

S1 Physical Sciences Concepts

The student demonstrates conceptual understanding by using a concept accurately to explain observations and make predictions and by representing the concept in multiple ways (through words, diagrams, graphs or charts, as appropriate). Both aspects of understanding—explaining and representing—are required to meet this standard.

The student produces evidence that demonstrates understanding of:

S1 a Structure of atoms, such as atomic composition, nuclear forces, and radioactivity.

S1 b Structure and properties of matter, such as elements and compounds; bonding and molecular interaction; and characteristics of phase changes.

S1 c Chemical reactions, such as everyday examples of chemical reactions; electrons, protons, and energy transfer; and factors that affect reaction rates such as catalysts.

S1 d Motions and forces, such as gravitational and electrical; net forces and magnetism.

S1 e Conservation of energy and increase in disorder, such as kinetic and potential energy; energy conduction, convection, and radiation; random motion; and effects of heat and pressure.

S1 f Interactions of energy and matter, such as waves, absorption and emission of light, and conductivity.

Examples of activities through which students might demonstrate conceptual understanding of physical sciences include:

- Debate the relative merits of harnessing nuclear fission and fusion as energy sources. **1a, 1b, 1c, E3b**
- Predict the age of a hypothetical fossil based on the rate of radioactive decay of several radioactive isotopes. **1a, 2c, 3a, 3b, 3c, 3d**
- Research the history of the periodic table; take and defend a position on the configuration that best illustrates properties of elements. **1a, 1b, 1c, 4e**
- Determine the characteristics for a dinner table candle that will keep the candle burning longer. **1c, 1e**
- Explain why a local urban area has smog and what can be done about it. **1a, 1b, 1c, 1e, 4d**
- Make an informational videotape describing how an understanding of acceleration and velocity can make one a better driver. **1d, 1e, 7d**
- Explain how electric motors and generators illustrate the relationship between electricity and magnetism. **1c, 1d, 1e, 4a, 4b**
- Explain to a younger student the difference between temperature and heat. **1e, 7d**
- Compare the efficiency and energy consumption of several different methods of generating electricity that could be used locally. **1e, 1f, 4b, 4d**
- Earn the Energy Merit Badge (Boy Scouts of America) and explain how it helped you to understand the interactions of matter and energy. **1f, 4b, 4d**
- Trace the transformations of energy from the electric current that enters a CD player or boombox to a sound that can be heard as music. **1f, 4b**

S2 Life Sciences Concepts

The student demonstrates conceptual understanding by using a concept accurately to explain observations and make predictions and by representing the concept in multiple ways (through words, diagrams, graphs or charts, as appropriate). Both aspects of understanding—explaining and representing—are required to meet this standard.

The student produces evidence that demonstrates understanding of:

S2 a The cell, such as cell structure and function relationships; regulation and biochemistry; and energy and photosynthesis.

S2 b Molecular basis of heredity, such as DNA, genes, chromosomes, and mutations.

S2 c Biological evolution, such as speciation, biodiversity, natural selection, and biological classification.

S2 d Interdependence of organisms, such as conservation of matter; cooperation and competition among organisms in ecosystems; and human effects on the environment.

S2 e Matter, energy, and organization in living systems, such as matter and energy flow through different levels of organization; and environmental constraints.

S2 f Behavior of organisms, such as nervous system regulation; behavioral responses; and connections with anthropology, sociology, and psychology.

Examples of activities through which students might demonstrate conceptual understanding of life sciences include:

- Create a picture book to explain how a producer converts solar energy to chemical energy through an ecosystem. **2a, 1c, 3a**
- Explain how cell functions are regulated to allow organisms to respond to the environment and to control and coordinate growth and differentiation. **2a, 2b, 2c, 2f, 1c**
- Predict how long a plant will live planted in a closed glass jar located by a window; and explain what additional information regarding the plant and the surrounding environment would be needed to improve the prediction. **2a, 1a, 3a, 3b**
- Create a working model to show how the instructions for specifying an organism's characteristics are carried in DNA and its subunits. **2b, 2c, 5c**
- Make a videotape debating the possible explanations for the extinction of dinosaurs. **2c, 2d, 7d**
- Make a storyboard and give a presentation to younger students explaining the increasing prevalence of dark forms of moths 150 years ago and the more recent return to light forms. **2b, 2c, 2d, 7d, E3c**
- Make a humorous travel brochure describing the pathway of a carbon dioxide molecule and an oxygen molecule through the living and non-living components of the biosphere. **2e, 1b**
- Earn the Ecology Merit Badge (Girl Scouts of the U.S.A.) or the Environmental Science Merit Badge (Boy Scouts of America) and explain how it helped you to understand the interdependence of organisms. **2d, 2e**
- Trace a candy bar from the time it is purchased to the time it is completely expended. **2e**
- Develop a recycling outreach program as part of a community service project to illustrate the limited availability of matter and energy in the ecosystem. **2c, 2d, 1c, 4b**
- Conduct an investigation to determine how different kinds of plants respond to various environmental stimuli. **2f**
- Research the development of, and recent advances in the theory of, evolutionary psychology. **2c, 2f, 4e**

S3 Earth and Space Sciences Concepts

The student demonstrates conceptual understanding by using a concept accurately to explain observations and make predictions and by representing the concept in multiple ways (through words, diagrams, graphs or charts, as appropriate). Both aspects of understanding—explaining and representing—are required to meet this standard.

The student produces evidence that demonstrates understanding of:

S3 a Energy in the Earth system, such as radioactive decay, gravity, the Sun's energy, convection, and changes in global climate.

S3 b Geochemical cycles, such as conservation of matter; chemical resources and movement of matter between chemical reservoirs.

S3 c Origin and evolution of the Earth system, such as geologic time and the age of life forms; origin of life; and evolution of the Solar System.

S3 d Origin and evolution of the universe, such as the "big bang" theory; formation of stars and elements; and nuclear reactions.

S3 e Natural resource management.

Examples of activities through which students might demonstrate conceptual understanding of Earth and space sciences include:

▲ Make a brochure providing an orientation to the climate of the local region to a newcomer; and explain the likely weather in that context. **3a**

▲ Explain the relationship between gravity and energy. **3a, 1d**

▲ Analyze the risk of natural disasters in the local region and make recommendations for actions that can be taken to mitigate the damage. **3a, 3b, 4b**

▲ Germinate seeds on a rotating platform and explain the observed growth pattern. **3a, 1d, 2e**

▲ Conduct a study of the geology of an area near the school; and describe the likely history of the region, using observations and reference materials. **3b, 3c**

▲ Diagram the birth, development, and death of a human; contrast with the geologic time frame of the origin and evolution of the Earth system or the universe. **3c, 3d, 2c**

▲ Work with other students to become an "expert panel" to describe the historical events leading to the development of the "big bang" theory. **3c, 3d, 5f**

▲ Write a research paper to explain how stars produce energy from nuclear reactions and how these processes led to the formation of other elements. **3d, 1a, 1b, 1c, 1f, E2a**

▲ Identify a place that is subject to periodic flooding, evaluate its positive and negative effects, and study different ways of maintaining, reducing, or eliminating the likelihood of flooding. **3e**

S4 Scientific Connections and Applications

The student demonstrates conceptual understanding by using the concept to explain observations and make predictions and by representing the concept in multiple ways (through words, diagrams, graphs or charts, as appropriate). Both aspects of understanding—explaining and representing—are required to meet this standard.

The student produces evidence that demonstrates understanding of:

S4 a Big ideas and unifying concepts, such as order and organization; models, form and function; change and constancy; and cause and effect.

S4 b The designed world, such as the reciprocal relationship between science and technology; the development of agricultural techniques; and the reasonableness of technological designs.

S4 c Health, such as nutrition and exercise; disease and epidemiology; personal and environmental safety; and resources, environmental stress, and population growth.

S4 d Impact of technology, such as constraints and trade-offs; feedback; benefits and risks; and problems and solutions.

S4 e Impact of science, such as historical and contemporary contributions; and interactions between science and society.

Examples of activities through which students might demonstrate conceptual understanding of scientific connections and applications include:

▲ Construct a computer-controlled robot arm that mimics the form and function of a human hand and forearm. **4a, 4b, 4c, 2a**

▲ Work with other students to give a presentation based on scientific principles arguing for a systemic solution to an environmental problem that concerns the school or community. **4a, 4b, 4c, 4d, 1a, 2d, 2e, A1b**

▲ Propose modifications to improve skateboards, in-line skates, bicycles, or similar objects to make them safer, faster, or less expensive. **4b, 4c, 1a, A1b**

▲ Conduct a study of the school cafeteria including: food storage and preparation, nutrition, and student preferences; and make recommendations for improvement. **4c, 4d**

▲ Debate the positive and negative consequences of a recently developed technological innovation. **4b, 4d, 4e, E3b**

▲ Earn the Food, Fibers, and Farming Merit Badge (Girl Scouts of the U.S.A.) and make a poster that shows understanding of agriculture or technology. **4b, 4c, 4d, 4e**

Samples of student work that illustrate standard-setting performances for these standards can be found on pages 86-105.

The examples that follow the performance descriptions for each standard are examples of the work students might do to demonstrate their achievement. The examples also indicate the nature and complexity of activities that are appropriate to expect of students at the high school level.

The cross-references that follow the examples highlight examples for which the same activity, and possibly even the same piece of work, may enable students to demonstrate their achievement in relation to more than one standard. In some cases, the cross-references highlight examples of activities through which students might demonstrate their achievement in relation to standards for more than one subject matter.

Performance Descriptions *Science*

To see how these performance descriptions compare with the expectations for elementary school and middle school, turn to pages 160-167.

The Science standards are founded upon both the National Research Council's *National Science Education Standards* and the American Association for the Advancement of Science's Project 2061 *Benchmarks for Science Literacy*. These documents, each of which runs to several hundred pages, contain detail that amplifies the meaning of the terms used in the performance descriptions.

S5 Scientific Thinking

The student demonstrates skill in scientific inquiry and problem solving by using thoughtful questioning and reasoning strategies, common sense and diverse conceptual understanding, and appropriate ideas and methods to investigate science; that is, the student:

S5 a Frames questions to distinguish cause and effect; and identifies or controls variables in experimental and non-experimental research settings.

S5 b Uses concepts from Science Standards 1 to 4 to explain a variety of observations and phenomena.

S5 c Uses evidence from reliable sources to develop descriptions, explanations, and models; and makes appropriate adjustments and improvements based on additional data or logical arguments.

S5 d Proposes, recognizes, analyzes, considers, and critiques alternative explanations; and distinguishes between fact and opinion.

S5 e Identifies problems; proposes and implements solutions; and evaluates the accuracy, design, and outcomes of investigations.

S5 f Works individually and in teams to collect and share information and ideas.

Examples of activities through which students might demonstrate skill in scientific thinking include:

▲ Evaluate the claims and potential benefits and risks of steroid use and apply the scientific evidence to a reported "case study" of an athlete. **5a, 5b, 5c, 5d**

▲ Predict how long a plant will live, planted in moist soil in a closed glass jar located by a window; explain what additional information would be needed to make a better prediction. **5a, 5b, 5c**

▲ Compare and contrast the nutritional value of several common brands of cereals. **5b, 5c, 5d**

▲ Compare and contrast lines of evidence for theories of dinosaur extinction. **5b, 5c, 5d, 2c, 2d**

▲ Explain the chain of inference in DNA testing and debate both positions regarding its inclusion as evidence in a capital trial. **5c, 5d, 1b, 1c, 2a, 2b, 4d**

S6 Scientific Tools and Technologies

The student demonstrates competence with the tools and technologies of science by using them to collect data, make observations, analyze results, and accomplish tasks effectively; that is, the student:

S6 a Uses technology and tools (such as traditional laboratory equipment, video, and computer aids) to observe and measure objects, organisms, and phenomena, directly, indirectly, and remotely, with appropriate consideration of accuracy and precision.

S6 b Records and stores data using a variety of formats, such as data bases, audiotapes, and videotapes.

S6 c Collects and analyzes data using concepts and techniques in Mathematics Standard 4, such as mean, median, and mode; outcome probability and reliability; and appropriate data displays.

S6 d Acquires information from multiple sources, such as print, the Internet, computer data bases, and experimentation.

S6 e Recognizes and limits sources of bias in data, such as observer and sample biases.

Examples of activities through which students might demonstrate competence in the tools and technologies of science include:

▲ Work with other students to repeat a historical series of experiments, such as those leading to the current understanding of photosynthesis, and write an essay comparing and contrasting the differences in available tools and technologies. **6d, 2a, 4d, 4e, 5c, 7b**

▲ Evaluate the accuracy and timeliness of information reported during the "life" of a hurricane or tropical storm. **6d, 3a, 4a, 5c**

▲ Use the Internet to get current information on a rapidly changing scientific topic. **6d**

▲ Use a computer interface to measure the velocity of objects. **6d, 1d, 5c**

▲ Use telecommunications to compare data on similar investigations with students in another state. **6d**

▲ Earn the Orienteering Merit Badge (Boy Scouts of America) and teach another student what to do if he or she gets lost. **6d, 3a, 5c, 7d**

S7 Scientific Communication

The student demonstrates effective scientific communication by clearly describing aspects of the natural world using accurate data, graphs, or other appropriate media to convey depth of conceptual understanding in science; that is, the student:

S7 a Represents data and results in multiple ways, such as numbers, tables, and graphs; drawings, diagrams, and artwork; technical and creative writing; and selects the most effective way to convey the scientific information.

S7 b Argues from evidence, such as data produced through his or her own experimentation or data produced by others.

S7 c Critiques published materials, such as popular magazines and academic journals.

S7 d Explains a scientific concept or procedure to other students.

S7 e Communicates in a form suited to the purpose and the audience, such as by writing instructions that others can follow; critiquing written and oral explanations; and using data to resolve disagreements.

Examples of activities through which students might demonstrate competence in scientific communication include:

▲ Analyze a ballot initiative on a local endangered species. **7a, 7b, 2c, 4d, 5a**

▲ Critique a *Time* article which reports on something you have studied. **7c**

▲ Make a "claymation" video illustrating in simple terms how a virus attacks the human body. **7c, 2d, 4c, 5c**

▲ Give an oral report describing the change over time in local air quality. **7d, 2d, 3e, 4d, E3c**

▲ Earn the Model Design and Building Merit Badge (Boy Scouts of America) and explain what constitutes an effective model. **7d, 4b, 5c**

▲ Write an advertisement for a cold relief product that explains how it works. **7e, 4c, 5c, 5d, 6d**

S8 Scientific Investigation

The student demonstrates scientific competence by completing projects drawn from the following kinds of investigation, including at least one full investigation each year and, over the course of high school, investigations that integrate several aspects of Science Standards 1 to 7 and represent all four of the kinds of investigation:

S8 a Controlled experiment.

S8 b Fieldwork.

S8 c Design.

S8 d Secondary research.

A single project may draw on more than one type of investigation. A full investigation includes:

• Questions that can be studied using the resources available.

• Procedures that are safe, humane, and ethical; and that respect privacy and property rights.

• Data that have been collected and recorded (see also Science Standard 6) in ways that others can verify, and analyzed using skills expected at this grade level (see also Mathematics Standard 4).

• Data and results that have been represented (see also Science Standard 7) in ways that fit the context.

• Recommendations, decisions, and conclusions based on evidence.

• Acknowledgment of references and contributions of others.

• Results that are communicated appropriately to audiences.

• Reflection and defense of conclusions and recommendations from other sources and peer review.

Examples of projects through which students might demonstrate competence in scientific investigation include:

▲ Investigate the effectiveness of common household cleaners on bacterial growth. **8a, 1c, 2a, 4c**

▲ Conduct research to determine if the incidence of asthma is related to weather. **8b, 3a, 4c**

▲ Conduct a study of the geology of an area near the school and describe the likely history of the region, using observations and reference materials. **8b, 8d, 3c, 6d**

▲ Compare and contrast the designs of different sports shoes and evaluate the designs considering the varying demands of different sports. **8c**

▲ Conduct an investigation to determine if the shape of a stereo speaker container affects sound quality. **8c, 1f**

▲ Study the distribution of a species in the region or state and discuss the likelihood of it becoming endangered. **8d, 2c, 5c, 6c**

Samples of student work that illustrate standard-setting performances for these standards can be found on pages 86-105.

The examples that follow the performance descriptions for each standard are examples of the work students might do to demonstrate their achievement. The examples also indicate the nature and complexity of activities that are appropriate to expect of students at the high school level.

The cross-references that follow the examples highlight examples for which the same activity, and possibly even the same piece of work, may enable students to demonstrate their achievement in relation to more than one standard. In some cases, the cross-references highlight examples of activities through which students might demonstrate their achievement in relation to standards for more than one subject matter.

Work Sample & Commentary: *Density of Sand*

The task

This work sample was an entry in a Golden State Examination Science Portfolio for the category "problem solving investigation." Students were required to submit a piece of work and the "Self-Reflection Sheet." In this case, the student designed and conducted an investigation to determine the density of sand.

Circumstances of performance

This sample of student work was produced under the following conditions:

alone	√ in a group
√ in class	as homework
√ with teacher feedback	√ with peer feedback
timed	√ opportunity for revision

The work was done with a partner and written up individually.

What the work shows

S1 b Physical Sciences Concepts: The student produces evidence that demonstrates understanding of the structure and properties of matter....

A **B** **C** Throughout the work, the student explained the relationship between mass, volume, and density, often with a level of detail revealing excellent conceptual understanding. There is also ample evidence that the student appreciated the relevance of density in everyday situations.

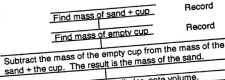

The Density of Sand

Purpose: To determine the density of a sample of sand with air around the sand granules and then the density of the sand alone.

Procedure:

J

Find mass of sand + cup		Record
Find mass of empty cup		Record
Subtract the mass of the empty cup from the mass of the sand + the cup. The result is the mass of the sand.		Record
Put sand in a graduated cylinder, note volume.		Record
Remove sand, put 20 mL water in graduated cylinder.		
Add sand to water, note volume of sand + water		Record
Subtract the volume of the water (20 mL) from the volume of the water + the sand. The result is the volume of the sand.		Record

Data:

Mass of sand + cup (g)	Mass of cup (g)	Mass of sand (g)
17.30	1.85	15.45

Volume of water + sand(mL)	Volume of water(mL)	Volume of sand (w/o air)mL
26.0	20.0	6.0

Volume of with air: 10.4 mL

Density with air: $\frac{M}{V}$ $\frac{15.45 \text{ g}}{10.4 \text{ mL}}$ = 1.49 g/mL

Density without air: $\frac{M}{V}$ $\frac{15.45 \text{ g}}{6.0 \text{ mL}}$ = 2.6 g/mL

S5 a Scientific Thinking: The student frames questions to distinguish cause and effect; and identifies or controls variables in experimental and non-experimental research settings.

D Here and throughout, the work displays evidence of appropriate scientific thinking and use of experimental data to reach conclusions.

S5 e Scientific Thinking: The student identifies problems; proposes and implements solutions; and evaluates the accuracy, design, and outcomes of investigations.

E **F** **G** The student continually evaluated and critiqued the appropriateness of the experimental design and the accuracy of the measuring process, and described the situations in which the techniques employed would be most effective.

Physical Sciences Concepts **S1**

Life Sciences Concepts

Earth and Space Sciences Concepts

Scientific Connections and Applications

Scientific Thinking **S5**

Scientific Tools and Technologies **S6**

Scientific Communication **S7**

Scientific Investigation

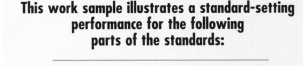

This work sample illustrates a standard-setting performance for the following parts of the standards:

S1 b Physical Sciences Concepts: Structure and properties of matter.

S5 a Scientific Thinking: Frame questions to distinguish cause and effect; and identify or control variables.

S5 e Scientific Thinking: Evaluate the accuracy, design, and outcomes of investigations.

S5 f Scientific Thinking: Work individually and in teams.

S6 a Scientific Tools and Technologies: Use technology and tools.

S7 e Scientific Communication: Write instructions that others can follow.

Density of Sand

Calculations and Analysis:

1. This lab was conducted using sand sample A. The mass of the sand was found by finding the mass of the sand in the cup, and then subtracting the mass of the cup. The mass of the sand was 15.45 g. The sand's volume with air, which was found by placing the sand in a graduated cylinder, was 10.4 mL. The sand's volume without air, which was found using the water displacement method, was 6.0 mL.

2. The density of the sand with air was found to be 1.49 g/mL, and the density of the sand alone was 2.6 g/mL. The sand with the air had a lower density than the sand alone. The equation for density is mass divided by volume. For both density calculations, the mass of the sand was the same. However, the volume of the sand with the air was larger than the volume of the sand alone. This is because the grains of sand were separated by air, which made the volume larger than it would be if air was not present. Since the volume of the sand with air was larger, it had a lower density.

3. Our answers were compared with those of four other groups.

    group #1:   density with air   1.4 g/ mL
                density without air   2.5 g/ mL

    group #2   density with air   0.65 g/ mL
                density without air   1.02 g/ mL

    group #3   density with air   3.0 g/ mL
                density without air   1.5 g/ mL

    group #4   density with air   1.49 g/mL
                density without air   2.73 g/mL

4. Three out of the four groups we compared results with had answers very similar to our own. One group, #2, had results that were very different. Since density is an intensive property, the difference in sample sizes among the other groups should not have affected the results. Other groups also may have made errors in their measurements or in their procedures. By double-checking each group's measurements and calculations, it would be possible to determine which group had the most accurate results.

5. The procedure utilized in this lab would work well for small, irregular solids such as sand. Many objects, however, would be far too large to place in a graduated cylinder and use the water displacement method. In their instance larger containers could be used. It also would also be much easier to determine the density of regular solids using calculations of length, width, and other dimensions in conjunction mathematical formulas. This method was extremely successful in this example.

S5 f Scientific Thinking: The student works individually and in teams to collect and share information.

E Comparison of results among groups provided partial confirmation of results.

H The student has acknowledged the benefits of collaboration.

S6 a Scientific Tools and Technologies: The student uses technology and tools (such as traditional laboratory equipment…) to…measure objects directly, indirectly…, and with appropriate consideration of accuracy and precision.

I The student used traditional methods and

F understood them.

E Comparison of results among groups was an effective method for judging accuracy.

S7 e Scientific Communication: The student communicates in a form suited to the purpose and the audience, such as by writing instructions that others can follow….

J

GSE SELF-REFLECTION SHEET

GSE Self-reflection Sheet: Problem-solving Investigation

1. *Thoroughly* explain the scientific concept you are investigating in this entry. Give specific examples that show how this concept relates to your Problem-solving Investigation.

    The purpose of this experiment was to determine the density of sand with air around it and the density of sand alone. The main concept in this lab is how the density of a substance is affected by its mass and volume, namely through the presence or the absence of air around the sand when determining the volume of the sample. This investigation introduces the idea that density is an intensive property, a concept that is reinforced by providing for different groups to use varied amounts of sand when performing these calculations. Density of a given substance remains constant regardless of the size of the sample used. ✓

2. Describe, *in detail*, the part or parts of this investigation YOU personally designed.

    This lab contained only a purpose, not a procedure. It was up to the students to design the entire method of determining the density of the sand both with and without air. I designed the plan to use the water displacement method for the volume of the sand without air, and to simply place the sand in a graduated cylinder in order to find it's volume with air. Please see the procedure section on page 1.

3. Describe how the scientific concept you investigated in this component is related to a real-world issue or personal experience (you may include issues that affect society or the environment).

    The difference in density of objects around us is an integral part of our world. It would be rather difficult to float in the bathtub if water's density were as low as that of air, and just as difficult if water had a density similar to that of a solid. In the same way, it is crucial to our way of thinking and living that density be an intensive property. If the density of a given substance varied with the size of the sample measured, the results could be catastrophic. Imagine buying a 4"x4"x4" block of wood with which to build your home, and finding it to be of a much different consistency and stability than a 50"x50"x50" block of the same type of wood! Everyday we rely on the properties of density for our most basic functions and activities. This experiment simply made us aware of them.

GSE Self-reflection Sheet: Problem-solving Investigation (cont'd)

4. Describe how working with others on this investigation helped to increase your understanding of science.

    Although a hypothesis was not necessary in this investigation, my group worked together to develop a procedure in order to fulfill the purpose of this experiment. My partner and I brainstormed for a great length of time, debating the most efficient set-up and procedures to achieve the most accurate results. This involved many ideas being rejected as inefficient or inaccurate. For example, our first instinct was to simply spill the sand out onto the triple beam balance when determining its mass. Careful thought and discussion, however, caused us to realize that this would result in lost sand and therefore inaccurate results. We then devised a more accurate plan of weighing the sand within the cup, and then removing the sand from the cup and weighing the cup alone. We then subtracted the mass of the empty cup from the mass of the cup and the sand, and indirectly determined the mass of the sand. The entire procedure for this investigation was the result of a collaborative effort between my partner and I.

5. What did you conclude from the investigation? Was the conclusion the same as or different from what you expected? Describe how your observations and data support your conclusions.

    From this investigation, we concluded that a sample of sand has a lower density when it is surrounded by air than when air is not present. My partner and I found sand surrounded by air to have a density of 1.49 g/mL, whereas sand that was not surrounded by air had a density of 2.6 g/mL. My partner and I found it interesting to discover that the presence or absence of air affects the density of a substance. This discovery was shown by the difference in our calculations of the density of the sand with air and without air. By comparing our results with those of other lab teams, we concluded that density is an intensive property. Although all of the teams used different amounts of sand in their calculations, their results were very similar, and in some cases identical to our own. This means that the density of a given substance does not change with the size of the sample measured.

H In chemistry, as in most areas in life, collaborative efforts achieve the most accurate results in the most efficient manner. Working with a partner or a with a group enables individuals to master concepts and ideas that would be difficult or impossible for them to understand on their own. While brainstorming ideas for the procedure, my partner and I were able to "bounce" ideas off of one another and receive feedback and new ideas in return. In the same manner, if one partner had overlooked a small detail that might impede the obtaining of accurate results, the second partner was quick to see that potential problem and propose a solution. Through exchanging ideas, critique, questions, and information, my partner and I were able to understand the concepts presented in this investigation.

S1 Physical Sciences Concepts

Life Sciences Concepts

Earth and Space Sciences Concepts

Scientific Connections and Applications

S5 Scientific Thinking

S6 Scientific Tools and Technologies

S7 Scientific Communication

Scientific Investigation

Work Sample & Commentary: *Photosynthesis*

The task

This work sample was an entry in a Golden State Examination Science Portfolio for the category "Problem-solving investigation." Students were required to submit a piece of work and the "Self-Reflection Sheet." In this case, the student designed and conducted an investigation of the factors that affect the rate of photosynthesis.

Circumstances of performance

This sample of student work was produced under the following conditions:

alone	√ in a group
√ in class	as homework
√ with teacher feedback	√ with peer feedback
timed	√ opportunity for revision

The work was done with a partner and written up individually. It followed a unit on biochemistry and photosynthesis.

What the work shows

S1 c Physical Sciences Concepts: The student produces evidence that demonstrates understanding of chemical reactions, such as…electrons, protons, and energy transfer….

A B In his descriptions of photosynthesis, the student explained the chemical reactions and interactions of energy and matter, often with sophisticated detail. This understanding is evident throughout the work.

The quotations from the Science performance descriptions in this commentary are excerpted. The complete performance descriptions are shown on pages 82-85.

Physical Sciences Concepts **S1**

Life Sciences Concepts **S2**

Earth and Space Sciences Concepts

Scientific Connections and Applications

Scientific Thinking **S5**

Scientific Tools and Technologies **S6**

Scientific Communication **S7**

Scientific Investigation

PHOTOSYNTHESIS LAB

Introduction:

Photosynthesis is an important process that is carried out within the chloroplast of plants. This reaction uses 6 CO_2 and the electrons from six water molecules (6 H_2O) to make glucose ($C_6H_{12}O_6$) and free oxygen (O_2), which will be explained in the conclusion. This reaction is powered by light, as the name implies (photo means light). The purpose of this lab is to discover how different wavelengths of visible light; red, orange, blue, and so on affect the process of photosynthesis. My hypothesis is that the water plant elodea will produce the lowest rate of photosynthesis when exposed to the green light, the highest with full spectrum white light, (because we see that green light is reflected by the plant and not absorbed by the plant) with the other wavelengths somewhere in between.

Procedures:

The elodea plants will be placed in a solution of sodium carbonate in a test tube. An identical test tube of sodium carbonate without any plant material will be used to demonstrate that the sodium carbonate alone produces no reaction when exposed to the various wavelengths of light.

1. Place a 5 cm length of elodea in a test tube, then carefully add 10 ml of sodium carbonate, making sure that no bubbles form around the plant. If bubbles do appear, gently flick the tube until they disappear. Place the test tube in the test tube rack.
2. Prepare a second tube of 10 ml of sodium carbonate, leaving the plant out, and place it in the test tube rack next to the first tube.
3. Shine a full spectrum white light on the two tubes for 3 minutes, and count the number of bubbles which float to the surface. Record your results in the data table below.
4. Repeat the experiment, using colored cellophane over the white light source until all of the colors of cellophane have been tested and recorded.

Results:

During the test we saw bubbles form on the elodea leaves and counted only those bubbles that actually broke free from the leaves and floated to the surface of the sodium carbonate solution. The bubbles were produced the fastest when the white light was shining on the plant. No bubbles were produced in any of the plain sodium carbonate tubes.

Color of Light	# of bubbles over 3 min.
White	8
Red	5
Green	2
Yellow	3
Blue	2

Rate of Photosynthesis

This work sample illustrates a standard-setting performance for the following parts of the standards:

S1 c **Physical Sciences Concepts: Chemical reactions.**

S1 f **Physical Sciences Concepts: Interactions of energy and matter.**

S2 a **Life Sciences Concepts: The cell.**

S2 e **Life Sciences Concepts: Matter, energy, and organization in living systems.**

S5 a **Scientific Thinking: Frame questions to distinguish cause and effect; and identify or control variables.**

S6 a **Scientific Tools and Technologies: Use technology and tools.**

S7 a **Scientific Communication: Represent data in multiple ways.**

S1 f Physical Sciences Concepts: The student produces evidence that demonstrates understanding of interactions of energy and matter, such as waves, absorption and emission of light, and conductivity.

C Here and elsewhere, the work shows evidence of understanding the interactions of matter and energy through the discussion of wavelengths of light. An alternative or additional explanation for the high rate of photosynthesis for the white light is that all of the colored filters reduced the intensity of the light, meaning that fewer photons reached the leaf. There is no mention of the intensity of the light, but from the description of the procedure it is unlikely that this variable was not controlled.

Photosynthesis

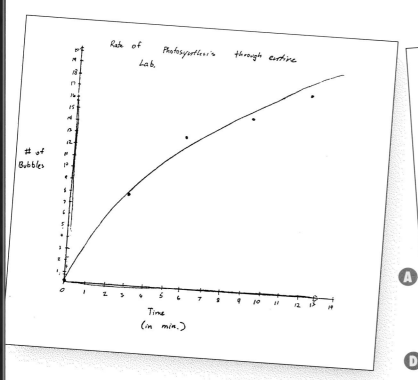

Rate of Photosynthesis through entire Lab.

# of Bubbles

Time (in min.)

Conclusion:

We expected the green light to produce the least or no bubbles from the stem. Our hypothesis was partially correct. The tubes exposed to the green and blue light each gave off only two bubble.. The tube exposed to the yellow light gave off 3 bubbles, red light gave off 5, and the white light gave off 8 bubbles.

The concept of this lab is photosynthesis. Photosynthesis is the process in which carbon dioxide and water is turned to simple sugars and oxygen. In this reaction, chlorophyll (the catalyst) and light (the energy source) must be present.

$$6\ CO_2 + 18\ H_2O \rightarrow C_6H_{12}O_6 + 6\ O_2 + 6\ H_2O$$
(Carbon Dioxide) + (Water) → (Glucose) + (Oxygen) + (Water)

In this lab, we soaked the plant stem in water and sodium carbonate. Sodium carbonate provided carbon dioxide within the water, giving the plant the materials needed for photosynthesis to occur. Photosynthesis occurs in two basic reactions, light and dark reactions. The light reaction occurs first, oxidizing water to oxygen, and the dark reaction combines the hydrogen with carbon dioxide to form simple carbohydrates. Oxygen is given off as a waste product, which were what the bubbles we saw coming out of the plant stem were. The more bubbles, the more oxygen is produced from the plant and in turn, the more oxygen, the faster the rate of photosynthesis of the plant because more H_2O is being split to O_2 in the light reaction.

A Within, the chloroplasts of the plant, there are chlorophyll, which is capable of absorbing light energy and exciting water molecules, oxidizing H_2O to O_2. As water is being oxidized into oxygen, energy rich ATP and NADPH are produced. Then, in the dark reaction, this energy rich ATP and NADPH are utilized in the Calvin cycle to convert CO_2 to carbohydrates. The electrons of this reaction come from the oxygen of H_2O. **B**

G NADPH and ATP are high energy. After Calvin cycle NADPH and ADP are low energy

D Light H_2O Chloroplast CO_2
Chlorophyll NADPH ATP Calvin Cycle Dark reaction
Light Reaction NADP ADP
O_2 Glucose

For photosynthesis to be most efficient, two wavelengths of light must be present, one wavelength greater than 650nm (red) and one wavelength less than 650nm. This is why the white light had the fastest rate of photosynthesis. White light contains the whole visible color spectrum. In our lab, it seems that light with lower wavelengths don't supply energy as well as light with higher wavelengths since green, yellow, and blue light all had a slower rate of photosynthesis. We know this because our plant produced the least oxygen under these light conditions. **C**

H All life on earth is dependant on photosynthesis, directly or indirectly. Plants are the bottom of the food chain. They make food for themselves and are food for higher life forms. If all photosynthesis-capable life forms disappear, animals would slowly,

one by one would die of starvation. Also plants, during photosynthesis, produce oxygen for oxygen breathing life forms. Animals use oxygen and create carbon dioxide as waste while plants complete the cycle by using carbon dioxide and creating oxygen as waste. Without plants, we would have no oxygen to breath.

Our conclusion is that different wavelengths of light does effect the rate of photosynthesis; generally, the higher the wavelength, the faster the rate of photosynthesis and the lower the wavelength, the slower the rate of photosynthesis. Our background information states that violet would also be an effective wavelength for photosynthesis. Unfortunately, we did not get a chance to test this color.

If there are any errors in conducting the experiment, it may have been in the experimental design. We could have weighed the plants as an additional control. We could have let the tubes stand in the light longer than 3 minutes, but I don't think either of these changes would have significantly changed the results of the experiment.

FURTHER TOPICS OF STUDY
*Does the intensity of the light effect the rate of photosynthesis?

S2 a Life Sciences Concepts: The student produces evidence that demonstrates understanding of the cell, such as cell structure and function relationships; regulation and biochemistry; and energy and photosynthesis.

D In describing what happens in the chloroplast of the cell, the work shows evidence of understanding the structure and function relationships inside the cell. The entire piece of work demonstrates understanding of photosynthesis.

S2 e Life Sciences Concepts: The student produces evidence that demonstrates understanding of matter, energy, and organization in living systems, such as matter and energy flow through different levels of organization; and environmental constraints.

E F The explanation of the flow of energy offers evidence of sophisticated understanding of the dynamic process whereby plants produce energy and other organisms rely on that energy for survival.

G The phrase "energy rich ATP and NADPH" appears above and adjacent to the cell drawing. It is true that NADPH has reducing power, but it is not an energy source, although ATP is.

S1 Physical Sciences Concepts

S2 Life Sciences Concepts

Earth and Space Sciences Concepts

Scientific Connections and Applications

S5 Scientific Thinking

S6 Scientific Tools and Technologies

S7 Scientific Communication

Scientific Investigation

Photosynthesis

S5 a Scientific Thinking: The student frames questions to distinguish cause and effect; and identifies or controls variables in experimental and non-experimental research settings.

H Here and throughout, the work displays evidence of appropriate scientific thinking and use of experimental data to reach conclusions.

S6 a Scientific Tools and Technologies: The student uses technology and tools (such as traditional laboratory equipment, video, and computer aids) to observe and measure objects, organisms, and phenomena directly, indirectly, and remotely; and with appropriate consideration of accuracy and precision.

Appropriate tools and technologies are used effectively and procedures are executed thoughtfully.

S7 a Scientific Communication: The student represents data and results in multiple ways, such as numbers, tables, and graphs; drawings, diagrams, and artwork; technical and creative writing; and selects the most effective way to convey the scientific information.

Throughout the work, multiple representations (e.g., graphs, diagrams, and text) are effectively employed to enhance the communication of the scientific concepts.

Physical Sciences Concepts **S1**

Life Sciences Concepts **S2**

Earth and Space Sciences Concepts

Scientific Connections and Applications

Scientific Thinking **S5**

Scientific Tools and Technologies **S6**

Scientific Communication **S7**

Scientific Investigation

GSE SELF-REFLECTION SHEET

1. *Thoroughly* explain the scientific concept you are investigating in this entry. Give specific examples that show how this concept relates to your Problem-solving Investigation.

> Every time we take in a breath of air, we breath in oxygen. This oxygen is no infinite. It comes from plants carrying out photosynthesis, a complicated and beautiful process in which water and carbon dioxide is turned to oxygen and glucose. We breath in the oxygen, a waste product given off from the plants, while the plant uses the glucose. Normally, what powers this process is light from the sun. The purpose of this investigation is to explore how different wavelengths of light, or different power sources, effect the rate of photosynthesis. We investigated this by measuring the output of oxygen under different light sources. The more oxygen is produced, the faster photosynthesis had to run in the plant to produce this oxygen. (More info in Conclusion)

2. Describe, *in detail*, the part or parts of this investigation YOU personally designed.

> I thought of what wavelengths of light we should investigate. I made sure that the choices were evenly spread over the color spectrum, to insure that most of the wavelengths of light are tested. I also designed the amount of time we should spend on each test counting bubbles, which was 3 minutes. I had to make sure that the time was long enough to get accurate test results while not so long that precious lab time is wasted.

3. Describe how the scientific concept you investigated in this component is related to a real-world issue or personal experience (you may include issues that affect society or the environment).

> Every time we eat something, like hamburgers, hot dogs, spinach, and other foods, we are either directly or indirectly consuming the products of photosynthesis. It's obvious that when we eat plants, we are eating plants that nurtures itself with the glucose produced in photosynthesis. When we eat animals, those animals may have eaten other animals which may have eaten other animals which finally may have eaten the plant. The point is that if photosynthesis ceased to exist, there be no plants, which means there will be no animals because they feed on the non-existing plants and life on earth would just not be possible. Photosynthesis is a process we take for granted.

E

GSE Self-reflection Sheet: Problem-solving Investigation (cont'd)

4. Describe how working with others on this investigation helped to increase your understanding of science.

> Before the lab, every single one of us was confused in their own way. When we got together and started discussing about it, our knowledge started to fill each other's gaps until we had the whole scientific concept of photosynthesis in our minds. Personally, I had no idea why the output of oxygen would tell us the rate of photosynthesis within the plant. I just knew the basic fact that the more oxygen produced, the faster photosynthesis is occurring. Now, we all know that the plant is not really trying to produce oxygen, but is producing glucose to nurture itself and oxygen just happened to be a waste product we need to survive produced while producing the glucose the plants need to survive.

F

5. What did you conclude from the investigation? Was the conclusion the same as or different from what you expected? Describe how your observations and data support your conclusions.

> We concluded that different wavelengths of light do indeed effect the rate of photosynthesis. Our data shows oxygen being given off from the plant faster when red or white light was shined on the plant. We concluded that in the presence of red or white light, photosynthesis was occurring faster because the rate of oxygen being released indicated the speed of photosynthesis. We weren't surprised that white light was so effective because white light, unlike other colors, is not just one wavelength of light, but the whole spectrum of wavelengths of light combined. From the white light, the plant had access of every wavelength of light. We also found that in the presence of green light, the rate oxygen was being released was extremely slow compared to the other wavelengths of light, which means the rate of photosynthesis was also extremely slow. We conclude this is so because green is refracted from the leaves. When green light is shown on the plant, the plant probably reflects it back out instead of absorbs it because we could see the refracted green light. This is why plants are green. The results we saw was mostly what we expected because before starting the lab, we had the chance to get a lot of background information.

Work Sample & Commentary: *Bio-poem*

The task

Students in a high school biology class were asked to write a bio-poem about something they had learned. The biographical form required the students to include in their poems specific statements about characteristics, siblings, and needs.

Circumstances of performance

This sample of student work was produced under the following conditions:

√ alone   in a group

√ in class   as homework

    with teacher feedback   with peer feedback

    timed   opportunity for revision

This task resulted from a series of assignments which allowed the students to express the relationships between living things in creative ways.

What the work shows

S2a   Life Sciences Concepts: The student produces evidence that demonstrates understanding of the cell, such as cell structure and function relationships;... and energy and photosynthesis.

Ⓐ

S2e   Life Sciences Concepts: The student produces evidence that demonstrates understanding of matter, energy, and organization in living systems, such as matter and energy flow through different levels of organization....

Ⓑ The student clearly identified the needs of plants and displayed understanding of the flow of energy between levels (plants to heterotrophs).

> Plant
>
> Makes its own food, produces spores through meiosis,
> captures energy from sunlight in thylakoid membranes, and passes
> on genetic information to daughter cells
> Sibling of fellow plant cells formed by mitosis
> Lover of fertilizer, light, and heat
> Who feels at rest in winter, refreshed after rain,
> and dehydrated in hot weather
> Who needs carbon dioxide, sunlight, and water
> Who gives oxygen, carbohydrates, and the sole
> source of energy for all heterotrophs
> Who fears acid rain, weeds, and insects
> Who would like to see more greenhouses,
> preservation of rainforests, and less pollution
> Resident of a leaf
> Cell

Ⓐ **Ⓑ** **Ⓒ**

This work sample illustrates a standard-setting performance for the following parts of the standards:

S2a   **Life Sciences Concepts: The cell.**

S2e   **Life Sciences Concepts: Matter, energy, and organization in living systems.**

S4a   **Scientific Connections and Applications: Big ideas and unifying concepts.**

S7d   **Scientific Communication: Explain a scientific concept or procedure to other students.**

S4a   Scientific Connections and Applications: The student produces evidence that demonstrates understanding of big ideas and unifying concepts, such as order and organization...; change and constancy....

The student demonstrated a complex understanding of biology throughout the work. By relating genetics and reproduction to the physiological needs of the plant and the products of photosynthesis, the student integrated many important ideas of science.

S7d   Scientific Communication: The student explains a scientific concept or procedure to other students.

Ⓒ Using the bio-poem form, the student correctly explained several complex concepts related to plants. These concepts are complex to explain in simple language. In producing this type of poem the student demonstrated a deep understanding of the needs of, desirable conditions for, and energy flow through plants.

The use of "sibling" with respect to mitosis is a consequence of the literary form, not a misunderstanding of mitosis.

The quotations from the Science performance descriptions in this commentary are excerpted. The complete performance descriptions are shown on pages 82-85.

Work Sample & Commentary: *Erosion on the Minnehaha Creek*

The task

The National Student Research Center (NSRC) encourages the establishment of student research centers in schools in the United States and around the world. The Center facilitates the exchange of information by publishing a journal of student investigations and by use of the Internet (nsrcmms@aol.com). It provides a standard format that students use to report their results. The format requires that students state a purpose and hypothesis; report their methods, data analysis, and conclusions; and suggest applications for their results.

Circumstances of performance

This sample of student work was produced under the following conditions:

√ alone   in a group

√ in class   √ as homework

√ with teacher feedback   √ with peer feedback

  timed   √ opportunity for revision

What the work shows

S3 e Earth and Space Sciences Concepts: The student produces evidence that demonstrates understanding of natural resource management.

A The student produced a list of hypotheses which is really a list of explanations that give evidence of conceptual understanding of the mechanisms of erosion.

The quotations from the Science performance descriptions in this commentary are excerpted. The complete performance descriptions are shown on pages 82-85.

S6 makes explicit reference to using telecommunications to acquire and share information. A recent National Center on Education Statistics survey recently reported that only 50% of schools and fewer than 9% of instructional rooms currently have access to the Internet. We know this is an equity issue—that far more than 9% of the homes in the United States have access to the Internet and that schools must make sure that students' access to information and ideas does not depend on what they get at home—so we have crafted performance standards that would use the Internet so that people will make sure that all students have access to it. New Standards partners have made a commitment to create the learning environments where students can develop the knowledge and skills delineated here.

Physical Sciences Concepts

Life Sciences Concepts

Earth and Space Sciences Concepts **◄S3**

Scientific Connections and Applications

Scientific Thinking **◄S5**

Scientific Tools and Technologies **◄S6**

Scientific Communication

Scientific Investigation

Title: Erosion on the Minnehaha Creek

I. Statement of Purpose and Hypothesis:

The Minnehaha weaves through the city as a quiet creek that adds to the charm, beauty, and wildlife of the city. The creek is a recreational park that allows fishing, tubing, canoeing, and walks along the bank. The banks are eroding in many places causing problems such as damage to yards, houses, and city parks. Narrower and lost walkways along the parks prevent bikes, running, and walking along the creek. In addition, a significant amount of funds is required to correct the damage every year caused by erosion. A recent television program talked about erosion in the creek as a major problem for Minneapolis Park Board. **◄E**

◄B For these reasons, I chose my project to find more ways to prevent erosion along the creek and eliminate these problems. The questions I would like to answer include whether erosion control factors such as bank vegetation, trees, rocks, and storm drains reduce the amount of erosion along the Minnehaha Creek. This study may provide answers on how we can prevent erosion along it's banks. I want to know if erosion, as measured by the Erosion Index, is **◄A** more where there is less erosion control present along the Minnehaha Creek. Specifically, the hypotheses to test include: 1) Erosion, as measured by the Erosion Index, is more at narrow and deep bends along the creek. 2) Erosion, as measured by the Erosion Index, occurs at places with less vegetation. These are places where there are no roots to hold the soil from being washed away by the water runoff. 3) Erosion, as measured by the Erosion Index, occurs where storm drains are not located along the creek. These places have higher erosion due to runoff from the rain making gullies and crevices. 4) Erosion, as measured by the Erosion Index, occurs at places with less trees on the banks.

This study will tell us whether these factors are important in controlling erosion along the creek. If so, these factors can be changed or implemented to provide a cost effective way of preventing erosion.

II. Methodology:

This study design will be an observational study to quantify the amount of erosion and erosion control factors that occur along the Minnehaha Creek. I hopes to determine what factors play a role in erosion. Two independent observers will walk along a specific section of the creek to measure the

The Student Researcher. Used by permission of the National Student Research Center, Dr. John I Swang, Mandeville Middle School, 2525 Soult Street, Mandeville, Louisiana 70448. 504-626-5980 or nsrcmms@aol.com.

> ### This work sample illustrates a standard-setting performance for the following parts of the standards:
>
> **S3 e** Earth and Space Sciences Concepts: **Natural resource management.**
>
> **S5 a** Scientific Thinking: **Frame questions to distinguish cause and effect; and identify or control variables.**
>
> **S5 b** Scientific Thinking: **Use concepts from Standards 1 to 4 to explain observations and phenomena.**
>
> **S5 c** Scientific Thinking: **Use evidence from reliable sources.**
>
> **S5 d** Scientific Thinking: **Distinguish between fact and opinion.**
>
> **S5 e** Scientific Thinking: **Identify problems and propose solutions.**
>
> **S5 f** Scientific Thinking: **Work individually and in teams.**
>
> **S6 a** Scientific Tools and Technologies: **Use technology and tools.**

S5 a Scientific Thinking: The student frames questions to distinguish cause and effect; and identifies or controls variables in experimental and non-experimental research settings.

B C The work shows that a number of steps were taken to measure erosion, although the Erosion Index that plays a critical role in the study is not explained. However, there is detailed evidence that most of the critical variables were identified and controlled.

S5 b Scientific Thinking: The student uses concepts from Standards 1 to 4 to explain a variety of observations and phenomena.

A

Erosion on the Minnehaha Creek

S5c Scientific Thinking: The student uses evidence from reliable sources to develop descriptions [and] explanations...; and makes appropriate adjustments and improvements based on additional data or logical arguments.

D The explanation of erosion control factors and probability is strong evidence of this student using data from the field study to reach a defensible conclusion.

S5d Scientific Thinking: The student...distinguishes between fact and opinion.

D The student explained the mathematical basis upon which he built his conclusion.

S5e Scientific Thinking: The student identifies problems; proposes...solutions....

E F The work shows that the student clearly identified and defined the problem and used data to back up the conclusions, recommending a practice to solve part of the problem.

S5f Scientific Thinking: The student works individually and in teams to collect and share information and ideas.

S6a Scientific Tools and Technologies: The student uses technology and tools (such as traditional laboratory equipment...) to observe and measure objects, organisms, and phenomena, directly, indirectly, and remotely, with appropriate consideration of accuracy and precision.

The student displayed attention to accuracy and precision by including the following steps: deciding on a representative sample, developing an observation form with help from experts, training independent observers, and taking observations from both sides of the creek.

amount of erosion and erosion control factors using the Erosion Index. I will obtain a map of about 10 blocks of the Minnehaha Creek from the Old Mill Dam in Edina to the city of Minneapolis. On the basis of on my preliminary observations, I feel this is a representative sample of the Creek that includes many areas of erosion and has had erosion control efforts completed to prevent erosion. In addition, this area is heavily used by pedestrians and is heavily populated with houses that may be effected by the erosion. First, I had to develop an index to score erosion and to score the presence of the erosion control factors. I did this with the help of the City of Minneapolis Park Board staff and specific references from my review of the literature. **G** Then I designed a form for the observers to score the amount of erosion and erosion control factors as they walk along the creek. We needed two observers on both sides of the creek to make sure that the data collected was reliable. A score will be placed on the form for each block and each side of the creek **C** inspected. Then I will add the scores up and compare the sum with the number in the erosion index that correlates to the bank and section. In addition, I will compare both of the numbers in a statistical analysis. This will include comparing the total of erosion control scores between blocks that have low erosion scores with an equal number of blocks that have high erosion scores.

III. Analysis of Data:

Three out of the 7 erosion control factors seem to correlate with less erosion or have a negative correlation with erosion. These are straight creek flow, shallow creek levels, and the rocks on the banks.

IV. Summary and Conclusion:

I have learned that most of the control factors are not a sure bet and that you cannot completely stop erosion. In addition, even if someone had all the **D** factors they could not completely stop erosion. The best prevention is unfortunately not manmade and includes a straight creek and shallow water. If someone is trying to stop erosion and they do not live on a section of the creek that is straight, I would recommend that rocks and trees would work the **F** best. Although the total correlation of all factors is close to zero the p-value (probability) is .83 which means that there is a big variance in the amount that erosion control factors effect erosion.

In general, I found out that when there were less Erosion Control Factors there was more erosion and when there was more Erosion Control Factors there was less erosion.

Application

I can apply this information in two ways. First, I can educate people on how to prevent erosion. Second, I can be more careful on how I treat the creek myself.

The Student Researcher. Used by permission of the National Student Research Center, Dr. John I Swang, Mandeville Middle School, 2525 Soult Street, Mandeville, Louisiana 70448. 504-626-5980 or nsrcmms@aol.com.

Physical Sciences Concepts

Life Sciences Concepts

S3 Earth and Space Sciences Concepts

Scientific Connections and Applications

S5 Scientific Thinking

S6 Scientific Tools and Technologies

Scientific Communication

Scientific Investigation

Work Sample & Commentary: *Are Oysters Safe to Eat?*

The task

The National Student Research Center (NSRC) encourages the establishment of student research centers in schools in the United States and around the world. The Center facilitates the exchange of information by publishing a journal of student investigations and by use of the Internet (nsrcmms@aol.com). It provides a standard format that students use to report their results. The format requires that students state a purpose and hypothesis; report their methods, data analysis, and conclusions; and suggest applications for their results.

The quotations from the Science performance descriptions in this commentary are excerpted. The complete performance descriptions are shown on pages 82-85.

Circumstances of performance

This sample of student work was produced under the following conditions:

√ alone   in a group

√ in class   as homework

√ with teacher feedback   with peer feedback

    timed   √ opportunity for revision

What the work shows

S2 d Life Sciences Concepts: The student produces evidence that demonstrates understanding of interdependence of organisms, such as...cooperation and competition among organisms in ecosystems....

Physical Sciences Concepts

Life Sciences Concepts **S2**

Earth and Space Sciences Concepts

Scientific Connections and Applications **S4**

Scientific Thinking **S5**

Scientific Tools and Technologies **S6**

Scientific Communication

Scientific Investigation **S8**

TITLE: Louisiana Oysters: Are They Safe to Eat?

I. STATEMENT OF PURPOSE AND HYPOTHESIS:

The purpose of my research is to try and find out if raw Louisiana oysters, that many people love, are safe to eat. Studies have been done on the oysters to find out if they are harmful to humans, and many of these studies contradict one another. My hypothesis states that forms of salmonella and e. coli bacteria will be present in the oysters I test.

II. METHODOLOGY:

I began my research by stating my hypothesis and doing a review of the literature about the diseases caused by the eating of raw oysters. With this information, I developed a methodology and list of materials that would help me measure the amount of bacteria present in oysters, the amount of the bacteria that can be safely consumed, and the length of time needed to cook the oysters so that they are safe to eat.

For materials, I used twenty raw Louisiana oysters, boiling water for sterilization, a sterilized blender, an incubator, sterile swabs, four petri dishes, a tryptic soy agar with 5% sheep blood.

I began by sterilizing all equipment with boiling water for ten minutes. I then took five of the raw oysters and placed them in the blender until they were ground up. Then, using one of the sterile swabs, I smudged a small amount of the liquid from the oysters onto a petri dish. I then steamed five oysters for one minute, another five for three minutes, and another five for five minutes. I then ground up each of these groups of oysters separately and smudged a small amount of the liquid from each onto three different petri dishes. Next, I incubated all four of the petri dishes for about forty-eight hours. Then I counted the colonies and identified the types of bacteria that were present in each petri dish. I also determined what amount of each type of bacteria could be safely consumed.

III. ANALYSIS OF DATA:

The bacteria count in the raw oysters was much greater than in the steamed oysters because the steaming did kill many of the bacteria. However, the oysters that were steamed for three minutes contained less bacteria than the ones that were steamed for five minutes. This may have been due to the fact that I had a random selection of unweighed oysters in each group of oysters. Some of the oysters were larger than others and the heated steam may not have penetrated as deeply into them. Therefore the larger oysters may not have been as fully cooked and the bacteria in them not fully killed, causing this result.

In the five types of colonies found, one was a vibrio which is the worst bacteria and the second worst thing you could eat in an oyster. Vibrio cause gastroenteritis that may lead to bacturimia if the bacteria moves into the blood. The other four colony were types of pseudomonas that aren't harmful to humans unless you eat too many or have a health condition. Both vibrio types and the pseudomonas types are naturally found in the water that oysters are raised in, polluted or not.

The Student Researcher. Used by permission of the National Student Research Center, Dr. John I Swang, Mandeville Middle School, 2525 Soult Street, Mandeville, Louisiana 70448. 504-626-5980 or nsrcmms@aol.com.

This work sample illustrates a standard-setting performance for the following parts of the standards:

S2 d Life Sciences Concepts: Interdependence of organisms.

S2 e Life Sciences Concepts: Matter, energy, and organization in living systems.

S4 c Scientific Connections and Applications: Health, personal and environmental safety.

S5 a Scientific Thinking: Frame questions to distinguish cause and effect; and identify or control variables.

S5 b Scientific Thinking: Use concepts from Standards 1 to 4 to explain observations and phenomena.

S5 c Scientific Thinking: Use evidence from reliable sources.

S5 d Scientific Thinking: Distinguish between fact and opinion.

S6 a Scientific Tools and Technologies: Use technology and tools.

S6 d Scientific Tools and Technologies: Acquire information from multiple sources.

S8 a Scientific Investigation: Controlled experiment.

A Many animals and bacteria live in cooperation. The identification of bacterial forms that are naturally found in waters with oysters demonstrates understanding of this relationship.

B The use of agar as a growth medium and the identification of the need for sterile equipment provide evidence of understanding how bacteria grow as well as the importance of appropriate scientific procedures.

S2 e Life Sciences Concepts: The student produces evidence that demonstrates understanding of...organization in living systems, such as...environmental constraints.

C The student related the rate of bacteria growth to temperature and season.

S4 c Scientific Connections and Applications: The student produces evidence that demonstrates understanding of health, such as...personal and environmental safety....

The student offered two types of warnings regarding bacteria and oysters.

Are Oysters Safe to Eat?

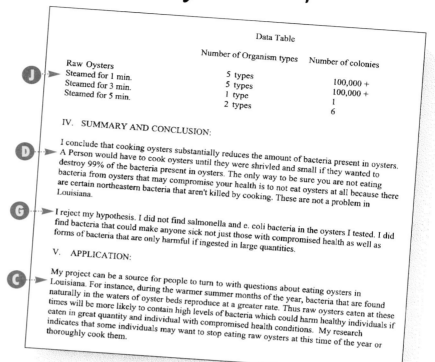

D The first gives a method to reduce risk of bacterial infection significantly.

C The second indicates different levels of risk by season.

Both provide evidence of the quality of work expected at the high school level.

S5 a Scientific Thinking: The student frames questions to distinguish cause and effect; identifies and controls variables in experimental...research settings.

E The evaluation of data offers evidence that the student understood both variables she controlled and those she may have needed to control. The data analysis is focused and findings are used appropriately to answer the initial experimental question.

S5 b Scientific Thinking: The student uses concepts from Science Standards 1 to 4 to explain a variety of observations and phenomena.

F The student used concepts from **S2 d** here.

S5 c Scientific Thinking: The student uses evidence from reliable sources to develop descriptions, explanations...and makes appropriate adjustments and improvements based on additional data or logical arguments.

E G Discussion of unexpected results and critique of one's own procedures are the kind of scientific thinking that is required by this part of the standard.

S5 d Scientific Thinking: The student...distinguishes between fact and opinion.

G

S6 a Scientific Tools and Technologies: The student uses technology and tools (such as traditional laboratory equipment)...with appropriate consideration of accuracy and precision.

H The procedures are clearly reported, which makes it possible to find ample evidence that this part of the standard has been met. The use of sterile equipment was necessary for this investigation and shows appropriate attention to detail that is reflected in the reporting of the procedures.

S6 d Scientific Tools and Technologies: The student acquires information from multiple sources, such as print, the Internet...and experimentation.

The report is not explicit about how the bacteria were identified. Identifying bacteria is sophisticated work for a high school student. Assistance would have been appropriate (and should have been acknowledged).

Data Table

Raw Oysters	Number of Organism types	Number of colonies
Steamed for 1 min.	5 types	
Steamed for 3 min.	5 types	100,000 +
Steamed for 5 min.	1 type	100,000 +
	2 types	1
		6

J

IV. SUMMARY AND CONCLUSION:

D I conclude that cooking oysters substantially reduces the amount of bacteria present in oysters. A Person would have to cook oysters until they were shriveled and small if they wanted to destroy 99% of the bacteria present in oysters. The only way to be sure you are not eating bacteria from oysters that may compromise your health is to not eat oysters at all because there are certain northeastern bacteria that aren't killed by cooking. These are not a problem in Louisiana.

G I reject my hypothesis. I did not find salmonella and e. coli bacteria in the oysters I tested. I did find bacteria that could make anyone sick not just those with compromised health as well as forms of bacteria that are only harmful if ingested in large quantities.

V. APPLICATION:

C My project can be a source for people to turn to with questions about eating oysters in Louisiana. For instance, during the warmer summer months of the year, bacteria that are found naturally in the waters of oyster beds reproduce at a greater rate. Thus raw oysters eaten at these times will be more likely to contain high levels of bacteria which could harm healthy individuals if eaten in great quantity and individual with compromised health conditions. My research indicates that some individuals may want to stop eating raw oysters at this time of the year or thoroughly cook them.

The Student Researcher. Used by permission of the National Student Research Center, Dr. John I Swang, Mandeville Middle School, 2525 Soult Street, Mandeville, Louisiana 70448. 504-626-5980 or nsrcmms@aol.com.

S8 a Scientific Investigation: The student demonstrates scientific competence by completing a controlled experiment. A full investigation includes:

• Questions that can be studied using the resources available.

I

• Procedures that are safe, humane, and ethical; and that respect privacy and property rights.

H

• Data that have been collected and recorded (see also Science Standard 6) in ways that others can verify, and analyzed using skills expected at this grade level (see also Mathematics Standard 4).

H J

• Data and results that have been represented (see also Science Standard 7) in ways that fit the context.

J

• Recommendations, decisions, and conclusions based on evidence.

C D

• Acknowledgment of references and contributions of others.

• Results that are communicated appropriately to audiences.

C D

• Reflection and defense of conclusions and recommendations from other sources and peer review.

The student, as part of the NSRC format, loaded this work up onto the Internet for peer review. It is not stated whether this review informed the final report.

Physical Sciences Concepts

S2 Life Sciences Concepts

Earth and Space Sciences Concepts

S4 Scientific Connections and Applications

S5 Scientific Thinking

S6 Scientific Tools and Technologies

Scientific Communication

S8 Scientific Investigation

Work Sample & Commentary: *Interview With Aspirin*

The quotations from the Science performance descriptions in this commentary are excerpted. The complete performance descriptions are shown on pages 82-85.

The task

Students were asked to write a report on the benefits and risks of common medications. This student compared three medications: aspirin, acetaminophen, and ibuprofen.

Circumstances of performance

This sample of student work was produced under the following conditions:

√ alone   in a group

√ in class   as homework

√ with teacher feedback   with peer feedback

    timed   √ opportunity for revision

What the work shows

S2 f   **Life Sciences Concepts:** The student produces evidence that demonstrates understanding of behavior of organisms, such as nervous system regulation....

A The discussion of the effects of aspirin demonstrates understanding of homeostatic mechanisms on clotting and bleeding.

B The connection between overdose and effects on the central nervous system clearly shows conceptual understanding of system control, maintenance, and the benefits and risks of medication.

C The understanding that human systems are regulated by the production of specific chemicals is consistently demonstrated throughout this work.

Aspirin, Acetaminophen, and Ibuprofen

An Interview with Aspirin

As I approached my interviewee, I noticed his appearance and attitude. He was white and powdery, and slightly bitter. Mr. Acet Asalicylic Acid, despite his insipid appearance, actually plays a very part important part in the pain relief of approximately 30 million people each week. The following is my recorded interview Mr. A. A. Acid.

Me: Mr. Acetasalicylic Acid . . .

Aspirin: Please, call me Aspirin, all of my friends do.

Me: Very well then. So Aspirin, millions of people use you weekly. How does it feel to be so wanted.

Aspirin: It feels great. Absolutely fantastic, which is how all my users feel after they have ingested a tablet or two of me.

Me: You have an unusual talent, do you not. Tell me about this remarkable ability of yours.

Aspirin: Well, I don't like to brag, but I have an uncanny ability to relieve the pain which frustrates millions of people every day.

Me: What specifically do people use you for?

Aspirin: I relieve musculoskelatal pain (pain dealing with the muscles and bones), fevers, and inflammation. I'm used mainly for non-migraine headaches, joint pain, muscle cramps, fever, inflammation, tennis elbow, menstrual cramps, toothaches, and surface cuts and bruises. I'm virtually ineffective with visceral pain, or pain dealing with organs. I can also be used for pain after childbirth, since I have just as much pain relieving power or more than any of the narcotics such as codeine or proporyphine.

Me: Could you tell me how you manage to relieve such pain.

Aspirin: It's rather simple. Let me go through the process. When there is pain, prostaglandins are synthesized from arachidonic acid with the help of the enzyme cyclo-oxygenase. These prostaglandins sensitizes peripheral pain receptors which then send impulses telling of pain or trauma from that particular area to the brain. When ingested, I simply inhibit the active site of cyclo-oxygenase, thereby preventing the synthesis of prostaglandins, which ultimately leads to the relief of pain. **C**

Me: Now tell me, when, where, and by whom were your talents discovered.

Aspirin: I was not particularly known until the 1830's when I was isolated from willow bark. Willow bark, back in those days, was commonly used to reduce fever and pain when steeped in tea. I was synthesized in a chemical laboratory. Being a form of salicylic acid, they named me Acetasalicylic acid. I have many other relatives, or salicylates, some of which are also used to relieve pain. There are more than 200 different products containing salicylates. After my discovery, Germany's Bayer Company became rich and famous.

This work sample illustrates a standard-setting performance for the following parts of the standards:

S2 f   **Life Sciences Concepts: Behavior of organisms.**

S4 c   **Scientific Connections and Applications: Health.**

S7 a   **Scientific Communication: Represent data in multiple ways.**

S7 b   **Scientific Communication: Argue from evidence.**

S7 d   **Scientific Communication: Explain a scientific concept or procedure to other students.**

S7 e   **Scientific Communication: Communicate in a form suited to the purpose and audience.**

E2 a   **Writing: Produce a report.**

S4 c   Scientific Connections and Applications: The student produces evidence that demonstrates understanding of health, such as...disease...; personal and environmental safety....

D **E** Understanding of health is evident throughout this piece. For example, the distinction between curing ailments, reducing pain and fever, and the summary of the three medications shows understanding as well as detail.

S7 a   Scientific Communication: The student represents data and results in multiple ways, such as...technical and creative writing.

The interview format is a creative way to provide a great amount of detail. This form requires the student to have a great deal of background knowledge and adequate understanding of the underlying concepts in order to present the information accurately.

Reading

Writing   **E2**

Speaking, Listening, and Viewing

Conventions, Grammar, and Usage of the English Language

Literature

Public Documents

Functional Documents

Physical Sciences Concepts

Life Sciences Concepts   **S2**

Earth and Space Sciences Concepts

Scientific Connections and Applications   **S4**

Scientific Thinking

Scientific Tools and Technologies

Scientific Communication   **S7**

Scientific Investigation

Interview With Aspirin

Reading

E2 ▶ Writing

Speaking, Listening, and Viewing

Conventions, Grammar, and Usage of the English Language

Literature

Public Documents

Functional Documents

S7 b Scientific Communication: The student argues from evidence, such as data produced through his or her own experimentation or...by others.

The work covers a range of information from uses to benefits and risks, giving a complete explanation and summary from varied sources. It does not consider the biases of these sources of information and this (apparently) uncritical acceptance of the information is a shortcoming of the piece.

S7 d Scientific Communication: The student explains a scientific concept or procedure to other students.

F The construction of the interview questions frames the topic in a way that allows an explanation of each medication to be given in depth. Careful attention to detail in the discussion of the effects of overdoses and how aspirin chemically blocks pain provides the clarity necessary to illustrate this part of **S7**.

S7 e Scientific Communication: The student communicates in a form suited to the purpose and the audience....

The format for the comparison, an interview with each of the pain relievers, is an effective way of presenting information that could be tedious to read if presented in a traditional report. However, the format limits the depth of conceptual understanding that is demonstrated.

Me: Is Arachidonic acid one of your relatives?

Aspirin: No, but we both share the same parent group.

Me: You also have some undesirable traits, or, shall we say, side effects. Could you tell me about them.

Aspirin: I do. I usually don't like to talk about them, but I'll tell them to you, since you appear to be an intelligent, bright, shrewd, and acute young man. The side effects I have are many, but mainly affect those who are either allergic to me, or have stomachs that are irritated by me. It's their fault, not mine. Very few of my users experience any side effects. Anyway, my side effects are: ulcers, severe bleeding, inflammation of mucous membranes, diarrhea, stomach cramps, asthma, severe breathing difficulty, skin rashes, shock, insulin shock, jaundice, kidney damage, ringing in the ears, nausea, blurred vision, mental confusion, vomiting, indigestion, and death. Many of the side effects for those who have problems digesting me can be taken care of if they take buffered aspirin. Less than 1% of the population is allergic to me. Those that are allergic to me are morons, and should stay away from me. I don't want them to have me or my analgesic effects anyway. Pregnant peoples and children, especially children with influenza or chickenpox, should restrain from taking me. As difficult as that may be for them, I am a potential hazard for such people. It is believed that I increase the risk of having Reye's Syndrome in children with the flu or chickenpox viruses; though, it has not yet been clearly proven that I do so.

Me: Do you not also have an effect on the clotting of blood.

Aspirin: Yes, I do. I compromise the homeostatic mechanism which controls the oozing type of capillary bleeding by irreversibly inhibiting platelet aggregation. Basically, in lay person's terms, I prevent the blood from clotting. In fact, after taking a single dose, or 650 mg, this effect can double bleeding time of, lets say, a tooth extraction, from 4 to 7 days. This is the reason why I'm not recommended for hemophiliacs, who naturally have poor blood clotting. **A**

Me: What happens when someone takes too much of you? **F**

Aspirin: Oh, nothing drastic. Overdoses with me are categorized as mild, moderate, and severe. The symptoms for an overdose are: lethargy, tinnitus, tachynea and pulmonary edema, convulsions, coma, nausea, vomiting, hemorrhage, and dehydration. I also cause noticeable acid base disturbances. These range from respiratory alkalosis to metabolic acidosis. I can also cause severe internal bleeding. If there is a chronic loss of blood in the Gastrointestinal tract resulting from the continued use of me, this blood loss can cause an iron-deficiency anemia and alter hematological indices. Aspirin overdoses accounted for 37% of the non-prescription analgesic overdoses, which is the second most compared to the 40% of that other loser Acetaminophen. Those who take too much of me in a single dose should note that increased doses increase the risk of side effects and doesn't significantly add to pain relief. I'm sure the people that take overdoses of me are wonderful people, I just don't want them die.

Me: Tell me about your competition.

Aspirin: What's there to say, my competition sucks. Let's look at Acetaminophen. Its ability to relieve pain and severe headaches is very similar to mine, but Acetaminophen has only weak anti-inflammatory activity, whereas I have superior anti-inflammatory activity. The only reason people use Acetaminophen is because those people can't use me. Anyway, there's a significant number of people in which Acetaminophen is less effective than me.

Me: How do you compare to Ibuprofen?

Aspirin: Uh -- um -- umm. Ibuprofen. I've never heard the bum. I'm sure Ibuprofen is a loser just like Acetaminophen.

Me: Well, thanks for your time, information, opinions, etc., etc.

An Interview with Acetaminophen

Acetaminophen is also an analgesic and antipyretic. This drug stars in several products such as Tylenol, Panadol, and Tempra, as well as many other non-aspirin pain relievers. This interview was done after that of Aspirin. The following is my interview with Mr. Acet Aminophen.

Me: Mr. Aminophen, as an analgesic, what kind of ailments do you cure. **D**

Acet: Well, I don't really cure anything. I do, however, reduce pain and fever. I am commonly used for headaches, fever, and muscle and joint pains. I am also best for pain secondary to dental surgery and episiotomy.

Me: Who are your consumers?

Acet: Mainly children, who aren't supposed to take Aspirin. After all, Aspirin is the primary cause of death by poisoning among children under five. Aspirin has also been linked to the sometimes fatal complication of chickenpox and influenza viruses called Reye's Syndrome. Other users are Aspirin-allergic peoples, and people with hemophilia. They are also unable to take Aspirin. Other users are people who just trust me over Aspirin and Ibuprofen, knowing that I have no real side effects, unless taken in large overdoses.

Me: Since I couldn't find anything about your history, we'll have to skip that part. So, how do you work to relieve pain?

Acet: Unlike Aspirin and Ibuprofen who produce analgesia by a peripheral effect, I produce analgesia through the Central Nervous System (i.e. the brain and spinal cord). Since I work on the CNS, I cannot really do much with inflammation. And again, since you couldn't find the specifics; I can't really answer your question.

Me: Tell me what happens to people who do take large overdoses of you.

Acet: I mainly cause permanent damage to the liver and kidney. Symptoms of an Acetaminophen overdose are: nausea, vomiting, drowsiness, confusion, low blood pressure, and abdominal pain. Symptoms of severe overdoses are: CNS stimulation, excitement, cardiac arrythmias, low blood pressure, and delirium. These are followed by CNS depression with a stupor, hypothermia, shock, and coma. Jaundice may also occur in severe overdosages. Many of these symptoms come from my effect on the CNS. **B**

Me: How would you rate yourself to Aspirin and Ibuprofen.

Acet: Well, I am better than them in the fact that I have no side effects and that I have no effect on platelet aggregation as both Aspirin and Ibuprofen do. I am just as effective and efficient as Aspirin is at relieving severe headaches and muscle pain. And though I am less efficient than Ibuprofen, meaning that it takes less of Ibuprofen of than myself to do what we do, I am just as effective as Ibuprofen is at relieving headaches and muscle pain. But of course, I'm still the best non-prescription analgesic in the business.

Physical Sciences Concepts

S2 ▶ Life Sciences Concepts

Earth and Space Sciences Concepts

S4 ▶ Scientific Connections and Applications

Scientific Thinking

Scientific Tools and Technologies

S7 ▶ Scientific Communication

Scientific Investigation

Reading

Writing **E2**

Speaking,
Listening,
and Viewing

Conventions,
Grammar,
and Usage
of the English
Language

Literature

Public
Documents

Functional
Documents

Physical
Sciences
Concepts

Life
Sciences
Concepts **S2**

Earth and
Space Sciences
Concepts

Scientific
Connections and **S4**
Applications

Scientific
Thinking

Scientific Tools
and
Technologies

Scientific **S7**
Communication

Scientific
Investigation

Interview With Aspirin

E2a Writing: The student produces a report that:

- engages the reader by establishing a context, creating a persona, and otherwise developing reader interest;

- develops a controlling idea that conveys a perspective on the subject;

- creates an organizing structure appropriate to purpose, audience, and context;

- includes appropriate facts and details;

- excludes extraneous and inappropriate information;

- uses a range of appropriate strategies, such as providing facts and details, describing or analyzing the subject, narrating a relevant anecdote, comparing and contrasting, naming, explaining benefits or limitations, demonstrating claims or assertions, and providing a scenario to illustrate;

- provides a sense of closure to the writing.

The work is presented within the controlling idea of a series of interviews.

The reader's interest is engaged through the establishment of three independent personas in a familiar "interview-with-a-celebrity" format.

C The organizing structure of the interviews allowed the student to convey information to his teacher and fellow students in an interesting and memorable fashion.

The three sections, for the most part, include parallel facts and details, allowing for a useful comparison among the three pain relievers.

The student employed the strategy of communicating facts and details within a narrative.

E The student provided a clear sense of closure by summarizing the benefits and risks of three common medications.

An Interview with Ibuprofen

Last, but not least, came my interview with Ibuprofen. Ibuprofen is a much more recently developed analgesic, antipyretic, and anti-inflammatory drug. In these respects, it is much like Aspirin. Ibuprofen is found in Motrin, Nuprin, and Advil. Now, my interview with Mr. Ibu Profen.

Me: How do you work to reduce pain?

Ibu: I work just as Aspirin does to relieve pain.

Me: Mr. Profen, you are very similar to Aspirin, aren't you?

Ibu: Yes, except I' m not chemically formulated the same and I am much better. Another difference is that I am classified as a nonsteroidal anti-inflammatory drug. Why I'm classified as something different than Aspirin is beyond me. Maybe it's because I am so much better.

Me: How are you better than Aspirin?

Ibu: Well, I have a reversible effect on platelet aggregation. The effect is reversed after 24 hours of the discontinuation of my use. I have a higher potential than aspirin for fast, long acting pain relief for mild to moderate pain.

Me: How are you better than Acetaminophen.

Ibu: I'm more efficient on a mg to mg basis than Acetaminophen as well as Aspirin. And I can reduce inflammation, fever, and pain whereas Acetaminophen can reduce only pain and fever.

Me: You also have side effects. Could you tell me about them?

Ibu: The only side effect I know of is my effect on platelet aggregation, which is like that of Aspirin except my effect is reversible. It is possible that I do have an effect on people that allergic to aspirin, but it's not proven. I don't know of any other side effects that I can cause.

Me: What are the symptoms of an Ibuprofen overdose.

Ibu: Symptoms are: nausea, vomiting, abdominal pain, lethargy, stupor, coma, nystagmus, dizziness, lightheadedness, hypotension, bridyeardea, tachnycardia, dyspensea, and painful breathing. Unlike some certain other analgesics, I only account for 15% of accidental overdoses with non-prescription analgesics. I guess people feel so relieved after the first dose, they realize they don't need much more.

Me: Who uses you?

Ibu: It's not who uses me, it's who can't use me. I'm not recommended for hemophiliacs. I am sometimes recommended for people allergic to Aspirin, but not often. Basically, there are very few people who can't use me.   **E**

A Comparative Summary on Aspirin, Acetaminophen, and Ibuprofen

Ibuprofen is more potent as an analgesic than either aspirin or acetaminophen. Ibuprofen, unlike aspirin, produces a reversible effect on platelet aggregation. Acetaminóphen is preferred for those who have a history with hemophilia, for children, and for aspirin allergic people. Aspirin, despite it relative shortcomings, is still used as a common analgesic.

Bibliography

Snyder, Solomon H. ed. Drugs & Pain, Encyclopedia of Psychoactive Drugs Series 2. New York: Chelsea House Publishers, 1978.

American Pharmaceutical Company. Handbook of Nonprescription Drugs. 10th ed. (1993).

Turkington, Carol. Poisons and Antidotes. New York: Maple-Vail Book Manufacturing Group, 1994.

Work Sample & Commentary: *A Geographical Report*

The task

Students were assigned to write a report for science class using at least five sources, only two of which could be encyclopedias. They were encouraged to include clarifications or illustrations of key points and a complete bibliography.

Circumstances of performance

This sample of student work was produced under the following conditions:

√ alone   in a group

   in class   √ as homework

√ with teacher feedback   √ with peer feedback

   timed   √ opportunity for revision

What the work shows

S2 d Life Sciences Concepts: The student produces evidence that demonstrates understanding of the interdependence of organisms, such as…cooperation and competition among organisms in ecosystems; and human effects on the environment.

A The student pointed out the necessity of having rabbits at the vernal pools to eat and then spread the seeds of digested plants.

B The pressure placed on this ecosystem is noted in the initial question.

This work sample illustrates a standard-setting performance for the following parts of the standards:

S2 d Life Sciences Concepts: Interdependence of organisms.

S3 e Earth and Space Sciences Concepts: Natural resource management.

S5 a Scientific Thinking: Frame questions to distinguish cause and effect.

S5 b Scientific Thinking: Use concepts from Standards 1 to 4 to explain observations and phenomena.

S5 c Scientific Thinking: Use evidence from reliable sources.

S5 d Scientific Thinking: Consider alternative explanations.

S7 a Scientific Communication: Represent data and results in multiple ways.

S7 d Scientific Communication: Explain a scientific concept to other students.

S7 e Scientific Communication: Communicate in a form suited to the purpose and audience.

S8 c Scientific Investigation: Design.

S8 d Scientific Investigation: Secondary research.

A GEOGRAPHICAL CONFLICT

My report is on a very rare and unique wetland that many people do not even know exists. They occur only in a few places around the world.

My topic is created by a specific geographical condition. Vernal pools in San Diego occur only on the local mesas and terraces, where soil conditions allow, but these are the ideal place for much of the city's urban and agricultural development. Is it possible to find a balance between the two conflicting purposes of expansion and preservation? **B**

This raises an interesting question; how can you establish vernal pools being thought of as a geographical asset?

METHODS

To answer my question I had to get information on vernal pools: what they are, where they are, and how they are a sensitive natural habitat. Then I needed to examine how city expansion is affecting vernal pools, and if it is apt to continue. I needed to know what the City thinks about the problem and what they are planning to do.

First I looked for any information available on vernal pools at public libraries, but I couldn't find what I was looking for. The topic is apparently too obscure. Next I went to a university library that had an environmental department, to get as much information as possible (University of San Diego).

I also interviewed several authorities in the field: the district representative for the U.S. Army Corps of Engineers, the federal agency **J** responsible for the protection of wetlands; a senior environmental planner with the City of San Diego, who wrote the City's Resource Protection Ordinance

3

C The student offered further explanation of human impact on this ecosystem.

D E The student made suggestions to minimize the damage caused by development.

S3 e Earth and Space Sciences Concepts: The student produces evidence that demonstrates understanding of…natural resource management.

F G H The student constructed a strong argument for the protection of the vernal pools.

S5 a Scientific Thinking: The student frames questions to distinguish cause and effect….

S5 b Scientific Thinking: The student uses concepts from Science Standards 1 to 4 to explain a variety of observations and phenomena.

I The student used conceptual information here and throughout the work to explain the pools and to develop the view of these wetlands as a geographical asset.

The quotations from the Science performance descriptions in this commentary are excerpted. The complete performance descriptions are shown on pages 82-85.

The standards for middle school are set at a level of performance approximately equivalent to the end of eighth grade and for high school at the end of tenth grade. It is expected that some students might achieve these levels earlier and others later than these grades. It is the expected quality of work rather than the age or grade of the student that govern the selection of work to illustrate the standards. This work sample appears in *New Standards Performance Standards* Volume 2 to illustrate a standard-setting performance for writing a report for the English Language Arts standards at the middle school level. The conceptual understanding in science, however, is at the level expected for high school. Thus, we have included the piece again here despite the age or grade of the student who produced it.

Physical Sciences Concepts

S2 Life Sciences Concepts

S3 Earth and Space Sciences Concepts

Scientific Connections and Applications

S5 Scientific Thinking

Scientific Tools and Technologies

S7 Scientific Communication

S8 Scientific Investigation

A Geographical Report

(RPO); the Station botanist at Miramar Naval Air Station, who is in charge of their vernal pool management plan on the land that has the largest number of pools remaining in the City of San Diego; a biologist working for RECON (Regional Environmental Consultants), a firm which is mapping the vernal pools for the City of Hemet, (another city in San Diego County facing the same issues); and finally a geographer working for SANDAG (San Diego Association of Governments), a regional organization that gathers, records, and analyzes data associated with regional planning and environmental issues. They answered many questions and offered their own ideas and information, including additional articles on my subject. I looked at several maps and photos of vernal pool locations, and charts of changing land use.

To decide how much education may be needed about vernal pools, I made a questionnaire, and surveyed two classrooms of elementary students, and a group of forty-two adults, trying to cover most age groups.

WHAT VERNAL POOLS ARE

Vernal pools are a unique and rare form of wetland. Wetlands are areas that are covered or soaked by water enough to support plants that grow only in moist ground. Some examples of wetlands are bogs, swamps, marshes, and edges of lakes and streams. These are what people think of when they hear "wetland". But vernal pools are different than these other types of wetlands. They are located on dry and flat places. No one would expect to find a wetland in such a dry area! **I**

San Diego vernal pools are surrounded by small mounds called "mima mounds". The name mima mounds comes from the Mima Prairie near Olympia, Washington. People don't know for sure how mima mounds are formed. Some

4

think that they were formed by gophers piling up the earth. Others think that ice wedges from glaciers caused the upheaval, or maybe the wind pushed loose dirt, catching in clumps of shrubs. Mounds can be found on prairies or terraces with a hardpan or clay layer underneath.

Vernal pools are depressions between the mima mounds. In winter the pools are filled by rain storms. In spring the pools look their best, when plants are in full splendor. By summer the pools are dry and look only like a dry pothole. (See illustration of pool cycles and typical cross section.) A vernal pool does not dry by soaking into the ground; the layer of clay or rock underneath the pool prevents the water from soaking through. Instead they dry out from evaporation, or use by the plants. The mima mounds are not impervious so one pool tends to drain into another. Therefore, the pools have to be on flat land; the pools cannot be on a slope or the water would run off, and the pools would not be filled.

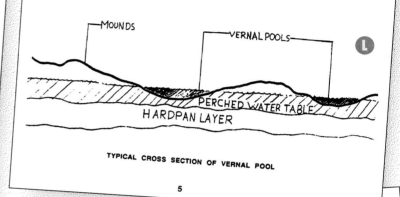

TYPICAL CROSS SECTION OF VERNAL POOL

5

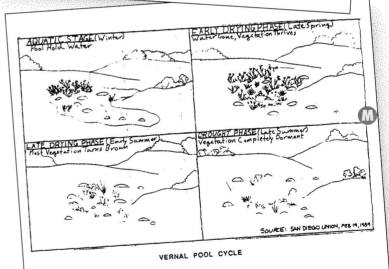

VERNAL POOL CYCLE

WHY VERNAL POOLS ARE SO IMPORTANT

Vernal pools are a very rare, specific habitat. Hardly any are left, so we don't have many to lose. There used to be vernal pools on many of the mesas and terraces of San Diego County, and the Central Valley of California. Now there are almost no vernal pools in the Central Valley, and an estimated 97% have been lost in San Diego County. An estimated 80% of the remaining pools in San Diego are located on Miramar Naval Air Station. (See map, next page.)

6

S5c Scientific Thinking: The student uses evidence from reliable sources to develop descriptions, explanations....

J **K** The student did not limit the work to what could be found at public libraries, but conducted interviews and a significant literature search to find the information needed.

S5d Scientific Thinking: The student proposes, recognizes, analyzes, considers, and critiques alternative explanations; and distinguishes between fact and opinion.

K Consideration of alternative explanations or solutions is not evident in the text itself, but the depth and breadth of the bibliography suggest that the work took into account a diversity of ideas.

S7a Scientific Communication: The student represents data and results in multiple ways, such as...graphs; drawings, diagrams, and artwork; technical...writing; and selects the most effective way to convey the scientific information.

The student used a combination of clear writing, diagrams, and references to other portions of the work to clearly communicate the structure and cycles of these pools.

L **M** **N** The diagrams are particularly effective.

A Geographical Report

S7d Scientific Communication: The student explains a scientific concept...to other students.

L **M** These drawings, which explain the cross-section of a vernal pool and the vernal pool cycle, are especially good examples.

S7e Scientific Communication: The student communicates in a form suited to the purpose and the audience....

Throughout the work, the text succeeds in explaining and persuading.

S8c Scientific Investigation: The student demonstrates scientific competence by completing a design project.

S8d Scientific Investigation: The student demonstrates scientific competence by completing a secondary research project.

A full investigation includes:

• Questions that can be studied using the resources available.

• Procedures that are safe, humane, and ethical; and that respect privacy and property rights.

• Data that have been collected and recorded (see also Science Standard 6) in ways that others can verify, and analyzed using skills expected at this grade level (see also Mathematics Standard 4).

Throughout the work, the student left a clear path for another student to follow in order to replicate the investigation or verify the conclusions.

• Data and results that have been represented (see also Science Standard 7) in ways that fit the context.

• Recommendations, decisions, and conclusions based on evidence.

E **N** The student argued from evidence to draw conclusions and make recommendations in a way that is focused and coherent.

• Acknowledgment of references and contributions of others.

O

• Results that are communicated appropriately to audiences.

• Reflection and defense of conclusions and recommendations from other sources and peer review.

Peer review is not included in the work. However, the extensive communication with experts shows that the conclusions were informed, in part, with the help of iterative external review.

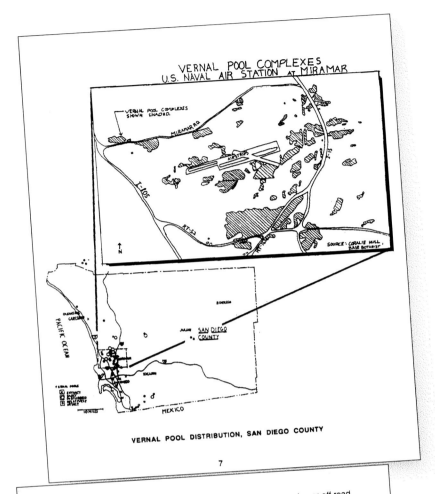

VERNAL POOL COMPLEXES
U.S. NAVAL AIR STATION AT MIRAMAR

VERNAL POOL DISTRIBUTION, SAN DIEGO COUNTY

7

C It does not take much to disturb a vernal pool. Even grazing or off road vehicle use in the summer, when pool species are dormant and people could think they are just a dry hole, can damage them. Most are disturbed by grading and flattening of their habitat, or by breakup of the impervious layer. With just flat land there would be no depressions for vernal pools to form; what would form would be "vernal mud". With no impervious layer the water would just sink into the ground, and would be there only for a short period of time, not enough for wetland plants.

The mima mounds have to be protected too. If the watershed for the pools is changed, the condition of the pools changes. If there isn't enough water from runoff, then all plant or animal life in them disappears, because they need enough moisture at the right time, to live. If there is too much water, then the pool may turn into another kind of wetland, such as a bog.

Although people have begun to study them, there is still a lot to learn. One thing scientists know is that they are a part of a larger environment. Many **F** animals travel from other areas to feed on plants or animals , or drink from the vernal pools. For example, water fowl from many other places will stop at the pools to eat the fairy shrimp and snack on the plants.

Vernal pools have a large assortment of rare and exotic flora and fauna (plants and animals). Five of them are on the federal list of endangered **G** species, and one more is a candidate for listing. The plants and animals in vernal pools are unusual because they have only developed recently compared to other changes in evolution. As scientists study the pools more intently they are finding more and more unknown species. There are temporary pools in other places around the world, but California's vernal pools are different because of their long drought phase, which causes the plants and animals to adapt to the climate. They go into a dormant phase. For example, fairy shrimp

8

A Geographical Report

lay eggs before the drought which hatch when it gets moist enough to be active. Some plants, in a short period of time, develop seeds; others appear to die out, but quickly sprout again from the rain. Many of these species cannot survive outside vernal pools, and some are "endemic" (species found only in a very restricted geographical area).

PROTECTION TECHNIQUES

The first step is to try to keep development away from vernal pools. But to do this you first need to know where the pools are. Thanks to regional mapping efforts, existing vernal pools have been fairly well identified in San Diego County.

There are already laws against disturbances of vernal pools. You could go to jail or get fined a large sum of money for disturbing a wetland. The U.S. Fish and Wildlife Service protects the listed endangered species present, and the U.S. Army Corps of Engineers makes sure you don't fill any kind of wetland habitat, including vernal pools. The local office of the U.S. Army Corps of Engineers has submitted a proposal to Washington for a stricter permit process for vernal pools.

When possible the vernal pools should be part of a large preserve of open space. That way the pools would not be isolated islands, but part of their natural communities, and would be protected by a buffer of distance. Fences should not be put directly around the vernal pools unless it cannot be avoided, because it would keep some animals out, such as rabbits which spread plant seeds around when they eat them.

It is important to educate people about vernal pools so they know how important they are and what they look like, and so they know how to preserve

them. To see how much education may be needed in San Diego, I surveyed ninety-two people (forty-two adults and fifty elementary students to try to cover all age groups). I asked them if they had heard of vernal pools, and if they knew what they were. About 21% thought they had heard of them, but only 7% really knew what they were. (See pie chart.) I found that much education is needed.

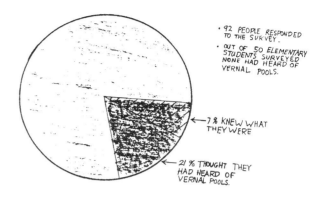

- 92 PEOPLE RESPONDED TO THE SURVEY.
- OUT OF 50 ELEMENTARY STUDENTS SURVEYED NONE HAD HEARD OF VERNAL POOLS.

← 7% KNEW WHAT THEY WERE

← 21% THOUGHT THEY HAD HEARD OF VERNAL POOLS.

SURVEY RESULTS

At N.A.S. Miramar the Station botanist has been putting articles dealing with vernal pools in almost every issue of the base newspaper. Now most people on the base know about vernal pools, and know how valuable they are.

RECOGNIZING AN ASSET

Education is a key to preserving vernal pools. Vernal pools are very unique and we do not have many to lose. Making new ones does not work. Studies done at the University of California, Santa Barbara, have shown that after five years their complexity goes down.

First, vernal pools must be protected. There could be different ranges of accessibility, from remote (available to research only), somewhat accessible (good for guided seasonal visits), to readily accessible (which may have to be protected by fencing or supervision). The most accessible ones would be a great educational opportunity for the general public. The pools closer to development could be developed into nature centers, with raised boardwalks to protect the habitat, as is done over the hot springs in Yellowstone. (See illustration.)

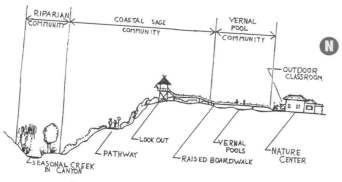

CROSS SECTION OF POSSIBLE NATURE CENTER

Interpretive signs and docents could provide information. Being very unique, vernal pools would make interesting learning centers. People would learn how the plants and animals adapt to the seasonal changes. This would teach people the importance of vernal pools, how complex they are, how to identify them, and how to preserve them when wet or dry. A park in the Sacramento area has an adjacent vernal pool with hiking trails around it; and it seems to work there because the people there know how important and delicate it is.

Ecotourism, a popular concept now, would be another idea. San Diego is a place where tourists already come. The very climate and geography that brings people here is what created vernal pools. Ecotourism would be easy to add to the other attractions, and would indirectly benefit the city. A tour company might be authorized to place advertisements to bring people to learn the importance of vernal pools and their ecosystem. With many people outside San Diego knowing about vernal pools and concerned about their well-being, there would be widespread support for vernal pool protection.

CONCLUSION

The problem of endangering vernal pools will not go away, because the City will need more land to develop. However, vernal pools remain a rare and unique wetland, and need protection. Even though there are laws made to protect them, pools are still being lost. Education is needed. Widespread education showing how important vernal pools are, and how easy they are to disturb, will create widespread support for protection.

A balance between expansion and preservation will not come easily, but if the public views vernal pools as a geographical asset, the balance will shift toward long-term vernal pool preservation.

A Geographical Report

K

BIBLIOGRAPHY

Ashworth, William. "Vernal Pool". The Encyclopedia of Environmental Studies, 1991, p. 412.

Barbour, Michael G. and Major, Jack, ed. Terrestrial Vegetation of California. New York: John Wiley and Sons, 1977.

Baskin, Yvonne. "California's Ephemeral Vernal Pools May be a Good Model for Speciation". BioScience, vol. 44 no. 6, June 1994, pp. 384-388.

City of San Diego Mima Mound-Vernal Pool Guidelines. July 20, 1993.

City of San Diego Municipal Code, Section 101.0462. "Resource Protection Ordinance".

Franklin, Jerry F., and Dyrness, C.T.. "Natural Vegetation of Oregon and Washington". Portland, Oregon: Pacific Northwest Forest and Range Experiment Station (General Technical Report PNW-8), 1973.

Hutchison, Steven M. "A Phenomenon of Spring: Vernal Pools". Environment Southwest, no. 480, Winter 1978.

Jenny, Hans. "The Soil Resource: Origin and Behavior". New York; Springer, 1980, pp. 228-231, 280-282, 356.

Martin, Glen. "Spring Fever". Discover, vol. 11 no. 3, March 1990, pp. 70-74.

Osment, Noel. "Dwindling Treasures: Unique Desert / Marsh Habitats Vanishing Fast". San Diego Union, February 19, 1989.

"Regulatory Permit Program". U.S. Army Corps of Engineers, Los Angeles District (SPL PAM 1130-2-1), Nov., 1993.

SANDAG. "A Look at San Diego's Future". INFO, January-February, 1994.

SANDAG. "Land Use in the San Diego Region". INFO, January-February, 1993.

White, Scott D. "Vernal Pools in the San Jacinto Valley". Fremontia, vol. 22 no. 4, October 1994, pp. 17-19.

Zedler, Paul H.. "The Ecology of Southern California Vernal Pools: A Community Profile". U.S.D.I. Fish and Wildlife Service, Washington D.C. (Biological Report 85 (7.11)), May 1987.

13

INTERVIEWS

_____ Senior research analyst. SANDAG (San Diego Association of Governments). January 6, 1995.

_____ Station botanist. U.S. Naval Air Station, Miramar. November 21, 1994.

_____ Director of biological services. RECON (Regional Environmental Consultants). December 6, 1994.

_____ Biologist. U.S. Army Corps of Engineers, San Diego Field Office. November 23, 1994.

_____ Senior Planner. City of San Diego, Environmental Services Department. December 7, 1994.

O

ACKNOWLEDGMENTS

First I would like to thank the library at the University of San Diego for supplying me with information and help. I would also like to thank all the people I interviewed, especially _____ for supplying me with two slides of a vernal pool. Also my uncle, _____ Department of Geography, Indiana University-Purdue University, Indianapolis, for information on mima mounds; and _____ Biology Department, University of San Diego, and _____ RECON, for recommending people to interview. I would like to thank Ms. _____ my former sixth grade teacher, and _____ Elementary School, for letting their classes take my survey.

Physical Sciences Concepts

S2 Life Sciences Concepts

S3 Earth and Space Sciences Concepts

Scientific Connections and Applications

S5 Scientific Thinking

Scientific Tools and Technologies

S7 Scientific Communication

S8 Scientific Investigation

Work Sample & Commentary: *Compost*

The task

Students were asked to design and conduct an experimental project that would improve the environment at their high school. The assignment, given to students in an environmental science class, followed a unit on the chemistry and biology of ground and water pollution.

Circumstances of performance

This sample of student work was produced under the following conditions:

alone	√ in a group
√ in class	as homework
with teacher feedback	√ with peer feedback
timed	√ opportunity for revision

The quotations from the Science performance descriptions in this commentary are excerpted. The complete performance descriptions are shown on pages 82-85.

What the work shows

S2d Life Sciences Concepts: The student produces evidence that demonstrates understanding of the interdependence of organisms, such as...cooperation and competition among organisms in ecosystems....

A B The work shows understanding of the interdependence of organisms, including populations, ecosystems, and food webs.

S4a Scientific Connections and Applications: The student produces evidence that demonstrates understanding of the big ideas and unifying concepts, such as...models, form and function; change and constancy; and cause and effect.

C The compost bottle was a small scale model in which the variables could be controlled, then scaled up to the compost pile recommended in the conclusions.

This work sample illustrates a standard-setting performance for the following parts of the standards:

S2d **Life Sciences Concepts:** Interdependence of organisms.

S4a **Scientific Connections and Applications:** Big ideas and unifying concepts.

S6a **Scientific Tools and Technologies:** Use technology and tools.

S6d **Scientific Tools and Technologies:** Acquire information from multiple sources.

S7a **Scientific Communication:** Represent data and results in multiple ways.

S8a **Scientific Investigation:** Controlled experiment.

Our Compost Pile Project:

A Plan: We want to find out what kinds of insects help compost turn from just waste to useable mulch and soil helper. We also would like to know what conditions help to speed up the breaking down of the compost. Our final goal is to recommend the best placement of the school compost pile we are recommending to Mr. W___. This will depend on light and water needed and if the pile needs insects that he might see as not desirable near a school. roaches, flies etc.)

Procedure:

E 1. The materials we used for the Compost Column were : 8, 2 liter bottles and the cutting thing (with razor blade) and glue guns. We used the instructions for making the bottles from the Bottle Biology book.

2. Construct two bottles (see our drawing)

3. We filled the compost part of the bottles with grass clippings, fruit waste, and leaves. we put the same stuff in both bottles. We mixed the compost up in a pail and placed half in one and half in the other. We also measured the mass of the bottle with the compost in it to make certain. We adjusted the amount to account for a 12 gram difference in the bottles because of extra glue on one.

4. We put one bottle in a direct sunlight part of the room and the other in a location that only has sunlight in the morning. We selected right in the middle window in the back of the room facing south with full sun from 7AM until 6PM and on the east side of Mr. G___'s room where there is sun only from 7AM until about noon. We found that the south window also gets about 10 degrees hotter. This may effect our results. (these two locations are similar to the sun times of our two proposed sites for the school compost pile).

5. We watered both bottles and recorded the amount of water added each day. This needed to be the same in both bottles because we did not want to get more than one variable in our light experiment.

I 5. We took out a small sample of the compost (YUCK) and examined it with a hand lens and the microscope). WASH your hands and only do this again when you really have to! We recorded our observations in the data. (later we voted to use gloves).

6. We did this for 2 weeks until we could identify some of the animals that came in with the compost and are helping to decompose the stuff (we think). We used a book on biology to help with identification. This was the most difficult part.

J 7. We were asked to throw the bottles away (it was very wasteful) after five weeks because they seemed to be the home of a big bunch of fruit flies. We decided to keep one compost column going and cover the top with a fine mesh cloth to keep the fruit flies in and continue our experiment. Also we wanted to use it when we present our idea of a compost pile to Mr. W

D The discussion of the earwigs' niche shows an understanding of the interdependence of growth, population stress, and predator/prey relationships, all evidence of an understanding of change and constancy, and of cause and effect.

S6a Scientific Tools and Technologies: The student uses technology and tools (such as traditional laboratory equipment...) to observe and measure...organisms and phenomena, directly....

E The students created the tools to make this investigation possible, overcoming the obstacle and impracticality of two full-size compost piles.

S6d Scientific Tools and Technologies: The student acquires information from multiple sources such as print...and experimentation.

B D

Physical Sciences Concepts

Life Sciences Concepts **S2**

Earth and Space Sciences Concepts

Scientific Connections and Applications **S4**

Scientific Thinking

Scientific Tools and Technologies **S6**

Scientific Communication **S7**

Scientific Investigation **S8**

Compost

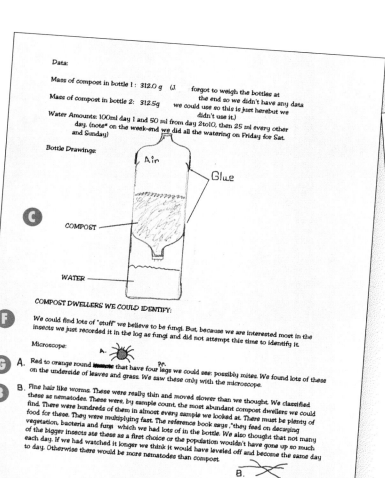

Data:

Mass of compost in bottle 1: 312.0 g   (J. forgot to weigh the bottles at the end so we didn't have any data we could use so this is just here but we didn't use it)

Mass of compost in bottle 2: 312.5g

Water Amounts: 100ml day 1 and 50 ml from day 2 to 10, then 25 ml every other day. (note* on the week-end we did all the watering on Friday for Sat. and Sunday)

Bottle Drawings:

Air
Glue
COMPOST
WATER

COMPOST DWELLERS WE COULD IDENTIFY:

We could find lots of "stuff" we believe to be fungi. But, because we are interested most in the insects we just recorded it in the log as fungi and did not attempt this time to identify it.

Microscope:

A. Red to orange round insects that have four legs we could see: possibly mites. We found lots of these on the underside of leaves and grass. We saw these only with the microscope.

B. Fine hair like worms. These were really thin and moved slower than we thought. We classified these as nematodes. These were, by sample count, the most abundant compost dwellers we could find. There were hundreds of them in almost every sample we looked at. There must be plenty of food for these. They were multiplying fast. The reference book says, "they feed on decaying vegetation, bacteria and fungi which we had lots of in the bottle. We also thought that not many of the bigger insects ate these as a first choice or the population wouldn't have gone up so much each day. If we had watched it longer we think it would have leveled off and become the same day to day. Otherwise there would be more nematodes than compost.

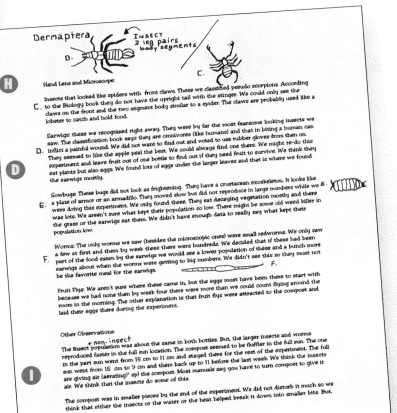

Dermaptera

INSECT
3 leg pairs
body segments

Hand Lens and Microscope:

C. Insects that looked like spiders with front claws. These we classified pseudo scorpions. According to the Biology book they do not have the upright tail with the stinger. We could only see the claws on the front and the two segment body similar to a spider. The claws are probably used like a lobster to catch and hold food.

D. Earwigs: these we recognised right away. They were by far the most fearsome looking insects we saw. The classification book says they are omnivores (like humans) and that in biting a human can inflict a painful wound. We did not want to find out and voted to use rubber gloves from then on. They seemed to like the apple peal the best. We could always find one there. We might re-do this experiment and leave fruit out of one bottle to find out if they need fruit to survive. We think they eat plants but also eggs. We found lots of eggs under the larger leaves and that is where we found the earwigs mostly.

E. Sowbugs: These bugs did not look as frightening. They have a crustacean exoskeleton. It looks like a plate of armor or an armadillo. They moved slow but did not reproduce in large numbers while we were doing this experiment. We only found three. They eat decaying vegetation mostly and there was lots. We aren't sure what kept their population so low. There might be some old weed killer in the grass or the earwigs eat them. We didn't have enough data to really say what kept their population low.

F. Worms: The only worms we saw (besides the microscopic ones) were small redworms. We only saw a few at first and them by week three there were hundreds. We decided that if these had been part of the food eaten by the earwigs we would see a lower population of these and a bunch more earwigs about when the worms were getting to big numbers. We didn't see this so they must not be the favorite meal for the earwigs.

Fruit Flys: We aren't sure where these came in, but the eggs must have been there to start with because we had none then by week four there were more than we could count flying around the room in the morning. The other explanation is that fruit flys were attracted to the compost and laid their eggs there during the experiment.

Other Observations:
The insect population was about the same in both bottles. But, the larger insects and worms reproduced faster in the full sun location. The compost seemed to be fluffier in the full sun. The one in the part sun went from 15 cm to 11 cm and stayed there for the rest of the experiment. The full sun went from 15 cm to 9 cm and then back up to 11 before the last week. We think the insects are giving air (aerating? sp) the compost. Most manuals say you have to turn compost to give it air. We think that the insects do some of this.

The compost was in smaller pieces by the end of the experiment. We did not disturb it much so we think that either the insects or the water or the heat helped break it down into smaller bits. But,

since the bits went smaller faster in the sunny bottle, the sun/temperature may have had a lot to do with it

CONCLUSIONS:

Our recommendation is that the compost pile be placed on the south side of the building just behind the driver's ed. simulator trailer. This location gets full sun all day and is close to a water faucet. The insects we saw with our experiment were not harmful. We saw no roaches or house flies or maggots. We do think that you should only use yard waste and maybe fruit waste from the cafeteria (salad stuff is OK too). We did not use any meat food waste and that might draw more flies. If we have time we will experiment to find out which insects do the most good in a compost pile and see what we can add to the pile to make their numbers go up. We think that it is a waste to throw all that yard waste from all the grass away when we could make compost that other's could use for gardens or soil building. Since our experiments showed that the full sunlight bottle broke into smaller pieces faster and seemed to decompose faster, the full sun location would be better. This is because we would like the compost to break down quicker so that it can be used. The smell of the compost goes down after the first week. But, if you are constantly adding material to the pile it may stay a little smelly. The only disadvantage of this location is that the wind usually blows out of the southwest and the pile will be upwind from the new building. We thought that by placing it by the simulator it would be far enough away (112 feet we measured) to dilute the smell and not cause a problem. The smell is the only bad effect of this location. The location was the best sun and the closest to water. We think we could find a way to cut down the smell if it became a problem. We are willing to contact local lumberyards to see if they will donate the chickenwire and the 2 x 4s to construct a compost pile that we can start using in May. Thank you for your time and reading our lab report.

S7a Scientific Communication: The student represents data and results in multiple ways, such as…drawings…[and] technical writing….

F G The precision of the language, "we believe to be fungi" and "possibly mites," is excellent.

C H Drawings are used effectively.

S8a Scientific Investigation: The student demonstrates scientific competence by completing a controlled experiment. A full investigation includes:

• Questions that can be studied using the resources available.

The work shows consideration of appropriate resources by scaling down the compost pile to conduct the investigation accurately and practically in a pop bottle.

• Procedures that are safe, humane, and ethical; and that respect privacy and property rights.

I J The work also shows attention to safety and consideration for others.

• Data that have been collected and recorded (see also Science Standard 6) in ways that others can verify, and analyzed using skills expected at this grade level (see also Mathematics Standard 4).

This work shows thorough and appropriate documentation, both in the procedures and in the descriptions of the organisms that provide enough detailed information for others to replicate the investigation.

• Data and results that have been represented (see also Science Standard 7) in ways that fit the context.

C F G H

The writing contains some spelling and grammatical errors, but these do not detract from the quality of the report.

• Recommendations, decisions, and conclusions based on evidence.

I The conclusion is drawn from evidence.

• Acknowledgment of references and contributions of others.

B E

• Results that are communicated appropriately to audiences.

K The conclusion of the report is an appropriate recommendation to the school principal, "Mr. W.," as to where the school should keep a compost pile.

• Reflection and defense of conclusions and recommendation from other sources and peer review.

Evidence of peer review is not included in this report.

Introduction to the performance standards for

Applied Learning

Applied Learning focuses on the capabilities people need to be productive members of society, as individuals who apply the knowledge gained in school and elsewhere to analyze problems and propose solutions, to communicate effectively and coordinate action with others, and to use the tools of the information age workplace. It connects the work students do in school with the demands of the twenty-first century workplace.

As a newer focus of study, Applied Learning does not have a distinct professional constituency producing content standards on which performance standards can be built. However, the Secretary's Commission on Achieving Necessary Skills (SCANS) laid a foundation for the field in its report, *Learning a Living: A Blueprint for High Performance* (1992) which defined the concept of "Workplace Know-how." We worked from this foundation and from comparable international work to produce our own "Framework for Applied Learning" (New Standards, 1994). That framework delineated nine areas of competence and spelled out their elements. The nine areas of competence were as follows:

• Collecting, analyzing, and organizing information;

• Communicating ideas and information;

• Planning and organizing resources;

• Working with others and in teams;

• Solving problems;

• Using mathematical ideas and techniques;

• Using technology;

• Teaching and learning on demand;

• Understanding and designing systems.

The Applied Learning performance standards have been built upon this framework. The standards have also been built on the experience of the Fort Worth Independent School District's applied learning initiative and the application projects developed by Mountlake Terrace High School in Washington.

We adopted the approach of developing distinct standards for Applied Learning rather than weaving them through the standards for the core subject areas. The advantage of establishing distinct standards for Applied Learning is that it focuses attention on the requirements of these standards and asserts an explicit role for Applied Learning as a domain for assessment and reporting of student achievement. "Cross-curricular" standards run the risk of being absorbed and lost within the expectations of the different subjects. However, the disadvantage of this approach is that it may be interpreted as advocating the development of Applied Learning as a subject in its own right to be studied in isolation from subject content. That is not the intention of these standards. We do not advocate development of Applied Learning as a separate subject. We expect that the work students do to meet the Applied

Learning performance standards will take place generally within the context of a subject or will draw on content from more than one subject area. This expectation is stated in the performance description for **A1**, Problem Solving.

There are five performance standards for Applied Learning:

A1 Problem Solving;

A2 Communication Tools and Techniques;

A3 Information Tools and Techniques;

A4 Learning and Self-management Tools and Techniques;

A5 Tools and Techniques for Working With Others.

A1, Problem Solving is the centerpiece of the standards. The performance description defines problem solving projects focused on productive activity and organized around three kinds of problem solving:

• Design a product, service or system in which the student identifies needs that could be met by new products, services, or systems and creates solutions for meeting them;

• Improve a System in which the student develops an understanding of the way systems of people, machines, and processes work; troubleshoots problems in their operation and devises strategies for improving their effectiveness;

• Plan and organize an event or an activity in which the student takes responsibility for all aspects of planning and organizing an event or an activity from concept to completion.

The performance description specifies the criteria for each kind of problem solving project. These criteria become progressively more demanding from elementary school to high school.

The four "tools and techniques" standards are designed to work in concert with the Problem Solving standard. Each of these standards describes tools and techniques that are needed for success in completing projects of the kinds outlined above.

The tools and techniques described in **A2**-**A5** (such as gathering information, making a multi-media presentation, learning from models, and working as a member of a self-directed team) are only meaningful when considered in the context of work that has a genuine purpose and audience. The key to effective use of these tools and techniques is the capacity to put them to use in an integrated way in the course of completing a real task. It is critical, therefore, that they be learned and used in such contexts rather than practiced in a piecemeal way as skills for their own

sake. Students are expected to demonstrate their achievement of the tools and techniques standards in the context of problem solving projects. This is reflected in the examples listed under the performance descriptions. At the same time, it is unlikely that any one project will allow students to demonstrate their achievement in relation to all of the standards. This is evident from the work samples and commentaries. In fact, it is likely that a project that attempts to cover all of the parts of the standards will accomplish none of them well.

The Applied Learning performance standards reflect the nine areas of competence defined in the "Framework for Applied Learning." But the match is not complete. **M6**, **M8**, **S6**, and **S8** embody many of the competencies that were defined by the "Framework for Applied Learning" in "Using mathematical tools and techniques" and "Using technology." These competencies have not been duplicated in Applied Learning. However, the Applied Learning standards do include an explicit requirement that students use information technology to assist in gathering, organizing, and presenting information. At the high school level, the requirements include using appropriate software to create documents, data bases, and spreadsheets, in addition to using on-line sources. Given the importance of ensuring all students develop the capacity to make effective use of information technology, we resolved that the overlap among the standards in this area was warranted. (See "Introduction to the performance standards for Science," page 80, for discussion of the resource issues related to this requirement.)

Another area in which we decided that some overlap was warranted relates to **A2**. The first part of this standard, which involves an oral presentation, is similar to one of the requirements of the Speaking, Listening, and Viewing standard in English Language Arts (**E3**). The difference is that the Applied Learning standard focuses explicitly on presenting project plans or results to an audience with expertise in the relevant subject matter, while the purpose and audience for the presentation are not specified in **E3**. As the cross-referencing of examples under the performance descriptions indicates, oral presentations that meet the requirements of **A2** a may also satisfy the requirements of **E3** c; however, the reverse would not necessarily be the case. **A2** b is also similar to the report included in **E3** c. However, **A2** b requires a specific purpose and audience, whereas these are not specified by the Writing standard. Accordingly, a report produced to meet the requirements of **A2** b may also satisfy the requirements of **E2** c, but the reverse would not necessarily be true.

The capacities defined by the tools and techniques standards (**A2**-**A5**) are difficult to pin down. There is a tendency to describe them in terms of general dispositions that render them almost impossible to assess in any credible way. Each part of these standards is defined in terms of a work product or performance that students can use to provide concrete evidence of their achievement. The overall set of products and performances required to meet the standards is similar at each grade level, but the specific requirements differ and grow in demand from elementary to high school. (See "Appendix IV: The Grade Levels Compared: Applied Learning," page 168.)

The first year of developmental testing of Applied Learning portfolios in 1995-96 provided an opportunity to test these performance standards (as they were presented in the *Consultation Draft*) in practice. Students in about 50 classrooms conducted projects designed around the standards. Their experience and the experience of the teachers who supported them was a valuable source of information for refining the performance descriptions. Refinements were also made in response to reviews by representatives of business and industry groups and community youth organizations, such as 4-H, Girl Scouts of the U.S.A., Boy Scouts of America, Junior Achievement, and Girls and Boys Clubs of America. The refinements were largely confined to the detail of the performance descriptions, but there were two more significant changes, both related to **A3**. The first was the definition of more explicit requirements for using information technology, especially at the high school level, in response to comments from business and industry representatives. The second was the inclusion of a specific requirement for "research" as set out in **A3** a. Research was implicit in the draft performance standards. The decision to make it explicit arose in the process of review of student projects where it was clear that the successful projects were those in which students had invested energy in research and could demonstrate that research in the work they produced.

Experience in using the standards to shape student work raised several issues. It was notable that most projects focused on "design" and on "planning and organizing." There were fewer examples of "improving a system." This was not surprising, but indicates the need to focus attention on gathering examples of such projects.

The circumstances in which the projects were conducted varied markedly. Some projects were initiated by the teacher and some were initiated by students; some projects were conducted by whole classes, some by small groups of students, and some by individuals; some projects were conducted as part of classwork and some were conducted largely outside class. It was clear, however, that regardless of how a project was initiated, a critical part of its success was the development of a sense of responsibility among the students involved for figuring out the work that needed to be done to complete the project and for making sure that the work got done. What was less clear were the relative merits of different arrangements of whole class, small group, and individual projects. A further question was the appropriate level of scaffolding of projects by teachers and the degree of scaffolding that is appropriate at different grade levels. Our capacity to resolve this last issue was complicated by the fact that, for most of the teachers and students involved, these were the first projects of this sort they had ever undertaken. The work samples and commentaries should be read with this fact in mind. These are issues that can only be resolved through practice and experience.

Performance Descriptions *Applied Learning*

A1 Problem Solving

Apply problem solving strategies in purposeful ways, both in situations where the problem and desirable solutions are clearly evident and in situations requiring a creative approach to achieve an outcome.

The student conducts projects involving at least two of the following kinds of problem solving each year and, over the course of high school, conducts projects involving all three kinds of problem solving.

- Design a Product, Service, or System: Identify needs that could be met by new products, services, or systems; and create solutions for meeting them.
- Improve a System: Develop an understanding of the way systems of people, machines, and processes work; troubleshoot problems in their operation; and devise strategies for improving their effectiveness.
- Plan and Organize an Event or an Activity: Take responsibility for all aspects of planning and organizing an event or activity from concept to completion, making good use of the resources of people, time, money, and materials and facilities.

Each project should involve subject matter related to the standards for English Language Arts, and/or Mathematics, and/or Science, and/or other appropriate subject content.

Design a Product, Service, or System
A1 a The student designs and creates a product, service, or system to meet an identified need; that is, the student:

- develops a design proposal that:
- shows how the ideas for the design were developed;
- reflects awareness of similar work done by others and of relevant design standards and regulations;
- justifies the choices made in finalizing the design with reference, for example, to functional, aesthetic, social, economic, and environmental considerations;
- establishes criteria for evaluating the product, service, or system;
- uses appropriate conventions to represent the design;
- plans and implements the steps needed to create the product, service, or system;
- makes adjustments as needed to conform with specified standards or regulations regarding quality or safety;
- evaluates the product, service, or system in terms of the criteria established in the design proposal, and with reference to:
- information gathered from sources such as impact studies, product testing, or market research;
- comparisons with similar work done by others.

Examples of designing a product, service, or system include:
- Design software for managing portfolio work. **2b, 4a**
- Design an electricity-powered vehicle to enter in a competition. **2a, 5a, S1d, S1e, S4a, S4b**
- Design a plan for development of a park recreation area. **2a, 2c, 5a, 5b, S3e, S4b**
- Design and build a staircase. **M2i, M6e, M6l, M8c**
- Design a market research service, providing advice on best-value products. **3b, 5b, M4b, M4c, M4d, M4e**
- Design a business plan for publication of a magazine. **M3a, M3i, M8**
- Design and build a cantilevered wooden deck. **2a, M2a, M2d, M2i, M6e, M6l, M8c**
- Design a tourist guide for the local area. **2c, 3b, 5c, E7b**
- Design a tutoring program in desktop publishing. **3b, 5b**

Improve a System
A1 b The student troubleshoots problems in the operation of a system in need of repair or devises and tests ways of improving the effectiveness of a system in operation; that is, the student:

- explains the structure of the system in terms of its:
- logic, sequences, and control;
- operating principles, that is, the mathematical, scientific, and/or organizational principles underlying the system;
- analyzes the way the system works, taking account of its functional, aesthetic, social, environmental, and commercial requirements, as appropriate, and using a relevant kind of modeling or systems analysis;
- evaluates the operation of the system, using qualitative methods and/or quantitative measurements of performance;
- develops and tests strategies to put the system back in operation and/or optimize its performance;
- evaluates the effectiveness of the strategies for improving the system and supports the evaluation with evidence.

Examples of troubleshooting problems in the operation of a system or improving the effectiveness of a system in operation include:
- Troubleshoot and repair faults in the operation of an automobile, tractor, or computer based communications system.
- Customize applications software for financial management to better suit a specific use. **2b, 4a, 5c**
- Improve the system of waste management in a community access area. **2c, S1c, S2d, S4b**
- Improve the yield of a farm or garden plot. **2a, 3a, S2b, S4b**
- Improve the system for emergency evacuation of the school. **2a, 2b, 5c**

Plan and Organize an Event or an Activity
A1 c The student plans and organizes an event or an activity; that is, the student:

- develops a planning schedule that:
- is sensible in terms of the goals of the event or activity;
- is logical and achievable;
- reflects research into relevant precedents and regulations;
- takes account of all relevant factors;
- communicates clearly so that a peer or colleague could use it;
- implements and adjusts the planning schedule in ways that:
- make efficient use of time, money, people, resources, facilities;
- reflect established priorities;
- respond effectively to unforeseen circumstances;
- evaluates the success of the event or activity using qualitative and/or quantitative methods;
- makes recommendations for planning and organizing subsequent similar events or activities.

Examples of planning and organizing an event or activity include:
- Organize a public exhibition of student artwork. **4a**
- Organize a weekend volunteer cleanup of a neighborhood. **3a**
- Arrange a series of career information seminars. **5a**
- Organize a community festival to promote local businesses.
- Organize a team sports tournament. **M1i, M5**
- Organize a schedule for practices and events at the school gymnasium and swimming pool, taking account of home and away games, junior varsity and varsity, and boys' and girls' teams. **M1i, M3a, M3i, M5**

To see how these performance descriptions compare with the expectations for elementary school and middle school, turn to pages 168-173.

The examples that follow the performance descriptions for each standard are examples of the work students might do to demonstrate their achievement. The examples also indicate the nature and complexity of activities that are appropriate to expect of students at the high school level.

The cross-references that follow the examples highlight examples for which the same activity, and possibly even the same piece of work, may enable students to demonstrate their achievement in relation to more than one standard. In some cases, the cross-references highlight examples of activities through which students might demonstrate their achievement in relation to standards for more than one subject matter.

A2 Communication Tools and Techniques

Communicate information and ideas in ways that are appropriate to the purpose and audience through spoken, written, and graphic means of expression.

A2 a The student makes an oral presentation of project plans or findings to an audience with expertise in the relevant subject matter; that is, the student:

• organizes the presentation in a logical way appropriate to its purpose;

• adjusts the style of presentation to suit its purpose and audience;

• speaks clearly and presents confidently;

• responds appropriately to questions from the audience;

• evaluates the effectiveness of the presentation and identifies appropriate revisions for a future presentation.

Examples of oral presentations include:

▲ A presentation of designs for a building or cantilevered wooden deck to an audience including an architect and civil engineer; or designs for a vehicle to an audience including a person with expertise in electronics. **1a, 5a, E3c**

▲ A presentation of proposals for design of a recreation area to the local parks authority. **1a, 2c, 5a, 5b, E3c**

▲ A presentation of findings of research into the system for emergency evacuation of the school to a panel including representatives of the police and fire departments. **1b, 2b, 5c, E3c**

▲ A presentation of a report on improving the yield of a farm or garden plot at an agricultural field day or horticultural show. **1b, 3a, E3c**

A2 b The student prepares a formal written proposal or report to an organization beyond the school; that is, the student:

• organizes the information in the proposal or report in a logical way appropriate to its purpose;

• produces the proposal or report in a format similar to that used in professionally produced documents for a similar purpose and audience.

Examples of written proposals and reports include:

▲ A proposal to a software design company for marketing software. **1a, 4a**

▲ A submission to a community organization in response to its request for a proposal to develop customized financial management software. **1b, 4a, 5c**

▲ A briefing for the school board on results of the investigation of the system for emergency evacuation of the school. **1b, 2a, 5c**

A2 c The student develops a multi-media presentation, combining text, images, and/or sound; that is, the student:

• selects an appropriate medium for each element of the presentation;

• uses the selected media skillfully, including editing and monitoring for quality;

• achieves coherence in the presentation as a whole;

• communicates the information effectively, testing audience response and revising the presentation accordingly.

Examples of multi-media presentations include:

▲ A presentation of proposals for design of a recreation area, combining video, graphics, and text. **1a, 2a, 5a, 5b**

▲ An oral presentation incorporating electronically produced graphics and videotape to explain proposals for improving waste management. **1b, E3c**

▲ A videotaped guide to tourist attractions in the area, combining music, still and moving images, and text. **1a, 3a, 3b, 5c**

Samples of student work that illustrate standard-setting performances for these standards can be found on pages 112-137.

The cross-references that follow the examples illustrate some of the ways by which a single Applied Learning project may provide a vehicle for demonstrating achievement of several parts of the standards. The cross-references are based on the examples that are linked to the Problem Solving standard. It is intended that students demonstrate their achievement of the four Tools and Techniques standards in conjunction with Problem Solving projects.

A3 Information Tools and Techniques

Use information gathering techniques, analyze and evaluate information, and use information technology to assist in collecting, analyzing, organizing, and presenting information.

A3 a The student gathers information to assist in completing project work; that is, the student:

• identifies potential sources of information to assist in completing the project;

• uses appropriate techniques to collect the information, e.g., considers sampling issues in conducting a survey;

• interprets and analyzes the information;

• evaluates the information in terms of completeness, relevance, and validity;

• shows evidence of research in the completed project.

Examples of gathering information to assist in completing project work include:

▲ Research information about soil types and their impact on productivity to assist in a project to improve the yield of a farm or garden plot. **1b, 2a**

▲ Research local public safety regulations to assist in organizing a weekend volunteer cleanup of a neighborhood. **1c**

▲ Research the history of local landmarks to assist in preparing a tourist guide for the local area. **1a, 2c, 3b, 5c**

A3 b The student uses on-line sources to exchange information for specific purposes; that is, the student:

• uses E-mail to correspond with peers and specialists in the subject matter of their projects;

• incorporates into E-mail correspondence data of different file types and applications.

A3 c The student uses word-processing software to produce a multi-page document; that is, the student:

• uses features of the software to create and edit the document;

• uses features of the software to format the document, including a table of contents, index, tabular columns, charts, and graphics;

• uses features of the software to create templates and style sheets for the document.

Examples of using word-processing software to produce a document include:

▲ Produce the proposal to the local parks authority for design of a recreation area. **1a, 2a, 5a**

▲ Produce a proposal to a software design company for marketing software. **1a, 2b, 4a**

▲ Produce submission to a community organization in response to a request for a proposal to develop customized financial management software. **1b, 2b, 3e, 4a, 5c**

A3 d The student writes, adds content to, and analyzes a data base program that uses a relational data base; that is, the student:

• writes a program capable of handling data with at least two files;

• creates macros to facilitate data entry, analysis, and manipulation;

• creates multiple report formats that include summary information;

• merges data from the data base with other files.

Examples of creating a data base include:

▲ Create a data base of volunteers for the weekend cleanup of a neighborhood. **1c, 3a**

▲ Create a data base of participants in a team sports tournament. **1c**

▲ Create a data base of works to be exhibited in a public exhibition of student artwork. **1c, 4a**

A3 e The student creates, edits, and analyzes a spreadsheet of information that displays data in tabular, numeric format and includes multiple graphs; that is, the student:

• creates a spreadsheet that displays the use of formulas and functions;

• uses features of the software to sort, arrange, display, and extract data for specific purposes;

• uses features of the software to create multiple spreadsheets and to synthesize the spreadsheets into a single presentation.

Examples of creating a spreadsheet include:

▲ Create a spreadsheet to record and analyze data related to the performance of a vehicle designed to enter in a competition. **1a, 2a, 5a**

▲ Create a spreadsheet as part of customizing applications software for financial management. **1b, 2b, 3c, 4a, 5c**

▲ Create a spreadsheet to record and analyze data related to improving the productivity of a farm or garden plot. **1b, 2a**

To see how these performance descriptions compare with the expectations for elementary school and middle school, turn to pages 168-173.

The examples that follow the performance descriptions for each standard are examples of the work students might do to demonstrate their achievement. The examples also indicate the nature and complexity of activities that are appropriate to expect of students at the high school level.

The cross-references that follow the examples highlight examples for which the same activity, and possibly even the same piece of work, may enable students to demonstrate their achievement in relation to more than one standard. In some cases, the cross-references highlight examples of activities through which students might demonstrate their achievement in relation to standards for more than one subject matter.

Applied Learning

A4 Learning and Self-management Tools and Techniques

Manage and direct one's own learning.

A4 a The student learns from models; that is, the student:

- consults with and observes other students and adults at work and analyzes their roles to determine the critical demands, such as demands for knowledge and skills, judgment and decision making;
- identifies models for the results of project work, such as professionally produced publications, and analyzes their qualities;
- uses what he or she learns from models in planning and conducting project activities.

Examples of learning from models include:

- Shadow a software designer at work. **1a, 2b**
- Undertake volunteer work in a community organization and assist in the management of financial records. **1b, 2b, 5c**
- Gain work experience in a museum and study the work of a curator in mounting an exhibition. **1c**

A4 b The student reviews his or her own progress in completing work activities and adjusts priorities as needed to meet deadlines; that is, the student:

- develops and maintains work schedules that reflect consideration of priorities;
- manages time;
- monitors progress towards meeting deadlines and adjusts priorities as necessary.

Examples of using tools and techniques for reviewing one's own progress include:

- Maintain project log books.
- Use project management software.
- Develop flow charts for determining the sequence in which tasks need to be tackled.

A4 c The student evaluates his or her performance; that is, the student:

- establishes expectations for his or her own achievement;
- critiques his or her work in light of the established expectations;
- seeks and responds to advice and criticism from others.

Examples of using tools for evaluating one's own performance include:

- Have a friend videotape an oral performance to allow for review.
- Ask a professional in the relevant field to review a draft design.
- Ask a friend to review a draft report.

A5 Tools and Techniques for Working With Others

Work with others to achieve a shared goal, help other people to learn on-the-job, and respond effectively to the needs of a client.

A5 a The student participates in the establishment and operation of self-directed work teams; that is, the student:

- defines roles and shares responsibilities among team members;
- sets objectives and time frames for the work to be completed;
- establishes processes for group decision making;
- reviews progress and makes adjustments as required.

Examples of working in teams include:

- Work in a team to design and build a vehicle to enter in a competition. **1a, 2a**
- Work in a team to design a recreational area. **1a, 2a, 2c, 5b**
- Work in a team to organize a series of seminars on careers. **1c**

A5 b The student plans and carries out a strategy for including at least one new member in a work program; that is, the student:

- plans and conducts an initial activity to introduce the new member to the work program;
- devises ways of providing continuing on-the-job support and advice;
- monitors the new member's progress in joining the program, and revises the kinds and ways of providing support and advice accordingly;
- reviews the success of the overall strategy.

Examples of including new members in a work program include:

- Respond to growth in demand for a market research service by including a partner in the enterprise. **1a, 3b**
- Provide training to other students on how to develop and conduct a tutoring program, based on experience in devising and running a tutoring program on desktop publishing. **1a, 3b**
- Include a student new to the school in an ongoing project, such as a project to design a proposal for use of a park recreation area. **1a, 2a, 2c, 5a**

A5 c The student completes a task in response to a commission from a client; that is, the student:

- negotiates with the client to arrive at a plan for meeting the client's needs that is acceptable to the client, achievable within available resources, and includes agreed-upon criteria for successful completion;
- monitors client satisfaction with the work in progress and makes adjustments accordingly;
- evaluates the result in terms of the negotiated plan and the client's evaluation of the result.

Examples of responding to a commission from a client include:

- Produce a tourist guide to the local area at the request of the local tourist authority. **1a, 2c, 3a, 3b**
- Customize applications software for financial management at the request of a community organization. **1b, 2b, 4a**
- Conduct an investigation of procedures for emergency evacuation of the school in response to a request from the school board. **1b, 2a, 2b**

Samples of student work that illustrate standard-setting performances for these standards can be found on pages 112-137.

The cross-references that follow the examples illustrate some of the ways by which a single Applied Learning project may provide a vehicle for demonstrating achievement of several parts of the standards. The cross-references are based on the examples that are linked to the Problem Solving standard. It is intended that students demonstrate their achievement of the four Tools and Techniques standards in conjunction with Problem Solving projects.

Work Sample & Commentary: *ElectroHawk 1*

The documentation presented from this project is not a comprehensive record of all work done as part of the project. It would be neither reasonable nor appropriate to ask students to keep detailed written records of every aspect of a project. This would defeat part of the purpose of applied learning which is for students to put their academic learning to work and to learn from projects that connect what they do at school to the demands of the twenty-first century workplace. Some of these standards lend themselves to assessment through observation and other less formal methods rather than through written work.

The task

Students were required to complete an application project that would develop their skills in gathering and using information, communication, and problem solving, and help them to become self-directed learners. The students defined the project and acquired a mentor from outside the school to assist them. The students were supervised by a teacher throughout the process of developing a proposal and planning a presentation of the project. This student designed an electric car for a local competition.

Circumstances of performance

The student worked as a member of a team to get most of the work done. This student was also the actual driver of the car in competition. The team worked with an adult mentor and a teacher advisor. The students were required to maintain a journal to record the time they spent on the project. The work culminated in a presentation to interested adults and peers.

What the work shows

A1 a Problem Solving: The student designs and creates a product, service, or system to meet an identified need; that is, the student:

- develops a design proposal that:
  - shows how the ideas for the design were developed;
  - reflects awareness of similar work done by others and of relevant design standards and regulations;
  - justifies the choices made in finalizing the design with reference, for example, to functional, aesthetic, social, economic, and environmental considerations;
  - establishes criteria for evaluating the product, service, or system;
  - uses appropriate conventions to represent the design;

Application Project Proposal Paper

Have you ever wanted to go for a ride into the future? Or maybe drive an almost non-polluting vehicle? For my application project, I propose to build a full size, fully drivable, fully operational solar/electric car. I am currently, and will continue to build, and improve an electric vehicle. I, along with the aid of 4 other students, and the watchful eye of Mr._____, and Mr._____, am currently building this vehicle in the_____Technology Department. The vehicle, along with the many tests and upgrades, should be completed by the end of July.

I have chosen to build an electric car for my application project almost by coincidence. _____High School received an electric motor, a speed control, and two batteries from P.U.D in early November. In return, we must build an electric or, solar-electric vehicle. Immediately I jumped at the rare opportunity to build the ElectroHawk 1. Unfortunately it took us until after December to get a team together to build this vehicle. This is the main reason that I have started my application project in the middle of building this vehicle.

E ⤍ There are many skills that have helped me along the way, as well as many new skills I have acquired while building this vehicle. Some of the most important skills I have are those pertaining to my familiarity of the various tools (saws, drills, grinders, sanders, etc.) used to fabricate the vehicle. I have been around these different tools all of my life since my father owns a custom woodworking company. I have also taken many classes in the Technology Department, teaching me the safety skills necessary to operate all the tools. I also feel that I get along well with others which helps to build a stronger team, and more important, a higher quality electric vehicle. Without a high quality electric vehicle, somebody will get hurt.

E ⤍ The variety of skills I plan to attain from this project are those related to metal works. I have already learned how to "tack" or make small welds, as well as what is necessary to cut metals. I will also have a better

H
N

- plans and implements the steps needed to create the product, service, or system;
- makes adjustments as needed to conform with specified standards or regulations regarding quality or safety;
- evaluates the product, service, or system in terms of the criteria established in the design proposal, and with reference to:
  - information gathered from sources such as impact studies, product testing, or market research;
  - comparisons with similar work done by others.

The proposal explains the genesis of the project: the P.U.D. (Public Utilities Department) provided the school with an electric motor, a speed control, and two batteries as the basis for designing and building an electric or solar-electric vehicle for entry in a competition with other schools in the local area.

The process of design of the vehicle emerges through the "Proposal Paper," "Time Line," and journal. The proposal records the plan the student envisaged early in the process. This plan is reflected in the timeline. The journal provides insight into the reality of the design process, especially the ways in which the students responded to problems they encountered as the design took shape.

This work sample illustrates a standard-setting performance for the following parts of the standards:

A1 a **Problem Solving: Design a product, service, or system.**

A4 a **Learning and Self-management: Learn from models.**

A4 b **Learning and Self-management: Review own progress and adjust priorities as needed.**

A4 c **Learning and Self-management: Evaluate own performance.**

A5 a **Working With Others: Participate in the establishment and operation of self-directed work teams.**

Problem Solving **A1**

Communication Tools and Techniques

Information Tools and Techniques

Learning and Self-management Tools and Techniques **A4**

Tools and Techniques for Working With Others **A5**

ElectroHawk 1

understanding of what goes into the fabrication of any vehicle, be it cars, planes, or boats. I will also have the thrill of being able to drive something that I made, with the help of the best team I could ever hope to work with, with my own two hands.

(K) Finding a mentor has proven to be difficult since there are not that many people that build electric cars for a living. By coincidence however, Mr._____, a former student teacher at MTHS was part of a team that built an electric car for _____University and has agreed to be my mentor for the duration of the project.

(A) For this project we have needed, and received many donations. One of the most important has been the donation of wood for our mock up, as well as the donation of the steel used to build the vehicle. We are also looking for donations for dinners (for all of our late nights). To complete this vehicle we still have to wire it up so that it will run safely and efficiently. We also have to complete the front and rear axles which are necessary for any vehicle. Front wheels need to be found as well as tubes and tires that will fit them. It is also necessary that we find a chain as well as sprockets that fit. We additionally need to go over the rules and regulations to make sure we fit within required safety parameters. A body is also something that we would like to have, should time allow. Once the vehicle is built, we will then need to run many tests on it. Some of these tests will include structural testing, battery testing, and efficiency rating of the motor.

(H) First, to complete this project, we must complete welding on the chassis. To do this safely the team has decided to have Mr._____ do this. We decided upon this for two reasons, the first is the fact the he has experience in welding which would give us a much safer vehicle, and the second is the fact that none of us are comfortable doing the actual welding of the vehicle.

(B) Second, we need to finish work on the rear axle and suspension. To do this we need to figure out where the motor will be mounted on the suspension, how much room is necessary in the rear portion of the suspension for the wheel, and how we will attach it.

(B) Next we have to locate a chain as well as a sprocket that matches the required gear ratio of the rear wheel sprocket. Mr._____ has been putting his time in to locate these items since he seems to have the best understanding of exactly what we need.

(B)(L) After deciding what needs to be done on the rear suspension, and gearing, we need to begin work on the front axle and suspension. This task includes many variables such as: how the vehicle will be steered, how the suspension will attach to the vehicle, as well as wheel size. Mr._____ has told us that he knows someone who builds front suspension kits, and that it might be possible to order one. Mr._____ has told us about a unique front suspension he has designed based on three-wheel bikes he saw while visiting the Oregon coast.

(B) Once we have the entire chassis finished we can begin mounting and wiring all of the electrical components such as speed control, throttle, and batteries. Our vehicle is very compact, and finding adequate space will be difficult. We also need to wire up the vehicle, and from the schematics, it does not look easy.

(H) After everything is wired up, and in place we will begin going over all of the rules and regulations to make sure that we are legal and able to race. There will be a practice day when all of the competing vehicles will turn out at _____ Speed Way to take practice runs, as well as have a judge look over our vehicle for anything we may be missing.

(I) Finally, after everything is completed we will begin doing tests and trials. Our main goal of running the various tests will be to find any flaws in the structure that may be present and get the vehicle running at it's most efficient levels. We will also begin lightening the vehicle at this point to see what the least amount of material is needed to make the vehicle hold together.

When presentation time comes I will have many ways of showing what I have learned. I hope to have a journal, several pictures, and several graphs and charts showing the vehicles rating of efficiency increasing as

each modification to the vehicle is done. There is also a plan in the making to mount an in-car camera so that a video can be shown on presentation day giving my audience a feel of what it is like to ride in an electric car.

(D) When all of the dust has cleared from the construction and the frantic running around looking for all of the missing parts of the vehicle has ended, and there is a solid, well built, highly efficient electric vehicle left standing, I will know my job is done. I know that my project will receive only the highest grade because I will allow nothing but quality work to be put into the construction of this vehicle of the future. And I hope that when people look at the ElectroHawk 1, the will see nothing but quality.

(A) The students began by building a wooden mock up for the vehicle (not shown).

(B) The proposal records some of the design issues that the student envisaged would require resolution. These are reflected in the "Time Line."

(C) The journal records some of the problems the students encountered and the strategies they adopted to solve them.

The design solutions reached during the course of construction of the vehicle are justified in terms of functional considerations.

(D) The student established criteria for evaluating the design.

Apart from reference to the mock up (which is one of the ways of presenting a design for a product of this sort), there is no reference to the presentation of design plans.

(E) The proposal notes some of the skills the student identified he would need to learn in order to complete the project.

(F) (G) The time line records the planned steps for turning the design into a reality while the journal entries record the ways in which those steps were achieved in practice and the modifications to the process the students made along the way.

(H) The proposal and journal contain several references that demonstrate attention to relevant regulations and to matters related to safety.

(I) The students devoted a lot of time and energy to testing their design and to trying out strategies to improve its performance and efficiency. The strategies included analysis of records of performance.

(J) The students were very aware of comparisons with other vehicles built for the competition. Even the use of "XXX" in the journal indicates an awareness that other electric car developers could gain advantages from the information the students' gathered in their tests.

A1 Problem Solving

Communication Tools and Techniques

Information Tools and Techniques

Learning and Self-management Tools and Techniques **A4**

Tools and Techniques for Working With Others **A5**

ElectroHawk 1

F

Application Project
Time Line

March 30, 1995:   Completed

By this date the mock-up will be completed
and work on the metal chassis will
commence.

April 14, 1995:   Completed

By this date the chassis will be completed
and work on the rear suspension will commence.

April 21, 1995:   Completed

By this date the rear suspension will be completed
and work on the front suspension will commence.

May 9, 1995:

By this date work on the front suspension will be
completed and work on wiring the car will
commence.

May 6, 1995:

Work on wiring the car will be completed and
safety checks will be performed. As well as checks
to make sure our vehicle can satisfy the rules.

May 9, 1995:

By this date all safety parameters will be met,
and performance testing of the vehicles systems
will begin.

May 13, 1995:

The vehicle will be taken to _____ speedway
to get looked over by a judge that will check to make
sure that we meet all the necessary guidelines.

May 16, 1995:

Work on a body for the vehicle will begin as well as
any improvements that may need to be made to the
vehicle to improve efficiency.

May 26, 1995:

A body will be completed and test runs for the vehicle
will be made with a body on. We will also run the
batteries down to see what the speed the vehicle can
run at and maintain speed during the race.

May 27, 1995:

Race Day! The vehicle will be raced for one hour
at Evergreen speedway against other vehicles to see
which vehicle can travel the furthest distance without
running out of power.

May 30, 1995:

From here on out efficiency tests will be run on the
vehicle to improve our distance during race day's.
We will also make any necessary repairs to the vehicle
as they arise.

August 1995:

Will have improved the car to it's maximum efficiency and have competed
in at least 3 events.

December 1995:

Will have presented in Fall '95 presentation.

A4 a Learning and Self-management Tools and
Techniques: The student learns from models; that is,
the student:

- consults with and observes other students and
  adults at work and analyzes their roles to determine the critical demands, such as demands for
  knowledge and skills, judgment and decision
  making;

- identifies models for the results of project work,
  such as professionally produced publications, and
  analyzes their qualities;

- uses what he or she learns from models in planning
  and conducting project activities.

K The proposal records the difficulties the students
experienced in identifying a mentor, though they
eventually succeeded in finding a person who had
taken part in a similar project.

L The team also made extensive use of the assistance of teachers with knowledge and expertise in
areas such as welding. The student's recognition of
the importance of these models to the eventual result
is evident throughout the journal.

Problem Solving **A1**

Communication
Tools and
Techniques

Information
Tools and
Techniques

Learning and
Self-management **A4**
Tools and
Techniques

Tools and
Techniques for **A5**
Working
With Others

G 3/31-(2 hrs)

This evening I finally finished my goal statement for this
project after 3 rewrites. Several times I forgot to include little
details here and there. but now I have finished and am ready to go.
M → I also found out today that info for the front axle of the car didn't
come and is now over a week late, and if we don't get an order in by
the end of this week I will get a little concerned due to the time
factor which is quickly becoming an enemy to us as race day
approaches. Oh well, guess it just means longer hours.

4/11-(5 hrs)

Today we worked very hard to try and get a rear axial and
suspension finished but instead we had to settle for a nearly finished
M → rear axial. I expect we should be finished with the rear axial by our
next meeting. I also started work on a very unique front axle system
conceived by Mr. using the same concept as the 3 wheel "banana"
bikes at Seaside Or. I did manage to get a full mock-up of the system
built. We may also still use the front axial kit. Mr. _____ is going to
try and order one as soon as possible.

4/14-(4 hrs)

Today we made up our minds that we wanted the vehicle
driveable by 4/22. And to do this we needed to devise a plan of
M → attack. We made the decision to work this Saturday. I was given the
duty to try and get _____ Pizza to sponsor us by giving us a couple
of pizzas for lunch. We also decided to work late Tuesday and
Thursday since we needed to be done the following Saturday which
is when time trails and first inspection of the vehicle. It is not
absolutely necessary to have our vehicle ready on this date, but we
would still like to make a showing. As far as work goes we finished
the rear axial as well as the part that the axial attaches to the car.
We also built the mock-up of the battery box. There isn't a whole lot
of room for it, but we will do what we can.

4/15-(5hrs)

Today was the first Saturday we worked. We did manage to
C → get allot done. We put the final touches on the rear axial today only
to discover a minor flaw in our design. When we installed the rear
tire we realized we didn't leave enough room for it. We had welded

the brackets that hold the tire to far forward. To correct this we thought it would mean rebuilding the entire rear suspension. Fortunately I got the wheels upstairs turning and found an alternative. The piece in the front of the axle that was blocking the tire could just be cut off and moved forward. A roll bar was also put on the vehicle. Mr. also welded up the car instead of having us do it mainly for safety reasons. We also have a partially completed battery box to hold and keep the batteries from leaking and possible putting the driver in danger. A front axial also got started today as well, but it still needs allot of work.

4/18-(4 hrs)

Today I managed to get work off so I would have more time on the car. We got the rear axial completed and now all we have to do is attach it. This will take very precise work making it happen so that we can get the axial on straight. We also began major work on the front axial and suspension. This is proving to be more difficult then we were hoping trying to build the suspension around the axial itself using the unique system that we decided to use.

4/19-(5 hrs)

Today the magic happened. The rear axle and suspension was placed in the car. Before we did this though we had to cut some very precise holes into the frame to give the axle something to connect to. This means that we have 4 total holes that need to line up perfectly. And we are relying solely on our measurements. And when the moment of truth happened, the axial went in nice and snug, and the suspension had very little play. We also worked more on the battery compartment. It is nearly completed. We also began making decisions as to where we want to place electrical components onto the vehicle. We are going to be calling it very close. It will be a late night Thursday for sure.

4/20-(8 hrs)

Today we worked almost solely on the front suspension. I worked most of the day machining the front axial making it the correct size for the wheel to fit on. I am wondering if this axial is strong enough to support itself since it is barely 1/4" thick. I also got pizzas for dinner tonight donated by. I also completed a battery box

---

to protect the driver from acid spills in the event of a role-over. We also connected the support for the axle and completed the front axial.

4/21-(10 hrs)

Tonight was the longest night I have ever worked on this car yet. We worked until midnight. We kind of had to since the practice run is tomorrow. Tonight we worked on many things. Our first priority was to check if our front axial steering system was going to work. Apparently the angle the steering system was at wouldn't work. it didn't have a sharp enough turn. So to adjust it we had to increase the angle of slope. After doing this our turning radius was dramatically increased. We also attempted to wire the vehicle and place all of the insides of the vehicle. This proved easier said then done. The schematics made almost no sense at first but we managed to get most of it done. Mr._____spent most of his evening looking for things we needed such as correct sized nuts, sprockets, chains, mirrors, and other equipment. We all eventually got a little cranky by the time 12:00 rolled around so we decided to call it quits and return early in the morning to finish all of the little unimportant items.

4/22-(6 hrs)

Today was safety inspection and practice day. before we headed off for the race track we still had a few things that needed to be done. Some minor adjustments as well as electrical wiring. We worked hard and fast to get everything done that needed to be done. We still didn't get it all done. it came time to head off to the track so we packed up and decided to finish our work there. Once we arrived at the race track we immediately began work on the electrical system and gearing. And just as quickly as we got started working on the car peoples curiosity grew as other teams came over to get a glimpse of our unique steering system. After about two hours of hard work, and safety inspection we finally rolled the car onto the track. And then the moment of truth came with Mr. as our test pilot. He pushed the throttle forward, there was no response, he pushed the throttle again and still there was no response. I began going over all the wires in the system. Turns out to be a wire disconnected from the motor. Very quickly we got the wire connected back on only to realize that our chain wasn't tight so again we responded quickly moving the tire back. And then it was time to test our creation. Mr.

---

pushed the throttle forward, and very, very quietly the car rolled away. As Mr. picked up the speed our car looked better an better. Eventually he reached very comparable speeds to some of the fastest vehicles there. As he was driving we noticed a slight shimmy or fish tail action of the vehicle that raised a little concerned. Mr. finally came in after a series of test runs. We all were very pleased with the vehicles performance. And then we learned the Mr. hadn't even run the vehicle to its fullest potential. So we told him to get back in and push it as fast as it would go. And so he took the car around to the larger outer track. We were very pleased with the results. According to our calculations and estimation the car achieved a top speed of about 33 mph. We all think that we can improve this to around 35-40 mph after we run a few efficiency tests and put a body on the car. After about 5 laps he came in. And before I knew it I was being strapped into our creation. I rolled out onto the track put the accelerator on and with a few wobbly steps I became the 2nd to drive the first of a new breed of_____vehicles. It was just like flying. It was amazing, and it was the smoothest ride I have had in any vehicle. but I got a little too curious as to the vehicles potential. About the 4th lap around my front axial had exceeded its maximum load limit and buckled. Luckily I still had minimal control of the vehicle and brought it safely to a stop. So we packed up and called it a day.

4/25-(3 hours)

Today we worked mostly on disassembling the car. We also got a head-board made for the role bar. Mr._____finished up welding the car. The team also discussed ideas on the body and possible ways we could improve our vehicle.

4/27-(4 hours)

Today, we worked on getting the car back together. I worked most of the day trying to get another front axle made. It didn't work out though. We failed on two axles because we just didn't have the necessary equipment. So we decided to turn the job over to my fathers friend who is a professional metal worker and has all the necessary equipment. We also got masonite from my fathers shop to use for the body.

5/9-(4 hours)

Today we disassembled the car so that we could get our chassis painted. We also had to make a temporary paint room to do this. Brian also got to work on making his nose easier to remove. This evening, I was asked to make a spreadsheet and some charts showing our cars performance. We also made repairs to the body with fiber-glass.

5/10-(3 hours)

Today we painted the chassis so that it wouldn't rust on us. We also did a little analyzing of the charts I made. We concluded that our motor was running at to slow of R.P.M.'s.

5/11-(7 hours)

Today we painted the body completely white. I personally think it looks much better now. We also started working on the front brakes. A decision was made to change our gear ratio to XX/XX because Mr._____heard from somebody that a XX tooth sprocket is most efficient for the chain. And then we decided that our motor is most efficient running at XXXX R.P.M.'s. We also got some wheel covers to reduce drag from the wheel spokes.

5/16-(5 hours)

Today, we worked on getting the cars front brakes done. We also started the long process of putting humpty together again (electrical mostly). We also worked on the wheel covers, as well as the rear wheel and getting the sprocket. And we got the air-scoop for the motor put onto the body.

5/17-(4 hours)

Today we painted the air-scoop, and put the bottom and body on. We also got the rear top section made. And on top of that, our new nose cone for use with "in-car-cam" was completed as well as battery tests which told us that 2 of our 3 batteries are pretty much useless for the race.

ElectroHawk 1

I

5/18-(4 hours)

Today for some reason, Mr. _____discovered that one of our bad batteries was playing tricks on us. It only lasted 57 minutes of the required 60, but due to "amazo" battery that lasted 75 minutes, we figured that it should do just fine. But one draw-back is that we really don't have any idea of what amperage were running at. We also finished what we could to get the car ready for Saturday. The front brakes were completed. And we got the seat back in place, and the motor aligned. A speed control was also made to help keep us a little more efficient.

5/19-(2 hours)

Today we hurriedly put finishing touches on the car. Making sure that all bolts are tightened down. We got the sponsors on the car, and now all we really have to do is get the batteries wired up when we get to the track tomorrow.

5/20-(5 hours)

Race Day #2

Today was race day, and probably one of the most stressful days of my life. I honestly thought that we weren't going to get out onto the track. It all started with a wire suddenly bursting into flames from the driver's shut-off switch. Apparently it was touching one of the battery hook-ups. From the amount of smoke coming from that wire, I thought we had fried our speed control box for sure. Then another one of the guys got a wrench stuck between the positive and negative connections of a battery. And someone else got a drill-bit stuck in our axle on the right side which kept us from getting our wheel on. At this point there were ten minutes to race time. My grandfather told me later that he thought he was going to have a heart attack, had he not went and sat in his car. Luckily some of the officials came over and saved our lives by giving us a hand. The race was also held 10 minutes for us even though we insisted they go ahead. Finally I heard somebody yell "O.K., were ready!" And before I knew it I was being strapped in. And then as the green countdown began, I switched the car on and prayed. As the green flag flew signaling the start of the race I throttled up and jolted away very quickly to my surprise. Now the only thing that was on my mind was battery power, and the fact that we had done everything we can; all the tests, all the calculations. And I had to stay at 26

N

mph.(It was supposed to be 28-29 mph, but we weren't sure about how our batteries were.) This meant I had to let everybody pass me. And that is what they did. However, I also knew that we would do about 78(later ended up being 76) laps according to our calculations. And we knew that the most any of them there could do would be about 60-65 laps. So after about 40 minutes had gone by, I knew we had it because the first and second place holders beginning to slow, and be passed by me (who was still going strong at 26 mph.). And once the race was over, we won by seven laps (not including the victory lap I was <u>forced</u> to take. I have to say that I have never felt prouder in my entire life about something I did. Everything went almost exactly according to plan, aside from a few minor mishaps. And it couldn't have been done without the team work of Mr. _____, Mr. _____, and the best electric car crew I could ever hope to work with.

Note: We celebrated with some _____Sparkling Cider afterwards. Most of which ended up on Mr._____.

One thing we have to do after races from now on is keep our "insides" covered up. Allot of people were very curious about our gear ratio. One man brought a video camera over to try and get some footage of our car. Luckily my father covered the rear with a blanket.

5/23-(2 hours)

We just can't seem to stay away from this car. We got the results back from the "in-car-cam." They were a bit wobbly. The camera had apparently been jolted to the side of the car, so we got a nice view of what I think were the stands going by. Today we mostly talked about what needed to be done as well as make up a time line so that we don't end up doing last minute jobs at the track. I also have been talking about the possibility of getting a CB radio for communication through a grant for Application projects.

5/24-(3 hours)

C

Today we worked on getting the body of the car off. We have decided to make our front axle vertically shorter so that it doesn't stick out of our body. I also got the application for financial aid to get the CB. radios. We all hope this is the last time that we have to take the body off.

A4b Learning and Self-management Tools and Techniques: The student reviews his or her own progress in completing work activities and adjusts priorities as needed to meet deadlines; that is, the student:

- develops and maintains work schedules that reflect consideration of priorities;
- manages time;
- monitors progress towards meeting deadlines and adjusts priorities as necessary.

F The work schedule was established in the time-line.

M The journal records several instances in which the students found it necessary to adjust their priorities in order to deal with unforeseen problems and to meet deadlines.

A4c Learning and Self-management Tools and Techniques: The student evaluates his or her performance; that is, the student:

- establishes expectations for his or her own achievement;
- critiques his or her work in light of the established expectations;
- seeks and responds to advice and criticism from others.

The proposal and journal reflect the student's expectations for his own achievement. The journal also records the student's analysis of his work in light of those expectations. The entries focus on the efforts he and his fellow team members made to reach a satisfactory result, rather than a detailed analysis of the student's own performance. There is also evidence of seeking and responding to advice, especially from the teachers who provided assistance to the team.

The student's recognition of his accomplishment is evident throughout the written work, as is his pride which comes through in a humble voice.

ElectroHawk 1

1/2–1/5–(3 hours)

This week I have worked on getting the rest of my journal onto the computer translating it from _____ language into the English language so that everyone can enjoy the trials and triumphs of the Electro-Hawk 1. It is also good to note that work on the Electro-Hawk 2 has begun this week. I have also once again been trying to get the scanner to work without any luck. So I may use the advice Mrs. _____ gave me and go and see Mr. _____ in the Hawkeye room and use their scanner.

1/5–1/11 (1 hour)

This week I did finnally see Mr. _____. He said it would be fine for me to come in and scan. Now all I have to do is find time when both him and myself can meet. Unfortunaty this week has been hectick since I have been in charge of the Martin Luther King jr. assembly.

1/11–1/18 (1 hour)

Due to this weeks unusual schedule, I have not been able to meet with Mr. _____. I have however, organized my pictures, and reviewed some of the rave footage to decide what I would like to use for the presentation.

1/18 to 1/25 (3 hours)

This week I finnaly got into the Hawkeye room to scan some of my pictures. Most of them turned out looking pretty good. Unfortunaty, my computer at home only accepted a little more than a half due to some uncompatibility. I will try to correct the problem as time goes on, but for now I'm stumped.

1-25 to 2/1 (3 hours)

This week I have just completed the opening sequence of the presentation using some of the pictures I have availible to me. It is awsome! I am using music from the soundtrack to "Grand Canyon" and it is cool stuff. I plan to get some intervue's with some of the "guys" and edit it into the computer, along with some race footage. So far, there have been no prob's with the computer, other than a couple of freeze-ups.

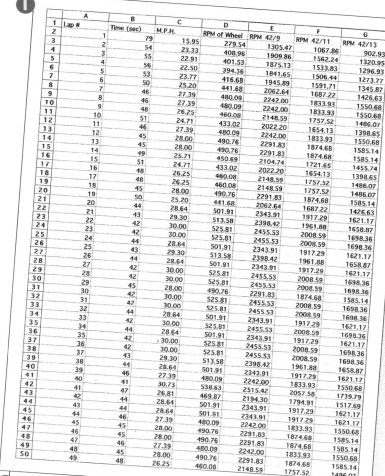

	A	B	C	D	E	F	G
1	Lap #	Time (sec)	M.P.H.	RPM of Wheel	RPM 42/9	RPM 42/11	RPM 42/13
2	1	79	15.95	279.54	1305.47	1067.86	902.93
3	2	54	23.33	408.96	1909.86	1562.24	1320.95
4	3	55	22.91	401.53	1875.13	1533.83	1296.93
5	4	56	22.50	394.36	1841.65	1506.44	1273.77
6	5	53	23.77	416.68	1945.89	1591.71	1345.87
7	6	50	25.20	441.68	2062.64	1687.22	1426.63
8	7	46	27.39	480.09	2242.00	1833.93	1550.68
9	8	46	27.39	480.09	2242.00	1833.93	1550.68
10	9	48	26.25	460.08	2148.59	1757.52	1486.07
11	10	51	24.71	433.02	2022.20	1654.13	1398.65
12	11	46	27.39	480.09	2242.00	1833.93	1550.68
13	12	45	28.00	490.76	2291.83	1874.68	1585.14
14	13	45	28.00	490.76	2291.83	1874.68	1585.14
15	14	49	25.71	450.69	2104.74	1721.65	1455.74
16	15	51	24.71	433.02	2022.20	1654.13	1398.65
17	16	48	26.25	460.08	2148.59	1757.52	1486.07
18	17	48	26.25	460.08	2148.59	1757.52	1486.07
19	18	45	28.00	490.76	2291.83	1874.68	1585.14
20	19	50	25.20	441.68	2062.64	1687.22	1426.63
21	20	44	28.64	501.91	2343.91	1917.29	1621.17
22	21	43	29.30	513.58	2398.42	1961.88	1658.87
23	22	42	30.00	525.81	2455.53	2008.59	1698.36
24	23	42	30.00	525.81	2455.53	2008.59	1698.36
25	24	44	28.64	501.91	2343.91	1917.29	1621.17
26	25	43	29.30	513.58	2398.42	1961.88	1658.87
27	26	44	28.64	501.91	2343.91	1917.29	1621.17
28	27	42	30.00	525.81	2455.53	2008.59	1698.36
29	28	42	30.00	525.81	2455.53	2008.59	1698.36
30	29	45	28.00	490.76	2291.83	1874.68	1585.14
31	30	42	30.00	525.81	2455.53	2008.59	1698.36
32	31	42	30.00	525.81	2455.53	2008.59	1698.36
33	32	44	28.64	501.91	2343.91	1917.29	1621.17
34	33	42	30.00	525.81	2455.53	2008.59	1698.36
35	34	44	28.64	501.91	2343.91	1917.29	1621.17
36	35	42	30.00	525.81	2455.53	2008.59	1698.36
37	36	42	30.00	525.81	2455.53	2008.59	1698.36
38	37	43	29.30	513.58	2398.42	1961.88	1658.87
39	38	44	28.64	501.91	2343.91	1917.29	1621.17
40	39	46	27.39	480.09	2242.00	1833.93	1550.68
41	40	41	30.73	538.63	2515.42	2057.58	1739.79
42	41	47	26.81	469.87	2194.30	1794.91	1517.69
43	42	44	28.64	501.91	2343.91	1917.29	1621.17
44	43	44	28.64	501.91	2343.91	1917.29	1621.17
45	44	46	27.39	480.09	2242.00	1833.93	1550.68
46	45	45	28.00	490.76	2291.83	1874.68	1585.14
47	46	45	28.00	490.76	2291.83	1874.68	1585.14
48	47	46	27.39	480.09	2242.00	1833.93	1550.68
49	48	45	28.00	490.76	2291.83	1874.68	1585.14
50	49	48	26.25	460.08	2148.59	1757.52	1486.07

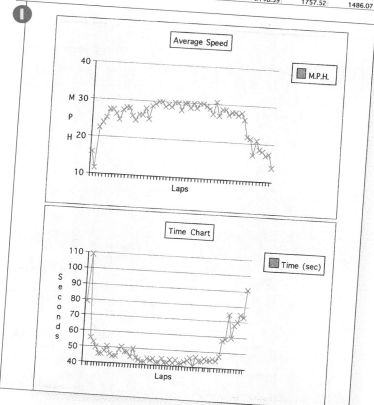

A5 a **Tools and Techniques for Working With Others:** The student participates in the establishment and operation of self-directed work teams; that is, the student:

- defines roles and shares responsibilities among team members;
- sets objectives and time frames for the work to be completed;
- establishes processes for group decision making;
- reviews progress and makes adjustments as required.

It is clear from the journal entries that the work was a team effort, though there are few references to the definition of roles and responsibilities or of the processes the team established for decision making. The journal also makes it clear that the students took responsibility for the project despite the close involvement and assistance of their advisors.

The proposal and timeline establish the objectives and time frame and the journal provides evidence that the team reviewed their progress and made adjustments as required.

N The student makes several references to the importance of teamwork in arriving at the goal of winning the competition. He notes also the connection between a strong team and the quality of the vehicle, and the connection between quality and safety.

The written work included with this project contains some errors, e.g., "parameters" is misspelled in the proposal; and the journal contains errors such as "allot" and "to" (instead of "too") and errors in the spelling of "available," "interview," and "awesome." Never-

theless, the narrative engages and maintains the reader's interest. The written work was completed primarily for personal use and to provide evidence of work on the project. It was not intended for wider publication.

A1 Problem Solving

Communication Tools and Techniques

Information Tools and Techniques

A4 Learning and Self-management Tools and Techniques

A5 Tools and Techniques for Working With Others

Work Sample & Commentary: *Caring for Your Campus Lawn*

The task

Chemistry students were asked to determine the most effective, economical, and environmentally safe grass fertilizer for the school district. The students were to produce an analytical report with detailed procedures and conclusions and to make a recommendation to the school district's Grounds and Maintenance Department.

Circumstances of performance

The students were given seven weeks to complete the project. They were responsible for all arrangements, such as making contacts with outside resources and obtaining permissions needed to complete the plan. Class time was used to visit other campuses for soil collection, and time outside the school day was also used to complete various parts of the project. The students divided into groups with responsibility for specific components of the project plan. The Director of the Grounds and Maintenance Department for the school district worked closely with the class during the project both as an advisor and as a client who would benefit from the project. The teacher facilitated the project and assisted the students as a resource person. Much of the work was completed as practical science work.

What the work shows

A1 b Problem Solving: The student troubleshoots problems in the operation of a system in need of repair or devises and tests ways of improving the effectiveness of a system in operation; that is, the student:

- explains the structure of the system in terms of its:
  - logic, sequences, and control;
  - operating principles, that is, the mathematical, scientific and/or organizational principles underlying the system;
- analyzes the way the system works, taking account of its functional, aesthetic, social, environmental,

and commercial requirements, as appropriate, and using a relevant kind of modeling or systems analysis;

- evaluates the operation of the system, using qualitative methods and/or quantitative measurements of performance;
- develops and tests strategies to put the system back in operation and/or optimize its performance;
- evaluates the effectiveness of the strategies for improving the system and supports the evaluation with evidence.

The students investigated the requirements for maintenance of campus lawns in the school district in order to arrive at recommendations to improve the effectiveness and efficiency of existing operations. The project documentation provides evidence that the students:

A **B** developed a procedure for undertaking the project;

C **D** **E** **F** **G** studied the scientific principles underlying the maintenance system, and analyzed the design and management of the system, especially with regard to environmental requirements and cost analysis;

The documentation presented from this project is not a comprehensive record of all work done as part of the project. It would be neither reasonable nor appropriate to ask students to keep detailed written records of every aspect of a project. This would defeat part of the purpose of applied learning which is for students to put their academic learning to work and to learn from projects that connect what they do at school to the demands of the twenty-first century workplace. Some of these standards lend themselves to assessment through observation and other less formal methods rather than through written work.

This work sample illustrates a standard-setting performance for the following parts of the standards:

A1 b Problem Solving: Improve a system.

A2 b Communication: Prepare a formal written proposal or report.

A5 a Working With Others: Participate in the establishment and operation of a self-directed work team.

A5 c Working With Others: Complete a task in response to a commission from a client.

Problem Solving **A1**

Communication Tools and Techniques **A2**

Information Tools and Techniques

Learning and Self-management Tools and Techniques

Tools and Techniques for Working With Others **A5**

A

To: Mr. _____ , Principal
From: Mr. _____ Period 1 Chemistry IB Class
Date: April 22, 1992
Subject: Proposal for funds for Applied Learning Project

For the next four to six weeks , our class is working on an Applied Learning Project called "The Chemistry of Soil and Fertilizers." This research is a part of Superintendent _____ C3 Project. The C3 Partnership not only addresses workplace readiness but also prepares students for success in higher education. The anticipated products of the C3 Project are a higher graduation rate, a practical alliance of schools and businesses linking the classroom with the world of work, and students who are better prepared to compete for entry-level jobs and to successfully complete college.

The purpose of our project is to determine the most effective, economical, and environmentally safe grass fertilizer for the Fort Worth Independent School District. The class will produce an analytical report with detailed procedures, conclusions, and recommendations for the Fort Worth Independent School District Grounds and Maintenance Department. The Grounds and Maintence Department will use the recommendations for future orders of fertilizer for the district.

The following is a list of the sequence of events to complete the project:

1. Prepare a basic project plan that will include projected costs and a research time table.
2. Prepare a proposal for submission to the principal (or other appropriate resources) requesting the necessary funds for the project.
3. Write to the Grounds and Maintenance Department of the school district requesting information on current fertilizing practices.
4. Write letters to plant nurseries and fertilizer companies requesting information on types of fertilizers and their percent compositions.
5. Interview a plant specialist to get ideas and gather information on grass types and fertilizers.
6. Research the basic grass types for the Fort Worth I.S.D.
7. Research the fertilizer requirements for different grasses on the school grounds.
8. Research the price, percent composition, and environmental safety of various brands of commercial fertilizers.
9. Based on our findings, we will determine the most effective, economical, and environmentally safe fertilizer for the school district campuses.
10. Write a letter to the Grounds Department either congratulating them on their choice of fertilizer or recommending a change in fertilizer.
11. Log all our efforts and produce a manual so that other students can monitor and/or replicate our efforts.

In order to complete this research, funds are needed. Our class has agreed that $100 will be sufficient to begin this important and worthwhile project. Please consider this proposal and help us obtain these necessary funds. A prompt response and your cooperation are greatly needed and appreciated.

Caring for Your Campus Lawn

(B) TIME TABLE

April 6 - April 10 Formed groups, study chemistry packet, call FWISD about current use of fertilizer, notes from parents, talk to Mr. _____ about the project.

Data/Control Group - Worked on proposal for money. Also typed a letter for the soil testing group. Set up folder and a list of all the groups.

Research Group - Made phone calls around to the various groundsmen. Read through Texas Master Gardner Hanbook, and other books for information. They also compared the A&M and chemistry packet for differences.

Soil Tester Group - Looked up varios schools and decided what schools to go to. Called and got permission to come out to campuses. Called _____ Nursery and asked about how to test the soil.

Interviewers ($) AT&T - Made phone calls. Got results from the different nurseries. Invited guest speaker _____. Wrote out questions to ask.

April 13 - April 16

Data/Control Group - Typed letter for money proposal . Typed a request letter for the Research group. Edited the letters and typed them up and sent them off.

Research Group - Recieved answeres from _____ Nursery. Recieved information from _____. Made questions to ask. Planned questions for _____. Made phone calls. Wrote a letter. Went to thelibrary for more information. Recieved a letter from _____

Soil Testers Group - Called schools to get permission. Planned to get soil samples but was put on hold. Went to the library.

Interviewers (&) AT&T - Called _____ again to set up date. Made more phone calls to different organizations. Made questions for FWISD representative. Wanted to see if other places would visit but there were no responses. Jason brought camera and taped different groups working.

April 20 - April 24

Data/Control Group - Our group took notes from the guest speaker _____. Wrote two thank you letters, one to _____ for visiting our class and the other to _____ for approving our proposal.

Research Group - Looked over information USDA sent. Made phone calls. Had visitor _____. Took notes. Found info. about organic fert. Wrote a paper about FWISD. Watched a tape to make sure facts were correct.

Soil Testers - Gathered soil from 4 different schools.

Interviewers (AT & T) - Made phone calls. Took notes over _____. Made a list of all the people called.

April 27 - May 1

Data/Control Groups - We typed reports and letters and edited the reports and letters. Several groups went out to measure the square feet of different schools. We sent out most of the letters we had to type.

Research - Edited letter and made changes for Stacy to type. Also, called _____ to find out about measuring lawns. He brought out his measure. Chose schools to measure. Received information. Went to certain schools and measured lawns.

Soil Testers - Got soil samples and took picture of schools and them working. Began testing the soil samples. Got results from testing the soil but they all came out the same.

Interviewers (AT&T) - Organized the notebook and went to measure the schools that were chosen. Also, collected money. Made phone calls to ask about prices of fertilizer.

May 4 - May 8

Data/Control Group - Made phone calls to get directions to three schools. Some of the groups went to measure the sq. footage of school campus front lawns. Typed letters and reports. Trying to bring project to a close.

Research - Went to schools to measure lawns of school campuses. Made phone calls. Compared organic to inorganice prices. Started

working on phamphlet. Looked over two handbooks for more information.

Soil Testers - Tested soil. Tried one soil test which didn't do so well. Then they got another more complicated soil testing kit after that failed, finally ended up sending soil samples to Texas A & M. Currently awaiting results.

Interviewers (AT & T) - Made phone calls.

May 11 - May 15

Data/Control Group - Started writing paper for journal. Typed out the averages of the schools front lawns. Typed testing procedures, safety, cleaning, and preparing soil samples. Worked on pamphlet. Wrote thank you letter to Dr. _____.

Research - Called to get info. on organic vs. inorganic. Called _____ for prices, compared prices, helped come up with conclusion.

Soil Testers - Received soil testing results from A&M. Analyzed data and made data table. Wrote conclusion.

Interviewers (AT&T) - Talked to _____ from Tarrant County Extension Service. Talked to _____ from Dallas who refused to speak to class. Contacted _____.

May 18 - May 22

Data/Control Group - Finished summary. Finished pamphlet. Sent pamphlet to all Fort Worth schools. Put pictures in notebook.

Research - Finished summary. Presented results to _____ with pamphlet.

Soil Testers - Analyzed data and proofed summary.

Interviewers (AT & T) - Contacted _____.

(C) (D) (E) (F) evaluated the system using quantitative measures; and

(H) made recommendations for improved techniques for managing the system based on analysis of fertilizers.

(H) (I) The students submitted their report to the Director of the Grounds and Maintenance Department and produced a set of procedures for revised practices in lawn maintenance to be used by grounds keepers, which was published by the Grounds and Maintenance Department.

This project illustrates an appropriate task for the high school level. Its scope extended beyond the school and immediate community of the students. It involved consideration of a range of factors including implications for cost. Finally, the project led to changes in practice.

A1 Problem Solving

A2 Communication Tools and Techniques

Information Tools and Techniques

Learning and Self-management Tools and Techniques

A5 Tools and Techniques for Working With Others

Caring for Your Campus Lawn

FWISD Grass Type

Bermudagrass

Bermudagrass is a low, creeping grass that grows year round. In the United States bermuda grass is a valuable lawn and pasture grass throughout the southern states.

Bermudagrass should be mowed at 1 1/4 inches every 5 to 6 days. Leaving grass clippings on the lawn contributes valuable nutrients to the soil.

Watering thoroughly and infrequently is best. During the summer, lawns require about 1 inch of water every 5 to 6 days. Watering in early morning is best because less water is lost in evaporation.

Bermudagrass requires 4 to 6 pounds of nitrogen per year to maintain color and density. Apply 2-3 pounds of fertilizer per 1,000 sq. ft. Apply the fertilizer at the following intervals: April 15, June 1, July 15, Sept. 1. By using a fertilizer containing sulfur-coated urea or ureaformaldhyde, a slow and even growth can be attained.

Current FWISD Fertilizing Practices

Athletic Field

During playing seasons, athletic fields in the FWISD grow turf grass. After the baseball season is over, fescue grass is grown. The current practices call for the fields to be fertilized four times during the warm season and twice during the cold season.

Front Lawns

The most common grass found on the FWISD campuses is bermuda. The front lawn fertilizing practices are as follows:

- 6 lbs. of Nitrogen per 1000 sq. ft. per year
- fertilize with 15-5-10 four times a year starting after the last freeze, approximately March 15
- other treatments follow eight weeks apart (5/15, 7/15, 9/15)
- 1 1/2 lbs. of Nitrogen is used each time

The FWISD uses ammonical based fertilizer for economical reasons. The ammonical based fertilizer runs about $175.00 per ton, while organic fertilizers cost between $275.00 and $325.00 a ton. Because of the amount of land needing to be fertilized and the expense of organic fertilizers, current practices continue to use ammonical based fertilizers.

Size of the Front Lawns in Fort Worth ISD

High Schools

1. Southwest High School
2. Arlington Heights — 41,045.5
3. Western Hills — 8,837
   — 15,788

Average 21,890 * 12 high schools => 262,680 sq. ft.

Middle Schools

1. Leonard
2. McLean — 6,831
3. Rosemont — 21,780
4. Wedgwood — 34,180
   — 6,877

Average 17,417 * 19 middle schools => 330,923 sq.ft.

Elementary Schools

1. Western Hills
2. Tanglewood — 8,070
3. Bruce Shulkey — 4,000
4. West Cliff — 3,966
5. Ridglea Hills — 4,364
6. Hubbard Heights — 3,640
7. West Park — 4,601
8. JT Stevens — 12,321
9. Woodway — 26,445
10. Westcreek — 37,318
11. Greenbriar — 11,520
12. South Hills — 13,230
13. South Hi Mount — 18,920
14. Glen Park — 12,561
    — 10,450

Average 12,243 * 68 elementary => 832,524 sq.ft.

Total of 1,426,127 sq.ft

* 1 acre has 43,560 sq.ft. 1,426,127/43,560=> 33 acres for the Fort Worth ISD

SOIL TESTING RESULTS
Ph, NITROGEN, PHOSPHORUS, AND POTASSIUM

SCHOOL	Ph	N	P	K
1. Arlington Heights H.S.	8.1	Low	Very High	Very High
2. Kirkpatrick Elementary	7.9	Very High	Very High	Very High
3. Meachum M. S.	7.9	Moderate	Very High	Very High
4. Northside H.S.	8.0	Moderate	Very High	Very High
5. South Hi Mount Elementary	7.8	High	Very High	Very High
6. Stripling M.S.	7.9	Very High	Very High	Very High
7. Forest Hill Elementary	8.0	Low	Very High	Very High
8. Forest Oak M.S.	7.6	Very High	Very High	Very High
9. Southwest H.S.	7.3	High	Very High	Very High
10. Tanglewood Elementary	8.0	High	Very High	Very High
11. Wedgwood M.S.	7.7	Very High	Very High	Very High
12. O.D.Wyatt H.S.	8.0	Low	Very High	Very High

Problem Solving **A1**
Communication Tools and Techniques **A2**
Information Tools and Techniques
Learning and Self-management Tools and Techniques
Tools and Techniques for Working With Others **A5**

Caring for Your Campus Lawn

SOIL TESTING OBSERVATIONS

Out of the 12 schools tested over the F.W.I.S.D., we found that all of the schools were abundant in phosphorus and potassium. Three of the schools were low in nitrogen, two were moderate, three were high, and four were very high in nitrogen.

The pH level ranged from 7.3 to 8.1 (7.3 lower, 8.1 higher). We found that five of the schools had a pH level of 8 or more. The seven remaining schools had a pH level of 7.3 to 7.9.

SAFETY

The poly bag of capsules should be returned to the storage chamber of the appropriate comparator after it has been washed and dried. Fit the caps on each comparator and make sure the color charts are in place. Replace all the components back into the package. The slide blister has been especially designed to be reused as a storage container. Store your kit indoors in clean, dry conditions, as you would store household cleaners. Keep out of the reach of childern.

CLEANING

Dispose of the test solutions by rinsing it down the sink. Empty gelatin capsules should be disposed of immediately with household waste. Remove the color charts. Wash the comparator and caps in warm, soapy water immediately after each use. Make sure any sediment or color staining is removed. Rinse well and dry. Replace the color chart on the appropriate comparators.

PREPARING SOIL SAMPLES

For lawns, annuals or plants, take the soil sample from about 2 - 3 inches below the surface. For perennials, especially shrubs, vegetables and fruits, the sample should be from 4 inches deep. Avoid touching the soil with your hands. Place the soil in one of the containers. Break the sample up with the trowel or spoon and allow it to dry out naturally. This is not essential, however; it makes working with the sample easier. Remove any small stones, organic material such as grass, weeds or roots, or hard particles of lime. Then, crumble the sample finely and mix it thoroughly.

Test different areas of your soil, as it may differ according to past cultivation, underlying soil difference of a local condition. It is preferable to make individual tests on several samples from different areas, than to make the samples together.

TESTING PROCEDURES

1. Fill the second container with 1 part of soil sample and 5 parts water.
2. Thoroughly shake or stir the soil and water together for at least one minute and then allow the mixture to settle out. Wait 10 minutes, longer if possible. The time for the mixture to settle will vary according to the type of soil you have. Fine clay soil will take longer than coarse sandy soil. The clarity of the solution will also vary from virtually clear to cloudy. Cloudiness will not affect the accuracy of the test.
3. Select the appropriate comp-arator for the test you wish to make. Remove the cap and take out the poly bag of capsules which should be the same color as the cap. Make sure the color chart (film) is in place and avoid interchanging color charts between comparators.
4. Using the dropper provided, fill the test and reference chambers, to the fill mark on the chart, with solution from your soil sample. Avoid disturbing the sediment - transfer only liquid.
5. Fill the storage chamber to the same level with clean tap water.
6. Remove one of the appropriate colored capsules from its poly bag. Carefulley separate the two halves and pour the powder into the test chamber.
7. Fit the cap onto the comparator, making sure it is seated properly and caps tightly. Shake thoroughly.
8. Allow the color to develop in the test chamber for the following times; pH - 1 min.; Nitrogen - 10 mins.; Phosphorus and Potash - 5 mins. Before taking a reading, invert the comparator several times to obtain a uniform color, then compare the color of the solution in the test chamber to the color chart.

Organic vs. Inorganic

Inorganic
- cheaper
- soil polutants
- more readily available
- easier to apply
- need less per 1000 sq. feet
- contains lots of salt and nitrates that kill or repel beneficial organisms in soil
- does nothing for resistance to diseases
- decomposes slowly and can enter water system and harm us

Organic
- much more expensive
- better for soil
- harder to get
- harder to apply
- need more per 1000 sq. feet
- low levels of salts and nitrates, which kill or repel beneficial organisms in soil
- increases resistance to most diseases
- decomposes easily

* inorganic
33 acres -- 7 lbs./1000 sq.feet -- apply 4 times a year=> $ 3,000

* organic
33 acres -- 40 lbs./1000sq.feet -- apply 3 times a year=> $ 10,225

total difference is $ 7,225 less for inorganic

A1 ▶ Problem Solving

A2 ▶ Communication Tools and Techniques

Information Tools and Techniques

Learning and Self-management Tools and Techniques

A5 ▶ Tools and Techniques for Working With Others

Caring for Your Campus Lawn

D

Dear Dr. _____

Thank you for helping our class today on the telephone! We greatly appreciate your time and expertise. Our project objective is to determine the most effective, economical, and environmentally safe grass fertilizer for the Fort Worth I.S.D. Our plans are to produce an analytical report with detailed procedures and conclusions and a recommendation report for the Fort Worth I.S.D. Grounds and Maintenance Department. We only have 2 weeks to complete our research!

Please test these 12 soil samples for pH, N, P, and K. We are only concerned with the regular analysis. Thank you for running these reports at no charge. Please call us at _____ between 8:15 and 9:00 a.m. as soon as you have the results. Also, please send us the written reports with information on how to interpret the data.

Sincerely,

_____

E

SOIL TEST REPORT

PAGE 1

TEXAS AGRICULTURAL EXTENSION SERVICE -- THE TEXAS A & M UNIVERSITY SYSTEM
SOIL TESTING LABORATORY, COLLEGE STATION TX. 77843

EXTENSION SOIL CHEMIST

DATE RECEIVED : 5/8/92
DATE PROCESSED: 05/11/92
COUNTY : TARRANT
COUNTY#: 439
LAB # : 14962

INV# 004975
FOR: -SOUTHWEST HS
     4100 ALTAMESA BLVD
     FORT WORTH, TX
     76133
     FEE : $10.00

|SAMPLE ID#   2 *Kirkpatrick Elementary*

SOIL ANALYSIS

|SOIL TEST RATINGS - PPM ELEMENT (AVAILABLE FORM)|

PH ACIDITY	NITROGEN	PHOSPHO- RUS	POTASSIUM	CALCIUM	MAGNESIUM	SALINITY	ZINC	IRON	MANGANESE	COPPER	SODIUM	SULPHUR
											38. VERY LOW	141 HIGH
7.9 MILDLY ALKALINE	47. VERY HIGH	161. VERY HIGH	643. VERY HIGH	21294 VERY HIGH	585. HIGH	617. SLIGHT						

(PPM X 2 = LBS/ACRE 6 INCHES DEEP)

CROP AND YIELD RANGE: LAWN

SUGGESTED FERTILIZER RATES PER 1000 SQ/FT PRIOR TO SPRING GROWTH :
   SUGGESTED LAWN FERTILIZER RATE OF N-P205-K20 REQUIRED FOR YOUR SOIL
NUTRIENTS   WATER CONSERVATION
REQUIRED   RATE

NITROGEN (N)........   0 LBS
PHOSPHORUS (P205).....   0 LB
POTASSIUM (K20) .....   0 LB
                    TAEX LAWN FERTILIZING GUIDE

FIND YOUR SOIL'S   APPLY RATE THAT BEST MATCHES YOUR
SUGGESTED N-P205-K20   SUGGESTED N-P205-K20 RATE OR
RATE/1000 SQ FT   EQUIVALENT FROM THE FOLLOWING

                    5 LBS OF 21-0-0 OR 3 LBS OF 34-0-0 OR 2 LBS OF 45-0-0
1 -0 - 0   5 LBS OF 21-0-0 OR 1.5 LBS OF 34-0-0 OR 1 LB OF 45-0-0
0.5 - 0 - 0   2.5 LBS OF 21-0-0 OR 1.5 LBS OF 34-0-0 OR 1 LB OF 45-0-0
0 - 0 - 0   NO NITROGEN OR PHOSPHORUS NEEDED

   THERE IS A SLIGHT AMOUNT OF SOLUBLE SALTS IN THIS SAMPLE WHICH SHOULD NOT AFFECT THE
GROWTH OF PLANTS.   EXTRA IRRIGATION WATER SHOULD HELP REDUCE SALT LEVELS AND POSSIBLY
IMPROVE GROWTH .
   SUPPLEMENTAL NITROGEN : WHEN SOIL ANALYSIS STATES A NEED FOR NITROGEN TREN BROADCAST
3 LBS OF UREA, 4 LBS OF AMMONIUM NITRATE (IF CITY ORDINANCES PERMIT SALES) OR 5 LBS OF
AMMONIUM SULFATE EVERY 4 TO 6 WEEKS AS NEEDED. NOTE IF SULFUR LEVELIS BELOW 25 PPM
THEN USE OF AMMONIUM SULFATE WILL HELP CORRECT LOW SULFUR LEVEL.
   CALCIUM LEVEL IS GREATER THAN 3500 PPM IN THIS SAMPLE.   CONSIDER USING 4 LBS OF
IRON SULFATE PER 1000 SQ FT IF PLANTS ARE YELLOWING OR CHLOROTIC.

FURTHER INFORMATION AND ASSISTANCE CAN BE OBTAINED FROM YOUR COUNTY EXTENSION AGENT :
                                                   FORT WORTH TX.   76102

500 JONES 4B

F

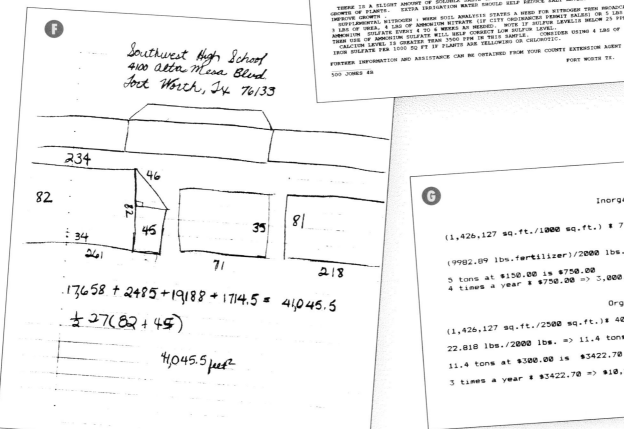

Southwest High School
4100 alta Mesa Blvd.
Fort Worth, Tx 76133

234
46
82
82
34
45
35
81
261
71
218

17,658 + 2485 + 19,188 + 1714.5 = 41,045.5
½ 27(82 + 45)

4,045.5 feet²

G

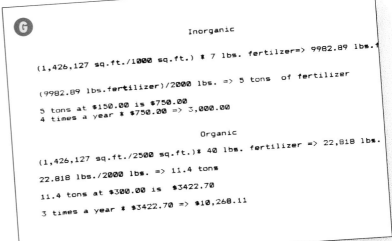

```
                      Inorganic

(1,426,127 sq.ft./1000 sq.ft.) * 7 lbs. fertilizer=> 9982.89 lbs.

(9982.89 lbs.fertilizer)/2000 lbs. => 5 tons  of fertilizer

5 tons at $150.00 is $750.00
4 times a year * $750.00 => 3,000.00

                       Organic

(1,426,127 sq.ft./2500 sq.ft.)* 40 lbs. fertilizer => 22,818 lbs.

22.818 lbs./2000 lbs. => 11.4 tons

11.4 tons at $300.00 is  $3422.70

3 times a year * $3422.70 => $10,268.11
```

Caring for Your Campus Lawn

A2 b Communication Tools and Techniques: The student prepares a formal written proposal or report to an organization beyond the school; that is, the student:

- organizes the information in the proposal or report in a logical way appropriate to its purpose;

- produces the proposal or report in a format similar to that used in professionally produced documents for a similar purpose and audience.

H The project led to the production of a formal written report to the Director of the Grounds and Maintenance Department for the school district. The report clearly sets out the procedures the students followed and their findings. It adopts a memorandum format appropriate to communicating a technical report of this sort, particularly one produced effectively in-house, and it is written in a style consistent with a memorandum.

I The students also chose the format of a memorandum for the pamphlet they prepared to communicate the project findings to grounds keepers, again an appropriate format. In this document, however, they adjusted the style, making it less discursive and more direct. This is appropriate, given the purpose of the pamphlet which was to provide directions. The information is set out clearly and logically, consistent with its purpose. See page 45 for commentary on this memorandum as a functional document within the requirements of the English Language Arts standards.

These documents are presented as finished work, as is appropriate to their purposes and audiences. The polish of these documents can be compared with the errors that appear in the Proposal to the Principal and with errors in some of the students' working documents.

H

To: Mr. _____ , F.W.I.S.D. Grounds and Maintenance Dept.

From: Mr. _____ Period 1 Fertilizer Research Group

Date: May 19, 1992

Subject: Fertilizer Project Report

This report summarizes the extensive research conducted by Mr. _____ first period chemistry class at _____ High School, 1991-1992. The data gathered support the following conclusions and recommendations.

Based on six weeks of library and field research, the most efficient, economical and environmentally safe fertilizer for the Fort Worth I. S.D. front lawns is inorganic fertilizer 15-5-10. This fertilizer should be applied at 7 lbs per 1,000 square feet four times annually on the following dates: April 15, June 1, July 15, and September 1. The approximate cost for the district is $3,000 a year based on a financial bid which the class was unauthorized to make.

The library and field research teams collected information on the current Fort Worth I.S.D. fertilizing practices, average size of Fort Worth I.S.D. front lawns, grass types, soil chemistry, and organic versus inorganic fertilizers. Plant nurseries, fertilizer companies, and soil and fertilizer chemistry experts were consulted.

Along with advice from experts, library research was conducted. Texas A & M University's *Texas Master Gardner Handbook* gave us several important facts and a list of experts to consult. _____ , Texas A & M soil chemistry professor, sent us information on soils, fertilizers, and plant nutrition. This information along with other sources answered questions about grass types, soil nutrients, and fertilizer chemistry.

Guest speakers were invited into the classroom to give us answers to many of our questions and to give the project better direction. One of these speakers was _____ _____ of the Fort Worth I.S.D. Grounds and Maintenance Department. He answered questions about current Fort Worth I.S.D. practices, lectured on the basics of soil chemistry, and helped focus the project.

According to several sources, organic fertilizer is more environmentally safe and productive compared to inorganic. After considering the economics of organic versus inorganic, inorganic is the choice fertilizer because it costs $7,000 less per year for the district. When the proper inorganic fertilizer percentage is applied at the proper time, it is just as efficient and effective as its organic counterpart.

After deciding that inorganic is the best fertilizer for Fort Worth I.S.D., the percentage of nitrogen, phosphorus, and potassium content had to be determined. Two soil testing kits were used to test the soil. Neither the _____ kit nor the _____ testing kit gave

conclusive data. After two weeks of soil testing, the soil was sent to Texas A & M University for analysis. The soil testing results revealed that most of the Fort Worth I.S.D. soil is in good shape. Some of the lawns need nitrogen, but all that were tested are high in phosphorus and potassium and the pH level is good also. After analyzing this data, a 15-5-10 inorganic fertilizer applied at 7 lbs. per 1,000 square feet about four times a year is recommended.

After organizing our data, the attached analytical pamphlet was compiled that includes fertilizing, mowing, and watering recommendations for the Fort Worth I.S.D. front lawns. The pamphlet was sent to the grounds keepers at all of the Fort Worth schools. The goal of the pamphlet is to help the grounds keepers improve and maintain the health and appearance of school front lawns.

The knowledge gained by Period 1 in the fields of fertilizer and soil chemistry is immeasureable. This applied learning project was practical, pertinent, interesting, hands-on, different from everyday textbook routine, multidisciplinary, and exciting. If you have any questions, please call _____ .

A1 Problem Solving

A2 Communication Tools and Techniques

Information Tools and Techniques

Learning and Self-management Tools and Techniques

A5 Tools and Techniques for Working With Others

Caring for Your Campus Lawn

A5ɑ Tools and Techniques for Working With Others: The student participates in the establishment and operation of self-directed work teams; that is, the student:

- defines roles and shares responsibilities among team members;
- sets objectives and time frames for the work to be completed;
- establishes processes for group decision making;
- reviews progress and makes adjustments as required.

B The timetable indicates that students shared the load of the work required for the project by forming groups, each with responsibility for a specific component of the project. The record suggests cooperation among the groups to set objectives and maintain time frames. However, the available evidence does not allow for commentary on the effectiveness of the work processes the students adopted or their strategies for reviewing progress.

A5c Tools and Techniques for Working With Others: The student completes a task in response to a commission from a client; that is, the student:

- negotiates with the client to arrive at a plan for meeting the client's needs that is acceptable to the client, achievable within available resources, and includes agreed-upon criteria for successful completion;
- monitors client satisfaction with the work in progress and makes adjustments accordingly;
- evaluates the result in terms of the negotiated plan and the client's evaluation of the result.

H **I** The client for this work was the Director of the Grounds and Maintenance Department for the school district. The memorandum to the Director documents communication between him and the students during the course of the project. But there is no evidence documenting negotiation of the plan or documenting the monitoring of the Director's satisfaction with the work in progress. The pamphlet the students wrote for grounds keepers, setting out procedures for lawn maintenance, appears under the title of the Grounds and Maintenance Department, which suggests that the Director was satisfied with the students' report and accepted their recommendations.

The written work included with this project contains some errors. For the main part the errors are confined to working documents which were not intended for publication. The three pieces of finished writing are the Proposal to the Principal (which contains an error in the spelling of "maintenance"), the memorandum to the Director, and the notice to grounds keepers.

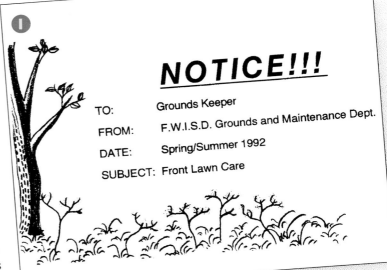

NOTICE!!!

TO: Grounds Keeper

FROM: F.W.I.S.D. Grounds and Maintenance Dept.

DATE: Spring/Summer 1992

SUBJECT: Front Lawn Care

PLEASE POST

CARING FOR YOUR CAMPUS LAWN

For a well maintained lawn follow these quick and easy steps!

FERTILIZATION

1. Measure the square footage of the lawn.
   To measure the square footage, multiply A and B together.

   A | To get A & B, simply walk off the number of feet.
   B

   Then, divide the answer of A and B by 1,000.
   Next, take the answer from above and multiply by 7. This gives you the amount of fertilizer in pounds for each time that you fertilize.
2. Fertilize on these dates for best results: *April 15, June 1, July 15, September 1*
3. Use **15-5-10** percentage fertilizer.
4. Requisition fertilizer from the F.W.I.S.D. warehouse.

MOWING

1. Mow the lawn at 2 inches weekly or when grass blade reaches one-third mowing height.
2. Leave grass clippings on the lawn--Don't Bag It!

WATERING

1. Water in early morning so less water is lost to evaporation.
2. Water thoroughly and infrequently making sure that in the summer the lawn gets 1 inch of water every week.

If you have any questions, please call _____ **at** _____.

This information is based on extensive research done in Mr. _____ first period chemistry class at _____ High School, 1991-1992.

The wide range of lawn areas of the various school campuses raises doubt about the adequacy of the sample used to arrive at the estimate of total lawn area. Given its derivation from the sample, the use of the exact figure (1,426,127 square feet) for some calculations is inaccurate. Rounding the figure to 33 acres is preferable, as used in "Organic vs. Inorganic."

Work Sample & Commentary: *Baseball Field*

The task

Students were required to complete an application project that would develop their skills in gathering and using information, communication, and problem solving, and help them to become self-directed learners. The students defined the project and acquired a mentor from outside the school to assist them. The students were supervised by a teacher throughout the process of developing a proposal and planning a presentation of the project. This student undertook the resurfacing of the high school's baseball field. The school district would not fund the renovation. Therefore, the student assumed responsibility for soliciting donations and materials, and planning for the restoration.

Circumstances of performance

The project to resurface the baseball field lasted for approximately five months, beginning in the fall semester. The student logged 157 hours in his journal. Parts of the project were fostered through assistance from a mentor (summer baseball coach), supportive parents, and a small group of volunteers. The student received feedback in class from his teacher and peers; however, much of the project was done outside class.

What the work shows

A1 b Problem Solving: The student plans and organizes an event or an activity; that is, the student:

- develops a planning schedule that:
  - is sensible in terms of the goals of the event or activity;
  - is logical and achievable;
  - reflects research into relevant precedents and regulations;
  - takes account of all relevant factors;
  - communicates clearly so that a peer or colleague could use it;
- implements and adjusts the planning schedule in ways that:
  - make efficient use of time, money, people, resources, facilities;
  - reflect established priorities;

This work sample illustrates a standard-setting performance for the following parts of the standards:

A1 b **Problem Solving: Improve a system.**

A4 a **Learning and Self-management: Learn from models.**

A4 b **Learning and Self-management: Review own progress and adjust priorities as needed.**

Proposal

For my application project, I plan to resurface the infield at the _____ High School baseball field during the fall season. I am a captain of the baseball team this year, and have endured, along with the rest of the team, the poor quality of the infield grass, pitchers mound, and base-paths. After playing on some fields with a flat surface and nicely cut grass this summer, I dream of raising my home field to that standard. Since the district does not provide funds, and will not improve the field unless it becomes a major physical hazard, I have decided I would like to renovate the field myself. My summer baseball coach, Mark _____ who is a coach and does maintenance at _____ Community College has agreed to help me. I have begun soliciting organizations for donations to the project. One donation already available comes from _____ Turf and Grass Farm, which has agreed to sell us sod for $.18 a square foot, which is half of the retail price. Several team members have offered to help me with some of the labor. My team is excited about the renovation and will do what it takes to help me improve our field. I am looking forward to doing a project like this because it will benefit myself, my team and our competitors. My baseball team along with the coaches will feel pride in our new "yard." The finished product may even attract more people to watch our games.

This project will require many hours of hard work. Because I do not have a primary source of money, I have and will continue to spend time on the phone with companies that sell equipment and materials that will be required for this project, hoping they will be willing to donate equipment to my cause. I also will ask more organizations for financial help. An organization that I have found success in, is the _____ _____ club. They have agreed to give us a financial donation and some help with the

---

- respond effectively to unforeseen circumstances;
- evaluates the success of the event or activity using qualitative and/or quantitative methods;
- makes recommendations for planning and organizing subsequent similar events or activities.

This project has characteristics both of improving a system and of planning and organizing an event or an activity. It is described, here, with respect to planning and organizing an event or an activity.

A The proposal establishes the problem to be solved. It describes the condition of the field: "…the poor quality of the infield grass, pitchers [sic] mound, and base-paths." The proposal contrasts this with the qualities of other baseball fields and describes the student's dream of turning his home field into a field of the quality that other teams would want to play on.

B The plan is logical and achievable. It takes account of relevant factors, such as the need for the materials and labor to complete the project, and the need to dispose of the materials removed from the site. The plan communicates clearly and would provide a useful checklist for anyone else embarking on a similar venture.

The documentation presented from this project is not a comprehensive record of all work done as part of the project. It would be neither reasonable nor appropriate to ask students to keep detailed written records of every aspect of a project. This would defeat part of the purpose of applied learning which is for students to put their academic learning to work and to learn from projects that connect what they do at school to the demands of the twenty-first century workplace. Some of these standards lend themselves to assessment through observation and other less formal methods rather than through written work.

A1 Problem Solving

Communication Tools and Techniques

Information Tools and Techniques

Learning and Self-management Tools and Techniques

A4

Tools and Techniques for Working With Others

Baseball Field

Page 2

Q labor that will be needed in the later stages of the project.. Bruce _____ is the _____ representative that is working with me. I think this is a great resource because it is a fairly large club that has many connections that may benefit my project.

B I will spend a lot of time working on the field. I need to remove the old sod, prepare the dirt for the new sod, set measurements of the base-paths and mound, and lay the new sod. Later on, I need to dig trenches to apply the irrigation system, and will maintain the grass until the Spring. The sod was laid on October 6th, and I expect the whole project to be complete with an irrigation system applied by December 1.

There are a number of traits that I already have or will learn to operate under to complete my project. Organization is something that will help my project become a success. I am keeping a record of everything I do on my computer which makes it easy to access. I have also maintained, with the rest of my team, the baseball field after practice and games. Through this experience, I have learned a lot about the care of grass and drainage. I am also good with money and am able to save a good percentage of my own money. This prepares me to look for the best deals and find which companies would be willing to donate equipment instead of paying for it. If the school district was to have a company do the project for them, it would cost them about $45,000. I expect this project to cost me about $3,741. If I find a way to get the irrigation system donated, the expense will be lowered to $2,400.

C Along with the skills that I already have to help me in this project, there are many things that I will learn. I am learning the strategies of growing grass. This will include the number of times to fertilize in a year and how often to water. I have chosen to try to get donations for an irrigation system that would be responsible to keep the grass wet. My mentor and I worked on a design for the sprinkler system. We drew a picture of the

Page 3

S piping going from our water source, to each sprinkler head. Now that we have that all ready, I can start petitioning companies for donations. Larry _____ of the _____ program has taught me about networking. Networking is using the resources, and people I know to help me find other people, that will help me get what I need to complete this project. For instance, Larry is a _____, which is a group with many members that have what I need to help me complete my project.

D Since it rains a lot here in Washington, I need to learn about how water drains. There is no real way we can fix the drainage system at the field right now unless we just started over with nothing. We can not do that since we will be playing on the field this spring. However, when I prepared the dirt for laying the grass, I sloped the field slightly from the mound to each base path to help water drain away from the field. That is the best I can do for drainage since the ground is as hard as a rock about 8-10" deep.

When the project is completed, I will have to make a presentation to my class, and to the public. I plan on orally going step-by-step through the process that I went through to make the project possible. For a visual aid, I will have before and after pictures, so that my audience can agree that my project was worth the effort. I will also give them a tour of the field so they can see what my project produced. This will give them a good picture of what went on and where, to make the field look as professional as it does. I am excited to show off the product of my hard work.

As you can see, this project of renovating the baseball infield will require a lot of time and dedication. I am still looking for donations to help me fund the project and so there is as little team fund raising as possible. I have been inspired by some fields that I have played on during the summer and wanted to help my home field become a quality that teams want to play on.

C D The plan is supplemented by the discussion in the proposal of factors involved in the renovation of the baseball field, in particular, the factors involved in irrigation of the field and renovation of the drainage system.

E F The student researched relevant precedents by obtaining information from the school district's athletics director and from sod dealers.

G H The student obtained information about the regulations governing the layout and dimensions of baseball fields. In his reflection, the student described the pleasure he experienced in "bringing perfection on to the field" by cutting out the required shapes and measuring the angles.

I He also attended to safety precautions such as not using sod with netting because, as he explained in the newspaper article, "spikes on shoes might get caught in it and injure the players."

J The extract from the student's journal records the implementation of the plan, beginning with 9/7. The steps to executing the plan are explained sensibly and could be followed by someone else.

B

Plan for Field Renovation

* Need a note book for the below information.
* Keep all the information on the computer in drive "A" on the disk there so you can put together something showing the process for the application project.
* Who are the people I need to talk to for permission to renovate the field? Keep a list of the names and phone numbers.
* Who do I need to talk to for money for the field?
* What materials will I need? List the ones that can be donated.
* What equipment will I need? List the equip. that can be donated.
* What time frames can I work with for: dirt work, layout, seeding, watering etc. Need to make a time chart with dates of expected completion of each segment. Use a calendar you can fill in.
* How much help, manual labor will I need? Who can I call on?
* When will the back-stop be put in?
* Who is the person in charge of that project. Need to coordinate both efforts together.
* Is a sprinkler system feasible for the infield?
* Needed lawn mowers.
* Progress report of the project to be sent to who?
* Where on site to put the old dirt and sod?

Baseball Field

E

Interview with Mr. _____

The Athletic Director for the _____ School District

* Brief explanation of the project. Mentors are.....
* What kinds of funds are available from the District elsewhere?
* Letters will be sent out for donations for the field. Does Mr. _____ have any ideas? _____, _____, Etc.
* What equipment does the District have to help? Like: Sod cutter, tractor, dump truck, roller, reel lawn mower, tamp-tool, transit.
* What supplies does the District have? Like: Plumbing for a sprinkler system, home plate, pitching rubber, grass seed/sod, fertilizer, 1" garden hose, dirt, sand, clay. Who do they use for these supplies?
* When is the back-stop to be taken down? Who is in charge of the project?
* When is the new back-stop to be installed? Who is in charge of that project?
* Need to know the size, location, and pressure of the water main near the field.
* Have contacted sod dealers for grass. Soil samples are very good.
* Have contacted the local newspapers for a story of the project.
* Review Site Improvement Proposal.
* Post season permit for field use.
* Require teams other than _____ to follow a permit and fee for field use. Requirements for use and some accountability system.

*

F

Questions to Ask the Sod Dealers

-What type of grasses are best for our application?

-What is the best growing season?

-What would be the latest date we would be able to seed the area?

-What equipment will we need for the job?

-Does your company have any equipment they could donate use of?

-What will we need to do to maintain the grass? (Fertilizer? Water?)

-Would seed or sod be the best for us now? What is the cost for each?

-What do we need to do for preparation prior to the grass going down for sod/seed?

-What should the soil makeup be for the base paths and around the non grassy area for the field?

-Netted or no net sod?

-We plan on contacting the local newspapers for a story on this project.
-We would be willing to do a sign in the outfield.
Called INTER.WPS

G

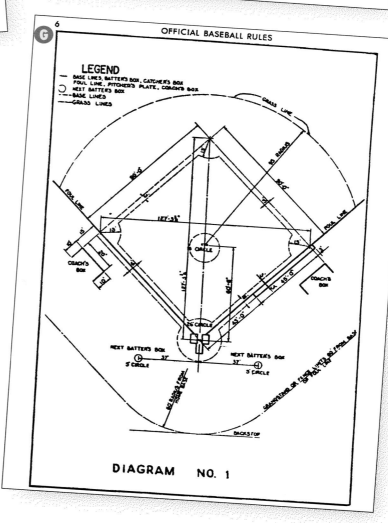

K The proposal devotes considerable attention to the need to obtain donations of materials and money to complete the project. This emphasis is reflected in the journal and in related materials.

L The press release outlines the student's strategy for obtaining the donations he needed to complete the project.

M The student documented several unforeseen problems that arose and the strategies he adopted to overcome them.

N A formal evaluation of the renovated field is not provided. However, the success of the project is implied in the newspaper article.

O The reflective statement, "Pretty much everything turned out as I had hoped," confirms that the project accomplishes most of the goals listed in the Proposal.

A1 Problem Solving

Communication Tools and Techniques

Information Tools and Techniques

Learning and **A4** Self-management Tools and Techniques

Tools and Techniques for Working With Others

Baseball Field

Reflection Paper

For my application project, I re-built the infield at
_____ High School. In early September, I
removed all of the old sod with a sod cutter that was
donated by_____Rents. Next, I leveled out the dirt, and
laid out the new sod. Then, I cut the base-paths, built the
pitcher's mound, and improved the drainage on the field.
Everything except for the new sod that was a part of this
project was donated.

From the very beginning, I had a good idea of the
amount of work that was going to be needed for this project.
I spent many more hours than I had expected on little things
like shoveling the dirt to build a slope for water to run
off. My favorite part of the project, was bringing
perfection on to the field. I liked cutting out the twenty-
eight foot circle at home plate, and measuring the angles of
the base paths.

To make the project successful, I needed to develop
some skills that would be helpful along the way. For
instance, at first, I had a hard time asking businesses for
donations. But after awhile, it soon became easier and

people were willing to help. I learned how tough it is for
grass to stay healthy during the winter Washington rain!

Along the way to completion, I ran into some difficult
times that I needed to plow through. When the old sod was
all rolled up, there was a guy that was going to load it all
up and haul it away. The night before, his dump truck broke
down. That night I went to the city council, and asked them
if they could haul the sod away for us. They liked my
project and agreed to help out with the sod and in other
ways also. The weather also was a stumbling block that
prevented my dad and me from working on the field. There
were some days that it pored rain and created a squishy
surface.

Through this project, I have learned many things. I
have never done anything like this before, so everything
that I did was all new to me. As a result of all of the
hours that I have put into the field, I now feel some
ownership. For instance, whenever I refer to the field, I
call it "My field." I am very particular about how it is
taken care of and still will continue to do most of the
maintenance on the field.

I am glad that I was able to do a project like this
with something that I love and had fun working on. Pretty
much everything turned out as I had hoped. I wish there

would have been some way that I could have protected the
grass from the heavy rain. The grass is not as thick and
healthy as it was when we installed it, but in the summer it
will bounce back. One of the major things that I have
enjoyed the most is working with my dad. He has helped me
so much in this project. I could not have done it without
him!

J

Journal

...9/7 30hrs
I talked to department of maintenance representative, Paul _____. I talked to Gene _____ at _____ turf farm, and received a deal of $.16 sod which is half price. I also talked to other turf farms. I wrote up plan of procedure for _____ field. I took dirt samples 8" below the field surface to observe the quality of the dirt. I wrote up a question sheet for turf dealers. Total hours: 30

9/8 1hr
I typed letters to businesses and procedure for the week. Total hours: 31

9/9 2hrs
I spent some time on the phone with businesses for donations. Total hours: 33

9/11 1hr
I worked on goal statement in class. Total hours: 34

9/12 5hrs
I spent all afternoon learning about donations and talked to the city council.
Total hours: 39

9/13 4hrs
My dad and I talked to Mr. _____ and set up a meeting. I talked to Bill _____ from _____ on the phone for a donation. I talked to the president of the _____ club. Wrote a letter to the _____ club. Total hours: 43

9/14 4hrs
Networked two more city council names for donations. Called news papers to cover the story. Finished goal statement. Total hours: 47

R ····▶ 9/16 2hrs
Talked to Larry_____ about raising funds. He said that everyone wants to give me something, I just have to ask and show them it is in their best interest to give it to me. Total hours: 49

9/17 2hrs
Laid out schedule for meeting with Mr. _____. Made up a bunch of questions that he could answer. Total hours: 51

9/18 3hrs
Talked to the _____. They will be doing a story with at picture at the end of the month. I transferred files on a new disk for the project. I also talked to Mr. _____ about _____'s offer. Total hours: 54

10/4 5 hrs
I dragged the field to make it smooth and flat. I used the tractor to take out fence poles and move dirt. Total hours: 88

10/5 5 hrs
Ten team members and I started laying out the sod. I also cut the grass to make the base paths, and prepared for the next day of laying sod. Total hours: 93

10/6 4 hrs
I finished laying out the sod with my team. Total hours: 97

10/17 1 hr
I worked on my proposal in class. Total hours: 98

10/19 2 hrs
I worked on my proposal in class. I also updated journal, and faxed off a wish list to the _____ club. Total hours: 100

10/26 2 hrs
I finished my proposal and timeline at home. I also updated my journal. I went to have Mark _____ sign the mentor forms and got all the other forms signed to release me from class. Total hours: 102

11/8 2 hrs
I went to the city council meeting to thank the council and tell them what we need. Ron _____ said he might be able to help with the irrigation, fence, and will give me dirt from the city. Total hours: 104

11/10 1 hr
I called Mark _____ and found out the specs for the mound and base paths. Total hours: 105

11/17 1 hr
I went out with my dad and measured the total amount of irrigation piping and equipment needed. Total hours: 106

11/20 2 hrs
I made a press release that gives all the information about the project that the press needs to know. Total hours: 108

11/21 2 hrs
I went to a meeting with _____ about the movement in teaching. I presented my project, and they agreed to do a story on it. Total hours: 110

L

Press Release

Who:
  Dustin _____
  _____
  _____
  _____

What:
  I am redoing the baseball infield at the _____ High School.

Where:
  _____ High School
  _____
  _____

Why:
  I have endured the poor quality of the infield grass, pitchers mound, and base-paths. After playing on some fields with a flat surface and nicely cut grass this summer, I dream of raising my home field to that standard.

Who is involved:
  My dad has helped me with just about everything that I have done. My mentor Mark _____ (Pitching coach _____ Community College) has also been a help with any questions I have. Some members of the team helped me lay sod.

How:
  My dad and I started with removing the old sod with a sod cutter. Next, we needed to get the old sod off the field. The city of _____ agreed to load the old sod and transport it to a provided site. Now that the grass is all gone, we prepared the soil for the new sod by roto-tilling, grading, and dragging to make level. After the soil was ready, the sod was delivered and laid. The largest obstacle is funding. The whole project will cost an expected $4,741. **We are paying this off with donations and selling outfield signs to businesses for $300.** We still have to build the pitchers mound, base-paths, and continue improving the drainage for the field.

Future:
  Applying an irrigation system.
  Building the Pitchers mound with 75% Clay and 25% dirt/sand.

Improve the base-paths with an infield mix.
Need 250' of 4' high fence with poles along the right field side to keep intruders from messing up the field.
Need a reel lawn mower to keep grass well manicured.
Need money!
Continue selling outfield signs for business advertisements for $300 each.

Who has helped:
  Lary_____ _____ club (Financial Donation)
  Chris_____ _____ Rents on Hwy 99 in _____ (All rental equipment that we needed was donated for free)
  _____ Turf and Grass Farm in Sumner (1/2 price sod. About 10,000 square feet)
  Diane_____, _____ manager donated burgers for all of the team members that helped lay sod.
  D.F. _____ Donated 150 lbs of fertilizer.

About me:
  I am 17 years old and one of the captains of the baseball team this year. I am #9 and play 3rd base. I have spent over 130 hours on the project so far.

If anything is unclear, or if you have any questions, call me at the number above!

A1 ▶ Problem Solving

Communication Tools and Techniques

Information Tools and Techniques

A4 ▶ Learning and Self-management Tools and Techniques

Tools and Techniques for Working With Others

Baseball Field

Reprinted by permission. By Leslie Moriarty, *The Herald*, Everett, WA.

A4 a Learning and Self-management Tools and Techniques: The student learns from models; that is, the student:

- consults with and observes other students and adults at work and analyzes their roles to determine the critical demands, such as demands for knowledge and skills, judgment, and decision making;

- identifies models for the results of project work, such as professionally produced publications, and analyzes their qualities;

- uses what he or she learns from models in planning and conducting project activities.

The documentation demonstrates consistent effort on the part of the student to learn from people who have expertise in areas that will benefit him.

P E Early on, the student acquired a mentor to support his efforts. The questions the student developed for his initial interview with the mentor indicate attention to the knowledge and skills needed to complete the job.

Q R S As the need to obtain donations became apparent, the student established contact with further mentors, members of the local Rotary club, who provided models for community networking.

L T U The press release, letter seeking donations, and wish list reflect the skills the student developed from these mentors.

Baseball Field

A4 b Learning and Self-management Tools and Techniques: The student reviews his or her own progress in completing work activities and adjusts priorities as needed to meet deadlines; that is, the student:

- develops and maintains work schedules that reflect consideration of priorities;
- manages time;
- monitors progress towards meeting deadlines and adjusts priorities as necessary.

B U The plan and wish list reflect development of work schedules that reflect consideration of priorities.

V The list of things to do provides evidence of time management.

The written work included with this project contains some errors. Most of the written work was completed for personal use and to provide evidence of work on the project, rather than for wider publication. The finished work consists of the press release, the letter, and the wish list. These contain virtually error free writing.

U

Wish List for the Project

1) Motorized equipment: 5-10 yard dump truck to haul the sod that has been cut from the field.
   Loader/backhoe to load the sod into the dump truck.
2) Need a site to dump the rolled sod.
3) Pea gravel or 5/8 minus for drainage. (Approx. 25 yards).
4) Soil for filling in low paarts of the grass areas. (Approx. 20 yards).
5) Fertilizer for the new grass to get a good start. (200#).
6) Grass seed to fill in the low spots. (30#)
7) Plumbing supplies for the irrigation sprinkler system. We have a design but need the supplies. This is to insure protection all year.
8) Small tractor for leveling areas to help drainage.
9) 1" rubber hose for manually watering the field.
10) 200' of 4' high fence with poles, concrete and supplies. This is for us to enclose the field to keep unwanted vehicles off the site.

Time table for the above items

Item #1:	Need this on October 3rd.
Item #2:	Same as above.
Item #3:	Same as above.
Item #4:	Sometime this winter.
Item #5:	Need on October 3rd.
Item #6:	This winter/spring.
Item #7:	The week of October 3rd.
Item #8:	This November/December.
Item #9:	Same as above.
Item #10:	Next spring.
Item #11:	Next spring.

CALLED NEEDS.WPS

Things to do this week
9/1/95

-Need maintenance man's name, address, & phone #.

-Need to send a letter to Mr._____to get written permission for what I am going to do. Explain that this is for my notebook. Name, address & phone #.

-Call Mr._____to get names, addresses, and phone #'s of who I need to talk to to get $ for the project. Schedule a time to meet those people.

-Have a plan of procedure written down to present to the people for the money.

-When is backstop being put in? Get name, address, and phone # of people involved.

-Keep track of time spent for the project.

Called 9-1-95.WPS

A1 Problem Solving

Communication Tools and Techniques

Information Tools and Techniques

A4 Learning and Self-management Tools and Techniques

Tools and Techniques for Working With Others

Work Sample & Commentary: *Fire and Home Safety*

The documentation presented from this project is not a comprehensive record of all work done as part of the project. It would be neither reasonable nor appropriate to ask students to keep detailed written records of every aspect of a project. This would defeat part of the purpose of applied learning which is for students to put their academic learning to work and to learn from projects that connect what they do at school to the demands of the twenty-first century workplace. Some of these standards lend themselves to assessment through observation and other less formal methods rather than through written work.

The task

Following several fire-related deaths in homes located in a community near the school campus, the students in a high school parenting class identified the need for local residents to become more aware of safety practices. The students assumed responsibility for planning and organizing a fire and home safety project in order to accomplish this goal. The project included home demonstrations of safety practices, installation of smoke detectors, and the distribution of first-aid kits and safety booklets.

Circumstances of performance

The students developed the safety project over a period of six weeks, in partnership with personnel from a local division of the fire department. Working usually in class or during the school day, the students produced work as individuals and in small groups and received feedback from peers and the teacher. The students were also assisted by other adults at the school. The teacher monitored the work to ensure that students accomplished content objectives.

What the work shows

A1 c Problem Solving: The student plans and organizes an event or an activity; that is, the student:

- develops a planning schedule that:
  - is sensible in terms of the goals of the event or activity;
  - is logical and achievable;
  - reflects research into relevant precedents and regulations;
  - takes account of all relevant factors;
  - communicates clearly so that a peer or colleague could use it;

A APPLIED LEARNING PARENTING CLASS JANUARY 17, 1996

Captain _____ met with the first period students
 Jaquita _____
 Candice _____
 TaShica _____
The students discussed concerns, dates, time, transportation and meals.

The following are the results of the meeting:

1. On January 22 Captain _____ will meet with periods 1 & 2 at 1:00 to demonstrate CPR. The fire department will supply the mannequins. We need your permission to talk to our first period classes and arrange to meet with second period.

   _____ Approval, Ms. _____, Principal 1/8/96

2. On January 29, 30, & 31 both classes will go together to the homes of five families. We will share the following information with the help of the fire department:

   a. install smoke detectors
   b. demonstrate CPR
   c. organize an escape route and a meeting place outside
   d. teach children how to Stop, Drop, and Roll; check closed doors, and crawl
   e. present & discuss the first aid kit and its contents
   f. 29th. we will work with 2 families from 9:00 am - 3:00 pm with the assistance of fire person Ms. Audi _____

   30th we will meet with 2 more families at the same time with Captain _____

   31st. we will meet with our last family from 9:00 am - 12:00 with the assistance of Captain _____

   Captain _____ has agreed to be responsible for transportation on all days and we have all signed permission forms from our parents to ride either in the school car or in a government vehicle.

   Also, if all goes well, Captain _____ and the fire department will be responsible for meals on two, hopefully three days.

Captain _____ did mention that if he could not get a van from the fire department, he will get in contact with Nina _____ and see if she will furnish one of those yellow buses.

3. We asked for a tour of one of the fire stations. Captain _____ suggested the largest, newest, and most equipped station at the Alliance Airport in between Fort worth and Denton. February 5th is the date chosen. With your approval we will proceed with this field trip.

   _____ Approval, Ms. _____, Principal 1/8/96

4. One last request was made for the fire department to assign a *female fire* person to talk about a career as a fire person, educational requirements, etc. Captain _____ volunteered Ms. Audi _____ for this request.

(left sidebar navigation)
Problem Solving **A1**
Communication Tools and Techniques **A2**
Information Tools and Techniques **A3**
Learning and Self-management Tools and Techniques **A4**
Tools and Techniques for Working With Others **A5**

This work sample illustrates a standard-setting performance for the following parts of the standards:

A1 c **Problem Solving: Plan and organize an event or an activity.**

A2 a **Communication: Make an oral presentation.**

A3 a **Information: Gather information.**

A4 a **Learning and Self-management: Learn from models.**

A5 a **Working With Others: Participate in the establishment and operation of a self-directed work team.**

- implements and adjusts the planning schedule in ways that:
  - make efficient use of time, money, people, resources, facilities;
  - reflect established priorities;
  - respond effectively to unforeseen circumstances;
- evaluates the success of the event or activity using qualitative and/or quantitative methods;
- makes recommendations for planning and organizing subsequent similar events or activities.

Having clearly defined a need and a goal, the students formulated a plan and followed it step by step

Fire and Home Safety

B

Itinerary for Fire and Home Safety Project

I. **Introduction**

    Candice _____

II. **Install smoke detectors**

    Lindsey _____
    Stacee _____
    Latoya _____

III. **Explain contents of the first aid kit**

    Catrina _____
    Roseanne _____
    Jennifer _____

IV. **Show how to:**
    make escape routes
    choose a meeting place outside the home
    Stop, Drop, and Roll

    TaShica _____
    Tamara _____
    JaQuita _____
    Danya _____

V. **Demonstrate CPR**

    Maria _____
    Catherine _____
    Candice _____

C

Home Safety Check List

*Post local emergency numbers(s).

*Have battery-operated smoke detectors.

*Keep medications safely and securely stored out of the reach of children.

*Keep cleansers and other poisonous materials safely and securly stored.

*Turn off the oven and other appliances after use.

*Keep a <u>working</u> fire extinguisher in your home.

*Have a emergency plan in the event of injury, sudden illness, or natural disaster.

*I practice emergency plans with my family or roommates.

*Wear a safety belt when driving or riding in a motor vehicle.

*Refrain from operating motor vehicles after drinking alcoholic beverages.

*If you own a gun, you should keep it unloaded and locked in a safe place.

*Stairs where you live should have rails.

*Use a stepladder or sturdy sstool to reach high, out-of-reach objects.

*Have adequate lighting in halls and stairways.

*Use good lifting techniques when lifting.

*You and your child should wear a helmet when riding a bicycle, motorcycle, or skateboarding.

*You and your child should wear a lifejacket when participating in activities on or near the water.

* You should use safety protection, such as goggles and hearing protection, and follow equipment safety recommendations when operating power tools.

to a successful conclusion. The students recorded the process in a scrapbook in such a way that other people can easily follow it. (All the documents and photographs shown here appeared originally in the scrapbook.)

A The project was proposed to the principal by a representative group from the class. The principal's approval is implied by her approval of this subsequent, related correspondence.

B The students accomplished the goal of increasing the families' awareness of safety practices by arranging to visit several homes. At the homes, they installed smoke detectors; demonstrated CPR, the Heimlich maneuver, and "Stop, Drop, Roll," and helped families chart escape routes in case of a fire.

A They made all the arrangements needed to organize the home visits. Their involvement of a captain from the local fire department provided the students with a direct (and essential) source of information and advice on relevant regulations. The captain trained them in administering CPR and the Heimlich maneuver. He also helped them install the smoke detectors when they visited the families.

C D After researching relevant procedures, the students wrote a "Home Safety Check List" for posting in the homes and designed a safety booklet for use by the families. These are extracts from the safety booklet.

D

-Preparing for emergencies

-Keep information about you and your family in a handy place, such as on the refrigerator door or in your automobile glove compartment.

-Keep medical and insurance records up-to-date.

- Find out if your community is served by an emergency 911 telephone number. If it is not, look up the numbers for the police or fire department, EMS, and poison control center. Emergency numbers are usually listed in the front of the telephone book. Teach everyone in your home how and when to use these numbers.

-Keep emergency telephone numbers in handy place, such as by the telephone or in the first aid kit. Include home and work numbers of family members and friends who can help. Be sure to keep both lists current.

-Keep a first aid kit handy in your home, automobile, workplace, and recreation area.

-Learn and practice first aid skills.

-Make sure your house or apartment number is easy to read. Numerals are easier to read than spelled out numbers.

-Wear a medical alert tag if you have the a potentially serious medical condition, such as epilepsy, diabetes, heart disease, or allergies.

D

Gun Safety

Every day in America, 12 children under the age of 19 are killed by a gun. Many more are wounded.
The numbers are shocking and disturbing. But, worst of all, they're growing. And what makes this problem especially painful is that it doesn't have to happen.
Parents who have guns in their homes, and even those who don't, should educate their children about the dangers of firearms. News reports state that nearly 90% of accidental shootings involving children are linked to easy-to-find, loaded handguns in the home. Here are some guidelines to help prevent you and your child from becoming victims of unnecessary tragedy.

* Guns should be stored and locked away so they are not accessible to children.

*Any gun that is in the house should be unloaded at all times.

*Ammunition should be stored to same way as guns - out of reach and out of sight. It should also be locked away in a different place that the gun.

*Ask your local police for education on safe storage and gun locks.

*In case children encounter a gun in their own home, at a friend or neighbor's house, or in a public place, they should be taught to follow these simple but i important rules:

A1 Problem Solving

A2 Communication Tools and Techniques

A3 Information Tools and Techniques

A4 Learning and Self-management Tools and Techniques

A5 Tools and Techniques for Working With Others

Fire and Home Safety

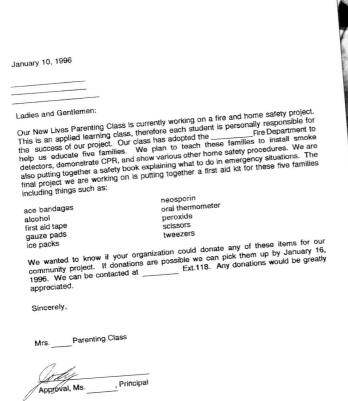

E

January 10, 1996

_____
_____

Ladies and Gentlemen:

Our New Lives Parenting Class is currently working on a fire and home safety project. This is an applied learning class, therefore each student is personally responsible for the success of our project. Our class has adopted the _____ Fire Department to help us educate five families. We plan to teach these families to install smoke detectors, demonstrate CPR, and show various other home safety procedures. We are also putting together a safety book explaining what to do in emergency situations. The final project we are working on is putting together a first aid kit for these five families including things such as:

ace bandages	neosporin
alcohol	oral thermometer
first aid tape	peroxide
gauze pads	scissors
ice packs	tweezers

We wanted to know if your organization could donate any of these items for our community project. If donations are possible we can pick them up by January 16, 1996. We can be contacted at _____ Ext.118. Any donations would be greatly appreciated.

Sincerely,

Mrs. _____ Parenting Class

_____
Approval, Ms. _____, Principal

G

Thank you letters that must be written.

Catherine 1. A letter to all parents for letting us come into their home and make the presentation.

Jaquita 2. A letter to Mr. John _____ for his patience and donation of reduced prices for the meals.

Candice 3. Captain _____ for walking us all over city hall after we had a delicious meal

Maria 4. Randy for driving and having a good time with us

5. Ms. _____ for going on the field trip with us *Collins*

6. Ms. _____ for going on the field trip with us

LaJoya 7. _____ for their donation of pizza

TaShica 8. _____ Fire Department for sharing two of their vans for transportation

Brandy 9. Mrs. _____ for furnishing the last family for us

Jennifer 10. Assistant city manager for sitting and encouraging us to pursue a career in life

Catrina 11. The acting mayor for the pens and for taking time from her busy schedule to talk to us.

Tanya 12. Mrs. _____ for her support and guidance/paying for transportation to _____

Lasenia 13. Mrs. _____ / Mrs. _____ for proof reading and checking the grammar on most of the papers we mailed or faxed from the building

Lindsey 14. A letter to all donators letting them know the project was a success and because of their donations we were able to help five families in this city

15. A letter to _____ Telegram (Class Acts) explaining our project and the success we had

Stacee 16. A write up to Channel __ (Family First) again explaining our project and the success.

E Later, the class collected supplies for first-aid kits that they gave to the families.

F The samples contain evidence that the students considered relevant factors and made efficient use of time, people, and resources. Because their resources for funding the project were limited, the students made strategic decisions to explore alternatives. They contacted representatives of several businesses and organizations, including the acting mayor, and asked for donations or supplies in order to provide families with first-aid kits and smoke detectors.

G The thank you list confirms their success.

H When possible, students located information written in Spanish and included it in their safety materials in order to accommodate bilingual families.

I J K The thank you note from one of the families and the students' own evaluations indicate the activity accomplished its goal. The students used professional practices, hence their assessment of the project as a success was based not only on their opinion but also on comparison of their performance with that of adults who perform these same tasks.

Problem Solving **A1**

Communication Tools and Techniques **A2**

Information Tools and Techniques **A3**

Learning and Self-management Tools and Techniques **A4**

Tools and Techniques for Working With Others **A5**

Fire and Home Safety

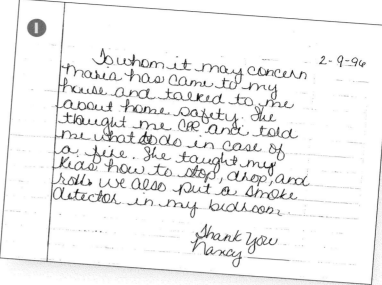

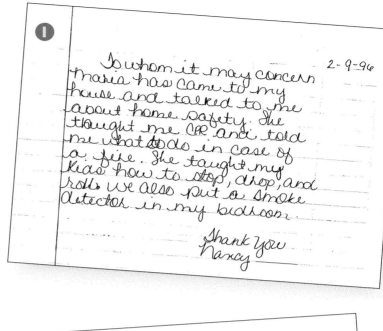

A2 a Communication Tools and Techniques: The student makes an oral presentation of project plans or findings to an audience with expertise in the relevant subject matter; that is, the student:

- organizes the presentation in a logical way appropriate to its purpose;

- adjusts the style of presentation to suit its purpose and audience;

- speaks clearly and presents confidently;

- responds appropriately to questions from the audience;

- evaluates the effectiveness of the presentation and identifies appropriate revisions for a future presentation.

L As an integral component of the project, the students made oral presentations in which they combined practical applications with providing useful information. The students used the data they collected to explain home safety practices and then utilized the training they had received in order to demonstrate safety procedures to several families.

M The students performed the presentation and demonstration in the presence of a safety expert who accompanied them to the homes of the families. The hands-on nature of the presentation was appropriate for the audience and purpose of the task. The complimentary letter from the expert verifies that the students did "an outstanding job of communicating with...and...instructing [the] families...."

A1 Problem Solving

A2 Communication Tools and Techniques

A3 Information Tools and Techniques

A4 Learning and Self-management Tools and Techniques

A5 Tools and Techniques for Working With Others

Fire and Home Safety

A3 a Information Tools and Techniques: The student gathers information to assist in completing project work; that is, the student:

- identifies potential sources of information to assist in completing the project;
- uses appropriate techniques to collect the information, e.g., considers sampling issues in conducting a survey;
- interprets and analyzes the information;
- evaluates the information in terms of completeness, relevance, and validity;
- shows evidence of research in the completed project.

The project required the collection of information about safety practices.

N **O** One group of students took responsibility for researching the effects of smoke inhalation and teaching the class about ways of avoiding these effects.

K

Final Evaluation

At the beginning of the project I really thought that it was a good idea. We were going to be able to teach families how important it is to be ready in case of a fire. I helped develop the home safety book, which included information on what to do in an emergency.

What I liked most about the project was that I got to interact with my classmates. Since I'm very shy it gave me the opportunity to work and get to know them. I wouldn't change anything about the project because it was all well organized. We provided all the information that was needed and was very important to know.

When we went out to the families I had to demonstrate CPR. We taught families what to do if an infant or grown-up is choking or not breathing. The group I worked with was very cooperative and friendly. We agreed on everything and helped each other. The visit to the families was fun. They were nice and generous with us. They listened to what we had to say and most important of all, they let us come into their homes.

What I learned during the project was that it is very important to be prepared in case of emergencies. That having an escape route and a meeting place can save many lives. The fire department educated us and in turn we educated the families. We adopted the _____ Fire Department. Captain _____ _____ works for the fire department educating people in the community about home safety. He was very helpful to us in this project because he provided transportation to families houses. Captain _____ also helped install the smoke detectors which he and the _____ Fire Department provided.

If I were grading myself I would give myself an A. The reason for this is that I think I explained CPR very good. I got along with my classmates and did what I was told to do. I also believe, for me being so shy I really came out and did my part for this project.

February 9, 1996

Maria _____   *Mrs. _____*

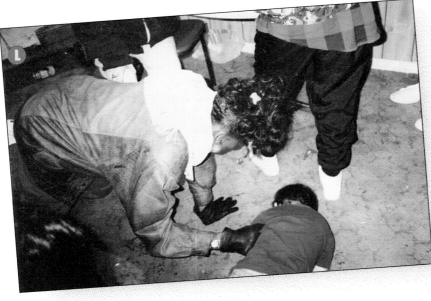

M

CITY OF _____

June 4, 1996

To Whom it May Concern;

It was my pleasure to work with the Parenting Students at _____ School to teach fire and home safety to five families in Fort Worth. The students and I went out to the homes of these five families and provided the following:

* CPR Training
* First Aid Training
* Rescue Breathing
* Installed Smoke Detectors
* Presented a Home Safety Book that discussed treatment and illustrated types of burns, insect bites, and poisonings. The book also included fire escape and tornado drill planning for homes, etc.
* Presented a Home safety kit with the essentials for common accidents in the home.

The _____ Parenting students did an outstanding job of communicating with the families and sharing very important and needed information. It was wonderful working with students that had a purpose and motivation to work with others in their neighborhood.

The students were excellent and did an outstanding job of instructing families. I strongly feel that this lifesaving information could possibly aid in saving a life in a fire or emergency medical situation.

Thank you,

Larry
Captain Larry _____

Fire and Home Safety

Sonya

Hilda

Dilantha

N What Smoke Inhalation does to your lungs in a fire and why it causes death.

When you breathe, air enters through the nose or mouth, passes through the pharynx, and then moves downward into the trachea, or windpipe. After it goes down the windpipe it goes into two large tubes called bronchial tubes. At the end of the bronchial tubes there are alveoli sacs. Oxygen and carbon dioxide exchange occurs in the alveoli. Blood then reaches the alveoli via capillaries which comes from the pulmonary arteries. In the alveoli, the level of carbon dioxide is low and the oxygen level is high. Under these conditions, the carbon dioxide in the blood diffuses into the alveoli and the oxygen in the alveoli diffuses into the blood. This is the breathing process for a normal person.

When smoke from a fire goes through, it passes the same way. The chemicals in the fire are absorbed by the lungs and transferred to other parts of the body to do damage. The irritant gases include chlorine, nitrogen dioxide, ammonia, and sulfur dioxide. These cause changes in the

airways, including inflammation and obstruction of the airways. There is an airway obstruction because of chemical tracheobronchitis caused by inhalation particulate debris and irritant volatile vapours from synthetic polymers on materials used in construction, furniture, and decorations. Instead of breathing in oxygen, you breathe in heated gas that cooks your lungs. You don't receive any oxygen and the only thing that your body has is the toxic gas, which eventually kills you. Most deaths from fires occur from smoke inhalation, and not from flames. Some of the most volatile vapors are in furniture, construction and decorations.

A4a Learning and Self-management Tools and Techniques: The student learns from models; that is, the student:

- consults with and observes other students and adults at work and analyzes their roles to determine the critical demands, such as demands for knowledge and skills, judgment, and decision making;
- identifies models for the results of project work, such as professionally produced publications, and analyzes their qualities;
- uses what he or she learns from models in planning and conducting project activities.

M The students modeled their work on the work of a safety expert, a captain from the local fire department. The safety expert provided training in the techniques the students were to demonstrate to the families and was in attendance at each of the home visits. There is evidence of the students making use of what they learned from their model in planning and conducting the project. The safety expert supported this in his evaluation of the students' work.

A5a Tools and Techniques for Working With Others: The student participates in the establishment and operation of self-directed work teams; that is, the student:

- defines roles and shares responsibilities among members;
- sets objectives and time frames for the work to be completed;
- establishes processes for group decision making;
- reviews progress and makes adjustments as required.

B The itinerary indicates that the students organized themselves into teams to conduct the project with each team taking responsibility for a specific aspect of the project.

J **K** The students' self-evaluations provide some evidence of the work processes established by the groups, but do not provide evidence on which to base specific commentary in relation to the criteria identified above.

The written work included with this project contains some errors. For the main part, the errors are confined to working documents which were not intended for publication. The three pieces of finished writing are the proposal, the Home Safety Check List, and the extracts from the safety booklet. These contain virtually error free writing.

A1 Problem Solving

A2 Communication Tools and Techniques

A3 Information Tools and Techniques

A4 Learning and Self-management Tools and Techniques

A5 Tools and Techniques for Working With Others

APPENDIX I

The elementary school standards are set at a level of performance approximately equivalent to the end of fourth grade. The middle school standards are set at a level of performance approximately equivalent to the end of eighth grade. The high school standards are set at a level of performance approximately equivalent to the end of tenth grade. It is expected that some students might achieve these levels earlier and others later than these grades.

An array of work is required to achieve any single standard. The work becomes increasing refined and sophisticated as students get older. The complexity of the tasks used to generate the work also increases. This notion of requiring students to hone the sophistication of their performances while simultaneously working with increasingly complex assignments cuts across all the English Language Arts standards.

These standards allow for oral performances of student work whenever appropriate.

Elementary School

E1 a The student reads at least twenty-five books or book equivalents each year. The quality and complexity of the materials to be read are illustrated in the sample reading list. The materials should include traditional and contemporary literature (both fiction and non-fiction) as well as magazines, newspapers, textbooks, and on-line materials. Such reading should represent a diverse collection of material from at least three different literary forms and from at least five different writers.

E1 b The student reads and comprehends at least four books (or book equivalents) about one issue or subject, or four books by a single writer, or four books in one genre, and produces evidence of reading that:

* makes and supports warranted and responsible assertions about the texts;

* supports assertions with elaborated and convincing evidence;

* draws the texts together to compare and contrast themes, characters, and ideas;

* makes perceptive and well developed connections;

* evaluates writing strategies and elements of the author's craft.

E1 c The student reads and comprehends informational materials to develop understanding and expertise and produces written or oral work that:

* restates or summarizes information;

* relates new information to prior knowledge and experience;

* extends ideas;

* makes connections to related topics or information.

E1 d The student reads aloud, accurately (in the range of 85-90%), familiar material of the quality and complexity illustrated in the sample reading list, and in a way that makes meaning clear to listeners by:

* self correcting when subsequent reading indicates an earlier miscue;

* using a range of cueing systems, e.g., phonics and context clues, to determine pronunciation and meanings;

* reading with a rhythm, flow, and meter that sounds like everyday speech.

Middle School

E1 a The student reads at least twenty-five books or book equivalents each year. The quality and complexity of the materials to be read are illustrated in the sample reading list. The materials should include traditional and contemporary literature (both fiction and non-fiction) as well as magazines, newspapers, textbooks, and on-line materials. Such reading should represent a diverse collection of material from at least three different literary forms and from at least five different writers.

E1 b The student reads and comprehends at least four books (or book equivalents) about one issue or subject, or four books by a single writer, or four books in one genre, and produces evidence of reading that:

* makes and supports warranted and responsible assertions about the texts;

* supports assertions with elaborated and convincing evidence;

* draws the texts together to compare and contrast themes, characters, and ideas;

* makes perceptive and well developed connections;

* evaluates writing strategies and elements of the author's craft.

E1 c The student reads and comprehends informational materials to develop understanding and expertise and produces written or oral work that:

* restates or summarizes information;

* relates new information to prior knowledge and experience;

* extends ideas;

* makes connections to related topics or information.

E1 d The student demonstrates familiarity with a variety of public documents (i.e., documents that focus on civic issues or matters of public policy at the community level and beyond) and produces written or oral work that does one or more of the following:

* identifies the social context of the document;

* identifies the author's purpose and stance;

* analyzes the arguments and positions advanced and the evidence offered in support of them, or formulates an argument and offers evidence to support it;

High School

E1 a The student reads at least twenty-five books or book equivalents each year. The quality and complexity of the materials to be read are illustrated in the sample reading list. The materials should include traditional and contemporary literature (both fiction and non-fiction) as well as magazines, newspapers, textbooks, and on-line materials. Such reading should represent a diverse collection of material from at least three different literary forms and from at least five different writers.

E1 b The student reads and comprehends at least four books (or book equivalents) about one issue or subject, or four books by a single writer, or four books in one genre, and produces evidence of reading that:

* makes and supports warranted and responsible assertions about the texts;

* supports assertions with elaborated and convincing evidence;

* draws the texts together to compare and contrast themes, characters, and ideas;

* makes perceptive and well developed connections;

* evaluates writing strategies and elements of the author's craft.

E1 c The student reads and comprehends informational materials to develop understanding and expertise and produces written or oral work that:

* restates or summarizes information;

* relates new information to prior knowledge and experience;

* extends ideas;

* makes connections to related topics or information.

E6 Public Documents

E6 a The student critiques public documents with an eye to strategies common in public discourse, including:

* effective use of argument;

* use of the power of anecdote;

* anticipation of counter-claims;

* appeal to audiences both friendly and hostile to the position presented;

* use of emotionally laden words and imagery;

* citing of appropriate references or authorities.

E6b The student produces public documents, in which the student:

- exhibits an awareness of the importance of precise word choice and the power of imagery and/or anecdote;

- utilizes and recognizes the power of logical arguments, arguments based on appealing to a reader's emotions, and arguments dependent upon the writer's persona;

- uses arguments that are appropriate in terms of the knowledge, values, and degree of understanding of the intended audience;

- uses a range of strategies to appeal to readers.

Functional Documents

E7a The student critiques functional documents with an eye to strategies common to effective functional documents, including:

- visual appeal, e.g., format, graphics, white space, headers;

- logic of the sequence in which the directions are given;

- awareness of possible reader misunderstandings.

E7b The student produces functional documents appropriate to audience and purpose, in which the student:

- reports, organizes, and conveys information and ideas accurately;

- includes relevant narrative details, such as scenarios, definitions, and examples;

- anticipates readers' problems, mistakes, and misunderstandings;

- uses a variety of formatting techniques, such as headings, subordinate terms, foregrounding of main ideas, hierarchical structures, graphics, and color;

- establishes a persona that is consistent with the document's purpose;

- employs word choices that are consistent with the persona and appropriate for the intended audience.

- examines or makes use of the appeal of a document to audiences both friendly and hostile to the position presented;

- identifies or uses commonly used persuasive techniques.

E1e The student demonstrates familiarity with a variety of functional documents (i.e., documents that exist in order to get things done) and produces written or oral work that does one or more of the following:

- identifies the institutional context of the document;

- identifies the sequence of activities needed to carry out a procedure;

- analyzes or uses the formatting techniques used to make a document user-friendly;

- identifies any information that is either extraneous or missing in terms of audience and purpose or makes effective use of relevant information.

Much writing can be classified as belonging to the public arena. New Standards, however, defines public documents to mean those pieces of text that are concerned with public policy, that address controversial issues confronting the public, or that arise in response to controversial issues or public policy. Public documents are included in the Reading standard at middle school level (**E1d**) and constitute a separate standard at high school level (**E5**). At the middle school level, the issues students write about come primarily from the school or local community. At high school, students should address issues which are of national importance.

Functional writing is writing that exists in order to get things done. Functional writing is ordinarily considered technical writing and, as such, is often not part of the typical English curriculum. New Standards requires students to demonstrate proficiency with functional writing because such writing is of increasing importance to the complex literacy of our culture. Functional documents are included in the Reading standard at middle school level (**E1e**) and constitute a separate standard at high school level (**E7**).

APPENDIX I

The number of books required for **E1 a** does not increase as students get older, but the length and complexity of what is read does increase (as indicated by the sample reading lists), so, this standard becomes increasingly formidable.

E1 a assumes an adequate library of appropriate reading material. In some places, library resources are too meager to support the amount of reading required for every student to achieve this standard. Where a shortage of books exists, better use of out-of-school resources must be made; for example, students may have to be assured access to local or county libraries.

Reading twenty-five books a year entails a substantial amount of time. Students may use materials read in conjunction with their regular class work, including courses other than English, to satisfy this requirement.

Elementary School

Fiction

Brink, *Caddie Woodlawn;*
Cleary, *Ramona and Her Father;*
Coerr, *The Josefina Story Quilt;*
Cohen, *Fat Jack;*
De Saint-Exupery, *The Little Prince;*
Hamilton, *Zeely;*
Hansen, *The Gift-Giver;*
Lord, *In the Year of the Boar and Jackie Robinson;*
Mendez and Byard, *The Black Snowman;*
Naidoo, *Journey to Jo'Burg;*
O'Dell, *Zia;*
Ringgold, *Tar Beach;*
Speare, *The Sign of the Beaver;*
Yep, *Child of the Owl.*

Non-Fiction

Aliki, *Corn Is Maize: The Gift of the Indians;*
Baylor, *The Way to Start a Day;*
Cherry, *The Great Kapok Tree;*
Epstein, *History of Women in Science for Young People;*
Greenfield, *Childtimes: A Three-Generation Memoir;*
Godkin, *Wolf Island;*
Hamilton, *Anthony Burns: The Defeat and Triumph of a Fugitive Slave;*
McKissack, *Frederick Douglass: The Black Lion;*
Politi, *Song of the Swallows;*
Sattler, *Dinosaurs of North America;*
Fritz, *And Then What Happened, Paul Revere?;*
McGovern, *The Secret Soldier: The Story of Deborah Sampson.*

Poetry

Ahlberg, *Heard It in the Playground;*
Blishen and Wildsmith, *Oxford Book of Poetry for Children;*
De Regniers, Moore, White, and Carr, eds., *Sing a Song of Popcorn;*
Giovanni, *Ego-Tripping and Other Poems for Young People;*
Greenfield, *Honey, I Love and Other Love Poems;*
Heard, *For the Good of the Earth and Sun;*
Janeczko, *Strings: A Gathering of Family Poems;*
Koch and Farrell, eds., *Talking to the Sun;*
Lobel, ed., *The Random House Book of Mother Goose;*
Manguel, ed., *Seasons;*
Mathis, *Red Dog, Blue Fly: Football Poems;*
Silverstein, *Where the Sidewalk Ends.*

Folklore

Griego y Maestas, *Cuentos: Tales From the Hispanic Southwest;*
French, *Snow White in New York;*
Huck and Lobel, *Princess Furball;*
Louie and Young, *Yeh-Shen: A Cinderella Story From China;*

Middle School

Fiction

Anaya, *Bless Me, Ultima;*
Armstrong, *Sounder;*
Bonham, *Durango Street;*
Cohen, *Tell Us Your Secret;*
Collier, *My Brother Sam Is Dead;*
Cormier, *I Am the Cheese;*
Danziger, *The Cat Ate My Gymsuit;*
Fast, *April Morning;*
Gaines, *A Gathering of Old Men;*
Goldman, *The Princess Bride;*
Greene, *Summer of My German Soldier;*
Hansen, *Which Way Freedom;*
Hinton, *The Outsiders;*
Holman, *Slake's Limbo;*
London, *The Call of the Wild;*
Mathis, *Listen for the Fig Tree;*
Mohr, *Nilda;*
Neufeld, *Lisa, Bright and Dark;*
O'Brien, *Z for Zachariah;*
Reiss, *The Upstairs Room;*
Schaefer, *Shane;*
Stevenson, *Treasure Island;*
Voigt, *Dicey's Song;*
Walker, *To Hell With Dying;*
Walter, *Because We Are;*
Zindel, *The Pigman.*

Non-Fiction

Amory, *The Cat Who Came for Christmas;*
Berck, *No Place to Be: Voices of Homeless Children;*
Frank, *The Diary of a Young Girl;*
George, *The Talking Earth;*
Gilbreth, *Cheaper by the Dozen;*
Haskins, *Outward Dreams;*
Hautzig, *Endless Steppe: A Girl in Exile;*
Herriott, *All Creatures Great and Small;*
Lester, *To Be a Slave;*
Meyers, *Pearson, a Harbor Seal Pup;*
Soto, *Living Up the Street;*
White, *Ryan White: My Own Story;*
Yates, *Amos Fortune, Free Man.*

Poetry

Adams, *Poetry of Earth and Sky;*
Eliot, *Old Possum's Book of Practical Cats;*
Frost, *You Come Too;*
Greenfield, *Night on Neighborhood Street;*
Livingston, *Cat Poems.*

Drama

Blinn, *Brian's Song;*
Davis, *Escape to Freedom;*
Gibson, *The Miracle Worker;*
Lawrence and Lee, *Inherit the Wind;*
Osborn, *On Borrowed Time;*

High School

Fiction

Carroll, *Alice in Wonderland;*
Cisneros, *The House on Mango Street;*
Clark, *The Ox-Bow Incident;*
Golding, *Lord of the Flies;*
Hawthorne, *The Scarlet Letter;*
Hemingway, *For Whom the Bell Tolls;*
Hentoff, *The Day They Came to Arrest the Book;*
Hilton, *Goodbye, Mr. Chips;*
Kinsella, *Shoeless Joe;*
Knowles, *A Separate Peace;*
Lee, *To Kill a Mockingbird;*
McCullers, *The Heart Is a Lonely Hunter;*
Orwell, *1984;*
Paulsen, *Canyons;*
Portis, *True Grit;*
Potok, *Davita's Harp;*
Stoker, *Dracula;*
Wartski, *A Boat to Nowhere;*
Welty, *The Golden Apples.*

Non-Fiction

Angell, *Late Innings;*
Angelou, *I Know Why the Caged Bird Sings;*
Ashe, *Days of Grace;*
Beal, *"I Will Fight No More Forever": Chief Joseph and the Nez Perce War;*
Bishop, *The Day Lincoln Was Shot;*
Bloom, *The Closing of the American Mind;*
Campbell, *The Power of Myth;*
Covey, *Seven Habits of Highly Effective People;*
Galarza, *Barrio Boy;*
Hawking, *A Brief History of Time;*
Houston, *Farewell to Manzanar;*
Kennedy, *Profiles in Courage;*
Kingsley and Levitz, *Count Us In: Growing Up With Down Syndrome;*
Kingston, *Woman Warrior;*
Mazer, ed., *Going Where I'm Coming From;*
Momaday, *The Way to Rainy Mountain;*
Rodriquez, *Hunger of Memory;*
Sternberg, *User's Guide to the Internet;*
Wright, *Black Boy.*

Poetry

Angelou, *I Shall Not be Moved;*
Bly, ed., *News of the Universe;*
Cummings, *Collected Poems;*
Dickinson, *Complete Poems;*
Randall, ed., *The Black Poets;*
Carruth, ed., *The Voice That Is Great Within Us;*
Hughes, *Selected Poems;*
Knudson and Swenson, eds., *American Sports Poems;*
Longfellow, *Evangeline;*
Wilbur, *Things of This World.*

Luenn, *The Dragon Kite*;
Goble, *Buffalo Woman*;
Steptoe, *Mufaro's Beautiful Daughters*;
Steptoe, *The Story of Jumping Mouse*;
Kipling, *The Elephant's Child*;
Lee, *Legend of the Milky Way*.

Modern Fantasy and Science Fiction

Andersen, *The Ugly Duckling*;
Bond, *A Bear Called Paddington*;
Dahl, *James and the Giant Peach*;
Grahame, *The Wind in the Willows*;
Lewis, *The Lion, the Witch and the Wardrobe*;
Norton, *The Borrowers*;
Van Allsburg, *Jumanji*;
White, *Charlotte's Web*.

Children's magazines

Weekly Reader;
Creative Classroom;
Social Studies for the Young Learner;
World (National Geographic);
News (Scholastic);
Action (Scholastic).

Other

Newspapers, manuals appropriate for elementary school children, e.g., video game instructions, computer manuals.

Shakespeare, *A Midsummer Night's Dream*;
Stone, *Metamora, or, the Last of the Wampanoags*.

Folklore/Mythology

Blair, *Tall Tale America*;
Bruchac, *The First Strawberries: A Cherokee Story*;
Bryan, *Beat the Story-Drum, Pum-Pum*;
D'Aulaire, *Norse Gods and Giants*;
Gallico, *The Snow Goose*;
Lee, *Toad Is the Uncle of Heaven: A Vietnamese Folk Tale*;
Pyle, *Merry Adventures of Robin Hood*.

Modern Fantasy and Science Fiction

Bradbury, *Dandelion Wine*;
Babbitt, *Tuck Everlasting*;
Cooper, *The Grey King*;
Hamilton, *The Magical Adventures of Pretty Pearl*;
L'Engle, *A Wrinkle in Time*;
Tolkien, *The Hobbit*;
Yep, *Dragon of the Lost Sea*.

Magazines/Periodicals

Scope (Scholastic);
World (National Geographic);
Junior Scholastic (Scholastic);
Science World (Scholastic);
Cobblestone (American history);
Calliope (world history);
Faces (anthropology);
Odyssey (science).

Other

Computer manuals; instructions; contracts. See also the reading lists included in award books corresponding to reading provided by the Girl Scouts of the U.S.A. and the Boy Scouts of America.

Drama

Christie, *And Then There Were None*;
Hansberry, *A Raisin in the Sun*;
McCullers, *The Member of the Wedding*;
Pomerance, *The Elephant Man*;
Rose, *Twelve Angry Men*;
Rostand, *Cyrano de Bergerac*;
Shakespeare, *Romeo and Juliet*; *Julius Caesar*;
Van Druten, *I Remember Mama*;
Wilder, *The Skin of Our Teeth*;
Wilson, *The Piano Lesson*.

Folklore/Mythology

Evslin, *Adventures of Ulysses*;
Pinsent, *Greek Mythology*;
Stewart, *The Crystal Cave*;
Burland, *North American Indian Mythology*;
White, *The Once and Future King*.

Modern Fantasy and Science Fiction

Adams, *Watership Down*;
Asimov, *Foundation*;
Bradbury, *The Martian Chronicles*;
Clarke, *2001: A Space Odyssey*;
Clarke, *Childhood's End*;
Frank, *Alas, Babylon*;
Herbert, *Dune*;
Lewis, *Out of the Silent Planet*;
McCaffrey, *Dragonflight*;
Twain, *A Connecticut Yankee in King Arthur's Court*;
Verne, *20,000 Leagues Under the Sea*.

Magazines and Newspapers

Omni;
Sports Illustrated;
Literary Cavalcade (Scholastic);
National Geographic;
Smithsonian;
Newsweek;
Time.

Other

Computer manuals; instructions; contracts; technical materials.

APPENDIX I

E2 b is meant to replace the repertoire of responses that students traditionally write when they respond to literature. This type of response requires an understanding of writing strategies.

The work students produce to meet the English Language Arts standards does not all have to come from an English class. Students should be encouraged to use work from subjects in addition to English to demonstrate their accomplishments. The work samples include some examples of work produced in other classes that meet requirements of these standards.

Elementary School

E2 a The student produces a report that:

- engages the reader by establishing a context, creating a persona, and otherwise developing reader interest;
- develops a controlling idea that conveys a perspective on the subject;
- creates an organizing structure appropriate to a specific purpose, audience, and context;
- includes appropriate facts and details;
- excludes extraneous and inappropriate information;
- uses a range of appropriate strategies, such as providing facts and details, describing or analyzing the subject, and narrating a relevant anecdote;
- provides a sense of closure to the writing.

E2 b The student produces a response to literature that:

- engages the reader by establishing a context, creating a persona, and otherwise developing reader interest;
- advances a judgment that is interpretive, analytic, evaluative, or reflective;
- supports judgment through references to the text, references to other works, authors, or non-print media, or references to personal knowledge;
- demonstrates an understanding of the literary work;
- provides a sense of closure to the writing.

E2 c The student produces a narrative account (fictional or autobiographical) that:

- engages the reader by establishing a context, creating a point of view, and otherwise developing reader interest;
- establishes a situation, plot, point of view, setting, and conflict (and for autobiography, the significance of events);
- creates an organizing structure;
- includes sensory details and concrete language to develop plot and character;
- excludes extraneous details and inconsistencies;
- develops complex characters;
- uses a range of appropriate strategies, such as dialogue and tension or suspense;
- provides a sense of closure to the writing.

Middle School

E2 a The student produces a report that:

- engages the reader by establishing a context, creating a persona, and otherwise developing reader interest;
- develops a controlling idea that conveys a perspective on the subject;
- creates an organizing structure appropriate to purpose, audience, and context;
- includes appropriate facts and details;
- excludes extraneous and inappropriate information;
- uses a range of appropriate strategies, such as providing facts and details, describing or analyzing the subject, narrating a relevant anecdote, comparing and contrasting, naming, and explaining benefits or limitations;
- provides a sense of closure to the writing.

E2 b The student produces a response to literature that:

- engages the reader through establishing a context, creating a persona, and otherwise developing reader interest;
- advances a judgment that is interpretive, analytic, evaluative, or reflective;
- supports a judgment through references to the text, references to other works, authors, or non-print media, or references to personal knowledge;
- demonstrates an understanding of the literary work;
- anticipates and answers a reader's questions;
- provides a sense of closure to the writing.

E2 c The student produces a narrative account (fictional or autobiographical) that:

- engages the reader by establishing a context, creating a point of view, and otherwise developing reader interest;
- establishes a situation, plot, point of view, setting, and conflict (and for autobiography, the significance of events and of conclusions that can be drawn from those events);
- creates an organizing structure;
- includes sensory details and concrete language to develop plot and character;
- excludes extraneous details and inconsistencies;

High School

E2 a The student produces a report that:

- engages the reader by establishing a context, creating a persona, and otherwise developing reader interest;
- develops a controlling idea that conveys a perspective on the subject;
- creates an organizing structure appropriate to purpose, audience, and context;
- includes appropriate facts and details;
- excludes extraneous and inappropriate information;
- uses a range of appropriate strategies, such as providing facts and details, describing or analyzing the subject, narrating a relevant anecdote, comparing and contrasting, naming, explaining benefits or limitations, demonstrating claims or assertions, and providing a scenario to illustrate;
- provides a sense of closure to the writing.

E2 b The student produces a response to literature that:

- engages the reader through establishing a context, creating a persona, and otherwise developing reader interest;
- advances a judgment that is interpretive, analytic, evaluative, or reflective;
- supports a judgment through references to the text, references to other works, authors, or non-print media, or references to personal knowledge;
- demonstrates understanding of the literary work through suggesting an interpretation;
- anticipates and answers a reader's questions;
- recognizes possible ambiguities, nuances, and complexities;
- provides a sense of closure to the writing.

E2 c The student produces a narrative account (fictional or autobiographical) that:

- engages the reader by establishing a context, creating a point of view, and otherwise developing reader interest;
- establishes a situation, plot, point of view, setting, and conflict (and for autobiography, the significance of events and of conclusions that can be drawn from those events);
- creates an organizing structure;
- includes sensory details and concrete language to develop plot and character;
- excludes extraneous details and inconsistencies;
- develops complex characters;
- uses a range of appropriate strategies, such as dialogue, tension or suspense, naming, pacing,

E2d The student produces a narrative procedure that:

- engages the reader by establishing a context, creating a persona, and otherwise developing reader interest;
- provides a guide to action that anticipates a reader's needs; creates expectations through predictable structures, e.g., headings; and provides transitions between steps;
- makes use of appropriate writing strategies such as creating a visual hierarchy and using white space and graphics as appropriate;
- includes relevant information;
- excludes extraneous information;
- anticipates problems, mistakes, and misunderstandings that might arise for the reader;
- provides a sense of closure to the writing.

- develops complex characters;
- uses a range of appropriate strategies, such as dialogue, tension or suspense, naming, and specific narrative action, e.g., movement, gestures, expressions;
- provides a sense of closure to the writing.

E2d The student produces a narrative procedure that:

- engages the reader by establishing a context, creating a persona, and otherwise developing reader interest;
- provides a guide to action for a relatively complicated procedure in order to anticipate a reader's needs; creates expectations through predictable structures, e.g., headings; and provides transitions between steps;
- makes use of appropriate writing strategies such as creating a visual hierarchy and using white space and graphics as appropriate;
- includes relevant information;
- excludes extraneous information;
- anticipates problems, mistakes, and misunderstandings that might arise for the reader;
- provides a sense of closure to the writing.

E2e The student produces a persuasive essay that:

- engages the reader by establishing a context, creating a persona, and otherwise developing reader interest;
- develops a controlling idea that makes a clear and knowledgeable judgment;
- creates and organizes a structure that is appropriate to the needs, values, and interests of a specified audience, and arranges details, reasons, examples, and anecdotes effectively and persuasively;
- includes appropriate information and arguments;
- excludes information and arguments that are irrelevant;
- anticipates and addresses reader concerns and counter-arguments;
- supports arguments with detailed evidence, citing sources of information as appropriate;
- provides a sense of closure to the writing.

- and specific narrative action, e.g., movement, gestures, expressions;
- provides a sense of closure to the writing.

E2d The student produces a narrative procedure that:

- engages the reader by establishing a context, creating a persona, and otherwise developing reader interest;
- provides a guide to action for a complicated procedure in order to anticipate a reader's needs; creates expectations through predictable structures, e.g., headings; and provides smooth transitions between steps;
- makes use of appropriate writing strategies, such as creating a visual hierarchy and using white space and graphics as appropriate;
- includes relevant information;
- excludes extraneous information;
- anticipates problems, mistakes, and misunderstandings that might arise for the reader;
- provides a sense of closure to the writing.

E2e The student produces a persuasive essay that:

- engages the reader by establishing a context, creating a persona, and otherwise developing reader interest;
- develops a controlling idea that makes a clear and knowledgeable judgment;
- creates an organizing structure that is appropriate to the needs, values, and interests of a specified audience, and arranges details, reasons, examples, and anecdotes effectively and persuasively;
- includes appropriate information and arguments;
- excludes information and arguments that are irrelevant;
- anticipates and addresses reader concerns and counter-arguments;
- supports arguments with detailed evidence, citing sources of information as appropriate;
- uses a range of strategies to elaborate and persuade, such as definitions, descriptions, illustrations, examples from evidence, and anecdotes;
- provides a sense of closure to the writing.

E2f The student produces a reflective essay that:

- engages the reader by establishing a context, creating a persona, and otherwise developing reader interest;
- analyzes a condition or situation of significance;
- develops a commonplace, concrete occasion as the basis for the reflection, e.g., personal observation or experience;
- creates an organizing structure appropriate to purpose and audience;
- uses a variety of writing strategies, such as concrete details, comparing and contrasting, naming, describing, creating a scenario;
- provides a sense of closure to the writing.

E3 Speaking, Listening, and Viewing

Elementary School

E3a The student participates in one-to-one conferences with a teacher, paraprofessional, or adult volunteer, in which the student:

- initiates new topics in addition to responding to adult-initiated topics;
- asks relevant questions;
- responds to questions with appropriate elaboration;
- uses language cues to indicate different levels of certainty or hypothesizing, e.g., "what if…," "very likely…," "I'm unsure whether…";
- confirms understanding by paraphrasing the adult's directions or suggestions.

E3b The student participates in group meetings, in which the student:

- displays appropriate turn-taking behaviors;
- actively solicits another person's comment or opinion;
- offers own opinion forcefully without dominating;
- responds appropriately to comments and questions;
- volunteers contributions and responds when directly solicited by teacher or discussion leader;
- gives reasons in support of opinions expressed;
- clarifies, illustrates, or expands on a response when asked to do so; asks classmates for similar expansions;

E3c The student prepares and delivers an individual presentation, in which the student:

- shapes information to achieve a particular purpose and to appeal to the interests and background knowledge of audience members;
- shapes content and organization according to criteria for importance and impact rather than according to availability of information in resource materials;
- uses notes or other memory aids to structure the presentation;
- engages the audience with appropriate verbal cues and eye contact;
- projects a sense of individuality and personality in selecting and organizing content, and in delivery.

Middle School

E3a The student participates in one-to-one conferences with a teacher, paraprofessional, or adult volunteer, in which the student:

- initiates new topics in addition to responding to adult-initiated topics;
- asks relevant questions;
- responds to questions with appropriate elaboration;
- uses language cues to indicate different levels of certainty or hypothesizing, e.g., "what if…," "very likely…," "I'm unsure whether…";
- confirms understanding by paraphrasing the adult's directions or suggestions.

E3b The student participates in group meetings, in which the student:

- displays appropriate turn-taking behaviors;
- actively solicits another person's comment or opinion;
- offers own opinion forcefully without dominating;
- responds appropriately to comments and questions;
- volunteers contributions and responds when directly solicited by teacher or discussion leader;
- gives reasons in support of opinions expressed;
- clarifies, illustrates, or expands on a response when asked to do so; asks classmates for similar expansions;
- employs a group decision-making technique such as brainstorming or a problem-solving sequence (e.g., recognize problem, define problem, identify possible solutions, select optimal solution, implement solution, evaluate solution).

E3c The student prepares and delivers an individual presentation in which the student:

- shapes information to achieve a particular purpose and to appeal to the interests and background knowledge of audience members;
- shapes content and organization according to criteria for importance and impact rather than according to availability of information in resource materials;
- uses notes or other memory aids to structure the presentation;

High School

E3a The student participates in one-to-one conferences with a teacher, paraprofessional, or adult volunteer, in which the student:

- initiates new topics in addition to responding to adult-initiated topics;
- asks relevant questions;
- responds to questions with appropriate elaboration;
- uses language cues to indicate different levels of certainty or hypothesizing, e.g., "what if…," "very likely…," "I'm unsure whether…";
- confirms understanding by paraphrasing the adult's directions or suggestions.

E3b The student participates in group meetings, in which the student:

- displays appropriate turn-taking behaviors;
- actively solicits another person's comment or opinion;
- offers own opinion forcefully without dominating;
- responds appropriately to comments and questions;
- volunteers contributions and responds when directly solicited by teacher or discussion leader;
- gives reasons in support of opinions expressed;
- clarifies, illustrates, or expands on a response when asked to do so; asks classmates for similar expansions;
- employs a group decision-making technique such as brainstorming or a problem-solving sequence (e.g., recognize problem, define problem, identify possible solutions, select optimal solution, implement solution, evaluate solution);
- divides labor so as to achieve the overall group goal efficiently.

E3c The student prepares and delivers an individual presentation, in which the student:

- shapes information to achieve a particular purpose and to appeal to the interests and background knowledge of audience members;
- shapes content and organization according to criteria for importance and impact rather than according to availability of information in resource materials;

⊞d The student makes informed judgments about television, radio, and film productions; that is, the student:

- demonstrates an awareness of the presence of the media in the daily lives of most people;
- evaluates the role of the media in focusing attention and in forming an opinion;
- judges the extent to which the media provide a source of entertainment as well as a source of information;
- defines the role of advertising as part of media presentation.

- develops several main points relating to a single thesis;
- engages the audience with appropriate verbal cues and eye contact;
- projects a sense of individuality and personality in selecting and organizing content, and in delivery.

⊞d The student makes informed judgments about television, radio, and film productions; that is, the student:

- demonstrates an awareness of the presence of the media in the daily lives of most people;
- evaluates the role of the media in focusing attention and in forming opinion;
- judges the extent to which the media are a source of entertainment as well as a source of information;
- defines the role of advertising as part of media presentation.

- uses notes or other memory aids to structure the presentation;
- develops several main points relating to a single thesis;
- engages the audience with appropriate verbal cues and eye contact;
- projects a sense of individuality and personality in selecting and organizing content, and in delivery.

⊞d The student makes informed judgments about television, radio, and film productions; that is, the student:

- demonstrates an awareness of the presence of the media in the daily lives of most people;
- evaluates the role of the media in focusing attention and in forming opinion;
- judges the extent to which the media are a source of entertainment as well as a source of information;
- defines the role of advertising as part of media presentation.

⊞e The student listens to and analyzes a public speaking performance; that is, the student:

- takes notes on salient information;
- identifies types of arguments (e.g., causation, authority, analogy) and identifies types of logical fallacies (e.g., ad hominem, inferring causation from correlation, over-generalization);
- accurately summarizes the essence of each speaker's remarks;
- formulates a judgment about the issues under discussion.

E4 Conventions, Grammar, and Usage of the English Language

Elementary School

E4a The student demonstrates a basic understanding of the rules of the English language in written and oral work, and selects the structures and features of language appropriate to the purpose, audience, and context of the work. The student demonstrates control of:

- grammar;
- paragraph structure;
- punctuation;
- sentence construction;
- spelling;
- usage.

E4b The student analyzes and subsequently revises work to clarify it or make it more effective in communicating the intended message or thought. The student's revisions should be made in light of the purposes, audiences, and contexts that apply to the work. Strategies for revising include:

- adding or deleting details;
- adding or deleting explanations;
- clarifying difficult passages;
- rearranging words, sentences, and paragraphs to improve or clarify meaning;
- sharpening the focus;
- reconsidering the organizational structure.

Middle School

E4a The student demonstrates an understanding of the rules of the English language in written and oral work, and selects the structures and features of language appropriate to the purpose, audience, and context of the work. The student demonstrates control of:

- grammar;
- paragraph structure;
- punctuation;
- sentence construction;
- spelling;
- usage.

E4b The student analyzes and subsequently revises work to clarify it or make it more effective in communicating the intended message or thought. The student's revisions should be made in light of the purposes, audiences, and contexts that apply to the work. Strategies for revising include:

- adding or deleting details;
- adding or deleting explanations;
- clarifying difficult passages;
- rearranging words, sentences, and paragraphs to improve or clarify meaning;
- sharpening the focus;
- reconsidering the organizational structure.

High School

E4a The student independently and habitually demonstrates an understanding of the rules of the English language in written and oral work, and selects the structures and features of language appropriate to the purpose, audience, and context of the work. The student demonstrates control of:

- grammar;
- paragraph structure;
- punctuation;
- sentence construction;
- spelling;
- usage.

E4b The student analyzes and subsequently revises work to clarify it or make it more effective in communicating the intended message or thought. The student's revisions should be made in light of the purposes, audiences, and contexts that apply to the work. Strategies for revising include:

- adding or deleting details;
- adding or deleting explanations;
- clarifying difficult passages;
- rearranging words, sentences, and paragraphs to improve or clarify meaning;
- sharpening the focus;
- reconsidering the organizational structure;
- rethinking and/or rewriting the piece in light of different audiences and purposes.

E5 Literature

Elementary School

E5 a The student responds to non-fiction, fiction, poetry, and drama using interpretive, critical, and evaluative processes; that is, the student:

- identifies recurring themes across works;
- analyzes the impact of authors' decisions regarding word choice and content;
- considers the differences among genres;
- evaluates literary merit;
- considers the function of point of view or persona;
- examines the reasons for a character's actions, taking into account the situation and basic motivation of the character;
- identifies stereotypical characters as opposed to fully developed characters;
- critiques the degree to which a plot is contrived or realistic;
- makes inferences and draws conclusions about contexts, events, characters, and settings.

E5 b The student produces work in at least one literary genre that follows the conventions of the genre.

Middle School

E5 a The student responds to non-fiction, fiction, poetry, and drama using interpretive, critical, and evaluative processes; that is, the student:

- identifies recurring themes across works;
- interprets the impact of authors' decisions regarding word choice, content, and literary elements;
- identifies the characteristics of literary forms and genres;
- evaluates literary merit;
- identifies the effect of point of view;
- analyzes the reasons for a character's actions, taking into account the situation and basic motivation of the character;
- makes inferences and draws conclusions about fictional and non-fictional contexts, events, characters, settings, and themes;
- identifies stereotypical characters as opposed to fully developed characters;
- identifies the effect of literary devices such as figurative language, allusion, diction, dialogue, and description.

E5 b The student produces work in at least one literary genre that follows the conventions of the genre.

High School

E5 a The student responds to non-fiction, fiction, poetry, and drama using interpretive, critical, and evaluative processes; that is, the student:

- makes thematic connections among literary texts, public discourse, and media;
- evaluates the impact of authors' decisions regarding word choice, style, content, and literary elements;
- analyzes the characteristics of literary forms and genres;
- evaluates literary merit;
- explains the effect of point of view;
- makes inferences and draws conclusions about fictional and non-fictional contexts, events, characters, settings, themes, and styles;
- interprets the effect of literary devices, such as figurative language, allusion, diction, dialogue, description, symbolism;
- evaluates the stance of a writer in shaping the presentation of a subject;
- interprets ambiguities, subtleties, contradictions, ironies, and nuances;
- understands the role of tone in presenting literature (both fictional and non-fictional);
- demonstrates how literary works (both fictional and non-fictional) reflect the culture that shaped them.

E5 b The student produces work in at least one literary genre that follows the conventions of the genre.

M1 Arithmetic and Number Concepts/Number and Operation Concepts

The elementary school standards are set at a level of performance approximately equivalent to the end of fourth grade. The middle school standards are set at a level of performance approximately equivalent to the end of eighth grade. The high school standards are set at a level of performance approximately equivalent to the end of tenth grade or the end of the common core. It is expected that some students might achieve these levels earlier and others later than these grades.

Elementary School

The student produces evidence that demonstrates understanding of arithmetic and number concepts; that is, the student:

M1 a Adds, subtracts, multiplies, and divides whole numbers, with and without calculators; that is:

- adds, i.e., joins things together, increases;

- subtracts, i.e., takes away, compares, finds the difference;

- multiplies, i.e., uses repeated addition, counts by multiples, combines things that come in groups, makes arrays, uses area models, computes simple scales, uses simple rates;

- divides, i.e., puts things into groups, shares equally; calculates simple rates;

- analyzes problem situations and contexts in order to figure out when to add, subtract, multiply, or divide;

- solves arithmetic problems by relating addition, subtraction, multiplication, and division to one another;

- computes answers mentally, e.g., 27 + 45, 30 x 4;

- uses simple concepts of negative numbers, e.g., on a number line, in counting, in temperature, "owing."

M1 b Demonstrates understanding of the base ten place value system and uses this knowledge to solve arithmetic tasks; that is:

- counts 1, 10, 100, or 1,000 more than or less than, e.g., 1 less than 10,000, 10 more than 380, 1,000 more than 23,000, 100 less than 9,000;

- uses knowledge about ones, tens, hundreds, and thousands to figure out answers to multiplication and division tasks, e.g., 36 x 10, 18 x 100, 7 x 1,000, 4,000 ÷ 4.

M1 c Estimates, approximates, rounds off, uses landmark numbers, or uses exact numbers, as appropriate, in calculations.

M1 d Describes and compares quantities by using concrete and real world models of simple fractions; that is:

- finds simple parts of wholes;

- recognizes simple fractions as instructions to divide, e.g., ¼ of something is the same as dividing something by 4;

- recognizes the place of fractions on number lines, e.g., in measurement;

Middle School

The student produces evidence that demonstrates understanding of number and operation concepts; that is, the student:

M1 a Consistently and accurately adds, subtracts, multiplies, and divides rational numbers using appropriate methods (e.g., the student can add ½ + % mentally or on paper but may opt to add ¹³⁄₂₄ + ⁵⁷⁄₆₈ on a calculator) and raises rational numbers to whole number powers. (Students should have facility with the different kinds and forms of rational numbers, i.e., integers, both whole numbers and negative integers; and other positive and negative rationals, written as decimals, as percents, or as proper, improper, or mixed fractions. Irrational numbers, i.e., those that cannot be written as a ratio of two integers, are not required content but are suitable for introduction, especially since the student should be familiar with the irrational number π.)

M1 b Uses and understands the inverse relationships between addition and subtraction, multiplication and division, and exponentiation and root-extraction (e.g., squares and square roots, cubes and cube roots); uses the inverse operation to determine unknown quantities in equations.

M1 c Consistently and accurately applies and converts the different kinds and forms of rational numbers.

M1 d Is familiar with characteristics of numbers (e.g., divisibility, prime factorization) and with properties of operations (e.g., commutativity and associativity), short of formal statements.

M1 e Interprets percent as part of 100 and as a means of comparing quantities of different sizes or changing sizes.

M1 f Uses ratios and rates to express "part-to-part" and "whole-to-whole" relationships, and reasons proportionally to solve problems involving equivalent fractions, equal ratios, or constant rates, recognizing the multiplicative nature of these problems in the constant factor of change.

M1 g Orders numbers with the > and < relationships and by location on a number line; estimates and compares rational numbers using sense of the magnitudes and relative magnitudes of numbers and of base-ten place values (e.g., recognizes relationships to "benchmark" numbers ½ and 1 to conclude that the sum ½ + % must be between 1 and 1½ (likewise, ¹³⁄₂₄ + ⁵⁷⁄₆₈)).

High School

The student produces evidence that demonstrates understanding of number and operation concepts; that is, the student:

M1 a Uses addition, subtraction, multiplication, division, exponentiation, and root-extraction in forming and working with numerical and algebraic expressions.

M1 b Understands and uses operations such as opposite, reciprocal, raising to a power, taking a root, and taking a logarithm.

M1 c Has facility with the mechanics of operations as well as understanding of their typical meaning and uses in applications.

M1 d Understands and uses number systems: natural, integer, rational, and real.

M1 e Represents numbers in decimal or fraction form and in scientific notation, and graphs numbers on the number line and number pairs in the coordinate plane.

M1 f Compares numbers using order relations, differences, ratios, proportions, percents, and proportional change.

M1 g Carries out proportional reasoning in cases involving part-whole relationships and in cases involving expansions and contractions.

M1 h Understands dimensionless numbers, such as proportions, percents, and multiplicative factors, as well as numbers with specific units of measure, such as numbers with length, time, and rate units.

M1 i Carries out counting procedures such as those involving sets (unions and intersections) and arrangements (permutations and combinations).

M1 j Uses concepts such as prime, relatively prime, factor, divisor, multiple, and divisibility in solving problems involving integers.

M1 k Uses a scientific calculator effectively and efficiently in carrying out complex calculations.

M1 l Recognizes and represents basic number patterns, such as patterns involving multiples, squares, or cubes.

- uses drawings, diagrams, or models to show what the numerator and denominator mean, including when adding like fractions, e.g., ⅛ + ⅜, or when showing that ¾ is more than ⅝;

- uses beginning proportional reasoning and simple ratios, e.g., "about half of the people."

M e Describes and compares quantities by using simple decimals; that is:

- adds, subtracts, multiplies, and divides money amounts;

- recognizes relationships among simple fractions, decimals, and percents, i.e., that ½ is the same as 0.5, and ½ is the same as 50%, with concrete materials, diagrams, and in real world situations, e.g., when discovering the chance of a coin landing on heads or tails.

M f Describes and compares quantities by using whole numbers up to 10,000; that is:

- connects ideas of quantities to the real world, e.g., how many people fit in the school's cafeteria; how far away is a kilometer;

- finds, identifies, and sorts numbers by their properties, e.g., odd, even, multiple, square.

M2 Geometry and Measurement Concepts

APPENDIX II

Elementary School

The student produces evidence that demonstrates understanding of geometry and measurement concepts; that is, the student:

M2 a Gives and responds to directions about location, e.g., by using words such as "in front of," "right," and "above."

M2 b Visualizes and represents two dimensional views of simple rectangular three dimensional shapes, e.g., by showing the front view and side view of a building made of cubes.

M2 c Uses simple two dimensional coordinate systems to find locations on a map and to represent points and simple figures.

M2 d Uses many types of figures (angles, triangles, squares, rectangles, rhombi, parallelograms, quadrilaterals, polygons, prisms, pyramids, cubes, circles, and spheres) and identifies the figures by their properties, e.g., symmetry, number of faces, two- or three-dimensionality, no right angles.

M2 e Solves problems by showing relationships between and among figures, e.g., using congruence and similarity, and using transformations including flips, slides, and rotations.

M2 f Extends and creates geometric patterns using concrete and pictorial models.

M2 g Uses basic ways of estimating and measuring the size of figures and objects in the real world, including length, width, perimeter, and area.

M2 h Uses models to reason about the relationship between the perimeter and area of rectangles in simple situations.

M2 i Selects and uses units, both formal and informal as appropriate, for estimating and measuring quantities such as weight, length, area, volume, and time.

M2 j Carries out simple unit conversions, such as between cm and m, and between hours and minutes.

M2 k Uses scales in maps, and uses, measures, and creates scales for rectangular scale drawings based on work with concrete models and graph paper.

Middle School

The student produces evidence that demonstrates understanding of geometry and measurement concepts in the following areas; that is, the student:

M2 a Is familiar with assorted two- and three-dimensional objects, including squares, triangles, other polygons, circles, cubes, rectangular prisms, pyramids, spheres, and cylinders.

M2 b Identifies similar and congruent shapes and uses transformations in the coordinate plane, i.e., translations, rotations, and reflections.

M2 c Identifies three dimensional shapes from two dimensional perspectives; draws two dimensional sketches of three dimensional objects that preserve significant features.

M2 d Determines and understands length, area, and volume (as well as the differences among these measurements), including perimeter and surface area; uses units, square units, and cubic units of measure correctly; computes areas of rectangles, triangles, and circles; computes volumes of prisms.

M2 e Recognizes similarity and rotational and bilateral symmetry in two- and three-dimensional figures.

M2 f Analyzes and generalizes geometric patterns, such as tessellations and sequences of shapes.

M2 g Measures angles, weights, capacities, times, and temperatures using appropriate units.

M2 h Chooses appropriate units of measure and converts measure with ease between like units, e.g., inches and miles, within a customary or metric system. (Conversions between customary and metric are not required.)

M2 i Reasons proportionally in situations with similar figures.

M2 j Reasons proportionally with measurements to interpret maps and to make smaller and larger scale drawings.

M2 k Models situations geometrically to formulate and solve problems.

High School

The student produces evidence that demonstrates understanding of geometry and measurement concepts; that is, the student:

M2 a Models situations geometrically to formulate and solve problems.

M2 b Works with two- and three-dimensional figures and their properties, including polygons and circles, cubes and pyramids, and cylinders, cones, and spheres.

M2 c Uses congruence and similarity in describing relationships between figures.

M2 d Visualizes objects, paths, and regions in space, including intersections and cross sections of three dimensional figures, and describes these using geometric language.

M2 e Knows, uses, and derives formulas for perimeter, circumference, area, surface area, and volume of many types of figures.

M2 f Uses the Pythagorean Theorem in many types of situations, and works through more than one proof of this theorem.

M2 g Works with similar triangles, and extends the ideas to include simple uses of the three basic trigonometric functions.

M2 h Analyzes figures in terms of their symmetries using, for example, concepts of reflection, rotation, and translation.

M2 i Compares slope (rise over run) and angle of elevation as measures of steepness.

M2 j Investigates geometric patterns, including sequences of growing shapes.

M2 k Works with geometric measures of length, area, volume, and angle; and non-geometric measures such as weight and time.

M2 l Uses quotient measures, such as speed and density, that give "per unit" amounts; and uses product measures, such as person-hours.

M2 m Understands the structure of standard measurement systems, both SI and customary, including unit conversions and dimensional analysis.

M2 n Solves problems involving scale, such as in maps and diagrams.

M2 o Represents geometric curves and graphs of functions in standard coordinate systems.

M2 p Analyzes geometric figures and proves simple things about them using deductive methods.

M2 q Explores geometry using computer programs such as CAD software, Sketchpad programs, or LOGO.

M3 Function and Algebra Concepts

Elementary School

The student produces evidence that demonstrates understanding of function and algebra concepts; that is, the student:

M3 a Uses linear patterns to solve problems; that is:

- shows how one quantity determines another in a linear ("repeating") pattern, i.e., describes, extends, and recognizes the linear pattern by its rule, such as, the total number of legs on a given number of horses can be calculated by counting by fours;

- shows how one quantity determines another quantity in a functional relationship based on a linear pattern, e.g., for the "number of people and total number of eyes," figure out how many eyes 100 people have all together.

M3 b Builds iterations of simple non-linear patterns, including multiplicative and squaring patterns (e.g., "growing" patterns) with concrete materials, and recognizes that these patterns are not linear.

M3 c Uses the understanding that an equality relationship between two quantities remains the same as long as the same change is made to both quantities.

M3 d Uses letters, boxes, or other symbols to stand for any number, measured quantity, or object in simple situations with concrete materials, i.e., demonstrates understanding and use of a beginning concept of a variable.

Middle School

The student produces evidence that demonstrates understanding of function and algebra concepts; that is, the student:

M3 a Discovers, describes, and generalizes patterns, including linear, exponential, and simple quadratic relationships, i.e., those of the form $f(n)=n^2$ or $f(n)=cn^2$, for constant c, including $A=\pi r^2$, and represents them with variables and expressions.

M3 b Represents relationships with tables, graphs in the coordinate plane, and verbal or symbolic rules.

M3 c Analyzes tables, graphs, and rules to determine functional relationships.

M3 d Finds solutions for unknown quantities in linear equations and in simple equations and inequalities.

High School

The student produces evidence that demonstrates understanding of function and algebra concepts; that is, the student:

M3 a Models given situations with formulas and functions, and interprets given formulas and functions in terms of situations.

M3 b Describes, generalizes, and uses basic types of functions: linear, exponential, power, rational, square and square root, and cube and cube root.

M3 c Utilizes the concepts of slope, evaluation, and inverse in working with functions.

M3 d Works with rates of many kinds, expressed numerically, symbolically, and graphically.

M3 e Represents constant rates as the slope of a straight line graph, and interprets slope as the amount of one quantity (y) per unit amount of another (x).

M3 f Understands and uses linear functions as a mathematical representation of proportional relationships.

M3 g Uses arithmetic sequences and geometric sequences and their sums, and sees these as the discrete forms of linear and exponential functions, respectively.

M3 h Defines, uses, and manipulates expressions involving variables, parameters, constants, and unknowns in work with formulas, functions, equations, and inequalities.

M3 i Represents functional relationships in formulas, tables, and graphs, and translates between pairs of these.

M3 j Solves equations symbolically, graphically, and numerically, especially linear, quadratic, and exponential equations; and knows how to use the quadratic formula for solving quadratic equations.

M3 k Makes predictions by interpolating or extrapolating from given data or a given graph.

M3 l Understands the basic algebraic structure of number systems.

M3 m Uses equations to represent curves such as lines, circles, and parabolas.

M3 n Uses technology such as graphics calculators to represent and analyze functions and their graphs.

M3 o Uses functions to analyze patterns and represent their structure.

APPENDIX II

M4 Statistics and Probability Concepts

Elementary School

The student produces evidence that demonstrates understanding of statistics and probability concepts in the following areas; that is, the student:

M4 a Collects and organizes data to answer a question or test a hypothesis by comparing sets of data.

M4 b Displays data in line plots, graphs, tables, and charts.

M4 c Makes statements and draws simple conclusions based on data; that is:

• reads data in line plots, graphs, tables, and charts;

• compares data in order to make true statements, e.g., "seven plants grew at least 5 cm";

• identifies and uses the mode necessary for making true statements, e.g., "more people chose red";

• makes true statements based on a simple concept of average (median and mean), for a small sample size and where the situation is made evident with concrete materials or clear representations;

• interprets data to determine the reasonableness of statements about the data, e.g., "twice as often," "three times faster";

• uses data, including statements about the data, to make a simple concluding statement about a situation, e.g., "This kind of plant grows better near sunlight because the seven plants that were near the window grew at least 5 cm."

M4 d Gathers data about an entire group or by sampling group members to understand the concept of sample, i.e., that a large sample leads to more reliable information, e.g., when flipping coins.

M4 e Predicts results, analyzes data, and finds out why some results are more likely, less likely, or equally likely.

M4 f Finds all possible combinations and arrangements within certain constraints involving a limited number of variables.

Middle School

The student produces evidence that demonstrates understanding of statistics and probability concepts; that is, the student:

M4 a Collects data, organizes data, and displays data with tables, charts, and graphs that are appropriate, i.e., consistent with the nature of the data.

M4 b Analyzes data with respect to characteristics of frequency and distribution, including mode and range.

M4 c Analyzes appropriately central tendencies of data by considering mean and median.

M4 d Makes conclusions and recommendations based on data analysis.

M4 e Critiques the conclusions and recommendations of others' statistics.

M4 f Considers the effects of missing or incorrect information.

M4 g Formulates hypotheses to answer a question and uses data to test hypotheses.

M4 h Represents and determines probability as a fraction of a set of equally likely outcomes; recognizes equally likely outcomes, and constructs sample spaces (including those described by numerical combinations and permutations).

M4 i Makes predictions based on experimental or theoretical probabilities.

M4 j Predicts the result of a series of trials once the probability for one trial is known.

High School

The student demonstrates understanding of statistics and probability concepts; that is, the student:

M4 a Organizes, analyzes, and displays single-variable data, choosing appropriate frequency distribution, circle graphs, line plots, histograms, and summary statistics.

M4 b Organizes, analyzes, and displays two-variable data using scatter plots, estimated regression lines, and computer generated regression lines and correlation coefficients.

M4 c Uses sampling techniques to draw inferences about large populations.

M4 d Understands that making an inference about a population from a sample always involves uncertainty and that the role of statistics is to estimate the size of that uncertainty.

M4 e Formulates hypotheses to answer a question and uses data to test hypotheses.

M4 f Interprets representations of data, compares distributions of data, and critiques conclusions and the use of statistics, both in school materials and in public documents.

M4 g Explores questions of experimental design, use of control groups, and reliability.

M4 h Creates and uses models of probabilistic situations and understands the role of assumptions in this process.

M4 i Uses concepts such as equally likely, sample space, outcome, and event in analyzing situations involving chance.

M4 j Constructs appropriate sample spaces, and applies the addition and multiplication principles for probabilities.

M4 k Uses the concept of a probability distribution to discuss whether an event is rare or reasonably likely.

M4 l Chooses an appropriate probability model and uses it to arrive at a theoretical probability for a chance event.

M4 m Uses relative frequencies based on empirical data to arrive at an experimental probability for a chance event.

M4 n Designs simulations including Monte Carlo simulations to estimate probabilities.

M4 o Works with the normal distribution in some of its basic applications.

APPENDIX II

M5 Problem Solving and Mathematical Reasoning

Elementary School

The student demonstrates logical reasoning throughout work in mathematics, i.e., concepts and skills, problem solving, and projects; demonstrates problem solving by using mathematical concepts and skills to solve non-routine problems that do not lay out specific and detailed steps to follow; and solves problems that make demands on all three aspects of the solution process—formulation, implementation, and conclusion.

Formulation

M5a Given the basic statement of a problem situation, the student:

- makes the important decisions about the approach, materials, and strategies to use, i.e., does not merely fill in a given chart, use a pre-specified manipulative, or go through a predetermined set of steps;

- uses previously learned strategies, skills, knowledge, and concepts to make decisions;

- uses strategies, such as using manipulatives or drawing sketches, to model problems.

Implementation

M5b The student makes the basic choices involved in planning and carrying out a solution; that is, the student:

- makes up and uses a variety of strategies and approaches to solving problems and uses or learns approaches that other people use, as appropriate;

- makes connections among concepts in order to solve problems;

- solves problems in ways that make sense and explains why these ways make sense, e.g., defends the reasoning, explains the solution.

Conclusion

M5c The student moves beyond a particular problem by making connections, extensions, and/or generalizations; for example, the student:

- explains a pattern that can be used in similar situations;

- explains how the problem is similar to other problems he or she has solved;

- explains how the mathematics used in the problem is like other concepts in mathematics;

- explains how the problem solution can be applied to other school subjects and in real world situations;

- makes the solution into a general rule that applies to other circumstances.

Middle School

The student demonstrates problem solving by using mathematical concepts and skills to solve non-routine problems that do not lay out specific and detailed steps to follow, and solves problems that make demands on all three aspects of the solution process—formulation, implementation, and conclusion.

Formulation

M5a The student participates in the formulation of problems; that is, given the basic statement of a problem situation, the student:

- formulates and solves a variety of meaningful problems;

- extracts pertinent information from situations and figures out what additional information is needed.

Implementation

M5b The student makes the basic choices involved in planning and carrying out a solution; that is, the student:

- uses and invents a variety of approaches and understands and evaluates those of others;

- invokes problem solving strategies, such as illustrating with sense-making sketches to clarify situations or organizing information in a table;

- determines, where helpful, how to break a problem into simpler parts;

- solves for unknown or undecided quantities using algebra, graphing, sound reasoning, and other strategies;

- integrates concepts and techniques from different areas of mathematics;

- works effectively in teams when the nature of the task or the allotted time makes this an appropriate strategy.

Conclusion

M5c The student provides closure to the solution process through summary statements and general conclusions; that is, the student:

- verifies and interprets results with respect to the original problem situation;

- generalizes solutions and strategies to new problem situations.

High School

The student demonstrates problem solving by using mathematical concepts and skills to solve non-routine problems that do not lay out specific and detailed steps to follow, and solves problems that make demands on all three aspects of the solution process—formulation, implementation, and conclusion.

Formulation

M5a The student participates in the formulation of problems; that is, given the statement of a problem situation, the student:

- fills out the formulation of a definite problem that is to be solved;

- extracts pertinent information from the situation as a basis for working on the problem;

- asks and answers a series of appropriate questions in pursuit of a solution and does so with minimal "scaffolding" in the form of detailed guiding questions.

Implementation

M5b The student makes the basic choices involved in planning and carrying out a solution; that is, the student:

- chooses and employs effective problem solving strategies in dealing with non-routine and multi-step problems;

- selects appropriate mathematical concepts and techniques from different areas of mathematics and applies them to the solution of the problem;

- applies mathematical concepts to new situations within mathematics and uses mathematics to model real world situations involving basic applications of mathematics in the physical and biological sciences, the social sciences, and business.

Conclusion

M5c The student provides closure to the solution process through summary statements and general conclusions; that is, the student:

- concludes a solution process with a useful summary of results;

- evaluates the degree to which the results obtained represent a good response to the initial problem;

- formulates generalizations of the results obtained;

- carries out extensions of the given problem to related problems.

Mathematical reasoning

M5 d The student demonstrates mathematical reasoning by generalizing patterns, making conjectures and explaining why they seem true, and by making sensible, justifiable statements; that is, the student:

- formulates conjectures and argues why they must be or seem true;

- makes sensible, reasonable estimates;

- makes justified, logical statements.

Mathematical reasoning

M5 d The student demonstrates mathematical reasoning by using logic to prove specific conjectures, by explaining the logic inherent in a solution process, by making generalizations and showing that they are valid, and by revealing mathematical patterns inherent in a situation. The student not only makes observations and states results but also justifies or proves why the results hold in general; that is, the student:

- employs forms of mathematical reasoning and proof appropriate to the solution of the problem at hand, including deductive and inductive reasoning, making and testing conjectures, and using counterexamples and indirect proof;

- differentiates clearly between giving examples that support a conjecture and giving a proof of the conjecture.

M6 Mathematical Skills and Tools

Elementary School

The student demonstrates fluency with basic and important skills by using these skills accurately and automatically, and demonstrates practical competence and persistence with other skills by using them effectively to accomplish a task, perhaps referring to notes, books, or other students, perhaps working to reconstruct a method; that is, the student:

M6a Adds, subtracts, multiplies, and divides whole numbers correctly; that is:

- knows single digit addition, subtraction, multiplication, and division facts;

- adds and subtracts numbers with several digits;

- multiplies and divides numbers with one or two digits;

- multiplies and divides three digit numbers by one digit numbers.

M6b Estimates numerically and spatially.

M6c Measures length, area, perimeter, circumference, diameter, height, weight, and volume accurately in both the customary and metric systems.

M6d Computes time (in hours and minutes) and money (in dollars and cents).

M6e Refers to geometric shapes and terms correctly with concrete objects or drawings, including triangle, square, rectangle, side, edge, face, cube, point, line, perimeter, area, and circle; and refers with assistance to rhombus, parallelogram, quadrilateral, polygon, polyhedron, angle, vertex, volume, diameter, circumference, sphere, prism, and pyramid.

M6f Uses +, -, x, ÷, /, ⎯ $, ¢, %, and . (decimal point) correctly in number sentences and expressions.

M6g Reads, creates, and represents data on line plots, charts, tables, diagrams, bar graphs, simple circle graphs, and coordinate graphs.

M6h Uses recall, mental computations, pencil and paper, measuring devices, mathematics texts, manipulatives, calculators, computers, and advice from peers, as appropriate, to achieve solutions; that is, uses measuring devices, graded appropriately for given situations, such as rulers (customary to the ⅛ inch; metric to the millimeter), graph paper (customary to the inch or half-inch; metric to the centimeter), measuring cups (customary to the ounce; metric to the milliliter), and scales (customary to the pound or ounce; metric to the kilogram or gram).

Middle School

The student demonstrates fluency with basic and important skills by using these skills accurately and automatically, and demonstrates practical competence and persistence with other skills by using them effectively to accomplish a task (perhaps referring to notes, or books, perhaps working to reconstruct a method); that is, the student:

M6a Computes accurately with arithmetic operations on rational numbers.

M6b Knows and uses the correct order of operations for arithmetic computations.

M6c Estimates numerically and spatially.

M6d Measures length, area, volume, weight, time, and temperature accurately.

M6e Refers to geometric shapes and terms correctly.

M6f Uses equations, formulas, and simple algebraic notation appropriately.

M6g Reads and organizes data on charts and graphs, including scatter plots, bar, line, and circle graphs, and Venn diagrams; calculates mean and median.

M6h Uses recall, mental computations, pencil and paper, measuring devices, mathematics texts, manipulatives, calculators, computers, and advice from peers, as appropriate, to achieve solutions.

High School

The student demonstrates fluency with basic and important skills by using these skills accurately and automatically, and demonstrates practical competence and persistence with other skills by using them effectively to accomplish a task, perhaps referring to notes, or books, perhaps working to reconstruct a method; that is, the student:

M6a Carries out numerical calculations and symbol manipulations effectively, using mental computations, pencil and paper, or other technological aids, as appropriate.

M6b Uses a variety of methods to estimate the values, in appropriate units, of quantities met in applications, and rounds numbers used in applications to an appropriate degree of accuracy.

M6c Evaluates and analyzes formulas and functions of many kinds, using both pencil and paper and more advanced technology.

M6d Uses basic geometric terminology accurately, and deduces information about basic geometric figures in solving problems.

M6e Makes and uses rough sketches, schematic diagrams, or precise scale diagrams to enhance a solution.

M6f Uses the number line and Cartesian coordinates in the plane and in space.

M6g Creates and interprets graphs of many kinds, such as function graphs, circle graphs, scatter plots, regression lines, and histograms.

M6h Sets up and solves equations symbolically (when possible) and graphically.

M6i Knows how to use algorithms in mathematics, such as the Euclidean Algorithm.

M6j Uses technology to create graphs or spreadsheets that contribute to the understanding of a problem.

M6k Writes a simple computer program to carry out a computation or simulation to be repeated many times.

M6l Uses tools such as rulers, tapes, compasses, and protractors in solving problems.

M6m Knows standard methods to solve basic problems and uses these methods in approaching more complex problems.

M7 Mathematical Communication

Elementary School

The student uses the language of mathematics, its symbols, notation, graphs, and expressions, to communicate through reading, writing, speaking, and listening, and communicates about mathematics by describing mathematical ideas and concepts and explaining reasoning and results; that is, the student:

M7 a Uses appropriate mathematical terms, vocabulary, and language, based on prior conceptual work.

M7 b Shows mathematical ideas in a variety of ways, including words, numbers, symbols, pictures, charts, graphs, tables, diagrams, and models.

M7 c Explains solutions to problems clearly and logically, and supports solutions with evidence, in both oral and written work.

M7 d Considers purpose and audience when communicating about mathematics.

M7 e Comprehends mathematics from reading assignments and from other sources.

Middle School

The student uses the language of mathematics, its symbols, notation, graphs, and expressions, to communicate through reading, writing, speaking, and listening, and communicates about mathematics by describing mathematical ideas and concepts and explaining reasoning and results; that is, the student:

M7 a Uses mathematical language and representations with appropriate accuracy, including numerical tables and equations, simple algebraic equations and formulas, charts, graphs, and diagrams.

M7 b Organizes work, explains facets of a solution orally and in writing, labels drawings, and uses other techniques to make meaning clear to the audience.

M7 c Uses mathematical language to make complex situations easier to understand.

M7 d Exhibits developing reasoning abilities by justifying statements and defending work.

M7 e Shows understanding of concepts by explaining ideas not only to teachers and assessors but to fellow students or younger children.

M7 f Comprehends mathematics from reading assignments and from other sources.

High School

The student uses the language of mathematics, its symbols, notation, graphs, and expressions, to communicate through reading, writing, speaking, and listening, and communicates about mathematics by describing mathematical ideas and concepts and explaining reasoning and results; that is, the student:

M7 a Is familiar with basic mathematical terminology, standard notation and use of symbols, common conventions for graphing, and general features of effective mathematical communication styles.

M7 b Uses mathematical representations with appropriate accuracy, including numerical tables, formulas, functions, equations, charts, graphs, and diagrams.

M7 c Organizes work and presents mathematical procedures and results clearly, systematically, succinctly, and correctly.

M7 d Communicates logical arguments clearly, showing why a result makes sense and why the reasoning is valid.

M7 e Presents mathematical ideas effectively both orally and in writing.

M7 f Explains mathematical concepts clearly enough to be of assistance to those who may be having difficulty with them.

M7 g Writes narrative accounts of the history and process of work on a mathematical problem or extended project.

M7 h Writes succinct accounts of the mathematical results obtained in a mathematical problem or extended project, with diagrams, graphs, tables, and formulas integrated into the text.

M7 i Keeps narrative accounts of process separate from succinct accounts of results, and realizes that doing so can enhance the effectiveness of each.

M7 j Reads mathematics texts and other writing about mathematics with understanding.

M8 Putting Mathematics to Work

Elementary School

The student conducts at least one large scale project each year, beginning in fourth grade, drawn from the following kinds and, over the course of elementary school, conducts projects drawn from at least two of the kinds.

A single project may draw on more than one kind.

M8 a Data study, in which the student:

- develops a question and a hypothesis in a situation where data could help make a decision or recommendation;

- decides on a group or groups to be sampled and makes predictions of the results, with specific percents, fractions, or numbers;

- collects, represents, and displays data in order to help make the decision or recommendation; compares the results with the predictions;

- writes a report that includes recommendations supported by diagrams, charts, and graphs, and acknowledges assistance received from parents, peers, and teachers.

M8 b Science study, in which the student:

- decides on a specific science question to study and identifies the mathematics that will be used, e.g., measurement;

- develops a prediction (a hypothesis) and develops procedures to test the hypothesis;

- collects and records data, represents and displays data, and compares results with predictions;

- writes a report that compares the results with the hypothesis; supports the results with diagrams, charts, and graphs; acknowledges assistance received from parents, peers, and teachers.

M8 c Design of a physical structure, in which the student:

- decides on a structure to design, the size and budget constraints, and the scale of design;

- makes a first draft of the design, and revises and improves the design in response to input from peers and teachers;

- makes a final draft and report of the design, drawn and written so that another person could make the structure; acknowledges assistance received from parents, peers, and teachers.

Middle School

The student conducts at least one large scale investigation or project each year drawn from the following kinds and, over the course of middle school, conducts investigations or projects drawn from three of the kinds.

A single investigation or project may draw on more than one kind.

M8 a Data study based on civic, economic, or social issues, in which the student:

- selects an issue to investigate;

- makes a hypothesis on an expected finding, if appropriate;

- gathers data;

- analyzes the data using concepts from Standard 4, e.g., considering mean and median, and the frequency and distribution of the data;

- shows how the study's results compare with the hypothesis;

- uses pertinent statistics to summarize;

- prepares a presentation or report that includes the question investigated, a detailed description of how the project was carried out, and an explanation of the findings.

M8 b Mathematical model of physical phenomena, often used in science studies, in which the student:

- carries out a study of a physical system using a mathematical representation of the structure;

- uses understanding from Standard 3, particularly with respect to the determination of the function governing behavior in the model;

- generalizes about the structure with a rule, i.e., a function, that clearly applies to the phenomenon and goes beyond statistical analysis of a pattern of numbers generated by the situation;

- prepares a presentation or report that includes the question investigated, a detailed description of how the project was carried out, and an explanation of the findings.

M8 c Design of a physical structure, in which the student:

- generates a plan to build something of value, not necessarily monetary value;

- uses mathematics from Standard 2 to make the design realistic or appropriate, e.g., areas and volumes in general and of specific geometric shapes;

High School

The student conducts at least one large scale investigation or project each year over the course of high school, conducts investigations or projects drawn from at least three of the kinds.

A single investigation or project may draw on more than one kind.

M8 a Data study, in which the student:

- carries out a study of data relevant to current civic, economic, scientific, health, or social issues;

- uses methods of statistical inference to generalize from the data;

- prepares a report that explains the purpose of the project, the organizational plan, and conclusions, and uses an appropriate balance of different ways of presenting information.

M8 b Mathematical model of a physical system or phenomenon, in which the student:

- carries out a study of a physical system or phenomenon by constructing a mathematical model based on functions to make generalizations about the structure of the system;

- uses structural analysis (a direct analysis of the structure of the system) rather than numerical or statistical analysis (an analysis of data about the system);

- prepares a report that explains the purpose of the project, the organizational plan, and conclusions, and uses an appropriate balance of different ways of presenting information.

M8 c Design of a physical structure, in which the student:

- creates a design for a physical structure;

- uses general mathematical ideas and techniques to discuss specifications for building the structure;

- prepares a report that explains the purpose of the project, the organizational plan, and conclusions, and uses an appropriate balance of different ways of presenting information.

M8 d Management and planning analysis, in which the student:

- carries out a study of a business or public policy situation involving issues such as optimization, cost-benefit projections, and risks;

- uses decision rules and strategies both to analyze options and balance trade-offs; and brings

M8d Management and planning, in which the student:

- decides on what to manage or plan, and the criteria to be used to see if the plan worked;
- identifies unexpected events that could disrupt the plan and further plans for such contingencies;
- identifies resources needed, e.g., materials, money, time, space, and other people;
- writes a detailed plan and revises and improves the plan in response to feedback from peers and teachers;
- carries out the plan (optional);
- writes a report on the plan that includes resources, budget, and schedule, and acknowledges assistance received from parents, peers, and teachers.
- writes a report that includes recommendations supported by diagrams, charts, and graphs, and acknowledges assistance received from parents, peers, and teachers.

M8e Pure mathematics investigation, in which the student:

- decides on the area of mathematics to investigate, e.g., numbers, shapes, patterns;
- describes a question or concept to investigate;
- decides on representations that will be used, e.g., numbers, symbols, diagrams, shapes, or physical models;
- carries out the investigation;
- writes a report that includes any generalizations drawn from the investigation, and acknowledges assistance received from parents, peers, and teachers.

- summarizes the important features of the structure;
- prepares a presentation or report that includes the question investigated, a detailed description of how the project was carried out, and an explanation of the findings.

M8d Management and planning, in which the student:

- determines the needs of the event to be managed or planned, e.g., cost, supply, scheduling;
- notes any constraints that will affect the plan;
- determines a plan;
- uses concepts from any of Standards 1 to 4, depending on the nature of the project;
- considers the possibility of a more efficient solution;
- prepares a presentation or report that includes the question investigated, a detailed description of how the project was carried out, and an explanation of the plan.

M8e Pure mathematics investigation, in which the student:

- extends or "plays with," as with mathematical puzzles, some mathematical feature, e.g., properties and patterns in numbers;
- uses concepts from any of Standards 1 to 4, e.g., an investigation of Pascal's triangle would have roots in Standard 1 but could tie in concepts from geometry, algebra, and probability; investigations of derivations of geometric formulas would be rooted in Standard 2 but could require algebra;
- determines and expresses generalizations from patterns;
- makes conjectures on apparent properties and argues, short of formal proof, why they seem true;
- prepares a presentation or report that includes the question investigated, a detailed description of how the project was carried out, and an explanation of the findings.

in mathematical ideas that serve to generalize the analysis across different conditions;

- prepares a report that explains the purpose of the project, the organizational plan, and conclusions, and uses an appropriate balance of different ways of presenting information.

M8e Pure mathematics investigation, in which the student:

- carries out a mathematical investigation of a phenomenon or concept in pure mathematics;
- uses methods of mathematical reasoning and justification to make generalizations about the phenomenon;
- prepares a report that explains the purpose of the project, the organizational plan, and conclusions, and uses an appropriate balance of different ways of presenting information.

M8f History of a mathematical idea, in which the student:

- carries out a historical study tracing the development of a mathematical concept and the people who contributed to it;
- includes a discussion of the actual mathematical content and its place in the curriculum of the present day;
- prepares a report that explains the purpose of the project, the organizational plan, and conclusions, and uses an appropriate balance of different ways of presenting information.

S1 Physical Sciences Concepts

APPENDIX III

The elementary school standards are set at a level of performance approximately equivalent to the end of fourth grade. The middle school standards are set at a level of performance approximately equivalent to the end of eighth grade. The high school standards are set at a level of performance approximately equivalent to the end of tenth grade. It is expected that some students might achieve these levels earlier and others later than these grades.

The Science standards are founded upon both the National Research Council's *National Science Education Standards* and the American Association for the Advancement of Science's Project 2061 *Benchmarks for Science Literacy*. These documents, each of which runs to several hundred pages, contain detailed explication of the concepts identified here.

Elementary School

The student produces evidence that demonstrates understanding of:

S1 a Properties of objects and materials, such as similarities and differences in the size, weight, and color of objects; the ability of materials to react with other substances; and different states of materials.

S1 b Position and motion of objects, such as how the motion of an object can be described by tracing and measuring its position over time; and how sound is produced by vibrating objects.

S1 c Light, heat, electricity, and magnetism, such as the variation of heat and temperature; how light travels in a straight line until it strikes an object or how electrical circuits work.

Middle School

The student produces evidence that demonstrates understanding of:

S1 a Properties and changes of properties in matter, such as density and boiling point; chemical reactivity; and conservation of matter.

S1 b Motions and forces, such as inertia and the net effects of balanced and unbalanced forces.

S1 c Transfer of energy, such as transformation of energy as heat; light; mechanical motion, and sound; and the nature of a chemical reaction.

High School

The student produces evidence that demonstrates understanding of:

S1 a Structure of atoms, such as atomic composition, nuclear forces, and radioactivity.

S1 b Structure and properties of matter, such as elements and compounds; bonding and molecular interaction; and characteristics of phase changes.

S1 c Chemical reactions, such as everyday examples of chemical reactions; electrons, protons, and energy transfer; and factors that affect reaction rates such as catalysts.

S1 d Motions and forces, such as gravitational and electrical; net forces and magnetism.

S1 e Conservation of energy and increase in disorder, such as kinetic and potential energy; energy conduction, convection, and radiation; random motion; and effects of heat and pressure.

S1 f Interactions of energy and matter, such as waves, absorption and emission of light, and conductivity.

S2 Life Sciences Concepts

Elementary School

The student produces evidence that demonstrates understanding of:

S2 a Characteristics of organisms, such as survival and environmental support; the relationship between structure and function; and variations in behavior.

S2 b Life cycles of organisms, such as how inheritance and environment determine the characteristics of an organism; and that all plants and animals have life cycles.

S2 c Organisms and environments, such as the interdependence of animals and plants in an ecosystem; and populations and their effects on the environment.

S2 d Change over time, such as evolution and fossil evidence depicting the great diversity of organisms developed over geologic history.

Middle School

The student produces evidence that demonstrates understanding of:

S2 a Structure and function in living systems, such as the complementary nature of structure and function in cells, organs, tissues, organ systems, whole organisms, and ecosystems.

S2 b Reproduction and heredity, such as sexual and asexual reproduction; and the role of genes and environment on trait expression.

S2 c Regulation and behavior, such as senses and behavior; and response to environmental stimuli.

S2 d Populations and ecosystems, such as the roles of producers, consumers, and decomposers in a food web; and the effects of resources and energy transfer on populations.

S2 e Evolution, diversity, and adaptation of organisms, such as common ancestry, speciation, adaptation, variation, and extinction.

High School

The student produces evidence that demonstrates understanding of:

S2 a The cell, such as cell structure and function relationships; regulation and biochemistry; and energy and photosynthesis.

S2 b Molecular basis of heredity, such as DNA, genes, chromosomes, and mutations.

S2 c Biological evolution, such as speciation, biodiversity, natural selection, and biological classification.

S2 d Interdependence of organisms, such as conservation of matter; cooperation and competition among organisms in ecosystems; and human effects on the environment.

S2 e Matter, energy, and organization in living systems, such as matter and energy flow through different levels of organization; and environmental constraints.

S2 f Behavior of organisms, such as nervous system regulation; behavioral responses; and connections with anthropology, sociology, and psychology.

S3 Earth and Space Sciences Concepts

Elementary School

The student produces evidence that demonstrates understanding of:

S3 a Properties of Earth materials, such as water and gases; and the properties of rocks and soils, such as texture, color, and ability to retain water.

S3 b Objects in the sky, such as Sun, Moon, planets, and other objects that can be observed and described; and the importance of the Sun to provide the light and heat necessary for survival.

S3 c Changes in Earth and sky, such as changes caused by weathering, volcanism, and earth-quakes; and the patterns of movement of objects in the sky.

Middle School

The student produces evidence that demonstrates understanding of:

S3 a Structure of the Earth system, such as crustal plates and land forms; water and rock cycles; oceans, weather, and climate.

S3 b Earth's history, such as Earth processes including erosion and movement of plates; change over time and fossil evidence.

S3 c Earth in the Solar System, such as the pre-dictable motion of planets, moons, and other objects in the Solar System including days, years, moon phases, and eclipses; and the role of the Sun as the major source of energy for phenome-na on the Earth's surface.

S3 d Natural resource management.

High School

The student produces evidence that demonstrates understanding of:

S3 a Energy in the Earth system, such as radioac-tive decay, gravity, the Sun's energy, convection, and changes in global climate.

S3 b Geochemical cycles, such as conservation of matter; chemical resources and movement of matter between chemical reservoirs.

S3 c Origin and evolution of the Earth system, such as geologic time and the age of life forms; origin of life; and evolution of the Solar System.

S3 d Origin and evolution of the universe, such as the "big bang" theory; formation of stars and elements; and nuclear reactions.

S3 e Natural resource management.

APPENDIX III

S4 Scientific Connections and Applications

Elementary School

The student produces evidence that demonstrates understanding of:

S4 a Big ideas and unifying concepts, such as order and organization; models, form and function; change and constancy; and cause and effect.

S4 b The designed world, such as development of agricultural techniques; and the viability of technological designs.

S4 c Personal health, such as nutrition, substance abuse, and exercise; germs and toxic substances; personal and environmental safety.

S4 d Science as a human endeavor, such as communication, cooperation, and diverse input in scientific research; and the importance of reason, intellectual honesty, and skepticism.

Middle School

The student produces evidence that demonstrates understanding of:

S4 a Big ideas and unifying concepts, such as order and organization; models, form, and function; change and constancy; and cause and effect.

S4 b The designed world, such as the reciprocal nature of science and technology; the development of agricultural techniques; and the viability of technological designs.

S4 c Health, such as nutrition, exercise, and disease; effects of drugs and toxic substances; personal and environmental safety; and resources and environmental stress.

S4 d Impact of technology, such as constraints and trade-offs; feedback; benefits and risks; and problems and solutions.

S4 e Impact of science, such as historical and contemporary contributions; and interactions between science and society.

High School

The student produces evidence that demonstrates understanding of:

S4 a Big ideas and unifying concepts, such as order and organization; models, form and function; change and constancy; and cause and effect.

S4 b The designed world, such as the reciprocal relationship between science and technology; the development of agricultural techniques; and the reasonableness of technological designs.

S4 c Health, such as nutrition and exercise; disease and epidemiology; personal and environmental safety; and resources, environmental stress, and population growth.

S4 d Impact of technology, such as constraints and trade-offs; feedback; benefits and risks; and problems and solutions.

S4 e Impact of science, such as historical and contemporary contributions; and interactions between science and society.

§5 Scientific Thinking

Elementary School

The student demonstrates scientific inquiry and problem solving by using thoughtful questioning and reasoning strategies, common sense and conceptual understanding from Science Standards 1 to 4, and appropriate methods to investigate the natural world; that is, the student:

§5 a Asks questions about natural phenomena; objects and organisms; and events and discoveries.

§5 b Uses concepts from Science Standards 1 to 4 to explain a variety of observations and phenomena.

§5 c Uses evidence from reliable sources to construct explanations.

§5 d Evaluates different points of view using relevant experiences, observations, and knowledge; and distinguishes between fact and opinion.

§5 e Identifies problems; proposes and implements solutions; and evaluates the accuracy, design, and outcomes of investigations.

§5 f Works individually and in teams to collect and share information and ideas.

Middle School

The student demonstrates scientific inquiry and problem solving by using thoughtful questioning and reasoning strategies, common sense and conceptual understanding from Science Standards 1 to 4, and appropriate methods to investigate the natural world; that is, the student:

§5 a Frames questions to distinguish cause and effect; and identifies or controls variables in experimental and non-experimental research settings.

§5 b Uses concepts from Science Standards 1 to 4 to explain a variety of observations and phenomena.

§5 c Uses evidence from reliable sources to develop descriptions, explanations, and models.

§5 d Proposes, recognizes, analyzes, considers, and critiques alternative explanations; and distinguishes between fact and opinion.

§5 e Identifies problems; proposes and implements solutions; and evaluates the accuracy, design, and outcomes of investigations.

§5 f Works individually and in teams to collect and share information and ideas.

High School

The student demonstrates skill in scientific inquiry and problem solving by using thoughtful questioning and reasoning strategies, common sense and diverse conceptual understanding, and appropriate ideas and methods to investigate science; that is, the student:

§5 a Frames questions to distinguish cause and effect; and identifies or controls variables in experimental and non-experimental research settings.

§5 b Uses concepts from Science Standards 1 to 4 to explain a variety of observations and phenomena.

§5 c Uses evidence from reliable sources to develop descriptions, explanations, and models; and makes appropriate adjustments and improvements based on additional data or logical arguments.

§5 d Proposes, recognizes, analyzes, considers, and critiques alternative explanations; and distinguishes between fact and opinion.

§5 e Identifies problems; proposes and implements solutions; and evaluates the accuracy, design, and outcomes of investigations.

§5 f Works individually and in teams to collect and share information and ideas.

S6 Scientific Tools and Technologies

S6 makes explicit reference to using telecommunications to acquire and share information. A recent National Center on Education Statistics survey recently reported that only 50% of schools and fewer than 9% of instructional rooms currently have access to the Internet. We know this is an equity issue—that far more than 9% of the homes in the United States have access to the Internet and that schools must make sure that students' access to information and ideas does not depend on what they get at home—so we have crafted performance standards that would use the Internet so that people will make sure that all students have access to it. New Standards partners have made a commitment to create the learning environments where students can develop the knowledge and skills delineated here.

Elementary School

The student demonstrates competence with the tools and technologies of science by using them to collect data, make observations, analyze results, and accomplish tasks effectively; that is, the student:

S6a Uses technology and tools (such as rulers, computers, balances, thermometers, watches, magnifiers, and microscopes) to gather data and extend the senses.

S6b Collects and analyzes data using concepts and techniques in Mathematics Standard 4, such as average, data displays, graphing, variability, and sampling.

S6c Acquires information from multiple sources, such as experimentation and print and non-print sources.

Middle School

The student demonstrates competence with the tools and technologies of science by using them to collect data, make observations, analyze results, and accomplish tasks effectively; that is, the student:

S6a Uses technology and tools (such as traditional laboratory equipment, video, and computer aids) to observe and measure objects, organisms, and phenomena, directly, indirectly, and remotely.

S6b Records and stores data using a variety of formats, such as data bases, audiotapes, and videotapes.

S6c Collects and analyzes data using concepts and techniques in Mathematics Standard 4, such as mean, median, and mode; outcome probability and reliability; and appropriate data displays.

S6d Acquires information from multiple sources, such as print, the Internet, computer data bases, and experimentation.

S6e Recognizes sources of bias in data, such as observer and sampling biases.

High School

The student demonstrates competence with the tools and technologies of science by using them to collect data, make observations, analyze results, and accomplish tasks effectively; that is, the student:

S6a Uses technology and tools (such as traditional laboratory equipment, video, and computer aids) to observe and measure objects, organisms, and phenomena, directly, indirectly, and remotely, with appropriate consideration of accuracy and precision.

S6b Records and stores data using a variety of formats, such as data bases, audiotapes, and videotapes.

S6c Collects and analyzes data using concepts and techniques in Mathematics Standard 4, such as mean, median, and mode; outcome probability and reliability; and appropriate data displays.

S6d Acquires information from multiple sources, such as print, the Internet, computer data bases, and experimentation.

S6e Recognizes and limits sources of bias in data, such as observer and sample biases.

S7 Scientific Communication

Elementary School

The student demonstrates effective scientific communication by clearly describing aspects of the natural world using accurate data, graphs, or other appropriate media to convey depth of conceptual understanding in science; that is, the student:

S7 a Represents data and results in multiple ways, such as numbers, tables, and graphs; drawings, diagrams, and artwork; and technical and creative writing.

S7 b Uses facts to support conclusions.

S7 c Communicates in a form suited to the purpose and the audience, such as writing instructions that others can follow.

S7 d Critiques written and oral explanations, and uses data to resolve disagreements.

Middle School

The student demonstrates effective scientific communication by clearly describing aspects of the natural world using accurate data, graphs, or other appropriate media to convey depth of conceptual understanding in science; that is, the student:

S7 a Represents data and results in multiple ways, such as numbers, tables, and graphs; drawings, diagrams, and artwork; and technical and creative writing.

S7 b Argues from evidence, such as data produced through his or her own experimentation or by others.

S7 c Critiques published materials.

S7 d Explains a scientific concept or procedure to other students.

S7 e Communicates in a form suited to the purpose and the audience, such as by writing instructions that others can follow; critiquing written and oral explanations; and using data to resolve disagreements.

High School

The student demonstrates effective scientific communication by clearly describing aspects of the natural world using accurate data, graphs, or other appropriate media to convey depth of conceptual understanding in science; that is, the student:

S7 a Represents data and results in multiple ways, such as numbers, tables, and graphs; drawings, diagrams, and artwork; technical and creative writing; and selects the most effective way to convey the scientific information.

S7 b Argues from evidence, such as data produced through his or her own experimentation or data produced by others.

S7 c Critiques published materials, such as popular magazines and academic journals.

S7 d Explains a scientific concept or procedure to other students.

S7 e Communicates in a form suited to the purpose and the audience, such as by writing instructions that others can follow; critiquing written and oral explanations; and using data to resolve disagreements.

S8 Scientific Investigation

APPENDIX III

Best practice in science has always included extensive inquiry and investigation, but these are frequently given less emphasis at the elementary level in the face of competing demands form English language arts and mathematics. There are many opportunities to learn science outside of school, including Scouts, Boys and Girls Clubs, 4-H, and Future Farmers of America. The work done in these venues can and should be used to provide evidence of meeting the standards.

Elementary School

The student demonstrates scientific competence by completing projects drawn from the following kinds of investigations, including at least one full investigation each year and, over the course of elementary school, investigations that integrate several aspects of Science Standards 1 to 7 and represent all four of the kinds of investigation:

S8 a An experiment, such as conducting a fair test.

S8 b A systematic observation, such as a field study.

S8 c A design, such as building a model or scientific apparatus.

S8 d Non-experimental research using print and electronic information, such as journals, video, or computers.

A single project may draw on more than one kind of investigation.

A full investigation includes:

• Questions that can be studied using the resources available.

• Procedures that are safe, humane, and ethical; and that respect privacy and property rights.

• Data that have been collected and recorded (see also Science Standard 6) in ways that others can verify and analyze using skills expected at this grade level (see also Mathematics Standard 4).

• Data and results that have been represented (see also Science Standard 7) in ways that fit the context.

• Recommendations, decisions, and conclusions based on evidence.

• Acknowledgment of references and contributions of others.

• Results that are communicated appropriately to audiences.

• Reflection and defense of conclusions and recommendations from other sources and peer review.

Middle School

The student demonstrates scientific competence by completing projects drawn from the following kinds of investigations, including at least one full investigation each year and, over the course of middle school, investigations that integrate several aspects of Science Standards 1 to 7 and represent all four of the kinds of investigation:

S8 a Controlled experiment.

S8 b Fieldwork.

S8 c Design.

S8 d Secondary research, such as use of others' data.

A single project may draw on more than one type of investigation.

A full investigation includes:

• Questions that can be studied using the resources available.

• Procedures that are safe, humane, and ethical; and that respect privacy and property rights.

• Data that have been collected and recorded (see also Science Standard 6) in ways that others can verify, and analyzed using skills expected at this grade level (see also Mathematics Standard 4).

• Data and results that have been represented (see also Science Standard 7) in ways that fit the context.

• Recommendations, decisions, and conclusions based on evidence.

• Acknowledgment of references and contributions of others.

• Results that are communicated appropriately to audiences.

• Reflection and defense of conclusions and recommendations from other sources and peer review.

High School

The student demonstrates scientific competence by completing projects drawn from the following kinds of investigation, including at least one full investigation each year and, over the course of high school, investigations that integrate several aspects of Science Standards 1 to 7 and represent all four of the kinds of investigation:

S8 a Controlled experiment.

S8 b Fieldwork.

S8 c Design.

S8 d Secondary research.

A single project may draw on more than one type of investigation.

A full investigation includes:

• Questions that can be studied using the resources available.

• Procedures that are safe, humane, and ethical; and that respect privacy and property rights.

• Data that have been collected and recorded (see also Science Standard 6) in ways that others can verify, and analyzed using skills expected at this grade level (see also Mathematics Standard 4).

• Data and results that have been represented (see also Science Standard 7) in ways that fit the context.

• Recommendations, decisions, and conclusions based on evidence.

• Acknowledgment of references and contributions of others.

• Results that are communicated appropriately to audiences.

• Reflection and defense of conclusions and recommendations from other sources and peer review.

APPENDIX IV

The elementary school standards are set at a level of performance approximately equivalent to the end of fourth grade. The middle school standards are set at a level of performance approximately equivalent to the end of eighth grade. The high school standards are set at a level of performance approximately equivalent to the end of tenth grade. It is expected that some students might achieve these levels earlier and others later than these grades.

Elementary School

The student conducts projects involving at least two of the following kinds of problem solving each year and, over the course of elementary school, conducts projects involving all three kinds of problem solving.

- Design a Product, Service, or System: Identify needs that could be met by new products, services, or systems and create solutions for meeting them.

- Improve a System: Develop an understanding of the way systems of people, machines, and processes work; troubleshoot problems in their operation and devise strategies for improving their effectiveness.

- Plan and Organize an Event or an Activity: Take responsibility for all aspects of planning and organizing an event or an activity from concept to completion, making good use of the resources of people, time, money, and materials and facilities.

Each project should involve subject matter related to the standards for English Language Arts, and/or Mathematics, and/or Science, and/or other appropriate subject content.

Design a Product, Service, or System

A1 a The student designs and creates a product, service, or system to meet an identified need; that is, the student:

- develops ideas for the design of the product, service, or system;

- chooses among the design ideas and justifies the choice;

- establishes criteria for judging the success of the design;

- uses an appropriate format to represent the design;

- plans and carries out the steps needed to turn the design into a reality;

- evaluates the design in terms of the criteria established for success.

Improve a System

A1 b The student troubleshoots problems in the operation of a system in need of repair or devises and tests ways of improving the effectiveness of a system in operation; that is, the student:

- identifies the parts of the system and the way the parts connect with each other;

Middle School

The student conducts projects involving at least two of the following kinds of problem solving each year and, over the course of middle school, conducts projects involving all three kinds of problem solving.

- Design a Product, Service, or System: Identify needs that could be met by new products, services, or systems and create solutions for meeting them.

- Improve a System: Develop an understanding of the way systems of people, machines, and processes work; troubleshoot problems in their operation and devise strategies for improving their effectiveness.

- Plan and Organize an Event or an Activity: Take responsibility for all aspects of planning and organizing an event or an activity from concept to completion, making good use of the resources of people, time, money, and materials and facilities.

Each project should involve subject matter related to the standards for English Language Arts, and/or Mathematics, and/or Science, and/or other appropriate subject content.

Design a Product, Service, or System

A1 a The student designs and creates a product, service, or system to meet an identified need; that is, the student:

- develops a range of ideas for design of the product, service, or system;

- selects one design option to pursue and justifies the choice with reference, for example, to functional, aesthetic, social, economic, or environmental considerations;

- establishes criteria for judging the success of the design;

- uses appropriate conventions to represent the design;

- plans and carries out the steps needed to create the product, service, or system;

- makes adjustments as needed to conform with specified standards or regulations regarding quality and safety;

- evaluates the quality of the design in terms of the criteria for success and by comparison with similar products, services, or systems.

High School

The student conducts projects involving at least two of the following kinds of problem solving each year and, over the course of high school, conducts projects involving all three kinds of problem solving.

- Design a Product, Service, or System: Identify needs that could be met by new products, services, or systems and create solutions for meeting them.

- Improve a System: Develop an understanding of the way systems of people, machines, and processes work; troubleshoot problems in their operation and devise strategies for improving their effectiveness.

- Plan and Organize an Event or an Activity: Take responsibility for all aspects of planning and organizing an event or activity from concept to completion, making good use of the resources of people, time, money, and materials and facilities.

Each project should involve subject matter related to the standards for English Language Arts, and/or Mathematics, and/or Science, and/or other appropriate subject content.

Design a Product, Service, or System

A1 a The student designs and creates a product, service, or system to meet an identified need; that is, the student:

- develops a design proposal that:

- shows how the ideas for the design were developed;

- reflects awareness of similar work done by others and of relevant design standards and regulations;

- justifies the choices made in finalizing the design with reference, for example, to functional, aesthetic, social, economic, and environmental considerations;

- establishes criteria for evaluating the product, service, or system;

- uses appropriate conventions to represent the design;

- plans and implements the steps needed to create the product, service, or system;

- makes adjustments as needed to conform with specified standards or regulations regarding quality or safety;

- evaluates the product, service, or system in terms of the criteria established in the design

- identifies parts or connections in the system that have broken down or that could be made to work better;
- devises ways of making the system work again or making it work better;
- evaluates the effectiveness of the strategies for improving the system and supports the evaluation with evidence.

Plan and Organize an Event or an Activity

A1 c The student plans and organizes an event or an activity; that is, the student:

- develops a plan for the event or activity that:
  - includes all the factors and variables that need to be considered;
  - shows the order in which things need to be done;
  - takes into account the resources available to put the plan into action, including people and time;
- implements the plan;
- evaluates the success of the event or activity by identifying the parts of the plan that worked best and the parts that could have been improved by better planning and organization;
- makes recommendations to others who might consider planning and organizing a similar event or activity.

Improve a System

A1 b The student troubleshoots problems in the operation of a system in need of repair or devises and tests ways of improving the effectiveness of a system in operation; that is, the student:

- describes the structure and management of the system in terms of its logic, sequences, and control;
- identifies the operating principles underlying the system, i.e., mathematical, scientific, organizational;
- evaluates the way the system operates;
- devises strategies for putting the system back in operation or improving its performance;
- evaluates the effectiveness of the strategies for improving the system and supports the evaluation with evidence.

Plan and Organize an Event or an Activity

A1 c The student plans and organizes an event or activity; that is, the student:

- develops a plan that:
  - reflects research into relevant precedents and regulations;
  - includes all the factors and variables that need to be considered;
  - shows the order in which things need to be done;
  - takes into account the resources available to put the plan into action, including people and time;
- implements the plan in ways that:
  - reflect the priorities established in the plan;
  - respond effectively to unforeseen circumstances;
- evaluates the success of the event or activity;
- makes recommendations to others who might consider planning and organizing a similar event or activity.

proposal, and with reference to:

- information gathered from sources such as impact studies, product testing, or market research;
- comparisons with similar work done by others.

Improve a System

A1 b The student troubleshoots problems in the operation of a system in need of repair or devises and tests ways of improving the effectiveness of a system in operation; that is, the student:

- explains the structure of the system in terms of its:
  - logic, sequences, and control;
  - operating principles, that is, the mathematical, scientific, and/or organizational principles underlying the system;
- analyzes the way the system works, taking account of its functional, aesthetic, social, environmental, and commercial requirements, as appropriate, and using a relevant kind of modeling or systems analysis;
- evaluates the operation of the system, using qualitative methods and/or quantitative measurements of performance;
- develops and tests strategies to put the system back in operation and/or optimize its performance;
- evaluates the effectiveness of the strategies for improving the system and supports the evaluation with evidence.

Plan and Organize an Event or an Activity

A1 c The student plans and organizes an event or an activity; that is, the student:

- develops a planning schedule that:
  - is sensible in terms of the goals of the event or activity;
  - is logical and achievable;
  - reflects research into relevant precedents and regulations;
  - takes account of all relevant factors;
  - communicates clearly so that a peer or colleague could use it;
- implements and adjusts the planning schedule in ways that:
  - make efficient use of time, money, people, resources, facilities;
  - reflect established priorities;
  - respond effectively to unforeseen circumstances;
- evaluates the success of the event or activity using qualitative and/or quantitative methods;
- makes recommendations for planning and organizing subsequent similar events or activities.

A2 Communication Tools and Techniques

Elementary School

A2 a The student makes an oral presentation of project plans or findings to an appropriate audience; that is, the student:

- organizes the presentation in a logical way appropriate to its purpose;
- speaks clearly and presents confidently;
- responds to questions from the audience;
- evaluates the effectiveness of the presentation.

A2 b The student composes and sends correspondence, such as thank-you letters and memoranda providing information; that is, the student:

- expresses the information or request clearly;
- writes in a style appropriate to the purpose of the correspondence.

A2 c The student writes and formats information for short publications, such as brochures or posters; that is, the student:

- organizes the information into an appropriate form for use in the publication;
- checks the information for accuracy;
- formats the publication so that it achieves its purpose.

Middle School

A2 a The student makes an oral presentation of project plans or findings to an audience beyond the school; that is, the student:

- organizes the presentation in a logical way appropriate to its purpose;
- adjusts the style of presentation to suit its purpose and audience;
- speaks clearly and presents confidently;
- responds appropriately to questions from the audience;
- evaluates the effectiveness of the presentation.

A2 b The student conducts formal written correspondence with an organization beyond the school; that is, the student:

- expresses the information or request clearly for the purpose and audience;
- writes in a style appropriate to the purpose and audience of the correspondence.

A2 c The student publishes information using several methods and formats, such as overhead transparencies, handouts, and computer generated graphs and charts; that is, the student:

- organizes the information into an appropriate form for use in the publication;
- checks the information for accuracy;
- formats the published material so that it achieves its purpose.

High School

A2 a The student makes an oral presentation of project plans or findings to an audience with expertise in the relevant subject matter; that is, the student:

- organizes the presentation in a logical way appropriate to its purpose;
- adjusts the style of presentation to suit its purpose and audience;
- speaks clearly and presents confidently;
- responds appropriately to questions from the audience;
- evaluates the effectiveness of the presentation and identifies appropriate revisions for a future presentation.

A2 b The student prepares a formal written proposal or report to an organization beyond the school; that is, the student:

- organizes the information in the proposal or report in a logical way appropriate to its purpose;
- produces the proposal or report in a format similar to that used in professionally produced documents for a similar purpose and audience.

A2 c The student develops a multi-media presentation, combining text, images, and/or sound; that is, the student:

- selects an appropriate medium for each element of the presentation;
- uses the selected media skillfully, including editing and monitoring for quality;
- achieves coherence in the presentation as a whole;
- communicates the information effectively, testing audience response and revising the presentation accordingly.

A3 Information Tools and Techniques

APPENDIX IV

Elementary School

A3 a The student gathers information to assist in completing project work; that is, the student:

- identifies potential sources of information to assist in completing the project;
- uses appropriate techniques to collect the information, e.g., considers sampling issues in conducting a survey;
- distinguishes relevant from irrelevant information;
- shows evidence of research in the completed project.

A3 b The student uses information technology to assist in gathering, organizing, and presenting information; that is, the student:

- acquires information for specific purposes from on-line sources, such as the Internet, and other electronic data bases, such as an electronic encyclopedia;
- uses word-processing, drawing, and painting programs to produce project reports and related materials.

Middle School

A3 a The student gathers information to assist in completing project work; that is, the student:

- identifies potential sources of information to assist in completing the project;
- uses appropriate techniques to collect the information, e.g., considers sampling issues in conducting a survey;
- interprets and analyzes the information;
- evaluates the information for completeness and relevance;
- shows evidence of research in the completed project.

A3 b The student uses information technology to assist in gathering, analyzing, organizing, and presenting information; that is, the student:

- acquires information for specific purposes from on-line sources, such as the Internet, and other electronic data bases, such as a scientific data base on CD ROM;
- uses word-processing, graphics, data base, and spreadsheet programs to produce project reports and related materials.

High School

A3 a The student gathers information to assist in completing project work; that is, the student:

- identifies potential sources of information to assist in completing the project;
- uses appropriate techniques to collect the information, e.g., considers sampling issues in conducting a survey;
- interprets and analyzes the information;
- evaluates the information in terms of completeness, relevance, and validity;
- shows evidence of research in the completed project.

A3 b The student uses on-line sources to exchange information for specific purposes; that is, the student:

- uses E-mail to correspond with peers and specialists in the subject matter of their projects;
- incorporates into E-mail correspondence data of different file types and applications.

A3 c The student uses word-processing software to produce a multi-page document; that is, the student:

- uses features of the software to create and edit the document;
- uses features of the software to format the document, including a table of contents, index, tabular columns, charts, and graphics;
- uses features of the software to create templates and style sheets for the document.

A3 d The student writes, adds content to, and analyzes a data base program that uses a relational data base; that is, the student:

- writes a program capable of handling data with at least two files;
- creates macros to facilitate data entry, analysis, and manipulation;
- creates multiple report formats that include summary information;
- merges data from the data base with other files.

A3 e The student creates, edits, and analyzes a spreadsheet of information that displays data in tabular, numeric format and includes multiple graphs; that is, the student:

- creates a spreadsheet that displays the use of formulas and functions;
- uses features of the software to sort, arrange, display, and extract data for specific purposes;
- uses features of the software to create multiple spreadsheets and to synthesize the spreadsheets into a single presentation.

A4 Learning and Self-management Tools and Techniques

Elementary School

A4 a The student learns from models; that is, the student:

- consults with or observes other students and adults at work, and identifies the main features of what they do and the way they go about their work;

- examines models for the results of project work, such as professionally produced publications, and analyzes their qualities;

- uses what he or she learns from models to assist in planning and conducting project activities.

A4 b The student keeps records of work activities in an orderly manner; that is, the student:

- sets up a system for storing records of work activities;

- maintains records of work activities in a way that makes it possible to find specific materials quickly and easily.

A4 c The student identifies strengths and weaknesses in his or her own work; that is, the student:

- understands and establishes criteria for judging the quality of work processes and products;

- assesses his or her own work processes and products.

Middle School

A4 a The student learns from models; that is, the student:

- consults with or observes other students and adults at work, and identifies the main features of what they do and the way they go about their work;

- identifies models for the results of project work, such as professionally produced publications, and analyzes their qualities;

- uses what he or she learns from models to assist in planning and conducting project activities.

A4 b The student develops and maintains a schedule of work activities; that is, the student:

- establishes a schedule of work activities that reflects priorities and deadlines;

- seeks advice on the management of conflicting priorities and deadlines;

- updates the schedule regularly.

A4 c The student sets goals for learning and reviews his or her progress; that is, the student:

- sets goals for learning;

- reviews his or her progress towards meeting the goals;

- seeks and responds to advice from others in setting goals and reviewing progress.

High School

A4 a The student learns from models; that is, the student:

- consults with and observes other students and adults at work and analyzes their roles to determine the critical demands, such as demands for knowledge and skills, judgment and decision making;

- identifies models for the results of project work, such as professionally produced publications, and analyzes their qualities;

- uses what he or she learns from models in planning and conducting project activities.

A4 b The student reviews his or her own progress in completing work activities and adjusts priorities as needed to meet deadlines; that is, the student:

- develops and maintains work schedules that reflect consideration of priorities;

- manages time;

- monitors progress towards meeting deadlines and adjusts priorities as necessary.

A4 c The student evaluates his or her performance; that is, the student:

- establishes expectations for his or her own achievement;

- critiques his or her work in light of the established expectations;

- seeks and responds to advice and criticism from others.

A5 Tools and Techniques for Working With Others

Elementary School

A5 a The student works with others to complete a task; that is, the student:

- reaches agreement with group members on what work needs to be done to complete the task and how the work will be tackled;
- takes a share of the responsibility for the work;
- consults with group members regularly during the task to check on progress in completing the task, to decide on any changes that are required, and to check that all parts have been completed at the end of the task.

A5 b The student shows or explains something clearly enough for someone else to be able to do it.

A5 c The student responds to a request from a client; that is, the student:

- interprets the client's request;
- asks questions to clarify the demands of a task.

Middle School

A5 a The student takes responsibility for a component of a team project; that is, the student:

- reaches agreement with team members on what work needs to be done to complete the task and how the work will be tackled;
- takes specific responsibility for a component of the project;
- takes all steps necessary to ensure appropriate completion of the specific component of the project within the agreed upon time frame.

A5 b The student coaches or tutors; that is, the student:

- assists one or more others to learn on the job;
- analyzes coaching or tutoring experience to identify more and less effective ways of providing assistance to support on-the-job learning;
- uses the analysis to inform subsequent coaching or tutoring activities.

A5 c The student responds to a request from a client; that is, the student:

- consults with a client to clarify the demands of a task;
- interprets the client's request and translates it into an initial plan for completing the task, taking account of available resources;
- negotiates with the client to arrive at an agreed upon plan.

High School

A5 a The student participates in the establishment and operation of self-directed work teams; that is, the student:

- defines roles and shares responsibilities among team members;
- sets objectives and time frames for the work to be completed;
- establishes processes for group decision making;
- reviews progress and makes adjustments as required.

A5 b The student plans and carries out a strategy for including at least one new member in a work program; that is, the student:

- plans and conducts an initial activity to introduce the new member to the work program;
- devises ways of providing continuing on-the-job support and advice;
- monitors the new member's progress in joining the program, and revises the kinds and ways of providing support and advice accordingly;
- reviews the success of the overall strategy.

A5 c The student completes a task in response to a commission from a client; that is, the student:

- negotiates with the client to arrive at a plan for meeting the client's needs that is acceptable to the client, achievable within available resources, and includes agreed-upon criteria for successful completion;
- monitors client satisfaction with the work in progress and makes adjustments accordingly;
- evaluates the result in terms of the negotiated plan and the client's evaluation of the result.

STANDARDS DEVELOPMENT STAFF

Harold Asturias, Academic Advancement, University of California Office of the President

Pam Beck, Academic Advancement, University of California Office of the President

Ann Borthwick, Learning Research and Development Center, University of Pittsburgh

Bill Calder, Fort Worth Independent School District, TX

Shannon C'de Baca, Thomas Jefferson High School, Council Bluffs, IA

Janet Coffey, Edmund Burke School, Washington, DC

Duane A. Cooper, Center for Mathematics Education and Department of Mathematics, University of Maryland

Phil Daro, Academic Advancement, University of California Office of the President

Mishaa DeGraw, Academic Advancement, University of California Office of the President

Diana Edwards, Learning Research and Development Center, University of Pittsburgh

Gary Eggan, Learning Research and Development Center, University of Pittsburgh

JoAnne Eresh, Learning Research and Development Center, University of Pittsburgh

Sally Hampton, Fort Worth Independent School District, TX

Drew Kravin, Cornell Elementary School, Albany, CA

Georgia Makris, Academic Advancement, University of California Office of the President

Mary Marsh, Fort Worth Independent School District, TX

Megan Martin, Academic Advancement, University of California Office of the President

Evy McPherson, Academic Advancement, University of California Office of the President

Kate Nolan, Learning Research and Development Center, University of Pittsburgh

Andy Plattner, National Center on Education and the Economy

Lonny Platzer, Learning Research and Development Center, University of Pittsburgh

Mark Rasmussen, Cornell Elementary School, Albany, CA

Jennifer Regen, Fort Worth Independent School District, TX

Christine Ross, Learning Research and Development Center, University of Pittsburgh

Annette Seitz, Learning Research and Development Center, University of Pittsburgh

Ann Shannon, University of California Office of the President

Liz Spalding, National Council of Teachers of English

Elizabeth Stage, Academic Advancement, University of California Office of the President

Dick Stanley, Dana Center, University of California at Berkeley

Cathy Sterling, Academic Advancement, University of California Office of the President

John Tanner, Fort Worth Independent School District, TX

Ginny Van Horne, Education and Human Resources, American Association for the Advancement of Science

ACKNOWLEDGMENTS

Peter Afflerbach, University of Maryland

Bob Anderson, California Department of Education

Laura Arndt, Eaglecrest High School, Aurora, CO

Rob Atterbury, San Diego City Schools, CA

Linda Ballenger, West Park Elementary, Fort Worth, TX

Jerry Bell, Education and Human Resources, American Association for the Advancement of Science

Neal Berkin, White Plains Schools, White Plains, NY

Victoria Bill, Institute for Learning, Learning Research and Development Center, University of Pittsburgh

Linda Block-Gandy, Mountainview Elementary, CO

Greg Bouljon, Bettendorf Middle School, IL

Rupi Boyd, Taft Junior High School, CA

Diane Briars, Pittsburgh Public Schools, PA

Melanie Broujos, Frick International Studies Academy, Pittsburgh, PA

Shirley Patton Brown, West Memphis High School, West Memphis, AR

Hugh Burkhardt, Shell Centre for Mathematics Education, Nottingham, England

Charlotte Burrell, Trimble Tech High School, Fort Worth, TX

Jill Calder, Wedgwood Sixth Grade School, Fort Worth, TX

Ruben Carriedo, San Diego City Schools, CA

Linda Carstens, San Diego City Schools, CA

Cynthia Carter, New York City Lab School, NY

Sharon Chambers, Forbes Elementary School, Penn Hills, PA

Miriam Chaplin, National Council of Teachers of English

Phyllis Chapman, Linden Elementary School, Pittsburgh, PA

Lynda Chittenden, Park Elementary, Mill Valley, CA

Fran Claggett, Forestville, CA

Doug Clarke, Australian Catholic University, Australia

Gill Close, King's College, University of London, England

Laurel Collins, Linton Middle School, Pittsburgh

Kathy Comfort, California Department of Education

John Davis, Langley High School, Pittsburgh, PA

Marshé DeLain, Delaware Department of Public Instruction

Dot Down, Dublin High School, CA

Mark Driscoll, Education Development Center, Newton, MA

Xandra Williams Earlie, Aldine Independent School District, Houston, TX

Phyllis Eisen, National Association of Manufacturers

Marcia Elliott, Somers Public Schools, CT

Ed Esty, Independent Consultant, Chevy Chase, MD

Alan Farstrup, International Reading Association

Harry Featherstone, Featherstone & Associates, Wooster, OH

Susan Fineman, East Hill ISA, PA

Donna Foley, Parker School, Chelmsford, MA

Amanda Frohberg, PS 41, New York, NY

Karen Fujii, Bucher Middle School, Santa Clara, CA

Matt Gandal, American Federation of Teachers

Don Geary, Linton Middle School, Pittsburgh, PA

Roger Gehman, Linton Middle School, Pittsburgh, PA

Karrie Gengo, Meadowdale High School, Lynnwood, WA

Judy Goldfeder, PS 116, New York, NY

Amy Granatire, Penn Hebron Elementary School, Pittsburgh, PA

Eunice Greer, University of Illinois

Susan Halbert, National 4-H Council

Mike Hale, Council Bluffs Community Schools, Council Bluffs, IA

Jerry Halpern, Langley High School, Pittsburgh, PA

Shirley Brice Heath, Stanford University

Rae Ann Hirsh, Penn Hebron Elementary School, Pittsburgh, PA

Bonnie Hole, Princeton Institute for Research, New Haven, CT

Bill Honig, San Francisco State University

Kathy Howard, Reizenstein Middle School, Pittsburgh, PA

David Hughes, Linton Middle School, Pittsburgh, PA

Beth Hulbert, Barre City Elementary School, VT

Sharon Woods Hussey, Girl Scouts of the U.S.A.

Robin Ittigson, Minadeo Elementary School, Pittsburgh, PA

Tom Jones, National Alliance for Restructuring Education

Nancy Kellogg, CONNECT, Colorado Department of Education

Don King, Department of Mathematics, Northeastern University, Boston, MA

Denis Krysinski, Vann Elementary School, Pittsburgh, PA

Brian Lawler, Eaglecrest High School, Aurora, CO

Lyn Le Countryman, Price Lab School, IA

Steve Leinwand, Connecticut State Department of Education

Jane Lester, New York City Lab School, NY

Denise Levine, New York City Community District 2, NY

Linda Lewis, Fort Worth Independent School District, TX

Debra Liberman, Fells High School, Philadelphia, PA

Bob Livingston, Pennsylvania Department of Education

Anthony Lucas, Duquesne University, Pittsburgh, PA

Denise Lutz, Peabody High School, Pittsburgh, PA

Susan MacArthur, South Portland High School, South Portland, ME

Gary MacDonald, Junior High School, Greely, CO

Shirley Malcom, American Association for the Advancement of Science

Kelly Maloney-Fermoile, Carrie E. Tompkins School, Croton-on-Hudson, NY

Rich Matthews, Pittsburgh Public Schools, PA

Ken McCaffrey, Brattleboro Union High School, VT

Jim Meadows, Mountlake Terrace High School, Mountlake Terrace, WA

David Mintz, National Alliance for Restructuring Education

Harriet Mosatche, Girl Scouts of the U.S.A.

Jo Ann Mosier, Kentucky Department of Education

Tim Moynihan, Mountlake Terrace High School, Mountlake Terrace, WA

Monty Multanen, Edmonds School District, WA

Sandy Murphy, University of California at Davis

Martha Murray-Zinn, Wedgwood Middle School, Fort Worth, TX

Miles Myers, National Council of Teachers of English

Tienne Myers, Hancock Elementary School, Philadelphia, PA

Christina Myren, Acacia Elementary School, Thousand Oaks, CA

Joseph Newkirk, School for the Physical City, New York, NY

Lee Odell, Rensselaer Polytechnic Institute, Troy, NY

Gary Oden, Institute for Learning, Learning Research and Development Center, University of Pittsburgh

Alan Olds, Standley Lake High School, Westminster, CO

Marian Opest, Penn Hills Senior School, Pittsburgh, PA

Ann Osborne, Linton Middle School, Pittsburgh, PA

Jean O'Shell, Linton Middle School, Pittsburgh, PA

Kevin Padian, Department of Integrative Biology, University of California at Berkeley

Dennie Palmer Wolf, Harvard PACE

Tim Patterson, Mountlake Terrace High School, Mountlake Terrace, WA

Risa Payne, Wedgwood Middle School, Fort Worth, TX

David Pearson, University of Illinois

Charles Peters, Oakland Michigan Schools, MI

Marge Petit, Vermont Institute for Mathematics, Science, and Technology

Cindy Phillips, Tri City Elementary, Myrtle Creek, OR

Marcia Pink, Newport High School, WA

John Porter, National Alliance for Restructuring Education

Robert Probst, University of Georgia

Fred Quinonez, Overland Trail Middle School, Brighton, CO

Susan Radley, Teachers College Writing Project at Columbia University, NY

Donald Raintree, Universal Dynamics Inc., Woodbridge, VA

Lynn Raith, Pittsburgh Public Schools, PA

Ginny Redish, Redish & Associates, Inc.

Eeva Reeder, Mountlake Terrace High School, Mountlake Terrace, WA

Susan Rowe, Bonnieville School, CT

Don Rubin, University of Georgia

Carmen Rubino, Eaglecrest High School, Aurora, CO

Robert Rueda, University of Southern California

Marge Sable, National Alliance for Restructuring Education

Sandy Short, Hillview Crest Elementary School, New Haven Unified School District, CA

Cheryl Sims, School for the Physical City, New York, NY

Sandy Smith, Harrison High School, Aurora, CO

Dave Steward, John Evans Jr. High School, Greely, CO

John Swang, National Student Research Center, Mandeville, LA

Carol Tateishi, Bay Area Writing Project

Johnny Tolliver, Delaware State University

Cathy Topping-Wiese, U-32 Junior/Senior High School, Montpelier, VT

Lora Turner, A. Leo Weil School, Pittsburgh, PA

Ann Tweed, Eaglecrest High School, Aurora, CO

Zalman Usiskin, The University of Chicago School Mathematics Project

John Vibber, Mt. Abraham Union High School, Briston, VT

Dale Vigil, San Diego City Schools, CA

Rhonda Wagner, Cherry Creek Schools, Englewood, CO

Brenda Wallace, New York, NY

Anne Weinstock, PS 116, New York, NY

Eric Weiss, U-32 Junior/Senior High School, Montpelier, VT

Sandra Wilcox, Michigan State University

Arnold Willens, PS 41, New York, NY

Ann Marie Williams, PS 41, New York, NY

Darby Williams, Sacramento County Office of Education, CA

Scott J. Wolff, Davenport West High School, IA

Victoria Young, Texas Education Agency

Judi Zawojewski, National-Louis University, Evanston, IL

MATERIALS USED WITH PERMISSION

"Two Poems About Sports" student work. From *Integrated English Language Arts Illustrative Material: Grade 10.* Copyright 1994, California Department of Education, 721 Capital Mall, 4th Floor, Sacramento, CA 95814.

"Miles of Words" and "Shopping Carts" tasks. The Balanced Assessment Project, University of California, Berkeley, CA 94720.

"Cubes" task. The Balanced Assessment Project, Graduate School of Education, University of California, Berkeley, CA 94720-1670.

"Designing a Theater for Galileo" assignment text. From *Discovering Geometry.* Copyright 1997 by Key Curriculum Press, P.O. Box 2304, Berkeley, CA 94702. Tel. 1-800-995-MATH.

"The Density of Sand" and "Photosynthesis Lab" the task's "Self-reflection Sheet" and student work. From the *Golden State Examination.* Copyright by California Department of Education, 721 Capital Mall, 4th Floor, Sacramento, CA 95814.

"Erosion on the Minnehaha Creek" and "Are Oysters Safe To Eat?" research format and student work. From *The Student Researcher.* National Student Research Center, Dr. John I. Swang, Mandeville Middle School, 2525 Soult Street, Mandeville, LA 70448. Tel. 504-626-5980 or nsrcmms@aol.com.

"Baseball Field" newspaper article titled "Diamond in the Rough." Reprinted with permission from Leslie Moriarty. *The Herald,* Everett, WA.

REFERENCES

American Association for the Advancement of Science. (1993). *Benchmarks for Science Literacy: Project 2061.* New York: Oxford University Press.

American Federation of Teachers. (1994). *Defining World Class Standards: A Publication Series.* Vol. 1-3. Washington, DC: Author.

American Federation of Teachers. (1995). *Making Standards Matter: A Fifty-State Progress Report on Efforts to Raise Academic Standards.* Washington, DC: Author.

Balanced Assessment Project. (In preparation). Schoenfeld, A. H., et al. *Twenty Plus Assessment Packages at Grades Four, Eight, Ten and Twelve.* Berkeley, CA: Graduate School of Education, University of CA at Berkeley.

Boy Scouts of America. (1990). *The Boy Scout Handbook.* Irving, TX: Author.

The Business Task Force on Student Standards. (1995). *The Challenge of Change: Standards To Make Education Work For All Our Children.* Washington, DC: Business Coalition for Education Reform.

Commission on Standards for School Mathematics. (1989). *Curriculum and Evaluation: Standards for School Mathematics.* Reston, VA: National Council of Teachers of Mathematics.

Girl Scouts of the U.S.A. (1995). *A Resource Book for Senior Girl Scouts.* New York: Author.

National Council of Teachers of English & International Reading Association. (1996). *Standards for the English Language Arts.* Urbana, IL and Newark, DE: NCTE and IRA.

National Education Goals Panel, Technical Planning Group. (1993). *Promises to Keep: Creating High Standards for American Students.* Washington, DC: Author.

National Research Council. (1996). *National Science Education Standards.* Washington, DC: National Academy Press.

New Standards Project. (1994). *The New Standards Framework for Applied Learning.* Discussion Draft. Washington, DC: Author.

Sallee, G. T., et al. (In preparation). *College Preparatory Mathematics.* Davis, CA: CRESS Center, University of California at Davis.

Secretary's Commission on Achieving Necessary Skills. (1992). *Learning A Living: A Blueprint for High Performance—A SCANS Report For America 2000.* Washington, DC: U.S. Department of Labor.

SELECT BIBLIOGRAPHY

Australian Education Council and Curriculum Corporation. (1991). *A National Statement on Mathematics for Australian Schools.* Carlton, Victoria: Curriculum Corporation.

California State Board of Education. (1987). *English-Language Arts Framework for California Public Schools.* Sacramento: Author.

California State Board of Education. (1985). *Mathematics Framework for California Public Schools.* Sacramento: Author.

California State Board of Education. (1990). *Science Framework for California Public Schools.* Sacramento: Author.

Colorado State Department of Education. (Draft). *Model Content Standards for Mathematics.* Denver: Author.

Colorado State Department of Education. (Draft). *Model Content Standards for Reading and Writing.* Denver: Author.

Colorado State Department of Education. (Draft). *Model Content Standards for Science*. Denver: Author.

Commission on Maine's Common Core of Learning. (1990). *Maine's Common Core of Learning: An investment in Maine's future*. Augusta, ME: Maine Department of Education.

Curriculum Corporation. (1994). *English—a curriculum profile for Australian schools*. Carlton, Victoria: Author.

Curriculum Corporation. (1994). *Mathematics—a curriculum profile for Australian schools*. Carlton, Victoria: Author.

Curriculum Corporation. (1994). *Science—a curriculum profile for Australian schools*. Carlton, Victoria: Author.

Der Kultusminister des Landes Nordrhein-Westfalen. (1989). *Grundschule in Nordrhein-Westfalen*. Köln, Bundesrepublik Deutschland: Greven Verlag Köln.

Dutch Ministry of Education and Science. (1993). *The Dutch National Curriculum for Primary School*. Typescript provided in translation by the Dutch Ministry of Education and Science.

Dutch Ministry of Education and Science. (1993). *Mathematics: General and Core Objectives*. Typescript provided in translation by the Dutch Ministry of Education and Science.

Educational and Cultural Exchange Division, UNESCO and International Affairs Department, Science and International Affairs Bureau, Ministry of Education, Science and Culture. (1983). *Course of Study for Elementary Schools in Japan*. (Notification No. 155 of Ministry of Education, Science and Culture.) Tokyo: Printing Bureau, Ministry of Finance.

Educational and Cultural Exchange Division, UNESCO and International Affairs Department, Science and International Affairs Bureau, Ministry of Education, Science and Culture. (1983). *Course of Study for Lower Secondary Schools in Japan*. (Notification No. 156 of Ministry of Education, Science and Culture.) Tokyo: Printing Bureau, Ministry of Finance.

Educational and Cultural Exchange Division, UNESCO and International Affairs Department, Science and International Affairs Bureau, Ministry of Education, Science and Culture. (1983). *Course of Study for Upper Secondary Schools in Japan*. (Notification No. 163 of Ministry of Education, Science and Culture.) Tokyo: Printing Bureau, Ministry of Finance.

Girl Scouts of the U.S.A. (1993). *Brownie Girl Scout Handbook*. New York: Author.

Girls Scouts of the U.S.A. (1995). *Cadette Girl Scout Handbook*. New York: Author.

Girls Scout of the U.S.A. (1995). *A Resource Book for Senior Girl Scouts*. New York: Author.

Illinois Academic Standards Project of the Illinois State Board of Education. (Draft). *Illinois Academic Standards, State Goals 1-10: English Language Arts and Mathematics*. Springfield, IL: Author.

Illinois Academic Standards Project of the Illinois State Board of Education. (Draft). *Illinois Academic Standards, State Goals 11-18: Science and Social Studies*. Springfield, IL: Author.

Iowa Department of Education. (1994). *Education is Iowa's Future: The State Plan for Educational Excellence in the 21st Century*. Des Moines, IA: Author.

Kentucky Department of Education. (1993). *Transformations: Kentucky's Curriculum Framework*. Frankfort, KY: Author.

Maine Department of Education. (Draft). *Learning Results*. Augusta, ME: Author.

Ministère de l'Éducation Nationale. (1985). *Collèges: Programmes et Instructions*. Paris: Centre National de Documentation Pédagogique.

Ministère de l'Éducation Nationale. (1994). *Évaluation à l'entrée en seconde générale et technologique: Français*. Paris: Direction de l'Évaluation et de la Prospective.

Ministère de l'Éducation Nationale de la Jeunesse et des Sports, Direction des Écoles. (1991). *Les cycles à l'école primaire*. Paris: Centre National de Documentation Pédagogique & Hachette Écoles.

Ministère de l'Éducation Nationale. (1991). *Baccalauréat Professionel: Enseignements généraux*. Paris: Centre National de Documentation Pédagogique.

Ministry of Education, New Zealand. (1994). *English in the New Zealand Curriculum*. Wellington, New Zealand: Learning Media Ltd.

Ministry of Education, New Zealand. (1994). *Mathematics in the New Zealand Curriculum*. Wellington, New Zealand: Learning Media Ltd.

Ministry of Education, New Zealand. (1994). *Science in the New Zealand Curriculum*. Wellington, New Zealand: Learning Media Ltd.

Ministry of Education and Research. (1987). *Curriculum Guidelines for Compulsory Education in Norway*. W. Nygaard, Norge: H. Aschehoug & Co.

Ministry of Education of the Russian Federation and the General School Education Institute of the Russian Academy of Education. (1993). *The Provisional State Education Standards, General Secondary Education: Mathematics*. Moscow: Author.

Ministry of Education and Training, Canada. (1993). *Provincial Standards: Mathematics*. Toronto, Ontario: Queen's Printer for Ontario.

Ministry of Education and Training, Canada. (1993). *The Common Curriculum, Grades 1-9*. Toronto, Ontario: Queen's Printer for Ontario.

Missouri Department of Education. (Draft). *Academic Performance Standards and Curriculum Frameworks*. Jefferson City, MO: Author.

National Science Teachers Association. (1992). *Scope, Sequence, and Coordination Content Core*. Washington, DC: Author.

Nolan, Kate. (1994). *Mathematics in Five Countries*. Pittsburgh, PA: New Standards.

Oregon Department of Education. (1993). *21st Century Schools: Information Packet*. Salem, OR: Author.

Oregon Department of Education. (1986). *English Language Arts: Common Curriculum Goals*. Salem, OR: Author.

Oregon Department of Education. (1986). *Essential Learning Skills*. Salem, OR: Author.

Oregon Department of Education. (1987). *Mathematics: Common Curriculum Goals*. Salem, OR: Author.

Rhode Island Department of Education. (1994). *First Draft: Mathematics Framework for Grades K-12*. Providence, RI: Author.

School Curriculum and Assessment Authority. (1994). *Design & Technology in the National Curriculum*. Draft Proposals. London: Author and the Central Office of Information.

School Curriculum and Assessment Authority. (1994). *English in the National Curriculum*. Draft Proposals. London: Author and the Central Office of Information.

School Curriculum and Assessment Authority. (1994). *Science in the National Curriculum*. Draft Proposals. London: Author and the Central Office of Information.

School-to-Work Transition Team. (1994). *Education for Employment in Rhode Island: The Report of the School-to-Work Opportunities Transition Team*. Providence, RI: Author.

Scottish Office Education Department. (1991). *Curriculum and Assessment in Scotland, National Guidelines: English Language 5-14*. Edinburgh: Author.

Southern Examining Group. (1992). *English: General Certificate of Secondary Education, National Curriculum Syllabus, 1994 Examinations*. Surrey, England: Author.

Speech Communication Association. (1996). *Speaking, Listening, and Media Literacy Standards For K through 12 Education*. Annendale, VA: Author.

State of Delaware. (1995). *English Language Arts Curriculum Framework: Volumes One and Two*. Dover, DE: Author.

State of Delaware. (1995). *Mathematics Curriculum Framework: Volumes One and Two*. Dover, DE: Author.

State of Delaware. (1995). *Science Curriculum Framework: Volumes One and Two*. Dover, DE: Author.

The State of Vermont Department of Education. (1995). *Content Standards: Working Draft*. Montpelier, VT: Author.

The State of Vermont Department of Education. (1995). *Performance Standards: Working Draft*. Montpelier, VT: Author.

The State of Vermont Department of Education. (1995). *Vermont's Common Core Framework for Curriculum and Assessment: Draft*. Montpelier, VT: Author.

Stigler, J. and Stevenson, H. W. (1991). "How Asian Teachers Polish Each Lesson to Perfection." *American Educator*. Spring, 1991, 12-20, 43-47.

Texas Education Agency. (1995). English Language *Arts Essential Elements: Chapter 75, Texas Administrative Code*. Austin, TX: Author.

Texas Education Agency. (1995). *Mathematics Essential Elements: Chapter 75, Texas Administrative Code*. Austin, TX: Author.

Texas Education Agency. (1995). *Science Essential Elements: Chapter 75, Texas Administrative Code*. Austin, TX: Author.

The University of the State of New York and The State Education Department. (1995). *Preliminary Draft Framework for Career Development and Occupational Studies*. Albany, NY: Authors.

The University of the State of New York and The State Education Department. (1994). *Preliminary Draft Framework for English Language Arts*. Albany, NY: Authors.

The University of the State of New York and The State Education Department. (1995). *Preliminary Draft Framework for Mathematics, Science and Technology*. Albany, NY: Authors.

Utbildningsdepartementet. (1993). *Kursplaner för Grundskolan*. Stockholm: Nordstedts Tryckeri AB.

NEW STANDARDS PRODUCTS AND SERVICES: WHERE TO FIND WHAT YOU NEED

These performance standards serve as the basis of design specifications for the New Standards reference examinations and portfolios, which in turn provide information about performance to students, teachers, and parents.

But the performance standards cannot by themselves provide all of the information students and teachers will need in order to improve student performance in the core subjects.

Therefore, we include here some of the common requests we encounter from people who have begun to use the performance standards, along with information about the New Standards resources available to answer those requests.

- **Where can I find samples of student work that do not yet meet the standards? What about rubrics and scoring guides?**

New Standards Released Tasks contain sample tasks, scoring rubrics, and samples of student work at all of the score points given in the rubrics. Released Tasks can be ordered from Harcourt Brace Educational Measurement (Tel. 800-228-0752).

- **Clearly, many parts of the performance standards can only be assessed through some kind of portfolio system. Does New Standards offer portfolios?**

Yes—the New Standards portfolios in Mathematics, Science, English Language Arts, and Applied Learning are constructed to link directly to the performance standards. Portfolios are available individually, in classroom sets, and in sampler packets. Portfolios can be ordered directly from New Standards (Tel. 888-361-6233).

- **Our school district is using the performance standards to improve teaching and learning. We want standardized tests that can tell us how our students are doing based on the standards. What does New Standards offer?**

The New Standards reference examinations are available in English Language Arts and Mathematics for grades 4, 8, and 10. The examinations are designed using the performance standards as their foundation. Score reports for the reference examinations tell teachers and students about the quality of student work by referring to the performance standards. To order reference examinations, call Harcourt Brace Educational Measurement (Tel. 800-228-0752).

- **In order to move to a standards-based district, we need professional development and consulting for teachers and central office staff. Can New Standards help us with this?**

New Standards consultants can provide on-site services in several areas, including professional development, public engagement, strategic planning, standards linking, and technical issues involved with performance assessment. To discuss services needed by your school or district, call the Office of State and Local Relations, located at the National Center on Education and the Economy (Tel. 202-783-3668).